Consciousness and

In *Consciousness and the Existence of God*, J.P. Moreland argues that the existence of finite, irreducible consciousness (or its regular, law-like correlation with physical states) provides evidence for the existence of God. Moreover, he analyzes and criticizes the top representative of rival approaches to explaining the origin of consciousness, including John Searle's contingent correlation, Timothy O'Connor's emergent necessitation, Colin McGinn's mysterian "naturalism," David Skrbina's panpsychism and Philip Clayton's pluralistic emergentist monism. Moreland concludes that these approaches should be rejected in favor of what he calls "the Argument from Consciousness."

J.P. Moreland is Distinguished Professor of Philosophy, Biola University. He has published over 60 articles in journals that include *Philosophy and Phenomenological Research*, *American Philosophical Quarterly*, *Australasian Journal of Philosophy* and *Metaphilosophy*. He has authored, edited or contributed to thirty-five books including *Universals* (McGill-Queen's), *Naturalism: A Critical Analysis* (Routledge) and *Does God Exist?* (Prometheus).

Routledge Studies in the Philosophy of Religion

Peter Byrne, Marcel Sarot, and Mark Wynn

1 **God and Goodness**
A natural theological perspective
Mark Wynn

2 **Divinity and Maximal Greatness**
Daniel Hill

3 **Providence, Evil, and the Openness of God**
William Hasker

4 **Consciousness and the Existence of God**
A theistic argument
J.P. Moreland

Consciousness and the Existence of God

A theistic argument

J.P. Moreland

NEW YORK AND LONDON

First published 2008
by Routledge
711 Third Ave, New York, NY 10017

Simultaneously published in the UK
by Routledge
2 Park Square, Milton Park, Abingdon, Oxon OX14 4RN

Routledge is an imprint of the Taylor & Francis Group, an informa business

Typeset in Sabon by
Taylor & Francis Books

Library of Congress Cataloging in Publication Data
Moreland, James Porter, 1948–
Consciousness and the existence of God: a theistic argument / By J.P. Moreland.
p. cm. – (Routledge studies in the philosophy of religion)
Includes bibliographical references and index.
1. Consciousness. 2. Naturalism. 3. Theism. I. Title.
B808.9.M67 2008
212′.1–dc22 2007037875

British Library Cataloguing in Publication Data
A catalogue record for this book is available from the British Library

ISBN 978-0-415-96240-7 (hbk)
ISBN 978-0-203-92933-9 (ebk)
ISBN 978-0-415-98953-4 (pbk)

J.P. Moreland's intriguing and well-informed book argues forcefully for the view that a theistic explanation of human consciousness is the only viable alternative to an implausibly strong form of reductive physicalism in the philosophy of mind. It deserves close attention from philosophical naturalists and theists alike, and is written in an engaging and accessible manner that makes it suitable material for upper-level undergraduate and graduate courses in the philosophy of mind, metaphysics, and philosophical theology.

E.J. Lowe, Durham University

In *Consciousness and the Existence of God*, J.P. Moreland develops a ground breaking, rigorous, systematic case against naturalism and for theism in light of the evident reality of consciousness. His engagement with contemporary naturalism is vigorous, thorough, and fair. This is essential reading for those with interests in metaphysics and epistemology in general, and philosophy of mind and philosophy of religion in particular.

Charles Taliaferro, St. Olaf College

To William Lane Craig

Φίλος και Συστρατιώτης κατα την ὁδόν

Contents

Preface x

1 The epistemic backdrop for locating consciousness in a naturalist ontology 1

2 The argument from consciousness 28

3 John Searle and contingent correlation 53

4 Timothy O'Connor and emergent necessitation 70

5 Colin McGinn and mysterian "naturalism" 95

6 David Skrbina and panpsychism 114

7 Philip Clayton and pluralistic emergentist monism 135

8 Science and strong physicalism 156

9 AC, dualism and the fear of God 175

Notes 195
Bibliography 221
Indexes 230

Preface

Two trends in philosophy and theology provide the rationale for this book. First, there has been an explosion of literature in philosophy of religion, philosophical theology, classic theology and religious studies. An important part of this explosion is a renewed vigor and excellence in discussions of the arguments for and against the existence of God. In the last three decades, philosophers trained in analytic philosophy have applied their craft to these discussions with the result that there is now a rich dialog taking place. Second, there is an interesting dialectic occurring in philosophy of mind. A large number, perhaps the majority, of philosophical naturalists (e. g. David Papineau, Frank Jackson and the Churchlands) hold that naturalism does not sit well with irreducible *sui generis* mental properties/events and advocate a (cottage industry of) strong form(s) of physicalism. However, there is a growing dissatisfaction with the various versions of strong physicalism, and more and more are breaking ranks by venturing into emergent property dualism (e.g. the evolution of Jaegwon Kim's thought in the last ten years), at least for phenomenal consciousness.

Curiously, these two trends—the explosion in philosophy of religion and the growing importance of clarifying the relationship between naturalism and the resurgence of emergent property dualism—are taking place largely in isolation from each other. However, *Consciousness and the Existence of God* seeks to remedy this isolation. To my knowledge, it is the only book-length attempt written from a theistic perspective to examine the issue of whether or not *sui generis* consciousness provides a significant defeater for naturalism and substantial evidence for theism. I believe that this book has the potential to open new territory of consideration, especially as more philosophers realize the relationship between finite consciousness and broader worldview considerations, including an exposure to the interface between the two trends mentioned above. I hope to introduce philosophers of religion to issues in philosophy of mind with which they often do not address and to introduce philosophers of mind, especially naturalists, to the way topics in philosophy of religion inform their area of reflection.

The book's central claim is that the existence of finite, irreducible consciousness (or its regular, law-like correlation with physical states) provides evidence (with a strength I characterize) for the existence of God. I call this *the Argument from Consciousness* (hereafter, AC). I provide some argumentation for irreducible consciousness, but the focus of the book is the conditional "If irreducible consciousness exists (or is regularly correlated with physical states), then this provides evidence (to a degree specified in chapter two) for God's existence."

In chapter one, I show how naturalist epistemic considerations along with a naturalist etiological account of how things have come-to-be provide constraints on a naturalist ontology. The constraints, along with other considerations, imply that positive naturalism (a form of naturalism that claims superiority over alternative worldviews due to its explanatory power) should be strong naturalism (all particulars, properties, relations and laws are physical). Weak naturalism accepts various forms of emergent entities that I classify. The upshot of chapter one is that the inner logic of naturalism places a severe burden of proof on those naturalists who would embrace (certain kinds of) emergent properties. In chapter two, I present three versions of AC, assess the strength of the evidence it supplies for theism, and clarify and defend its major premises. I conclude that the presence of AC as a rival to naturalism places an additional burden of proof on those who opt for weak naturalism.

In chapters three through seven, I analyze and criticize the top representative of rival approaches to explaining the origin of consciousness. Chapters three through five focus on naturalist approaches: John Searle and contingent correlation (chapter three), Timothy O'Connor and emergent necessitation (chapter four), Colin McGinn and mysterian "naturalism" (chapter five). In chapters six and seven, I consider views that I claim are not plausibly taken to be versions of (positive) naturalism: David Skrbina and panpsychism (chapter six) and Philip Clayton and pluralistic emergentist monism (chapter seven). I conclude that these approaches fail for various reasons and, in light of the considerations in chapters one and two, AC stands as the most plausible view currently available.

In light of this fact, a naturalist has an additional reason for opting for strong naturalism. Accordingly, he or she may claim that while possible, scientific evidence has made substance or emergent property dualism untenable. While it is not my main purpose to defend property dualism, I do lay out evidence for it in chapter one. Part of that evidence consists in providing some new insights into the Knowledge Argument and into issues surrounding intentionality that favor (at least) property dualism. In chapter eight, I argue that science provides virtually no evidence at all for strong physicalism and, in fact, the central issues at the core of the mind/body problem are philosophical and not scientific. Given that science does not justify physicalism and given that most physicalists claim that science is the main justification for the view, it is important to ask why physicalism is so popular among contemporary philosophers of mind. In chapter nine, I argue that the fear of God—what Nagel calls "the cosmic authority problem"—is the main reason for physicalism's popularity. I turn this claim into an argument against physicalism and show that it is the relationship between dualism (substance or property) and theism, especially as formulated in AC, which accounts for physicalism's hegemony.

I have intentionally included some repetition—indeed, more repetition than is often found in a philosophical monograph—in chapters one through seven. I have done this so that each of these chapters can stand alone and be used as supplemental reading in a course on the ontology of naturalism, on theistic arguments, or a course on the thinking of Searle, O'Connor, McGinn, Skrbina, or Clayton. Thus, while trying to keep this to a minimum, I have repeated important points, especially criticisms, so each chapter can be used in isolation from the others. I have also included the repetition of important citations from prominent naturalists so students who are exposed only to one chapter or a few chapters will see for themselves that my characterization of naturalism is not a caricature but, rather, one that self-reflective, prominent naturalists accept.

Several people helped me bring this book to completion. Appreciation goes to those who read portions of the manuscript or who heard me give paper presentations on related material and gave helpful, though not always heeded, feedback: Francis Beckwith, Paul Copan, Thomas Crisp, Garry DeWeese, Stewart Goetz, William Hasker, Chad Meister, Paul Moser, Jeffrey Schwartz, Richard Swinburne, and William Wainright. Chapter eight came from a much-appreciated plenary dialog with Peter van Inwagen at the Pacific Regional meeting of the Society of Christian Philosopher's in April 2002. Thanks also go to my graduate students at Biola University who participated in seminars in which I developed some of my ideas. I am deeply grateful to Joseph Gorra for proofreading the entire manuscript, providing me with philosophical insights and developing a bibliography and indices. Finally, I am grateful to the Discovery Institute (especially to Stephen Meyer) for a grant to work on the manuscript.

Special thanks goes to the editors and publishers of the following publications, who graciously supplied permission to use the following: "If You Can't Reduce, You Must Eliminate: Why Kim's Version of Physicalism Isn't Close Enough," *Philosophia Christi* 7:2 (Summer 2005): 463–73; "A Christian Perspective on the Impact of Modern Science on Philosophy of Mind," *Perspectives on Science and Christian Faith* 55 (March 2003): 2–12; "Searle's Biological Naturalism and the Argument from Consciousness," *Faith and Philosophy* 15 (January 1998): 68–91; "Timothy O'Connor and the Harmony Thesis: A Critique," *Metaphysica* 3:2 (2002): 5–40.

1 The epistemic backdrop for locating consciousness in a naturalist ontology

Leibniz's gauntlet

Consciousness is among the most mystifying features of the cosmos. During the emergence of the mechanical philosophy in the seventeenth century, Leibniz wrote the following as a challenge to mechanistic materialism:

> It must be confessed, moreover, that *perception*, and that which depends on it *are inexplicable by mechanical causes*, that is, by figures and motions. And, supposing there were a machine so constructed as to think, feel and have perception, we could conceive of it as enlarged and yet preserving the same proportions, so that we might enter it as a mill. And this granted, we should only find on visiting it, pieces which push one against another, but never anything by which to explain a perception. This must be sought for, therefore, in the simple substance and not in the composite or in the machine.[1]

And while different bells and whistles have been added to our conception of matter since Leibniz's time, scientific naturalist explanations for the emergence of consciousness are as inadequate today as they were when Leibniz threw down his gauntlet. Thus, Geoffrey Madell opines that "the emergence of consciousness, then is a mystery, and one to which materialism signally fails to provide an answer."[2] Colin McGinn claims that its arrival borders on sheer magic because there seems to be no naturalistic explanation for it: "How can mere matter originate consciousness? How did evolution convert the water of biological tissue into the wine of consciousness? Consciousness seems like a radical novelty in the universe, not prefigured by the after-effects of the Big Bang; so how did it contrive to spring into being from what preceded it?"[3]

Not only are adequate naturalistic explanations for irreducible consciousness hard to come by, there is a widespread suspicion, if not explicit acknowledgement that irreducible consciousness provides evidence for theism. Thus, Crispin Wright notes,

> A central dilemma in contemporary metaphysics is to find a place for certain anthropocentric subject-matters—for instance, semantic, moral, and psychological—in a world as conceived by modern naturalism: a stance which inflates the concepts and categories deployed by (finished) physical science into a metaphysics of the kind of thing the real world essentially and exhaustively is. On one horn, if we embrace this naturalism, it seems we are committed either to reductionism: that is, to a construal of the reference of, for example, semantic, moral and psychological vocabulary as somehow being within the physical domain—or to disputing that the discourses in question involve reference to what is real at all. On the other horn, if we reject this naturalism, then we accept that there is more to the world than can be embraced within a physicalist ontology—and so take on a commitment, it can seem, to a kind of eerie supernaturalism.[4]

Similarly, William Lyons notes that

> [physicalism] seem[s] to be in tune with the scientific materialism of the twentieth century because it [is] a harmonic of the general theme that all there is in the universe is matter and energy and motion and that humans are a product of the evolution of species just as much as buffaloes and beavers are. Evolution is a seamless garment with no holes wherein souls might be inserted from above.[5]

Wright's allusion to a commitment to "a kind of eerie supernaturalism," and Lyons' reference to souls being "inserted from above" appear to be veiled references to the explanatory power of theism for consciousness, viz., that if "souls" exist, they would have to be "inserted from above" since natural processes by themselves are "seamless." More generally, some argue that, while certain features of consciousness or other finite mental entities—construed as *sui generis* and non-physical—may be inexplicable on a naturalist worldview, they may be explained by theism, thereby furnishing evidence for God's existence.

It is clear that for the last two-thirds of the twentieth century, mental entities have been recalcitrant facts for naturalists. Indeed, for philosophers who take the issues and options in philosophy of mind to be significantly influenced by empirical considerations, the proliferation of a wild variety of physicalist specifications of a naturalist treatment of mental phenomena may fairly be taken as a sign that naturalism is in a period of Kuhnian paradigm crisis. The argument from consciousness for God's existence (hereafter, AC) provides a way of dethroning the naturalist hegemony. Moreover, by giving a more adequate analysis of and explanation for mental entities, it provides a way out of the crisis and, together with other lines of evidence, offers materials for a cumulative-case argument for theism, or so I shall argue in the pages to follow.

In the last twenty years or so, versions of naturalism have multiplied like rabbits, so before we examine AC and some of its rivals, it is important to clarify two factors that constitute the appropriate dialectical background for the arguments to follow. First, I shall unpack the ideational structure of a version of naturalism that follows most plausibly from taking it as a worldview that claims explanatory, epistemic superiority to its rivals. Second, I shall lay out the central epistemic conditions relevant to assessing the force of AC *vis-à-vis* naturalism.

Exactly what are the central features of contemporary scientific naturalism?[6] There will be different nuances given to naturalism by different thinkers, as one would expect with any widely accepted ideology. Nevertheless, it is both possible and desirable to give an accurate characterization of a specific form of philosophical naturalism (hereafter, simply naturalism or scientific naturalism) that is currently enjoying widespread acceptance. Moreover, by clarifying the relationship between a naturalist ontology on the one hand, and its epistemology and creation account on the other, a picture will emerge as to what *ought* to constitute that ontology. This picture will allow us to identify a substantial burden of proof for alternative naturalist ontologies that bloat naturalist metaphysical commitments beyond what is justifiable within the constraints that follow from the other two aspects of a naturalist worldview.

Fundamentally, and as a first attempt at characterization, naturalism is the view that the spatio-temporal universe of entities postulated by our best current (or ideal) theories in the physical sciences (or relevantly similar entities), particularly physics, is all there is. Scientific naturalism includes:

1 Different aspects of a naturalist epistemic attitude (e.g. acceptance of naturalized epistemology, a rejection of so-called first philosophy along with an acceptance of either weak or strong scientism);
2 An etiological account of how all entities whatsoever have come to be, constituted by an event-causal story (especially the atomic theory of matter and evolutionary biology) described in natural scientific terms; and
3 A general ontology in which the only entities allowed are ones that bear a relevant similarity to those thought to characterize a completed form of physics. Whether or not this ontology should be expanded to include *sui generis* emergent properties, e.g. secondary qualities, normative or mental properties, will occupy our attention shortly.

The ordering of these three ingredients is important. The naturalist epistemic attitude serves as justification for the naturalist etiology, which together justify the naturalist's ontological commitment. Moreover, naturalism seems to require coherence among what is postulated in these three different areas of the naturalistic turn. Thus, in setting up his naturalist project, David Papineau claims that we should set philosophy within science in the sense that philosophical investigation should be conducted within the framework of our best empirical theories. It follows, says Papineau, that "the task of the philosophers is to bring coherence and order to the set of assumptions we use to explain the empirical world."[7] By way of application, there should be coherence among third-person scientific ways of knowing, a physical, evolutionary account of how our sensory and cognitive processes came to be, and an ontological analysis of those processes themselves. Any entities that are taken to exist should bear a relevant similarity to entities that characterize our best (or ideal) physical theories, their coming-to-be should be intelligible in light of the naturalist causal story, and they should be knowable by scientific means.

The naturalist epistemic attitude

As with much of modern philosophy, naturalism is primarily an expression of an epistemic posture, specifically, a posture called scientism. In the early 1960s, Wilfrid Sellars expressed this posture when he said, "in the dimension of describing and explaining the world, science is the measure of all things, of what is that it is, and of what is not that it is not."[8] Steven Wagner and Richard Warner claim that naturalism is "the view that only natural science deserves full and unqualified credence."[9] Contemporary naturalists embrace either weak or strong scientism. According to the former, nonscientific fields are not worthless nor do they offer no intellectual results, but they are notably inferior to science in their epistemic standing and do not merit full credence. According to the latter, unqualified cognitive value resides in science and in nothing else. Either way, naturalists are extremely skeptical of any claims about reality that are not justified by scientific methodology in the hard sciences. For example, that methodology is a third-person one and the entities justified by it are capable of exhaustive description from a third-person perspective. Entities that require the first-person perspective as the basic mode of epistemic access to them are to be met with skepticism.

Naturalists believe that they are justified in this posture because of the success of science *vis-à-vis* other fields of inquiry. In addition, some naturalists justify this standpoint by appealing to the unity of science, though this argument is employed less frequently today than it was a few decades ago. For example, in the late 1970s, Roy Bhaskar asserted that "*naturalism* may be defined as the thesis that there is (or can be) an essential unity of method between the natural and the social sciences."[10] Moreover, as John Searle notes, since for these naturalists science exhausts what we can know, then belief in the unity of science turns out to be a belief in the unity of all knowledge because it is scientific knowledge:

> Every fact in the universe is in principle knowable and understandable by human investigators. Because reality is physical, and because science

> concerns the investigation of physical reality, and because there are no limits on what we can know of physical reality, it follows that all facts are knowable and understandable by us.[11]

For such naturalists, the exhaustive or elevated nature of scientific knowledge entails that either the only explanations that count or the ones with superior, unqualified acceptance are those employed in the hard sciences.[12]

We have seen that scientism is the core epistemic posture of the contemporary naturalist. From this core commitment, at least three philosophical theses follow that in one way or another elaborate the epistemic and methodological constraints for philosophy that are part of taking the naturalistic turn. First, there is no such thing as first philosophy. According to David Papineau, there is a continuity between philosophy and natural science:

> the task of the philosophers is to bring coherence and order to the total set of assumptions we use to explain the natural world.
>
> The question at issue is whether *all* philosophical theorizing is of this kind. Naturalists will say that it is. Those with a more traditional attitude to philosophy will disagree. These traditionalists will allow, of course, that some philosophical problems, problems in *applied* philosophy, as it were, will fit the above account. But they will insist that when we turn to "first philosophy," to the investigation of such fundamental categories as thought and knowledge, then philosophy must proceed independently of science. Naturalists will respond that there is no reason to place first philosophy outside of science.[13]

Second, the naturalist epistemology generates intellectual pressure to employ epistemology—or language which has become the surrogate epistemology for many naturalists—to deflate, eliminate or reduce ontological matters that are *prima facie* philosophical and not scientific to epistemic or linguistic ones. Thus, Paul Churchland replaces the first-person qualitative ontology of pain with a physicalist substitute because the latter is more epistemically acceptable from a naturalist perspective: the former is derived from a discredited first-person knowledge by acquaintance, whereas all one needs for explaining our notion of pain is linguistic know-how regarding the term "pain" discernible in terms of the third-person perspective.[14] Keith Campbell reduces the ontological notion of "abstract" (not existing in space or time) in debates about abstract objects to an epistemic notion (attending to a property-instance by disregarding a number of features in its noetic environment; an abstract particular is one that is brought before the mind by certain acts of noticing and disregarding).[15] David Papineau undercuts and, thus, places a substantial burden of proof on dualist ontological claims they take to be descriptive reports of events and properties with which they are introspectively acquainted. By contrast, Papineau employs a version of epistemic methodism to establish the terms of debate and thereby dismiss such dualist claims: A claim about mental entities is justified if and only if it is required by the categories of an ideal physics.[16]

These are not isolated incidents. They are expressions of a proper understanding of the impact on ontology of the naturalist epistemology and its certified creation account by three of naturalism's brightest lights. It is widely recognized that the sorts of naturalistic *reduction*—Nagelian and linguistic—that flourished from the 1930s to the 1960s was intellectually motivated by epistemic, specifically positivistic, concerns. Moreover, while positivism has gone the way of the dodo, its epistemic (or linguistic) remains are what underwrite the sorts of ontological moves illustrated by the naturalist triumvirate above.

Third, scientific theories that are paradigm cases of epistemic/explanatory success, e.g. the atomic theory of matter and evolutionary biology, employ combinatorial modes of explanation. Thus, any process that constitutes the Grand Story and any entity in the naturalist ontology should exhibit an ontological structure analyzable in terms that are isomorphic with such modes of explanation. Perhaps more than anyone, Colin McGinn has defended this idea along with what he takes it to entail, viz. the inability of naturalism to explain genuinely unique emergent properties:

> Can we gain any deeper insight into what makes the problem of consciousness run against the grain of our thinking? Are our modes of theorizing about the world of the wrong shape to extend to the nature of mind? I think we can discern a characteristic structure possessed by successful scientific theories, a structure that is unsuitable for explaining consciousness. ... Is there a "grammar" to science that fits the physical world but becomes shaky with applied to the mental world?
>
> Perhaps the most basic aspect of thought is the operation of *combination*. This is the way in which we think of complex entities as resulting from the arrangement of simpler parts. There are three aspects to this basic idea: the atoms we start with, the laws we use to combine them, and the resulting complexes ... I think it is clear that this mode of understanding is central to what we think of as scientific theory; our scientific faculty involves representing the world in this combinatorial style.[17]

We have looked at a number of philosophers who express different aspects of the naturalist epistemic attitude. Let us now turn to an overview of the naturalist's view of how things came to be.

The naturalist Grand Story

The naturalist has an account of how all things whatever came to be. Let us call this account the Grand Story. The details of the Grand Story need not concern us here. Some version of the Big Bang is the most reasonable view currently available. On this view, all of reality—space, time, and matter—came from the original "creation" event and the various galaxies, stars, and other heavenly bodies eventually developed as the expanding universe went through various stages. On at least one of those heavenly bodies—earth—some sort of pre-biotic soup scenario explains how living things came into being from non-living chemicals. Moreover, the processes of evolution, understood in either neo-Darwinian or punctuated equilibrium terms, gave rise to all the life forms we see including human beings. Thus, all organisms and their parts exist and are what they are because they contributed to (or at least did not hinder) the struggle for reproductive advantage, more specifically, because they contributed to the tasks of feeding, fighting, fleeing, and reproducing.

There are four important things to note about the Grand Story. First, at the core of the Grand Story are two theories that result from combinatorial modes of explanation: the atomic theory of matter and evolutionary theory. If we take John Searle to be representative of naturalists here, this means that causal explanations, specifically, bottom-up but not top-down causal explanations, are central to the (alleged) explanatory superiority of the Grand Story.[18]

Second, it is an expression of a scientistic version of philosophical monism. According to this view, everything that exists or happens in the world is susceptible to explanations by natural scientific methods. Whatever exists or happens in the world is natural in this sense. *Prima facie*, the most consistent way to understand naturalism in this regard is to see it as entailing some version of strong or strict physicalism: everything that exists is fundamentally matter, most likely, elementary "particles" (whether taken as points of potentiality, centers of mass/energy, units of spatially extended stuff/waves or reduced to/eliminated in favor of fields), organized in various ways according to the laws of nature.[19] By keeping track of these particles and their physical traits, we are keeping track of everything that exists. No non-physical entities exist, including emergent ones. This constitutes a strong sense of physicalism. When naturalists venture away from strong physicalism, however, they still argue that additions to a strong physicalist ontology must be depicted as rooted in, emergent from, dependent upon the physical states and events of the Grand Story. Whether or not emergent properties should be allowed in a naturalist ontology will occupy our attention throughout this book.

Third, the Grand Story is constituted by event causality. It eschews both irreducible teleology and agent causation in which the first relatum of the causal relation is in the category of substance and not event. Moreover, the Grand Story is deterministic in two senses: diachronically such that the state of the universe at any time t coupled with the laws of nature determine or fix the chances for the state of the universe at subsequent times; synchronically such that the features of and changes regarding macro-wholes are dependent on and determined by micro-phenomena.

Finally, while some naturalists eschew questions about the nature of existence itself, others have formulated an analysis of existence—sometimes called the Eleatic principle of existence—based on a naturalist epistemology and consistent with the Grand Story. Thus, Bruce Aune defines *a exists* as "a belongs to the space-time-causal system that is our world. Our world is, again, that system of (roughly) causally related objects."[20] Along similar lines, D. M. Armstrong says that for any entities, the following question settles the issue of whether or not those entities can be said to exist: "Are these entities, or are they not, capable of action upon the spatio-temporal system? Do these entities, or do they not, act in nature?"[21] Daniel Dennett claims that when we are trying to find out whether or not some entity like the self exists, what we must do is locate the entity within the causal fabric.[22] Keith Campbell applies the same reasoning to the question of the existence of emergent entities like social characteristics by claiming that the test of their existence turns on their ability to exhibit independent causality because "power has been recognized as the mark of being."[23] Finally, Jaegwon Kim says, "Causal powers and reality go hand in hand. To render mental events causally impotent is as good as banishing them from our ontology."[24] The sort of causal power characteristic of the entities most consistent with the processes, properties, relations and particulars that constitute the Grand Story is passive liability and not active power.

The naturalist ontology

Weak vs. strong naturalism

In order to characterize a naturalist ontology, we must distinguish global vs. local naturalism and weak vs. strong naturalism. Roughly, global naturalism is the view that the spatio-temporal universe of natural entities studied by science is all there is. Global naturalists (e.g. Wilfrid Sellars) reject abstract objects of any kind, including traditional realist properties. Local naturalists (e.g. Jeffrey Poland) either accept or are indifferent towards abstract objects but they insist that the spatio-temporal universe consists only of entities studied by the natural sciences. Local naturalists reject Cartesian souls, Aristotelian entelechies, and so forth.

A distinction also exists between strong and weak naturalists. Strong naturalists (e.g. David Papineau) accept a strong version of physicalism (all individuals, events, states of affairs, properties, relations and laws are entirely physical) for the natural world, while weak naturalists (e.g. John Searle) embrace various emergent entities. Elsewhere, I have argued against global naturalism because naturalists should eschew universals (construed as abstract objects) and other abstract objects yet such entities do, in fact, exist.[25] The debate about global naturalism will not be of concern in this book, except in chapter five in connection with evaluating McGinn's rejection of certain dualist rivals to his attempt to reconcile consciousness with naturalism.

The location problem

For our purposes, it is important to say a bit more about criteria for naturalist ontological commitments. A good place to start is with what Frank Jackson calls the "location problem."[26] According to Jackson, on the basis of the superiority of scientific ways of knowing exemplified by the hard sciences, naturalists are committed to a fairly widely-accepted physical story about how things came to be (the Grand Story) and what they are. The location problem is the task of locating or finding a place for some entity (for example, semantic contents, mind and agency) in that story.

For Jackson, the naturalist must either locate a problematic entity in the basic story or eliminate the entity. Roughly, an entity is located in the basic story just in case it is entailed by that story. Otherwise, the entity must be eliminated. At this point, it is worth recalling that Kim and others have complained that one does not *explain* a phenomenon by labeling it supervenient. Likewise, one might think that someone hasn't really "located" a puzzling phenomena if all one has done is point out that it necessarily covaries with this or that sort of physical phenomenon. In any case, Jackson provides three examples of location. First, just as density is a different property from mass and volume, it is not an additional feature of reality over and above mass and volume in at least this sense: an account of things in terms of mass and volume implicitly contains, i.e. entails the account in terms of density. Second, Jones being taller than Smith is not an additional feature of reality over and above Jones' and Smith's heights because the relational fact is entailed, and in this sense located by the latter.

More importantly, Jackson focuses on the location of macro-solidity. He acknowledges that prior to modern science there was a widely accepted commonsense notion of macro-solidity, viz., being everywhere dense. However, due to modern science, this notion has been replaced with being impenetrable. So understood, macro-solidity may be located in the basic micro-story: given a description of two macro-objects in terms of their atomic parts, lattice structures, and sub-atomic forces of repulsion, this description entails that one macro-object is impenetrable with respect to the other.

Jackson believes there are four important sorts of troublesome entities that the naturalist must locate: mental properties/events, facts associated with the first-person indexical, secondary qualities, and moral properties. Focusing on mental properties/events, Jackson claims that the naturalist must argue that they globally supervene on the physical. He unpacks this claim with two clarifications. First, he defines a minimal physical duplicate of our world as "a world that (a) is exactly like our world in every physical respect (instantiated property for instantiated property, law for law, relation for relation), and (b) contains nothing else in the sense of nothing more by way of kinds or particulars than it *must* to satisfy (a)."[27] Second, he advocates B*: "Any world which is a *minimal* physical duplicate of our world is a psychological duplicate of our world."[28]

Jackson concludes in this way:

> Let φ be the story as told in purely physical terms, which is true at the actual world and all the minimal physical duplicates of the actual world, and false elsewhere; φ is a hugely complex, purely physical account of our world. Let ψ be any true sentence which is about the psychological nature of our world in the sense that it can only come false by things being different psychologically from the way they actually are: every world at which ψ is false differs in some psychological way from our world. Intuitively, the idea is that ψ counts as being about the psychological nature of our world because making it false requires supposing a change in the distribution of psychological properties and relations. … [E]very world at which φ is true is a world at which ψ is true—that is, φ entails ψ.[29]

The logic of the mereological hierarchy

Jackson grasps the connection between accepting the epistemic superiority of naturalism and deciding between weak and strong naturalism. For Jackson, if naturalism is to have superior explanatory power, this entails strong naturalism. Jackson correctly understands that there are at least three constraints for developing a naturalist ontology and locating entities within it:

a Entities should conform to the naturalist epistemology.
b Entities should conform to the naturalist Grand Story.
c Entities should bear a relevant similarity to those found in chemistry and physics or merely be capable of one-to-one or one-to-many correlation with entities in chemistry or physics or be shown to depend necessarily on entities in chemistry and physics.

Regarding the naturalist epistemology, all entities should be subject to combinatorial modes of explanation and be entirely publicly accessible and, thus, should be knowable entirely by third-person scientific means. Regarding the Grand Story, one should be able to show how any entity *had* to appear in light of the naturalist event-causal story according to which the history of the cosmos amounts to a series of events governed by natural law in which micro-parts come together to form various aggregates with increasingly complex physical structures.

As we shall see in subsequent chapters, these constraints seem to rule out the existence of genuinely emergent properties. When construed in terms of emergent properties, the second disjunct of (c) "solves" the so-called hard problem of consciousness, the explanatory gap, by simply naming the problem and dismissing the need for a naturalist to do any further explanatory work. For many philosophers, including many naturalists, this strategy is inadequate. The second disjunct also suffers from the difficulty of justifying the existence of *sui generis* emergent entities in light of criteria (a) and (b). The third disjunct of (c) suffers from this latter problem and from difficulties with justifying the claim that emergent entities are "necessitated" by their subvenient physical bases. Clarifying and defending these claims are central to the desiderata of this book. But it may be useful at this stage of reflection to show how (a) and (b) justify the standard layered mereological hierarchy as the proper naturalist ontology.

Let us construe this hierarchy in terms of individual entities and properties rather than in terms of concepts or linguistic descriptions. So understood, the standard mereological hierarchy consists in an ascending level of entities in the category of individual such that for each level above the ground level of elementary micro-physics (at which entities have no further physically significant separable parts), wholes at that level are composed of the separable parts at lower levels. Thus, from bottom to top we get micro-physical entities (strings, waves, particles, fields?), sub-atomic parts, atoms, molecules, cells, living organisms, and so on. The relationship between individuals at level n and $n+1$ is the part/whole relation. But there are two kinds of parts relevant to the hierarchy—separable and inseparable.

p is a separable part of some whole W = def. p is a particular and p can exist if it is not a part of W.

p is an inseparable part of some whole W = def. p is a particular and p cannot exist if it is not a part of W.

In contemporary philosophy, inseparable parts were most fruitfully analyzed in the writings of Brentano, Husserl and their followers.[30] The paradigm case of an inseparable part in this tradition is a (monadic) property-instance or relation-instance. The mereological hierarchy explicitly employs and only employs separable parts.

For present purposes, there is an important point to make about the hierarchy in the category of individual (and as we will see below, the category of property): *The "hierarchy" is not really a hierarchy.* There is no ascending, no going up anything. Rather, the levels form spatio-temporally wider and wider wholes. So we should think of the "hierarchy" as going out, not up. To see this, consider the relationship between a water molecule and its constituent atoms. There are two ways to analyze the water molecule.

First, we may adopt the eliminativist line of Peter van Inwagen and Trenton Merricks and eliminate water molecules in favor of certain collections of proper separable parts arranged waterwise.[31] Let "the p's" stand for all and only the atomic simples that constitute such an arrangement. The difference between the p's and the p's being arranged waterwise is that the latter includes and the former does not include a relational structure. Elsewhere, I have defended a realist constituent ontology for properties/relations and their instances.[32] Nothing of importance here turns on this assumption, so for ease of exposition, let us grant it. It follows that the structure itself is nothing but a combination of relation-instances that stand between and among and only between and among the p's. On this view, it becomes clear that the molecule is not riding on top of anything because there is no such thing as a water molecule. Moreover, the-p's-arranged-waterwise is not something such that its relationship to its separable parts (the p's) is top/down. Rather, we have a relational structure that is spatio-temporally wider than any of its constituent proper separable parts. So if there is any hierarchy at all, that hierarchy does not move up and there is no top or down; it moves out: there are wider and wider relational arrangements in focus.

Second, we may resist the eliminativist line and provide an analysis of the water molecule that grounds its unity such that it is not exhaustively decomposable into a relevant collection of parts and an individuated structure. There are two main ways of doing this. The first is to attribute to the water molecule a particular sort of inseparable part called a boundary or surface. Arguably, entities at the microphysical level have boundaries/surfaces, so one may employ such an entity at "higher" levels of analysis without bloating one's basic ontological categories. By providing a metaphysical limit such that entities within the boundary or surface are constituents of the whole and those outside the boundary are not, it unifies and reifies the water molecule such that it cannot be exhaustively decomposed along eliminativist lines.[33]

The second is to attribute to the molecule an individuated essence of its own, e.g. a substantial form construed as an abstract particular, an individuated essence construed as an *infimae species*, or an haecceitas construed as a Leibnizian essence. There are at least two reasons why there is pressure for naturalists to reject this solution. First, this alternative commits one to a shopping-list approach to metaphysics in which one *sui generis* entity after another is added to one's ontology. Any self-respecting materialist should reject this bloated ontology because it is not simple and it means that in principle an ideal physics does not exhaustively carve the cosmos at its most basic joints. To be sure, there are several versions of *reduction*, but now is not the time to discuss them. However, if understood as the drive to keep one's ontology to a minimum in light of the Grand Story, the spirit of *reductio*n is at the heart of naturalism. Second, such an ontological pluralism and its voluminous list of brute facts stretch the explanatory resources of the naturalist epistemology and Grand Story beyond the breaking point.

Note carefully that such individuated essences are neither physical (they are not constituents over which physical theory quantifies) nor entailed by the Grand Story. Instead, they are metaphysical entities added to the naturalist ontology to solve distinctively philosophical problems for which science is silent. For example, to solve problems of individuation, Jackson acknowledges that it may well be the case that,

> The physicalist will need to require that minimal physical duplicates of our world be ones which, in addition to being identical in respect of physical properties, laws, and relations with our world, are identical in which *haecceities* are associated with which physical properties, laws, and relations.[34]

For Jackson, *haecceities* are entities not included in the physical description of the world. Such individuated essences were central to the Medieval Great Chain of Being, which remains the paradigm case of pluralistic shopping-list ontology, an ontology completely rejected with the rise of the mechanical philosophy.

If this is correct, then the two main naturalist alternatives for analyzing "higher level" individuals should be the eliminativist or the boundary/surface alternatives. On each alternative, "higher level" wholes are wider than and not higher than their constituent parts, and those wholes are capable of combinatorial explanation ultimately in terms of the micro-physical level in keeping with the naturalist epistemology and Grand Story. No non-structural, *sui generis* entities of which the lowest level is bereft are needed, and we have a macro-ontology in which entities are differentiated by individuated relational structures in keeping with ontological constraints (a) and (b) above.

So much for the category of individual. What about the category of property (and relation)? Are there ontological constraints for what sorts of properties a naturalist should include in the hierarchy? I believe there are, and to get at those constraints, note that as typically presented, the hierarchy entails the causal closure of the basic microphysical level along with the ontological dependence of entities and their activities at supervenient levels on entities and their activities at that basic level.

Causal closure and the related matter of top/down causation are controversial, and not all naturalists accept the former or reject the latter. But closure and a rejection of top/down causation are hard for a naturalist to avoid. As Kim nicely states, the basic naturalist argument in favor of causal closure is that if it is rejected, then

> you are ipso facto rejecting the in-principle completeability of physics—that is, the possibility of a complete and comprehensive physical theory of all physical phenomena. For you would be saying that any complete

> explanatory theory of the physical domain must invoke nonphysical causal agents. ... It is safe to assume that no serious physicalist could accept such a prospect.[35]

The so-called "completeability of physics" is not an arbitrary postulate in a naturalist worldview. It follows quite naturally once one understands the Grand Story. That Story gives the naturalist an account of how all things have come-to-be, and the Story's account is one according to which one begins at the Big Bang with a small number of physical entities and explains the origin and behavior of everything else in terms of the laws of physics and new combinations of micro-physical entities. The Story itself gives pride of place to micro-physical entities and it is bottom/up at its core. The completeability of physics is essential to the plausibility of the naturalist creation myth.

The causal closure principle is not arbitrary from a naturalist perspective nor is it an additional postulate that naturalists are intellectually free to reject. It follows from the combinatorial mode of causal explanation and the Grand Story's commitment to the sort of micro-macro constitution and determination at the core of the atomic theory of matter, evolutionary biology and other central theories of how things have come to be. As we shall see in later chapters, if a naturalist rejects closure he or she will have to accept *sui generis*, contingent brute facts. In turn, this undermines the claim that a naturalist worldview is superior to rivals because it can explain how all things have come to be.

There are two different ways to understand causal closure: (1) Every physical event has a physical cause. (2) No physical event has a non-physical cause. The Grand Story, as Kim correctly notes, implies a complete and comprehensive theory of the physical domain and, indeed, the cosmos and everything that occurs within it. Thus, the Grand Story provides a reason for preferring (2) to (1).

Besides closure, a related issue for deciding what sorts or properties should populate the hierarchy is the problem of top/down causation. I believe there is severe intellectual pressure that follows from the nature of naturalism itself for rejecting top/down causation for genuinely emergent *sui generis* properties. Moreover, the only way to save top/down causation is to reduce it to outside/in causation that occurs with respect to structural wholes at the same level as their parts via causal feedback. I also think that the price to be paid for retaining causal laws in the special sciences is to disallow emergent properties and allow only microphysically based structural properties constituted by microphysical parts, properties and relationships. If this is right, it follows that an adequate treatment of these desiderata (to preserve "top/down" causation and causal laws in the special sciences) entails that a naturalist ontology constituted by the standard mereological hierarchy can countenance structural wholes in the category of individual and structural supervenient properties in the category of property. But note that it cannot countenance genuine emergent properties, especially causally active emergent properties. All emergent properties, if such there be, must be epiphenomenal.

Before proceeding, I want to clarify the difference between emergent and structural properties and supervenience in a way that is apt for what follows. An emergent property is a unique, new kind of property different from those that characterize its subvenient base. Accordingly, emergent supervenience is the view that the supervenient property is a simple, intrinsically characterizeable, novel property different from and not composed of the parts, properties, relations, and events at the subvenient level. We may characterize "novel" as follows:

> Property P is a *novel* emergent property of some particular x at level l_n just in case P is an emergent property, x exemplifies P, and there are no determinates P' of the same determinable D as P such that some particular at a level below l_n exemplifies P or P'.[36]

By contrast, a structural property is one that is constituted by the parts, properties, relations, and events at the subvenient level. A structural property is identical to a configurational pattern among the subvenient entities. It is not a new kind of property; it is a new pattern, a new configuration of subvenient entities. In addition, many philosophers would characterize emergent and structural supervenience as causal and constitutive, respectively. Since I am contrasting emergent and structurally supervenient properties, I will use the notion of an emergent property as simply being a novel, *sui generis* property.

For two reasons, if we assume that mental properties are genuinely emergent *sui generis* qualities, then given the mereological hierarchy and its disallowance of top/down causation, the existence of emergent mental properties presents at least two problems for naturalism. First, for those naturalists who accept a causal criterion of existence, emergent mental properties are epiphenomenal and, thus, do not exist. One is then faced with a dilemma: Either one accepts phenomenal consciousness, which construes emergent mental properties along familiar lines as what-it-is-like to be such and such and rejects causal closure *or* one retains closure and rejects phenomenal consciousness because it is epiphenomenal. In my view, the latter option is the correct one for a naturalist to take. Nevertheless, irrespective of whether I am right, in subsequent chapters, we will be examining only versions of naturalism that accept emergent mental properties. For naturalists of this stripe, the problem of epiphenomenalism must be addressed in an adequate way.

Second, it is obvious that mental states are causal factors in our behavior. It is hard to see how knowledge and agency can be salvaged if this is denied. Indeed, if an analysis of mental states entails epiphenomenalism, this is widely recognized as fodder for a *reductio* against that analysis. This is why most naturalists think that the only way to save mental causation is in one way or another to identify it with the physical.

More than any other naturalist, Jaegwon Kim has pressed the problem of top/down mental causation for naturalism.[37] Kim correctly notes that the problem of mental causation arises from the very nature of physicalism itself, and not from a Cartesian view of mental substance and, indeed, mental causation is a difficulty in the category of property every bit as much as in the category of substance.

Kim's supervenience argument (a.k.a. the exclusion argument) purportedly shows that, given the irreducibility of the mental, there can be no mental causation in a world that is fundamentally physical, and according to Kim, this raises serious problems regarding cognition and agency, two features of our lives that are hard to give up. The supervenience argument, says Kim, may be construed to show that mental causation is inconsistent with the conjunction of four theses: (1) closure; (2) exclusion (no overdetermination); (3) supervenience (not construed simply as property covariance, but taken to entail dependence and synchronic determination); and (4) mental irreducibility. The fundamental idea of the supervenience argument is that "vertical determination excludes horizontal causation." To see this, Kim invites us to consider two physical events, p and p*, along with two mental events, m and m* such that (1) m and m* supervene on p and p* respectively (where supervenience includes the notion of dependence and determination, even if this is not taken to be efficient causality) and (2) p causes p*.

The argument proceeds in two stages. Stage 1: Focus on m to m* causation. Since m* obtains in virtue of p*, if m is going to cause m* it must do so by causing p*. Stage 2: Kim offers two different ways to complete the argument. Completion 1: Assuming causal closure and exclusion (no causal overdetermination), p will be the cause of p* and there is no room for m to be involved in bringing about p*. We have m and m* supervening on p and p*, respectively, and p causing p*, nothing more and nothing less. Completion 2: Granting that m causes m* by causing p*, if follows that m causes p*. By irreducibility, we have $m \neq p$. So m and p cause m*. By exclusion and closure, m is ruled out and p is selected as the only cause for p*. Completion 2 avoids reference to supervenience. On either way of completing stage two, we have m→m* and m→p* giving way to p→p*.

Some have not been persuaded by Kim's argument, though I am not among them.[38] More importantly, we have already examined reasons for why a naturalist should accept closure and reject top/down causation that follow naturally from the naturalist epistemic attitude and Grand Story. I will argue below that there are additional reasons for accepting closure and rejecting top/down causation if we limit our focus to emergent properties. Within this limitation, I believe that there are strong reasons to hold that top/down causation is disallowed by a naturalist view that entails the standard mereological model. If this is so, then mental causation can obtain only if the mental is not emergent but, rather, in some way or another identified with the physical. However, there have been counter-examples offered that allegedly show that top/down causation is real and consistent with the standard hierarchy. Roger Sperry offered a paradigm case of such a counterexample.[39] According to Sperry, there can be top/down causation without disrupting or intervening in the causal relations or micro-interactions at the elementary level. Such top/down causation does not disrupt the laws or behavior of entities at that level. Here is his example:

> A molecule within the rolling wheel, for example, though retaining its usual inter-molecular relations within the wheel, is at the same time, from the standpoint of an outside observer, being carried through particular patterns in space and time determined by the over-all properties of the wheel as a whole. There need be no "reconfiguring" of molecules relative to each other *within the wheel itself*. However, *relative to the rest of the world* the result is a major "reconfiguring" of the space-time trajectories of all components in the wheel's infrastructure.[40]

Unfortunately, for two reasons this analogy fails as an example of real top/down causation of emergent properties as we are assuming mental properties to be. Note first that the "over-all properties of the wheel as a whole" are not emergent properties caused by and on top of subvenient entities. They are mere structural complexes constitutively supervenient "on," that is, constituted by base entities. What we have is a wider relational context of molecules than would obtain as inter-molecular relations among a small set of the wheel's constituents if the larger context were annihilated. But the wheel and such a set of molecules are at the same level. Regarding the wheel's effect on some specific molecule, we have outside/in causation, not top/down. Second, the "reconfigured" space-time trajectory of some specific molecule is not an emergent property at all, at least not in the way we are treating mental properties. Mental properties are emergent in the sense that they are genuinely new *kinds* of properties that in no way characterize the base level. However, the "reconfigured" trajectory is merely a new combination of spatial and temporal properties that already characterize the base. The wheel case is merely an example of outside-in causal interaction due to wider structural relations at the base level. I believe similar problems beset other alleged cases of top/down causation.

There is also a problem with emergent causal powers and laws in the special sciences. To get at this problem, let us begin by examining Kim's treatment of the generalization problem.[41] According to Kim, if we grant property/event dualism, then given causal closure and the rejection of overdetermination, mental top/down causation cannot occur. He also argues that causal closure is not needed for the rejection of mental causation. If we reject the notion that there cannot be two sufficient efficient causes for some physical event that is, in fact, caused, and grant for the sake of argument that there is a mental cause for some physical event, then we have two competing causal stories. Why? Given the Grand Story and the assumption that the physical event in focus was caused, there is a clear story about antecedent physical causes for the event. However, there is no room for the higher mental story to be efficacious given that the supervenience of the higher story on the micro-physical story entails an ontological dependence and determination of the former on the latter. Thus, eschewal of top/down mental causation follows merely from supervenience (taken to include the dependence and determination of the emergent mental event on its physical base) and a rejection of overdetermination (and from the irreducibility of the mental).

But now we face the generalization problem: Does the causal impotency of higher-level mental properties/events threaten other higher-level properties in the special sciences, e.g. chemical, geological, biological properties? Kim offers a response to the generalization problem that he takes to be adequate for saving the causal powers in focus in the special sciences. His solution begins by rejecting the idea that the mind/brain supervenience relationship which renders the mental epiphenomenal is the same as the relationship between higher-level properties in special sciences like geology and lower-level micro-physical properties. Kim draws a distinction between different levels up the hierarchy and different orders within a single level. Now, if we focus on the supervenience of the mental on brain states, we are actually depicting higher-order mental properties as structural functional properties (for Kim, concepts) that are realized by brain states. In this case, the realization relation is the converse of the supervenience relation and we have either mere conceptual supervenience, structural supervenience or both.

So understood, the realization relation is different from the micro-macro relation, and the realization relation does not track up or down the levels of the hierarchy as does the micro-macro relation. The realization relation stays within one level and higher-order mental properties are at the same level as their physical realizers. Given that the supervenience relation between mental and brain properties and its converse (the realization relation) render mental properties causally impotent, says Kim, this problem is one of higher and lower orders within one level. Thus, it does not generalize to the macro-micro relation that connects different levels up the hierarchy and that is the relevant relation between special science properties and microphysical ones. For an object at a macro-level to have a micro-based property such as being water is for the property to be identical to a set of parts having their properties and standing in certain relations to each other. Being ten kilograms is a micro-based property of a table, says Kim, and it is causally efficacious. In the same way, micro-based properties of earthquakes are such that earthquakes cause things to occur.

Is Kim's solution to the generalization problem successful? If the generalization problem is understood in the specific way Kim frames it, it may well be. The distinction between intra-level higher order functional properties and lower order realizers on the one hand and inter-level micro-based properties along with the micro-macro relation that (allegedly) tracks up the hierarchy is a clear one. Given this distinction, the generalization from mental property causal impotence to properties in various special sciences is blocked.

However, in the context of *sui generis* mental properties and epiphenomenalism, Kim's solution comes at a price. It should be clear that his employment of micro-based properties entails that they are structural and not *sui generis* emergent properties. As such, they are exhaustively decomposable into parts, properties and relations at the subvenient level. These micro-physical constituents constitute micro-based properties. So construed, they may have "new" causal powers in the sense of additive sums of constituent powers or due to a new spatial shape resulting from a new arrangement of subvenient entities, but there are no new *kinds* of causal powers.

Moreover, as I have argued above, the macro-micro relation does not travel up anything. Rather, it ventures outward at the same level, including wider and wider relational structures. If the properties of the special sciences are emergent, then for the reasons we have investigated, they are epiphenomenal. *It is the hierarchy itself, along with the ontological dependency and determination of higher-level novel emergent properties on their subvenient bases that rules out top/down causation. And the hierarchy is not arbitrary for naturalism. The ontology flows out of the Grand Story, which, in turn, is certified by the hard sciences.* Novel emergent properties are like shadows produced by a flashlight. Moreover, if one accepts physical closure and rejects causal overdetermination, we have further reasons for rejecting the top/down causation of novel emergent properties.

Before we summarize our discussion of the naturalist ontology, I want to mention one final constraint on the sorts of properties it should include. If we limit ourselves to macro-properties, an appropriate limitation because consciousness is a macro-feature (except for certain versions of panpsychism—see chapter six), then the following principle seems to be *prima facie* justified:

Principle of Naturalist Exemplification (PNE): (x) Px→Ex

P stands for any property whatever and E stands for the property of being extended. Moreover, x ranges over and only over property-instances. Elsewhere I have defended a constituent ontology in which property-instances are complex entities, and I shall merely assume this ontology here.[42] According to this ontology, when some concrete particular e exemplifies a property P, then the-having-of-P-by-e is a property-instance that is modally distinct from both P and e. X is neither identical to P nor e. So understood, property-instances are certain sorts of states of affairs and, moreover, if the instantiation of P by e is temporal, then the property-instance becomes an event.

Note that P and e are constituents of x. If we focus on paradigm cases that satisfy PNE, it becomes reasonable to hold that the spatial extension of x is grounded in, obtains in virtue of the spatial extension of e. For example, when an apple is red, the-having-of-red-by-the-apple is a property-instance spread out through the extended region occupied by the apple. It is in virtue of the apple's extension that the particular instance of red is extended. This may be seen, for example, by noting that it is because the apple has a particular shape that its instance of red has that shape as well.

PNE says that if a property in the naturalist ontology is to be exemplified, then a necessary condition is that both the concrete particular that exemplifies P and the property-instance that results have spatial extension.

PNE seems to capture nicely the wide range of properties in macro-physics, chemistry, geology, neuro-science, and so forth. It could be objected that PNE fails because certain entities, e.g. some quantum entities are or the point particles of Roger Boscovich were unextended, and provide sufficient counter examples to PNE. I do not think this objection works. Regarding quantum entities, there are at least eight different empirically equivalent philosophical models of quantum reality and, at this stage, it is irresponsible to make dogmatic claims about the ontology of the quantum level.[43] Moreover, since I have limited PNE to the macro-level, we may set aside the quantum world for our purposes. Regarding entities such as Boscovich's point particles, rather than conclude that they are counter examples to PNE, their lack of spatial dimensionality may be taken as a *reductio* against them. And, indeed, this is how the history of physics ran. Boscovich's point particles fit more easily into a spiritualist ontology, e.g. Berkeley's, than in a straightforward version of materialism, and like action at a distance, they were rejected.

There is a debate about whether individual mental states such as pains and thoughts are extended. I cannot enter that debate here. Nevertheless, based on PNE, if it turns out that mental states are not extended, then PNE banishes them and their constituent properties from a naturalist ontology. In this case, PNE counts against any naturalist ontology that quantifies over emergent mental properties.

It is time to summarize what a naturalist ontology should look like.[44] In the category of individual, if we reject an eliminativist strategy, then all wholes "above" the microphysical level are structural, relational entities constituted by the parts, properties and relations at the microphysical level. Such wholes stand in a constituent/whole relation to these microphysical entities and are actually wider entities at the basic level. This is true whether we adopt an eliminativist line for such wholes (and accept atomic simples and various arrangements of them) or add some sort of boundary or surface.

Regarding the category of property, consider the following:

Emergence$_0$: New features that can be deduced from base (e.g. fractal patterns).

Emergence$_1$: Ordinary structural properties (e.g. being water, solidity)

Emergence$_{2a}$: *Sui generis*, simple, intrinsically characterizable, new kinds of properties relative to base that are also epiphenomenal (e.g. being painful construed epiphenomenally).

Emergence$_{2b}$: *Sui generis*, simple, intrinsically characterizable, new kinds of properties relative to base with new causal powers construed as passive liabilities (e.g. being painful understood as having top/down causal liabilities).

Emergence$_{2c}$: *Sui generis*, simple, intrinsically characterizable, new kinds of properties with active power (e.g. being active power that characterizes most versions of agent causation).

Emergence$_3$: An emergent, suitably unified mental subject or I with active power.

Clearly, emergence$_0$ and emergence$_1$ fit nicely in the mereological hierarchy and conform to the naturalist epistemology (e.g. combinatorial explanation) and Grand Story. But emergence$_{2a}$ through emergence$_3$ should be disallowed for reasons we have already investigated, e.g. they resist functionalization. It would seem that all a naturalist could do with them is simply to label them as contingent brute facts and assert that they are not a problem for the naturalist. We will look at different attempts to handle some of these sorts of properties in subsequent chapters. But we have already examined reasons to be highly suspicious of a naturalist view that accepts one or more of these sorts of properties and also claims that naturalism is explanatorily and epistemically superior to alternative worldviews.

Moreover, there is an increasingly heavy burden of proof on a naturalist ontology as one moves from emergence$_{2a}$ to emergence$_3$. All types of emergence fall prey to previous arguments against emergent entities. Emergence$_{2a}$ requires less justification than stronger forms of emergence because it does not require a rejection of closure. Emergence$_{2b}$ is subject to these arguments and additional difficulties with top/down causation and causal closure. But relative to emergence$_{2c}$ and emergence$_3$ it has the advantage of exhibiting the same sort of causal power—passive liability subject to law—that characterizes causal particulars at the microphysical level.

Emergence$_{2c}$ has all the problems exemplified by emergence$_{2b}$ and it also suffers from having a completely unique sort of causal power—active power—different from the causal powers that range throughout the naturalist ontology outside of agent causal events. Emergence$_3$ shares all of the difficulties with emergence$_{2c}$ and it also suffers from two further facts not easily accommodated in the naturalist ontology if they are taken as irreducible and uneliminable facts about the world: First, the indexical fact associated with "I." Second, difficulties with explaining how one can get a sort of primitive, substantial unity in which its various inseparable parts/faculties are internally related to the substantial subject from a mereological aggregate constituted by a structural arrangement of separable parts that stand in external relations to each other and their mereological whole.

D. M. Armstrong as a paradigm case naturalist

I have argued that the naturalist epistemology and Grand Story constrain the naturalist ontology and justify strong naturalism and a rejection of emergent entities. It may be worth noting that many naturalists who keep a steady eye on broader epistemological and metaphysical issues reach the same conclusion. More than anyone else, D. M. Armstrong had clearly reflected on this topic and he concludes that all entities in the naturalist ontology must be: 1) spatially located; 2) entities knowledge of which conform to an externalist causal epistemology; 3) capable of entering into causal relations; and 4) entities whose existence can be given a natural scientific causal explanation according to the Grand Story.

To illustrate these points in Armstrong, the following statement is an example where he uses a naturalist externalist epistemology to settle issues in ontology:

> If any entities outside this [spatio-temporal] realm are postulated, but it is stipulated further that they have no manner of causal action upon the particulars in this realm, then there is no compelling reason to postulate them.[45]

In this context, Armstrong is claiming that the only way something can interact with natural entities—including cognitive processes to be objects of knowledge—is by way of causation.

Armstrong also employs the Grand Story as a criterion for an acceptable naturalist ontology:

> I suppose that if the principles involved [in analyzing and explaining the origin of or processes of change in things within the single all-embracing spatio-temporal system which is reality] were completely different from the current principles of physics, in particular if they

> involved appeal to mental entities, such as purposes, we might then count the analysis as a falsification of Naturalism.[46]

Elsewhere, he uses the Grand Story, coupled with scientism and epistemic simplicity to justify a strong physicalist analysis of mental entities, along with a *reduction* of secondary qualities to micro-physical entities.[47] Regarding secondary qualities, Armstrong claims that while the naturalist should hold that secondary qualities are objective features of the external world, she

> cannot put them back into the world *alongside* and in *addition* to the properties that contemporary science attributes to physical objects. ... There really is no place in the physical world for such extra properties. What we must say, rather, is that these properties are respectable, but *micro-physical*, properties of objects, surfaces, and so on. ... The general idea is to find *micro-physical correlates* for the secondary qualities of physical objects and events and then to identify the qualities with these physical correlates.[48]

Further, as a naturalist, Armstrong explicitly rejects internal relations because they cannot be spatio-temporally located and thus, are disanalogous with other entities in the Grand Story. Their lack of spatial location also means they cannot enter into physical causal relations with the brain, which is a necessary condition to be an object of knowledge or justified belief in a naturalized externalist epistemology.[49] Armstrong clearly grasps the inner logic of naturalism.

Serious metaphysics, simplicity and emergent properties

Frank Jackson begins his attempt to develop a naturalistic account of the mental by contrasting two very different approaches to metaphysics. The first he calls serious metaphysics. Serious metaphysics is not content to draw up large pluralistic lists of *sui generis* entities. Advocates of serious metaphysics tend to approach the discipline with a prior epistemic commitment of some sort. This commitment functions as a criterion of knowledge or justified belief for quantifying over some entity and, thus, serious metaphysics usually goes hand in hand with epistemological methodism. For naturalists, this methodism expresses the various aspects of the naturalist epistemic attitude described earlier. Accordingly, serious metaphysics is primarily *explanatory* and not *descriptive* metaphysics. Thus, advocates seek to account for all entities in terms of a limited number of basic entities and in this way serious metaphysics is inherently *reductionistic*. For naturalists, these entities will constitute those at the core of the Grand Story: A property/event/object x exists iff it is contained within (truth functionally entailed by) the Grand Story.

The second perspective we may call a "shopping-list" approach whose primary goal is a careful description and categorial analysis of reality. Advocates of this approach tend to employ epistemological particularism, and it is no accident that Roderick Chisholm is the paradigm case of epistemological particularism and shopping-list metaphysics.[50]

Jackson claims that the scientific naturalist will prefer serious metaphysics and I think he is right about this. His naturalist approach to metaphysics expresses a certain form of the principle of simplicity and provides material content for that principle of simplicity most suited for a philosophical naturalist. To see this, let us compare two versions of the principle of simplicity, an epistemic and ontological version, respectively:

> Simplicity_E: Entities must not be multiplied beyond necessity.
>
> Simplicity_O: Our ontology or preferred theory about the world should be simple.

Of course, there are various ways to state each principle, but these will do for our purposes. Simplicity_E may not be easy to apply (one rival may be simple in one respect and the other in a different respect; one rival may be simpler and the other may be more empirically accurate), but its rationale is fairly straightforward. All things being equal, if a simpler theory does the epistemic job, then the more complicated theory has baggage that serves no important epistemic function. Ontological simplicity is quite different from epistemic simplicity and some philosophers conflate the two principles. For example, Kim rightly advocates epistemological simplicity for the same reason just mentioned. But he then passes over into ontological simplicity, apparently without noticing the equivocation. After embracing "entities must not be multiplied beyond necessity," he urges with no justification or further explanation that "we expect our basic laws to be reasonably simple, and we expect to explain complex phenomena by combining and iteratively applying these simple laws."[51]

Clearly, ontological simplicity does not follow from epistemic simplicity. In fact, it sometimes happens that progress in an area of science entails adopting a more complicated ontology even though both the simpler and more complicated ontologies are epistemically simple. The shift from the simpler ideal gas equation to the more complicated van der Waals equation is a case in point. That said, I believe that the naturalist should adopt both principles of simplicity, and Kim and Jackson give the reason why. Each refers to the Grand Story (which, in turn, is justified by the naturalist epistemology) which is inherently *reductio*nistic.

Moreover, if naturalism is to retain its claim to have epistemic/explanatory superiority over its rivals, then its employment of the Grand Story must be done in such a way that entities that cannot be identified with some structural combination of fundamental microphysical entities must be eliminated. Kim and Jackson both understand this, and while Jackson seeks to carry out this way of understanding the location project, Kim recently abandoned it a few years ago.[52] Still, Kim's appeal to ontological simplicity, every bit as much as Jackson's, provides a representative naturalist employment of the principle.

Moreover, their characterization of it provides a way of transforming the merely formal principle Simplicity$_{O}$ into a related version with material content. For Kim, we begin with simple, basic laws—and presumably microphysical particulars governed by them—and allow more complex entities into one's ontology only if they are subject to combinatorial modes of explanation that involve the iterative application of the basic laws. Similarly, Jackson says one should start with the Grand Story and allow entities into one's ontology only if they are entailed by that ontology.[53] For Jackson, this means accepting only structural entities that are emergent$_0$ or emergent$_1$. Expressed in terms of the appropriate naturalist material principle of simplicity, we have

> Simplicity$_{ON}$: Our ontology or preferred theory about the world should be simple in the sense that it contains the microphysical particulars, properties, relations and laws of an ideal physics or whose existence can be explained by the naturalist epistemology (e.g. combinatorial modes of explanation, are capable of exhaustive description from the third-person perspective) applied to the microphysical entities that constitute the Grand Story.

Simplicity$_{ON}$ would seem to rule out from a naturalist ontology entities that are emergent$_2$ or emergent$_3$.

A realist view of causation and emergent properties

We have seen reasons for adopting a *prima facie* burden of proof on any naturalist ontology that includes emergent entities. If such entities are accepted, then a naturalist would owe us a causal account of their coming-to-be. In closing this chapter, it is important to get before us certain constraints on such an account. In chapters to follow, we shall look at naturalist views that seek to conform to or disregard these constraints. But these constrains seem *prima facie* justified because they follow naturally from the naturalist epistemology, Grand Story and other aspects of the naturalist ontology.

Regarding emergent properties, though some demur, at least five reasons have been proffered for the claim that causal explanations in the natural sciences exhibit a kind of causal necessity, that on a typical realist construal of natural science, physical causal explanations must show—usually by citing a mechanism—why an effect must follow given the relevant causal conditions:

(1) Causal necessitation unpacks the deepest, core realist notion of causation, namely, causal production according to which a cause "brings about" or "produces" its effect.
(2) Causal necessitation fits the paradigm cases of causal explanation (e.g. macro-solidity/impenetrability in terms of micro-lattice structures, repulsive forces; mass proportions in chemical reactions in terms of atomic models of atoms/molecules, bonding orbitals, energy stability, charge distribution) central to the core theories (e.g. the atomic theory of matter) that constitute a naturalist worldview and in terms of which it is purported to have explanatory superiority to rival worldviews.
(3) Causal necessitation provides a way of distinguishing accidental generalizations or coincidences from true causal laws or sequences.
(4) Causal necessitation supports the derivation of counterfactuals (if that chunk of gold had been placed in aqua regia, then it would have dissolved) from causal laws (gold dissolves in aqua regia).
(5) Causal necessitation clarifies the direction of causality and rules out the attempt to explain a cause by its effect.

Three points of clarification are needed about causal necessity and the reasons for it. First, minimally, the sort of modality involved may be taken as physical necessity, a form of necessity that runs throughout possible worlds relevantly physically similar to our actual world (e.g. in having the same physical particulars, properties, relations and/or laws). Second, strong conceivability is the test that is used to judge causal necessitation (given the lattice structures and so forth of two macro-objects impenetrable with respect to each other, it is strongly inconceivable that one could penetrate the other).

Finally, principles (3)–(5) have sometimes been offered as additions to a covering law form of explanation to provide an adequate natural scientific causal explanation. Strictly speaking, a covering law "explanation" is just a description of what needs to be explained and not an explanation. However, by adding a causal model that underwrites it and that exhibits causal necessitation, the total package provides explanations for both what and why the phenomena are as they are. For brevity's sake, below I will talk as if a covering law explanation is, in fact, an explanation, but it should be understood that when I speak of a covering law explanation I include in it an underwriting causal model.

In this chapter, we have examined limitations on a naturalist ontology that follow from naturalism itself taken as a worldview epistemically/explanatorily superior to its rivals. Let N stand for the truth of naturalism and Emergence_{2a}. In the terms of epistemic appraisal proffered by Chisholm, it seems that, $\neg$ (N & Emergence_{2a}) is at least *epistemically in the clear* where a proposition is *epistemically in the clear* provided only that subject S is not more justified in withholding that proposition than in believing it. Alternatively, it is at least *reasonable to disbelieve* (N & Emergence_{2a}) (S is not more justified in withholding that proposition than in disbelieving it).[54]

However, there are additional limits placed on the naturalist ontology when a plausible rival worldview is brought into the picture. As Timothy O'Connor points out, emergent properties, especially mental properties, must be shown to arise by way of causal necessitation from a micro-physical base if we are to "render emergent phenomena naturalistically explicable."[55] Among his reasons for this claim is the assertion that if the link between micro-base and emergent properties is a contingent one, then the only explanation for the existence and constancy of the link is a theist explanation.[56] O'Connor's claim seems to me to be correct, and to probe this matter further, we turn to an examination of the theistic argument for God's existence from consciousness.

2 The argument from consciousness

Some argue that, while finite mental entities may be inexplicable on a naturalist worldview, they may be explained by theism, thereby furnishing evidence for God's existence. In this chapter, I shall clarify and defend this argument from consciousness (AC) by describing three issues in scientific theory acceptance relevant to assessing AC's force, presenting three forms of AC and offering a brief defense of its premises. Among other things, I hope to show that an important factor in theory acceptance—scientific or otherwise—is whether a specific theory has a rival. If not, then certain epistemic activities, e.g. labeling some phenomenon as basic for which only a description and not an explanation is needed, may be quite adequate not to impede the theory in question. But the adequacy of those same activities can change dramatically if a sufficient rival position is present. In chapter one, we saw reasons for a naturalist to deny the existence of emergent mental properties/events that followed solely from naturalism itself. In this chapter, we shall discover additional reasons for naturalists to eschew emergent mental entities that follow because of the presence of AC. The combined force of chapters one and two will place a severe (and increasing) burden of proof on any naturalist who seeks to reconcile the existence of emergent mental entities (from emergence$_{2a}$ to emergence$_3$) with naturalism.

Three issues in scientific theory acceptance

Basicality

While theism and naturalism are broad worldviews and not scientific theories, three issues that inform the adjudication between rival scientific theories are relevant to AC. While these are neither individually necessary nor jointly sufficient to justify one theory over its rivals, they are important characteristic marks whose presence or absence carries a great deal of epistemic weight in theory adjudication. The first issue involves deciding whether it is appropriate to take some phenomenon as *ontologically basic* such that only a description and not an explanation for it is required, or whether that phenomenon should be understood as something to be explained in terms of *more basic* phenomena. For example, attempts to explain uniform inertial motion are disallowed in Newtonian mechanics because such motion is ontologically basic on this view, but an Aristotelian had to explain how or why a particular body exhibited uniform inertial motion. Thus, what is basic to one theory may be derivative in another.

Ontological basicality should be distinguished from pre-theoretical basicality. According to the latter, the pre-theoretical description of an entity's nature is to remain in tact and the theoretician's aim is to explain the entity's origin or behavior but not to reduce it. Consciousness is ontologically basic for theism since it characterizes the fundamental being. The appearance of finite consciousness qua finite requires explanation and theism may employ the explanatory resources of its basic ontological inventory (e.g. consciousness in God) for that explanation. But consciousness *per se* is ontologically basic. Not so for a naturalist though he or she may treat consciousness as pre-theoretically basic. According to naturalism, consciousness is emergent, derivative and supervenient and both its finitude (Why did the Grand Story lead to and through consciousness as opposed to taking alternative paths?) and intrinsic nature require explanation.

Naturalness

Issue two is the *naturalness* of an accepted entity in light of the overall theory (or research program) of which it is a part. The types of entities embraced, along with the sorts of properties they possess and the relations they enter should be at home with other entities in the theory, and, in this sense, be natural for the theory. Some entity (particular thing, process, property, or relation) e is natural for a theory T just in case either e is a central, core entity of T or e bears a relevant similarity to central, core entities in e's category within T. If e is in a category such as substance, force, property, event, relation, or cause, e should bear a relevant similarity to other entities of T in that category. This is a formal definition and the material content given to it will depend on the theory in question. In chapter one, I argued that the basic entities constitutive of the Grand Story provide this material content for naturalism.

Moreover, given rivals R and S, the acceptance of e in R is *ad hoc* and question-begging against advocates of S if e bears a relevant similarity to the appropriate entities in S, and in this sense is "at home" in S, but fails to bear this relevant similarity to the appropriate entities in R.[1] The notion of "being *ad hoc*" is notoriously difficult to specify precisely. It is usually characterized as an intellectually inappropriate adjustment of a theory whose sole epistemic justification is to save the theory from falsification. Such an adjustment involves adding a new supposition to a theory not already implied by its other features. In the context of evaluating rivals R and S, the principle just mentioned provides a sufficient condition for the postulation of e to be *ad hoc* and question-begging. Moreover, in the presence of such a dialectical situation, advocates of R are under intellectual pressure to treat e along reductive or eliminativist lines.

The issue of *naturalness* is relevant to theory assessment between rivals because it provides a criterion for advocates of a theory to claim that their rivals have begged the question against them or adjusted their theory in an inappropriate, *ad hoc* way. And though this need not be the case, naturalness can be related to basicality in this way: Naturalness can provide a means of deciding the relative merits of accepting theory R, which depicts phenomenon e as basic, vs. embracing S, which takes e to be explainable in terms that are more basic. If e is natural in S but not in R, it will be difficult for advocates of R to justify the bald assertion that e is basic in R and that all proponents of R need to do is describe e and correlate it with other phenomena in R as opposed to explaining e. Such a claim by advocates of R will be even more problematic if S provides an explanation for e.[2]

By way of application, consider the following argument presented by Evan Fales:

> Darwinian evolution implies that human beings emerged through the blind operation of natural forces. It is mysterious how such forces could generate something nonphysical; all known causal laws that govern the physical relate physical states of affairs to other physical states of affairs. Since such processes evidently *have* produced consciousness, however construed, consciousness is evidently a natural phenomenon, and dependent on natural phenomena.[3]

Given the presence of theism and AC, it should be clear that this argument is *ad hoc* and question-begging, especially since it includes an acknowledgement of the unnaturalness of consciousness in light of the Grand Story (its forces and causal laws) and the rest of the naturalist ontology.

Epistemic values

Issue three involves *epistemic values*. Roughly, an epistemic value is a normative property, which, if possessed by a theory, confers some degree of rational justification on that theory. Examples of epistemic values are these: theories should be simple, descriptively accurate, predicatively successful, fruitful for guiding new research, capable of solving their internal and external conceptual problems, and use certain types of explanations or follow certain methodological rules and not others (e.g. "appeal to efficient and not final causes"). Studies in scientific theory assessment have made it clear that two rivals may solve a problem differently depending on the way each theory depicts the phenomenon to be solved.

Moreover, it is possible for two rivals to rank the relative merits of epistemic values in different ways or even give the same virtue a different meaning or application. Rivals can differ radically about the nature, application, and relative importance of a particular epistemic value. Thus, given rivals A and B, in arguing against B, it may be inappropriate for advocates of A to cite its superior comportment with an epistemic value when B's proponents do not weigh that value as heavily as they do a different one they take to be more central to B. For example, given rivals A and B, if A is simpler than B but B is more descriptively accurate than A, then it may be inappropriate—indeed, question-begging—for advocates of A to cite A's simplicity as grounds for judging it superior to B. I am not suggesting that rivals are incommensurable. In fact, I believe that seldom, if ever, is this the case. Only on an issue-by-issue basis can one appropriately make judgments about the epistemic impact of the conflict of disparate epistemic values.

For example, in philosophy of mind, property dualists will argue that descriptive accuracy is on their side since their position accurately captures the intrinsic features of mental states and this accuracy justifies viewing those features and not relational ones as what constitutes the essence of the mental states in dispute. Property dualists argue that descriptive accuracy is more important than simplicity considerations as employed by physicalist rivals because epistemic simplicity becomes a factor in selecting between rivals only after it is judged that "all things are equal" between those rivals. And based on descriptive accuracy, this is precisely what property dualists deny.

Ontological simplicity is another matter. Among other things, strong physicalists eschew irreducible, uneliminable mental properties and claim that ontological simplicity is on their side. Property dualists respond that this appeal to ontological simplicity is done at the cost of denying the obvious facts as they are accurately described from a first-person perspective. According to Kim, at this stage of the argument, "the only positive considerations [for strong physicalism] are broad metaphysical ones that might very well be accused of begging the question."[4]

It is clear that an essential part of assessing this debate is an analysis of the different epistemic values in play and their employment by the disputants. Applied to theism, the AC, and the characterization of robust, positive naturalism in chapter one, the central epistemic values of robust naturalism—including ontological simplicity, epistemic preference for the third-person point of view, and so on—place severe intellectual pressure on naturalists to be strong physicalists. Theists have no such pressure, and one aspect of evaluating AC is the asymmetrical pressure to avoid irreducible mental properties or other mental entities. The pressure towards some form of reductionism or eliminativism flows from the very nature of naturalism itself and is exacerbated by the presence of theism and AC as a rival.

The argument from consciousness

Three forms of the argument

Theists such as Angus Menuge[5], Robert Adams[6], and Richard Swinburne[7] have advanced different forms of an argument from consciousness for the existence of God. The argument may be construed as an inference to the best explanation, a Bayesian-style argument, or a straightforward deductive argument in which its premises are alleged to be more reasonable then their denials.

An inference to the best explanation begins with certain data to be explained (the existence of irreducible mental entities or their regular, law-like correlation with physical entities), assembles a pool of live options that explain the data, and usually on the basis of certain criteria—e.g. explanatory scope, explanatory power by making the data more epistemically likely than rivals, being less *ad hoc*—one option is chosen as the best explanation of the data. According to AC, on a theistic metaphysic, one already has an instance of consciousness and other mental entities, e.g. an unembodied mind, in God. Therefore, it is hardly surprising that finite consciousness or other mental entities should exist in the world. However, on a naturalist view, mental entities are so strange and out of place that their existence (or regular correlation with physical entities) defies adequate explanation. There appear to be two realms operating in causal harmony and theism provides the best explanation of this fact.

Richard Swinburne draws a distinction between a C-inductive (one in which the premises add to the probability and, in this sense, confirm the conclusion) and a P-inductive (one in which the premises make the conclusion more probable than not) argument. Understood as an inference to the best explanation, I will try to show in this book that AC is at least a correct C-inductive argument, though as a part of a cumulative case, consciousness contributes to a P-inductive theistic argument.[8]

Construed as a Bayesian argument, assuming the presence of background knowledge, we have:

$$Pr(T/C) = \frac{Pr(T) \times Pr(C/T)}{Pr(T) \times \mathrm{Pr}(C/T) + Pr(\neg\, T) \times \mathrm{Pr}(C/\neg\, T)}$$

T and C stand for theism and either the existence of conscious properties or their regular correlation with physical features. We will be assuming that naturalism and theism are the only live options under consideration (see below) and, thus, $\neg$T = N (naturalism).[9]

Relative to our background knowledge, Pr (T) is much higher than many naturalists concede. The problem is that many naturalists are either ignorant of or simply disregard the explosion of literature in the last twenty-five years or so providing sophisticated and powerful justification for theism. And the face of Anglo-American philosophy has been transformed as a result. In a recent article lamenting "the desecularization of academia that evolved in philosophy departments since the late 1960s," prominent naturalist philosopher Quentin Smith observes that "in philosophy, it became, almost overnight, 'academically respectable' to argue for theism, making philosophy a favored field of entry for the most intelligent and talented theists entering academia today."[10] He complains that "Naturalists passively watched as realist versions of theism ... began to sweep through the philosophical community, until today perhaps one-quarter or one-third of philosophy professors are theists, with most being orthodox Christians." He concludes, "God is not 'dead' in academia; he returned to life in the late 1960s and is now alive and well in his last academic stronghold, philosophy departments." This explosion of Christian philosophy includes fresh, highly sophisticated defenses of theism. In chapter nine, we will explore why this massive proliferation of Christian theism in philosophy is largely ignored by naturalist philosophers as seen by, among other things, a nearly complete lack of interaction with sophisticated versions of theism or substance dualism in their writings.

Pr (C/T) is highly probable (> > .5). Richard Swinburne's version of AC provides several grounds for this ranking of Pr (C/T). Here are two: First, given theism, mental properties are basic characteristics of the fundamental being that constitutes a theistic ontology, so the theist has no pressing issue regarding the existence or exemplification of the mental. Such is basic on theism. As a result, the theist is under no pressure to explain how the mental data of AC could exist in light of the Grand Story. Second, a basic datum of persons is that they are communal beings who love to share in meaningful relationships with others and who desire to bring other persons into being. Thus, theism would predict a proliferation of persons besides God Himself.

According to advocates of AC, Pr (¬T) x Pr (C/¬T) is highly improbable (< < .5). To see why, first recall that the formula is equivalent to Pr (N) × Pr (C/N). Let us set aside Pr (N) for the moment. Pr (C/N) is so low that it approximates to zero. Why? Recall that in the early days of emergentism in the eighteenth and early nineteenth centuries, emergent properties were characterized epistemically, viz., as those that were unpredictable, even from a God's-eye perspective, from a complete knowledge of the subvenient base. That subvenient base provided no explanatory or predictive grounds for emergent properties precisely as emergent entities. Now it makes no difference for the relevance of this point that today we construe emergent properties ontologically and not epistemically. Even on the ontological construal, emergent properties are completely *sui generis* relative to the entities and processes at the subvenient base. In this regard, the following characterization by Timothy O'Connor may be taken as canonical:

> An emergent property of type E will appear only in physical systems achieving some specific threshold of organized complexity. From an empirical point of view, this threshold will be arbitrary, one that would not be anticipated by a theorist whose understanding of the world was derived from theories developed entirely from observations of physical systems below the requisite complexity. In optimal circumstances, such a theorist would come to recognize the locally determinative interactive dispositions of basic physical entities. Hidden from his view, however, would be the tendency ... to generate an emergent state.[11]

As we saw in chapter one, applied to mental phenomena, it is almost impossible for advocates of a naturalist worldview to avoid admitting that these phenomena are explanatorily recalcitrant for them and must be admitted as brute facts. The sort of separable—part/whole framework and type of structural change at the core of the Grand Story is simply inadequate in principle for explaining consciousness. And this is to admit that Pr (C/N) is very, very low indeed. In this case, the denominator in Bayes' Theorem approaches the numerator and Pr (T/C) approaches 1. This is the claim of a Bayesian form of AC.

In response, a naturalist could argue as follows: It seems like the conclusion to draw from the fact that the explanatory connection between the natural world and consciousness is opaque is not that P(C/N) is low but that it is inscrutable. Suppose you think it is a brute, inexplicable fact that consciousness sometimes "pops into existence" when matter-energy is arranged a certain way. You learn then of a parallel universe with very different physical laws. Somehow, you come to have exhaustive knowledge of the distribution of matter/energy in that world, though you know nothing so far about whether there is consciousness in that world. So you wonder: *is* there? One could easily think the right attitude here is agnosticism: If it is a brute, inexplicable fact that consciousness emerges on certain configurations of matter/energy, then one simply would not know whether consciousness emerges from the configurations of matter/energy in this parallel universe. But if so, then the right thing to think about P(C/N) isn't that it's low, but that it's inscrutable.[12]

There are at least four things to say in response to this argument, and we are now in a position to understand the first rejoinder: The presence of theism and AC provide intellectual grounds for rejecting this move. Given the presence of AC as a rival to naturalism, the postulation of the appearance of consciousness as a brute, inexplicable fact is clearly *ad hoc* and question-begging. AC provides a clear and powerful explanation for finite consciousness. There is no good reason to postulate it as a brute fact, especially when it does not bear a relevant similarity to the rest of the naturalist ontology. Moreover, the Grand Story cannot explain it, and it is not fundamentally known from the third-person point of view as are the rest of the entities over which the naturalist quantifies.

This response is an example of a broader dialectic that theists often encounter in debates with atheists. The theist argues that the existence of God is the best explanation for P (the Big Bang, fine-tuning, the instantiation of normative properties, consciousness) and provides grounds for why this is so and for why atheism cannot adequately explain P. The atheist responds by suggesting that we hold the actual world constant including the reality of P, i.e., consider a duplicate world containing P, and just leave God out. Well then, he or she concludes, it looks like the existence of God is irrelevant to P. In light of what I have argued above in the context of scientific theory acceptance, this is argumentation by theft and not honest toil.

Second, naturalism itself provides intellectual pressure against brute, non-physical facts. Our knowledge of this world would give us positive reasons for not believing that irreducible consciousness would appear in it, e.g. the geometrical rearrangement of inert physical entities into different spatial structures hardly seems sufficient to explain the appearance of consciousness. Thus, naturalism itself provides positive reasons for rejecting irreducible consciousness and, thus, for rejecting the claim that its appearance is a brute, natural fact. Coupled with various epistemic constraints, e.g. ontological and epistemic simplicity, a commitment to serious metaphysics, the centrality of combinatorial modes of explanation, and an ontology exhaustively describable from the third-person point of view, naturalism entails an inherent drive towards some form of reductionism.

In a way, this entire book is an attempt to argue this point in the context of AC, and I shall offer detailed criticisms of the major non-theistic attempts to explain the appearance of consciousness or simply to label it as a brute fact. For now, I merely note that most naturalists who work in philosophy of mind hold to some sort of strong physicalism and rightly cast a suspicious eye towards those who allow for emergent mental properties because they correctly understand that the Grand Story nicely explains structural particulars and properties but not emergent ones. In addition, they realize that the postulation of consciousness as a brute fact leaves them vulnerable to alternative worldviews that offer an explanation for what they admit cannot be explained within naturalist constraints.

To cite one representative example, David Papineau warns that the naturalist ought to deny that mental properties are not identical to physical ones because if they do not, they will have to face the question

> *why* does consciousness emerge in just those cases [where physical properties correlate with them]. And to this question, [weak physicalism] seem[s] to provide no answer.
>
> I suspect that many philosophers regard the inability to answer this question as the fatal flaw in the physicalist approach to consciousness.

> Surely, they feel, any satisfactory philosophical view of consciousness ought to tell us why consciousness emerges in some physical systems but not others.
>
> I think that physicalists should simply reject the question. ... [T]he physicalist should simply deny that there are two properties here.[13]

Third, given that "popping into existence" is instantaneous and not a process, it is not something that can be governed by anything, e.g. natural constraints. Natural constraints such as the laws of nature govern processes of alteration for entities that already exist. If an entity does not exist, there is nothing on which the constraints can operate. Thus, there could be no reason in principle as to why consciousness as opposed to an angel or a Toyota Camry would appear. Thus, the regular "popping into existence" of consciousness when matter-energy is arranged in a certain way would be sheer magic, indeed, magic without a Magician. In fact, the very idea of "matter-energy being arranged in a certain way" would be utterly vacuous as an expression of constraints for consciousness and could only be characterized in a circular way.

The naturalist may respond that there are certain cases in which such constraints can be conceived, e.g. there would have to be space before a spatial entity could pop into existence, so in this case it is plausible to think there could be constrains even if coming-to-be is not a process. But for two reasons, this response fails. First, it is not analogous with the origin of consciousness. The reason that a spatial entity could not pop into existence without there being such a thing as space is the same as why a square circle could not pop into existence. In both cases, one is dealing with a logically contradictory state of affairs—a spatial entity existing without space and a square circle—so it is not a constraint that resists something popping into existence that is in play; rather, it is the inconsistency in the nature of the relevant states of affairs themselves. But there is no parallel contradictory nature to there being consciousness in a physical world. In my view, the reason a naturalist should not accept the reality of irreducible consciousness is not that such a state of affairs is *logically* contradictory, but that matter is bereft of what is needed to ground its origin. If one claims that consciousness does not pop into existence, but rather, is actualized from mental potentialities in matter, then as we shall see in chapters four through seven, this move amounts to an abandonment of naturalism in favor of something else, e.g. panpsychism.

Additionally, consider a non-spatial world. With no adjustments to that world, it is true that a table could not pop into existence for the reasons just mentioned. But there is no reason why a table and the necessary spatial conditions could not jointly pop into existence. So even in cases where there are *prima facie* constraints on what can pop into existence, when a broader state of affairs in taken into consideration, the constraints may be otiose.

Fourth, armed with the distinction between a state of affairs seeming to be impossible to a subject S vs. a state of affairs failing to seem possible to S, one could argue that he has strong defeasible modal intuitions that it is impossible for consciousness to arise from matter by way of purely natural, physical processes. This strategy could be undercut by a counter-claim according to which one either raises skeptical problems with modal intuitions in general or simply denies the relevant intuitions. Regarding modal skepticism, I think that modal intuitions of the sort just mentioned are ubiquitous in philosophy and, in fact, employed by physicalists in supporting their own views (e.g. it seems impossible—in some modal sense or other—to most physicalists that such different states as mental and physical ones could causally interact with each other). Regarding a failure to have the relevant intuitions, one could respond that the dualist intuition is the pervasive, commonsense one and the physicalist fails to share that intuition only because of a question-begging prior commitment to physicalism.

Finally, there is a third form of AC. Taken as a straightforward deductive argument, AC becomes the following:

(1) Mental events are genuine non-physical mental entities that exist.
(2) Specific mental event types are regularly correlated with specific physical event types.
(3) There is an explanation for these correlations.
(4) Personal explanation is different from natural scientific explanation.
(5) The explanation for these correlations is either a personal or natural scientific explanation.
(6) The explanation is not a natural scientific one.
(7) Therefore, the explanation is a personal one.
(8) If the explanation is personal, then it is theistic.
(9) Therefore, the explanation is theistic.

Overview of deductive premises

The relationship among these three forms of argumentation is controversial, e.g. is inference to the best explanation (IBE) reducible to other, perhaps Bayesian forms of argumentation. I do not wish to enter that controversy because I think that a defense of AC can be formulated based on one of the three argument forms I am presenting or based on three independent arguments. I do believe, however, that by stating the argument deductively we gain clarity on the precise considerations that most likely provide the basis for an IBE argument or for assignment of probabilities to key factors in the Bayesian approach. Therefore, I shall develop and defend the deductive form of the argument in some detail.

In my view, premises (3) and (6) are the most crucial ones for the success of AC since they are the premises most likely to come under naturalist attack. Let us set them aside for the moment.

We are assuming the truth of premise (1), since all the naturalist rivals of AC we are considering agree with it. There have been a number of variants on or alternatives to (1) that have been cited as problems which science cannot explain but which can be given a theistic personal explanation:

(a) the existence of mental properties themselves;[14]
(b) the fact that mental properties have come to be exemplified in the spatio-temporal world;[15]
(c) the nature of the relation, e.g., causal or supervenient, between mental and physical entities since it is as inexplicable from a naturalist perspective as is Cartesian causal interaction because the problem consists in the nature of the relation itself, along with the desperate nature of its relata, and is not a function of the category of the relata;[16]
(d) the fact that certain particular mental events are correlated with certain particular physical events;[17]
(e) the fact that the correlations mentioned in d are regular;[18]
(f) the existence of libertarian freedom and the type of agent necessary for it;[19]
(g) the aptness of our noetic equipment to serve as truth gatherers in our noetic environment;[20]
(h) the evolutionary advantage of having mental states as opposed to the evolution of organisms with direct stimulus-response mechanisms that have no mental intermediaries.[21]

Even though we are assuming the truth of (1), I want to make a few observations about the dialectical status of property dualism. My main argument in this book is that naturalists should be strict physicalists and, given property dualism, we have evidence against naturalism and for theism. A naturalist may well respond with a hearty "So what!" because strict physicalism is clearly the case. Of course, I reject strict physicalism, but more importantly, I believe certain issues are conspicuous by their absence in defenses of strict physicalism or criticisms of property dualism. In addition, I want to get these issues before the reader. So if you wish, consider the next several pages to be an excursus, though a relevant one.

Property dualists argue that mental states are in no sense physical since they (or at least some of them) possess *six* features that do not characterize physical states:

(a) There is a raw qualitative feel or a "what it is like" to a mental state such as a pain.
(b) At least many mental states have intentionality—*ofness* or *aboutness*—directed towards an object.
(c) Mental states exhibit certain epistemic features (direct access, private access, first-person epistemic authority, are expressed in intentional contexts, self-reflexivity associated with "I") that could not be the case if they were physical.

(d) They require a subjective ontology—namely, mental states are necessarily owned by the first-person, unified, sentient subjects who have them.
(e) Mental states fail to have crucial features (e.g. spatial extension, location) that characterize physical states and, in general, cannot be described using physical language.
(f) Libertarian free acts exemplify active power and not passive liability.

A few observations about (a)–(c) are important. Regarding (a), I believe the so-called Knowledge Argument has been misrepresented in two ways: what Mary comes to know is usually understated and the argument really is not an argument at all. Let us consider these in order.

A standard presentation of the argument has it that Mary, a brilliant scientist blind from birth, knows all the physical facts relevant to acts of perception. When she suddenly gains the ability to see, she gains knowledge of new facts. Since she knew all the physical facts before recovery of sight, and since she gains knowledge of new facts, these facts must not be physical facts and given Mary's situation, they must be mental facts.

To understand the richness of what Mary comes to know, we need to grasp the nature of self-presenting properties. Insights about self-presenting properties go back at least as far as Augustine, but, more than any other contemporary philosopher, Roderick Chisholm has done the best job of analyzing them.[22] While Chisholm proffered slightly different definitions of a self-presenting property, the following is representative of his views:

P is self-presenting = Df Every property that P entails includes the property of thinking.[23]

To understand this definition, we need to get clear on Chisholm's definitions of property entailment and inclusion.[24] Properties may sustain these different relations to each other:

Inclusion: Property P includes property Q = Df P is necessarily such that whatever exemplifies it exemplifies Q.

Entailment: Property P entails property Q = Df P is necessarily such that, for every x and every y, if y attributes P to x, then y attributes Q to x or, alternatively, believing something to be P includes believing something to be Q.

Inclusion requires it to be the case that the very same entity that exemplifies a property, P, must also exemplify the property P includes. Determinates (being red) include their determinables (being colorful). The notion of entailment contains the concept of attribution. In an attribution, one ascribes a property to something, e.g. a judgment or belief that x is F is an attribution of being F to x. For example, the property of believing there to be red circles entails the property of believing there to be things that are red.

I mention Chisholm's unique formulation of a self-presenting property to get before us a widely, though not universally accepted, characterization of it. Obviously, the notion has deep Cartesian roots in two aspects of Descartes' thought. First, when Descartes characterized the essential attributes of mind and body as thinking (i.e. consciousness) and extension, respectively, the former satisfies the definition of being self-presenting and the latter does not. Second, Descartes' approach to the mind was an expression of his view of epistemology as a distinctively first-person enterprise that, nowadays, would be described as a version of internalist foundationalism. On this view, a self-presenting property is that by way of which a first-person knowing subject can take other entities as objects of intentionality, including as objects of propositional knowledge. In different ways, self-presenting properties present their intentional objects and themselves to first-person knowing subjects. Thus, the twofold Cartesian roots of being self-presenting are such that, even though shared in his own way by Chisholm, they provide grounds for alternative formulations of being self-presenting other than those presented by Chisholm. For those who reject Chisholm's formulation, the notion of a self-presenting property could still be cashed out in a way relevant to the Knowledge Argument.

Self-presenting properties characterize thoughts, sensations, and other states of consciousness. For example, the property of being-appeared-to-redly entails the property of being-appeared-to and the latter property includes the property of thinking. By "thinking," Chisholm means the same thing as being conscious, and he claims that self-presenting properties are psychological or "Cartesian" properties. According to Chisholm, a thing is conscious if and only if it has a self-presenting property. From the fact that a person has a self-presenting property, it follows logically that the person is conscious but it does not follow that the person has any property that does not include consciousness.

Some and, perhaps, all mental states are constituted by self-presenting properties. I can be aware of the external, physical world only by means of my mental states, but I need not be aware of my mental states by means of anything else. In different ways, a self-presenting property presents to a subject the intentional object of that property and the self-presenting property itself. Such properties present other things to a subject intermediately by means of them, and they present themselves to a subject directly simply in virtue of the fact that he has them. In each case, in normal circumstances, it is by virtue of exemplifying the relevant self-presenting property that a subject comes to have knowledge by acquaintance with the intentional object of the property and with the property itself. Moreover, it is in virtue of exemplifying the relevant self-presenting property that a subject is *prima facie* justified in believing that the intentional object has a certain feature.

For example, it is by way of a sensation of red that one is aware of the surface color of an apple, but one is not aware of the sensation of red by way of another sensation. The red sensation makes the apple's surface present to one by virtue of one having the sensation; but the sensation also presents itself directly to one without another intermediary. A person sees red by means of the sensation of red and is made directly aware of (but does not actually see in the same way he sees the red on the apple's surface) the sensation itself by having that sensation. The person gains knowledge by acquaintance with the property of being red on the apple's surface and the property of being-an-appearing-of-red. Further, it is on the basis of the latter, viz., that the apple's surface seems red to one, that the person is *prima facie* justified in believing that the apple's surface is red.

When a person exemplifies a self-presenting property, he is modified in some way. We may put this by saying that when a person has a red sensation, the person is in the state of being-appeared-to-redly. Suppose the light is such that an orange jar looks red to Smith. If Smith says the object is red, his statement is about the jar is false. If Smith says, "I seem to see something red" or "the jar appears red to me", what he says is true because he is reporting a description of his own sensation. He is not talking about the jar. Smith's statements employ what is called a phenomenological use of "seems" or "appears." When people use "seems" or "appears" phenomenologically, they use them to report their own description of their self-presenting properties, i.e. to report the private, directly accessed mental states going on inside them.

By way of application, if one is appeared-to-redly while looking at a red apple, then we may say that this self-presenting property has two intentional objects. First, there is the primary intentional object, the red surface, which is the object of a focused awareness, in this case, a sensory awareness. Such an object requires a distinct mental state to be purposefully directed upon it. However, the self-presenting property also presents itself to the subject as a secondary, peripheral object. The self-presenting property being-appeared-to-redly is one that the subject is aware of but not in the sense that it is the primary intentional object of a distinct mental act. As a secondary, peripheral object, the self-presenting property presents itself to a subject by simply being instantiated by that subject, and it may, though it need not be the object of a distinct mental act of attending to it. So understood, no infinite regress is present.

In order to apply adequately the notion of a self-presenting property to the Knowledge Argument, let us review three different forms of knowledge. In keeping with the epistemic role of self-presenting properties in the Knowledge Argument, dualists will, or at least should argue that these three forms of knowledge are irreducible to each other. The three kinds of knowledge are: 1) *Knowledge by acquaintance*: This happens when we are directly aware of something, e.g. when I see an apple directly before me, I know it by acquaintance. One does not need a concept of an apple or a knowledge of how to use the word "apple" in English to have knowledge by acquaintance of an apple. A baby can see an apple without having the relevant concept or linguistic skills. 2) *Propositional knowledge:* This is knowledge that an entire proposition is true. For example, knowledge that "the object there is an apple" requires having a concept of an apple and knowing that the object under consideration satisfies the concept. 3) *Know-how*: This is the ability to do certain things, e.g. to use apples for certain purposes.

We may distinguish mere know-how from genuine know-how or skill. The latter is know-how based on knowledge and insight and is characteristic of skilled practitioners in some field. Mere know-how is the ability to engage in the correct behavioral movements, say by following the steps in a manual, with little or no knowledge of why one is performing these movements. In Searle's Chinese Room thought experiment, the person in the Chinese Room who does not know Chinese has mere know-how. A person in the room with a mastery of Chinese would have skill.

Moreover, since the Knowledge Argument captures a first-person internalist perspective regarding Mary as a knowing subject, advocates of the argument will claim that, in general, knowledge by acquaintance provides the epistemic basis for propositional knowledge which, in turn, provides the epistemic basis for genuine know-how, i.e. skill. It is because one sees the redness on the apple's surface that one knows that the apple's surface is red, and it is in virtue of one's knowledge of the apple's surface color that one has the skill to do things to or with that surface color.

We are now in a position to describe six different forms of knowledge that dualists should claim are central to the Knowledge Argument. To repeat the thought experiment, suppose Mary is a neuroscientist who lives thousands of years in the future. Mary knows all there is to know about the physics and neurophysiology of seeing. She can describe in complete detail what happens when light reflects off an object, interacts with the eye, optic nerve, and brain, and so on. However, suppose that Mary was born blind and, suddenly, gains sight for the first time and sees a red object. There will be some new facts Mary learns that were left out of her exhaustive knowledge of all the relevant physical facts prior to gaining vision. Since Mary knew all the physical facts before gaining sight, and since she now has knowledge of new facts, these facts are not physical facts; at least some are mental facts, facts involved in what it is like to see.

To expand the argument a bit, Mary comes to exemplify the self-presenting mental property of being-appeared-to-redly. In this way, Mary gains six new kinds of knowledge – she gains knowledge by acquaintance, and on that basis, propositional knowledge, and on that basis, skill regarding the color red. She also gains these three types of knowledge, along with a similar epistemic order among them, about the phenomenological aspects of her own red sensation. Moreover, it is in virtue of exemplifying the property of being-appeared-to-redly that Mary's knowledge by acquaintance with redness itself is both possible and justified.

Mary now knows by acquaintance what redness is. Upon further reflection and experience, based on this knowledge by acquaintance, she can now know things like: 1) Necessarily, red is a color. 2) Necessarily, something cannot be red and green all over at the same time. 3) Necessarily, red is darker than yellow.[25] Finally, based on this propositional knowledge, she gains skill about comparing or sorting objects based on their color, of how to arrange color patterns that are most beautiful or natural to the eyes, etc. Assuming a realist and not a representative dualist construal of secondary qualities, the three kinds of knowledge just listed are not themselves knowledge of mental facts, but the dualist can argue that they are forms of knowledge that can be gained only by way of mental states that exemplify the relevant self-presenting property.

She also gains knowledge about her sensation of red. She is now aware of having a sensation of red for the first time and can be aware of a specific sensation of red being pleasurable, vague, etc. For example, at the eye doctor, when someone reports a letter on the eye chart as appearing vague, he is accurately describing his sensation of the letter, not the letter itself. Indeed, the doctor can see that the letter on the chart has clear borders; however, he needs the person to tell him how it appears to him since the doctor has no access to the patient's inner mental sensation. Mary could now report things like this about her red sensations.

Based on the knowledge by acquaintance just mentioned, she also has propositional knowledge about her sensations. She could know that a sensation of red is more like a sensation of green than it is like a sour taste. She can know that the way the apple appears to her now is vivid, pleasant, or like the way the orange appeared to her (namely, redly) yesterday in bad lighting. Finally, based on this propositional knowledge, she has skill about her sensations. She can recall them to memory, re-image things in her mind, adjust her glasses until her sensations of color are vivid, etc. Mary had none of this knowledge prior to gaining color vision. These are all examples of knowledge of mental facts.

In addition to the richness of what Mary comes to know, there is the debate about precisely how the dualist employs the Knowledge Argument. From what we have seen about self-presenting properties, I believe the argument is not an "argument" at all. As I am using "argument," an argument begins with premises that are better known than the conclusion they support. However, the property dualist will, or at least should say that first-person awareness of phenomenal consciousness is epistemically primitive and provides the ultimate ground for the relevant properly basic beliefs. When one tries to establish the fact that an alleged primitive is, in fact, a primitive, there are two things she can do. She can show that a denial of the primitive leads to conclusions that are unacceptable or she can use examples that invite interlocutors to attend to the primitive carefully by becoming aware of it and the various relations it sustains to other things. I suggest the Knowledge Argument be understood in this way and not as an "argument."[26]

My purpose is not to defend the Knowledge Argument in detail, e.g. to defend against the claim that Mary already knew these things and merely gained a new way to access or talk about them. Rather, I am simply correcting what I believe to be two mistakes widely made in discussing the Knowledge Argument, viz., what Mary (allegedly) comes to know and the way dualists should present the "argument."

So much for (a). What about (b) and the issue of intentionality? The topic is too vast to cover in detail. However, it needs to be said that people regularly experience sequences of mental states that exhibit what Husserl called a fulfillment structure. In such cases, one forms a concept of something (e.g. that a specific book is waiting to be picked up in the university bookstore), and goes through a series of experiences (walking to the store instead of going swimming in the Pacific Ocean, entering the store, walking closer and closer to the relevant section of the store, seeing the book from a distance to being right next to it) that terminate in the experience of comparing one's initial concept of the thing to the thing itself to see if there is a match.

We all experience fulfillment structures regularly. What is important about them is that from a first-person perspective, one is able simply to grasp one's initial (vague) concept (Husserl called it an empty intention), understand (perhaps somewhat vaguely) what its intentional object is, infer a series of experiential steps that would help to verify or disconfirm the initial concept, and eventually compare the concept with the object. Fulfillment structures and the cognitive success to which they (often) lead require that whatever account of intentionality one gives, it must be such that (1) the essence of conceptual meanings can be grasped from the first-person perspective; (2) the intentionality of conceptual meanings and the nature of their objects can be grasped from a first-person perspective; and (3) the enduring I that remains identical through the series of mental events can experience the initial somewhat empty concept become fuller and fuller until the thing itself is present in knowledge by acquaintance.

I fear that most strong physicalist accounts of intentionality run amuck of these abilities. For example, certain functionalist *reductions* of intentionality entail the holism of the mental in that a specific mental state is individuated by its relation to one's entire psychology. How anyone could know what concept one was entertaining at a given moment or grasp its intentional features becomes quite opaque for such a view. I think similar difficulties confront attempts to identify beliefs (or thoughts) with indicators (a.k.a. "indicator meanings" or "representations") that satisfy some sort of functional or causal criterion. I suggest that the nature of fulfillment structures provides a test that any view of intentionality must meet on pain of being disregarded as inadequate. While I cannot argue the point here, I believe that (at least) property dualism for the relevant mental states is the only adequate solution that meets this criterion.

Finally, we come to (c), the fact that mental states exhibit various epistemic features. It is fairly typical for physicalists to attempt to undercut arguments associated with (c) because (1) epistemic modality should not be confused with metaphysical modality nor is the former a good guide to the latter; and (2) these arguments just show that there are two ways of knowing the same (physical) things, not that there are two things known. I think these responses are too dismissive and fail to grasp the fact that arguments associated with the epistemic phenomena captured by (c) are really ontological arguments and not epistemic ones at all.[27] The arguments are not simply pointing out that there are certain epistemic avenues to mental states (private access, direct access, first-person authoritative access) and there are other avenues to physical states. Rather, the arguments begin by surfacing these epistemic features of mental states and they go on to say that if strong physicalism were true, none of these features would obtain in the world. The arguments, then, move quickly to the sorts of properties, particulars and relations that characterize physical entities (e.g. brain states) and entail that if mental states were physical, they would exhibit and only exhibit these sorts of features. Because they do not, and because they would if they were physical, they are not physical after all. Successful or not, this sort of argument is not making a simple move from epistemic observations straightaway to a conclusion about dualism, and rebuttals like the ones mentioned above seem to me to be entirely irrelevant.

So much for (1). What about premise (2)? Physicalist treatments of the mental, multiple realization, and the existence/irreducibility of laws in the special sciences are irrelevant here because we are granting the existence of genuine mental events constituted by mental properties. Thus, such physicalist attempts to avoid the *reduction* of psychological to physical laws by denying such laws in the first place do not count against (2).[28] For example, both the functionalist account of the mental offered by Fodor and the anomalous monism of Davidson deny the existence of general exceptionless psychological or psycho-physical laws. But both positions depict the mental as being realized by the physical. Moreover, most are naturally associated with token physicalism when it comes to an ontological analysis of individual mental events.[29] Yet, if mental and physical events are what the argument from consciousness takes them to be, then it seems reasonable for individual events of both kinds to be instances of general types of events that could in principle be correlated.

Premise (2) would be accepted by an advocate of emergent physicalism since there are two desiderata for this position: non-reductive physicalism plus the dependency of supervenient entities on the physical. If one accepts premise (1) but denies (2), then the mental becomes too autonomous for naturalism. An example of such a view is weak dualism according to which the mind is a Humean bundle of mental states that neither belong to nor depend on a specific body but which at best are more or less generally associated with specific physical states.

The main justification for premise (4) is the difference between libertarian and event causal theories of agency. J. L. Mackie rejected (4), claiming that personal explanation is simply a sub-class of event causal explanation. Moreover, divine action, as it figures into Swinburne's account of personal explanation, involves the direct fulfillment of an intention on the part of God. But, argued Mackie, since human action is a type of efficient event causality between the relevant prior mental state (e.g. an intending, and a fulfillment which runs through and depends on a number of intermediate events which are part of a complex physical mechanism), there is a disanalogy between human intentional acts in which intentions are fulfilled indirectly and those of a god in which, supposedly, intentions are directly fulfilled. On Mackie's view, this disanalogy makes alleged divine action and the relevant sort of personal explanation mysterious and antecedently improbable. Thus, (4) is false and, even if it is true, it makes theistic personal explanation less, not more probable.

Is Mackie's argument successful against (4)? I don't think so. For one thing, pace Mackie, it is not at all clear that libertarian agency and the associated form of personal explanation are not to be preferred as accounts of human action to event causal accounts. Obviously, we cannot delve into this issue here, but if libertarian agency is correct, then Mackie is wrong in his claim that (4) is false.

Secondly, a defense of (4) may only require a *concept* of libertarian agency and personal explanation, even if we grant an event-causal theory of action for human acts. If we have such a clear conception, then even if human acts do not fall under it, under the right circumstances, it could be argued that a form of explanation clearly available to us is now to be employed. What those circumstances are and whether they obtain are more centrally related to premises (3) and (6) of AC and not (4). But since Mackie criticized (4) because if true it would make theistic explanation antecedently improbable, I want briefly to say something about what could justify the claim that a personal explanation of the libertarian sort should actually be used.

There have been a number of attempts to state necessary and sufficient conditions for personal action in event causal terms with John Bishop's account being the most sophisticated to date. But Bishop admits that our common sense concept of agency is different from and irreducible to event causality and is, in fact, libertarian.[30] For Bishop, the pervasiveness and power of the libertarian conception of agency places the burden of proof on the defender of a causal theory of action. Bishop claims that his own causal theory works only for worlds relevantly similar to ours in being naturalistic (strictly physical) worlds. He does not offer an analysis of action true across all possible worlds because he admits that our concept of action is libertarian and there are worlds in which it is satisfied. His justification of this minimal task is a prior assumption of naturalism, but such an assumption is clearly question-begging against AC. Therefore, if we have a clear, powerful and, *prima facie* justified libertarian conception of agency, Mackie's point about the mysteriousness and antecedent improbability of anything answering to this concept is seriously overstated.

Now, if we grant the non-physicality of mental states, then a causal theory of action for human acts will boil down to the claim that person P does some act e (raising one's hand to vote) if and only if some event b (the hand going up) which instantiates the type of state intrinsic to e-ing is caused by the appropriate mental state in the appropriate way. Note carefully that, regardless of the details of such an account, it will amount to nothing more than a causal correlation between certain physical states and the relevant mental events. According to premises (2) and (3) of AC, these correlations need and have an explanation. A causal theory of action will not do for the origin, regularity, and precise nature of these correlations, since these are what constitute a causal theory of action in the first place. If a causal theory of action presupposes mental states, then it will be important to explain the existence, regularity, and precise nature of those mental states themselves unless, of course, a divine causal theory of action is used. If this is so, and if we possess a clear concept of libertarian agency and personal explanation, then there is no good reason why a theist cannot use this type of explanation in this case.

However, when it comes to defending AC, I think one could deny a libertarian view of agency and personal explanation altogether and still defend (4). After all, some Christian theists, e.g. certain Calvinists, employ a causal theory for divine action. One could argue that there is some difference between normal physical event causality in physics and a causal theory of personal action. At the very least, the latter utilizes appropriately related mental states as parts of causal chains. Since (4) simply notes that there is a distinguishable difference between personal and natural scientific explanation, the alternative we are now considering may be all that AC needs to rebut Mackie. Bishop claims that for a naturalist causal theory of action must be combined with a strong physicalist theory of mental states.[31] I agree. I also reject a causal theory of action.[32] But setting this aside, since we are assuming the reality of mental states, Bishop's physicalist rendition of the causal theory of action simply does not apply here and a suitable statement of the nature and role of mental states in a causal theory could be all that is needed to distinguish personal from natural scientific explanation according to (4).

The presence of personal explanation as a unique argument form means that when it comes to explaining emergent properties such as those constitutive of consciousness, one does not need to acquiesce with Samuel Alexander's dictum that such properties are "to be accepted with the 'natural piety' of the investigator."[33] Thus, it is more than curious to find naturalists jump straightaway from the recognition that mental properties are genuinely emergent and incapable of naturalist explanation to the conclusion that we must take then as brute facts. To cite one example, speaking of the law-like correlations between emergent mental and physical properties, Kim says that

> [t]he emergent approach, therefore, asks us to accept these dangling laws as brute, unexplainable laws—that is, we are asked to count them among our fundamental laws, laws that are basic in the sense that no further explanation is possible for them. But this proposal is highly implausible, for we expect fundamental laws of nature to be reasonably simple, but these psychophysical correlations involve, on the physical side, tens of thousands of cells, millions and billions of molecules and basic particles.[34]

There are two sides to (5): Is personal explanation different from natural scientific explanation and are there other explanations for the facts mentioned in (1) and (2) besides these two? We have already dealt with the first question in conjunction with (4). Regarding question two, I think it is safe to say that, given the current intellectual climate, a personal theistic or a naturalistic explanation would exhaust at least the live, if not the logical, options. It is true that Thomas Nagel suggested that panpsychism might be necessary to explain the mental.[35] But it is widely recognized that panpsychism has serious problems in its own right, e.g. explaining what an incipient or proto-mental entity is or how the type of unity that appears to characterize the self could emerge from a mere system of parts standing together in various causal and spatio-temporal relations.[36] Moreover, panpsychism is arguably less reasonable than theism on other grounds, though I cannot pursue this point here. Further, it is not clear that panpsychism is an *explanation* of the phenomena in question. As Geoffrey Madell notes, "the sense that the mental and the physical are just inexplicably and gratuitously slapped together is hardly allayed by adopting … a panpsychist … view of the mind, for [it does not] have an explanation to offer as to why or how mental properties cohere with physical."[37] Interestingly, Nagel's own argument suggestive of panpsychism turns on a failure to consider a theistic explanation of the mental, coupled with an admission of the inadequacy of a natural scientific explanation:

> One unsettling consequence of such a theory [of mental/physical duality] is that it appears to lead to a form of panpsychism – since the mental properties of the complex organism must result from some properties of its basic components, suitably combined: and these cannot be merely physical properties or else in combination they will yield nothing but other physical properties. If any two hundred pound chunk of the universe contains the material needed to construct a person, and if we deny both psychophysical reductionism and a radical form of emergence, then everything, reduced to its elements, must have proto-mental properties.[38]

Actually, Nagel's statement is a near précis of AC. He accepts (1) and (2) in his denial of *reductionism*, he accepts (3) in his rejection of radical emergence which, I take it, would amount to the claim that the emergence of the mental from the physical is a brute case of something coming from nothing without explanation, and his whole argument rests on the acceptance of (6) as an implicit premise. Elsewhere, Nagel expresses a view about freedom and personal explanation according to which libertarian freedom is what we take ourselves to have, yet we cannot have it, given naturalism and the external, third-person scientific point of view.[39] Apparently, Nagel would accept some version of (4). That leaves (5) and, as far as I know, Nagel does not argue for the relative merits of theism vs. panpsychism. At the very least, we may be able to say this: If the other premises of AC are accepted, then scientific naturalism is false and there is an intramural debate left between theists and panpsychists. We will explore this dispute in chapter six. In chapter seven, we will examine Philip Clayton's pluralistic emergentist monism. There I will show that Clayton's position is an alternative to and not a plausible version of positive naturalism.

(7) follows from previous steps in the argument and asserts the adequacy of a personal explanation for the facts expressed in (1) and (2). One may reject (7) (or (5)) because personal explanation, theistic or otherwise, does not give us any real understanding of an explanandum, especially one like (1) and (2). Sometimes this objection assumes that an explanation must cite a mechanism before it can count as adequate. My response to this problem centers on the difference between libertarian and event causality and their associated forms of explanation.

Advocates of libertarian agency employ a form of personal explanation that stands in contrast to a covering law model. To understand this form of explanation, we need to look first at the difference between a basic and non-basic action. Often more than one thing is accomplished in a single exercise of agency. Some actions are done by doing others, e.g. I perform the act of going to the store to get bread by getting into my car and by driving to the store. Basic actions are fundamental to the performance of all others but are not done by doing something else. In general, S's φ-ing is basic iff there is no other non-equivalent action description "S's Ψ-ing" such that it is true that S φ-ed by Ψ-ing. My endeavoring to move my arm to get my keys is a basic action. A non-basic action contains basic actions as parts, which serve as means for realizing the ultimate intention of that non-basic action. To fulfill a non-basic intention, I must form an action plan certain ordered set of basic actions that I take to be an effective means of accomplishing my non-basic intention. The action plan that constitutes going to the store to get bread includes the acts of getting my keys and walking to my car.[40]

In my view, an action is something contained wholly within the boundaries of the agent. Thus, strictly speaking, in standard cases the results of an action are not proper parts of that action. A basic result of an action is an intended effect brought about immediately by the action. If I successfully endeavor to move my finger, the basic result is the moving of the finger. Non-basic results are more remote intended effects caused by basic results or chains of basic results plus more remote intended effects. The firing of the gun or the killing of Lincoln are respective illustrations of these types of non-basic results.

With this in mind, a personal explanation (divine or otherwise) of some basic result R brought about intentionally by person P where this bringing about of R is a basic action A will cite the intention I of P that R occur and the basic power B that P exercised to bring about R. P, I, and B provide a personal explanation of R: agent P brought about R by exercising power B in order to realize intention I as an irreducibly teleological goal. To illustrate, suppose we are trying to explain why Wesson simply moved his finger (R). We could explain this by saying that Wesson (P) performed an act of endeavoring to move his finger (A) in that he exercised his ability to move (or will to move) his finger (B) intending to move the finger (I). If Wesson's moving his finger was an expression of an intent to move a finger to fire a gun to kill Smith, then we can explain the non-basic results (the firing of the gun and the killing of Smith) by saying that Wesson (P) performed an act of killing Smith (I3) by endeavoring to move his finger (A) intentionally (I1) by exercising his power to do so (B), intending thereby to fire the gun (I2) in order to kill Smith. An explanation of the results of a non-basic action (like going to the store to get bread) will include a description of the action plan.[41]

By way of application, the adequacy of a personal explanation does not consist in offering a mechanism, but rather, in correctly citing the relevant person, his intentions, the basic power exercised, and in some cases, offering a description of the relevant action plan. Thus, if we have some model of God and His intentions for creating a world suitable for human persons (from revelation or otherwise), we can make reference to God, His intentions for creating a world with persons with mental states regularly correlated with their environment, and the adequacy of His power to bring about the basic results captured in (1) and (2).

Premise (8) seems fairly uncontroversial. To be sure, Humean-style arguments about the type, size, and number of deities involved could be raised at this point, but again, these issues would be intramural theistic problems of small comfort to someone like Searle committed to naturalism.[42] Moreover, if we take live options only, then it seems fair to limit our alternatives in (5) to theistic or naturalistic. If that is acceptable, at least for the purposes of arguing against Searle and other naturalists like him, then (8) should not be objectionable.

In the terms of epistemic appraisal proffered by Chisholm, it seems that, given AC and what we have seen about the naturalist ontology from chapter one, ¬(N & Emergence$_{2a}$) is at least *beyond reasonable doubt* where a proposition is *beyond reasonable doubt* for a subject S means that S is more justified in believing that proposition than in withholding it.

Alternatively, given AC, (N & $Emergence_{2a}$) is at least *reasonable to disbelieve* (S is more justified in disbelieving that proposition than in withholding it).[43] However, it would be premature to conclude that this is the correct epistemic appraisal of (N & $Emergence_{2a}$). We still need to look at premises (3) and (6). Rather than doing so directly, I shall examine them in chapters three through seven in the context of naturalist attempts that, if successful, would defeat (3) and (6).

Preview

In chapters one and two we have examined the naturalist ontology and AC as a rival to naturalism in explaining the appearance of consciousness or its law-like correlations with physical states. We have seen reasons that follow from the nature of naturalism itself and from the presence of AC as a rival for why a naturalist ought to be a strong physicalist. Unfortunately, strong physicalism is a tough sell and a growing number of philosophers are dissatisfied with it. Perhaps our conclusion that a naturalist ought to be a strong physicalist is premature. Maybe there are adequate naturalist accounts of the mental.

In chapters three through five we will look at representative samples of the major strategies employed to provide such an account in increasing order of strength. In chapter three we will examine a view expressed by Searle to the effect that all a naturalist needs to do is to provide contingent correlations between mental and physical states. In chapter four, we will investigate a view proffered by Timothy O'Connor to the effect that naturalists must go beyond contingent correlations and justify the claim that physical states necessitate in some appropriate modal sense the mental ones. In chapter five, we shall turn to a view advocated by Colin McGinn who asserts that all previous naturalist attempts to explain consciousness fail due to in-principle considerations about the phenomena to be explained and the evolutionary limitations on our noetic equipment. McGinn proffers a mysterian solution he claims to be consistent with naturalism. I will take Searle's, O'Connor's and McGinn's to be canonical representations of contingent emergent-correlation, necessary emergent and mysterian forms of naturalism.

In chapter six, we shall look at a position—panpsychism as proffered by its most able advocate, David Skrbina—that is most likely an alternative to and not a version of naturalism, but that is less extreme from a naturalist standpoint than a theistic solution. In chapter seven, we will look at Philip Clayton's pluralistic emergentist monism. Of all the positions we shall consider, I believe that Clayton's is the most plausible. But I hope to show that it is not an option for a naturalist who claims explanatory superiority for his/her worldview, nor is it preferable to classic theism and AC.

I will conclude that none of these solutions is adequate and that AC is to be preferred. If I am right about this, then the existence of finite mental states provides good evidence that God exists. The best thing for a naturalist to do in this case it to opt for a strong form of physicalism. In chapter eight, I will show that the main naturalist argument for physicalism, namely, an appeal to the hard sciences, is an abject and obvious failure. This will raise the question as to why physicalism enjoys the status it does in the academy today in spite of the lack of significant evidence for it. I try to answer this question in chapter nine.

3 John Searle and contingent correlation

The weakest position for a naturalist, who at least accepts emergent mental properties and events, is one according to which all the naturalist must adequately do to explain the mental is to establish contingent correlations between physical and mental states and leave it at that. The most prominent attempt to flesh out this approach is the biological naturalism of John Searle.

Searle's position

Contingent correlation

Searle actually acknowledges that such correlations are not enough for an adequate account of the mental, which should also include the transformation of correlations into causal relations by showing that the manipulation of the physical state alters the mental state and by providing a mechanism as to how this works.[1] But for three reasons I believe it is appropriate to take him as an example of a contingent correlation position. First, he takes such correlations to be adequate to justify the superiority of biological naturalism, so they are sufficient conditions for a naturalist account of consciousness.[2] Second, he explicitly claims that a causal explanation of consciousness may be in principle beyond our abilities to obtain. Moreover, even if this is the case, his biological naturalism remains standing.[3] Third, he argues against the need for a naturalist to meet some necessitation requirement according to which one can show that the relevant mental state *must* occur given a certain physical state.[4] That leaves us with correlations for which the establishment of counterfactual covariance would be nice but not necessary for biological naturalism to be adequate.

Biological naturalism

Searle has some pretty harsh things to say about the last fifty years or so of work in the philosophy of mind.[5] Specifically, he says that the field has contained numerous assertions that are obviously false and absurd and has cycled neurotically through various positions precisely because of the dominance of strong physicalism as the only live option for a naturalist. Searle's statement of the reason for this neurotic behavior is revealing:

> How is it that so many philosophers and cognitive scientists can say so many things that, to me at least, seem obviously false? . . . I believe one of the unstated assumptions behind the current batch of views is that they represent the only scientifically acceptable alternatives to the anti-scientism that went with traditional dualism, the belief in the immortality of the soul, spiritualism, and so on. Acceptance of the current views is motivated not so much by an independent conviction of their truth as by a terror of what are apparently the only alternatives. That is, the choice we are tacitly presented with is between a "scientific" approach, as represented by one or another of the current versions of "materialism," and an "unscientific" approach, as represented by Cartesianism or some other traditional religious conception of the mind.[6]

In other words, philosophy of mind has been dominated by scientific naturalism for fifty years and scientific naturalists have advanced different versions of strong physicalism, however implausible they may be in light of what is obviously known by us about consciousness, because strong physicalism was seen as a crucial implication of taking the naturalistic turn. For these naturalists, if one abandons strong physicalism one has rejected a scientific naturalist approach to the mind/body problem and opened himself up to the intrusion of religious concepts and arguments about the mental.

Searle offers his analysis of the mind as a naturalistic account because, he says, no one in the modern world can deny "the obvious facts of physics – for example, that the world is made up entirely of physical particles in fields of force."[7] An acceptance of naturalism is constituted by an acknowledgment of the atomic theory of matter and evolutionary biology both of which allow for micro-to-micro or micro-to-macro causal explanations, but not macro-to-micro ones.[8] According to Searle, dualism in any form is widely rejected because it is correctly considered inconsistent with the scientific worldview.[9] He also claims that because people educated in the contemporary scientific worldview know how the world works, the existence of God is no longer a serious candidate for truth.[10] But a commitment to naturalism and a concomitant rejection of dualism have blinded people to the point that they feel compelled to reject what is obvious to experience, namely, the obvious nature of consciousness and intentionality.

Searle's own solution to the mind/body problem is biological naturalism: consciousness, intentionality, and mental states in general, are emergent biological states and processes that supervene upon a suitably structured, functioning brain. Brain processes cause mental processes which are not reducible to the former. Consciousness is just an ordinary, i.e. physical feature of the brain and, as such, is merely an ordinary feature of the natural world.[11] Despite the frequent assertions by a number of philosophers that Searle is a property dualist, he denies the charge and seems puzzled by it.[12] However, in my view, Searle is indeed a property dualist and an epiphenomenalist one at that, though he also denies the latter charge as well.[13] To show this, let us consider the charge of property dualism first. Searle's characterization of neurophysiological and mental states are exactly those of the property dualist who insists that mental and physical properties are to be characterized in a certain way and that they are two, different types of properties. In light of Searle's descriptions of the mental and physical, it is obvious why most philosophers charge him with property dualism and the burden of proof is on him to show why he is not.

Searle's response to this problem is twofold.[14] First, he seems to think that a property dualist must accept the entire Cartesian metaphysics. Second, he says that dualists accept a false dichotomistic vocabulary in which something is either physical or mental but cannot be both. So biological naturalism is to be distinguished from property dualism in that the former does not include the entire Cartesian apparatus and it rejects this dichotomistic vocabulary. Now if this is how Searle distinguishes biological naturalism from property dualism, then his response is inadequate. For one thing, it is absurd to claim that one must accept the entire Cartesian metaphysics to be a property dualist. Thomas Aquinas was a certain sort of property (and substance) dualist, but obviously, he did not accept the Cartesian apparatus.[15] Swinburne defends Cartesian property and substance dualism without accepting Descartes' entire metaphysical scheme.[16] Moreover, Searle's own view has a dichotomistic vocabulary in which he distinguishes normal physical (e.g. neurophysiological) properties from emergent biological "physical" (i.e. mental) properties. So he has simply replaced one dualism with another one.

Perhaps there is a different and deeper distinction between (at least) Cartesian property dualism and biological naturalism for Searle. For the property dualist mental and physical properties are so different that it is inconceivable that one could emerge from the other by natural processes. However, for the biological naturalist, biological physical properties are normal physical properties in this sense: they are like solidity, liquidity, or the properties of digestion or other higher-level properties that can emerge by means of natural processes. I don't wish to comment further on this claim here except to say that Searle's employment of it to distinguish biological naturalism from property dualism amounts to nothing more than a mere assertion combined with a few undeveloped examples (e.g. liquidity) that are supposed to be good analogies to emergent mental states. But this assertion is simply question begging in light of AC and, as I will show later, it amounts to an abandonment of naturalism. At the very least, one should stop and ask why, if Searle's solution to the mind/body problem is at once obvious and not at all problematic for naturalists, a field of philosophy dominated by naturalists for fifty years has missed this obvious solution?

Searle and epiphenomenal property dualism

Searle's response to this question involves a specification of why it is that emergent mental states have no deep implications. We will look at this issue shortly, but for now, I want to show that Searle's biological naturalism implies an epiphenomenalist view of emergent mental states in spite of his denial that this is so. Searle's position is epiphenomenalist for at least three reasons. First, Searle takes scientific naturalism to imply that there is no macro-to-micro causation and, as we have seen, on this point, most naturalists would agree: Jaegwon Kim says "a physicalist must, it seems, accept some form of the principle that the physical domain is causally closed – that if a physical phenomenon is causally explainable, it must have an explanation within the physical domain."[17] He goes on to say that "Causal powers and reality go hand in hand. To render mental events causally impotent is as good as banishing them from our ontology."[18] For these reasons, Kim claims that a naturalist should be a strong and not a supervenient physicalist because the latter implies a problematic epiphenomenal view of the mental. David Papineau has endorsed the same point.[19]

Second, Searle distinguishes two types of emergent features. $Emergent_1$ features are caused by micro-level entities and do not exercise independent causality. $Emergent_2$ features are caused by micro-level entities and *are* capable of exercising independent causality once they exist. Searle rejects the existence of $emergent_2$ features because, among other things, they would violate the transitivity of causality. Since he holds that conscious states are $emergent_1$, it is hard to see how those states could have causal efficacy.

Third, Searle holds to the causal *reduction* of the mental. In causal *reduction*, the existence and "powers" of the emergent but causally reduced entity are explained by the causal powers of the reducing, base entities. It is hard to see how he could hold this and avoid epiphenomenalism. I conclude then, that despite protests to the contrary, Searle's biological naturalism is a certain type of epiphenomenal property dualism. According to the typology of chapter one, Searle accepts $emergence_{2a}$.

Searle's three reasons why biological naturalism is not a threat to naturalism

Why are there no deep metaphysical implications that follow from Searle's biological naturalism? Why is it that biological naturalism does not represent a rejection of scientific naturalism which, in turn, opens the door for religious concepts about and arguments from the mental? Searle's answer to this question is developed in three steps. First, he cites several examples of emergence (e.g. liquidity) that he takes to be unproblematic for a naturalist and argues by analogy that the emergent properties of consciousness are likewise unproblematic.

Step two is a formulation of two reasons why, appearances to the contrary notwithstanding, consciousness is not a problem for naturalists. First, Searle says that naturalists are troubled by the existence of irreducible mental entities because they are misled into thinking that the following is a coherent question that needs an answer: "How do unconscious bits of matter produce consciousness?"[20] Many "find it difficult, if not impossible to accept the idea that the real world, the world described by physics and chemistry and biology, contains an ineliminably subjective element. How could such a thing be? How can we possibly get a coherent world picture if the world contains these mysterious conscious entities?"[21]

For Searle, the question of how matter produces consciousness is simply a question about how the brain works to produce mental states even though individual neurons in the brain are not conscious. This question is easily answered in terms of specific though largely unknown neurobiological features of the brain. However, Searle thinks that many are misled into thinking this question is about something deeper and more puzzling. Setting consciousness aside, in all other cases of entities arranged in a part/whole hierarchy of systems, we could picture or image how emergent features arise because these systems and all their features are objective phenomena. Our problem is that we try to image how consciousness could arise from a system of unconscious bits of matter in the same way, but this is not possible because consciousness itself is not imageable and we cannot get at it through a visual metaphor.[22] Once we give up trying to imagine consciousness, any deep puzzlement about the emergence of consciousness, given naturalism, evaporates and the only question left is one about how the brain produces mental states.

There is another reason Searle offers as to why the emergence of consciousness has no deep metaphysical significance.[23] In standard cases of *reduction*, e.g. heat and color, an ontological *reduction* (color is nothing but a wavelength) is based on a causal *reduction* (color is caused by a wavelength). In these cases we can distinguish the appearance of heat and color from the reality, place the former in consciousness, leave the latter in the objective world, and go on to define the phenomenon itself in terms of its causes. We can do this because our interests are in the reality and not the appearance. The ontological *reduction* of heat to its causes leaves the appearance of heat the same. However, when it comes to mental states like pain, even though an ontological *reduction* cannot be found, there is a similar causal pattern, e.g. pain is caused by particular brain states.

So why do we regard heat as ontologically reducible but not pain? In the case of heat, we are interested in the physical causes and not the subjective appearances, but with pain, the subjective appearance itself interests us. If we wanted to, we could reduce pain to particular physical processes and go on to talk about pain appearances analogous to the heat case. However, in the case of consciousness, the reality is the appearance. Since the point of a *reduction* is to distinguish and separate reality from appearance in order to focus on underlying causes by definitionally identifying the reality with those causes, the point of a *reduction* for consciousness is missing, since it is the appearance itself that is the reality of interest. Therefore, the irreducibility of consciousness has no deep metaphysical consequences and is simply a result of the pattern of *reduction* that expresses our pragmatic interests.

In step three, Searle claims that an adequate scientific explanation of mental emergence is a set of very detailed, even law-like correlations between specific mental and physical states.[24]

Critique

Searle vs. Nagel on causal necessitation

Searle rejects an argument by Thomas Nagel, which denies that mere correlations amount to a scientific explanation. In terms of AC, Nagel would accept premise (6) (the explanation is not a natural scientific one) and deny that Searle's correlations count as scientific explanations. Searle rejects (6) and believes such correlations count as adequate scientific explanations. Nagel claims that in other cases of emergence like liquidity, a scientific explanation does not just tell us what happens, it explains why liquidity *must* emerge when a collection of water molecules gather under certain circumstances. In this case, scientific explanation offers physical causal necessity: given certain states of affairs, it is causally necessary that liquidity emerge and it is inconceivable that it not supervene. But, argues Nagel, no such necessity and no answer to a why question is given by a mere correlation between mental states and physical states in the brain.

Searle's response to Nagel is threefold.[25] First, he says that some explanations in science do not exhibit the type of causal necessity Nagel requires, e.g. the inverse square law is an account of gravity that does not show why bodies have to have gravitational attraction. This response is question-begging against Nagel because the inverse square law is merely a description of what happens and not an explanation of why it happens. Interestingly, Newton himself took the inverse square law to be a mere description of how gravity works but explained the nature of gravity itself (due to his views about action at a distance, the nature of spirit, and the mechanical nature of corpuscularian causation by contact) in terms of the activity of the Spirit of God. The point is not that Newton was right, but that he distinguished a description of gravity from an explanation of what it is and his explanation cannot be rebutted by citing the inverse square law. Rather, one needs a better explanatory model of gravity. Therefore, Searle's own example actually works against him.

Moreover, even if we grant that covering law explanations are, in fact, explanations in some sense, they are clearly different from explanations that offer a model of why things must take place given the model and its mechanisms. Since the argument from consciousness assumes the correlations and offers an answer to the why question, Searle's solution here is not really a rival explanation, but merely a claim that such correlations are basic, brute facts that just need to be listed. In light of what we have already seen, there are at least two further difficulties with Searle's claim.

First, given AC and the nature of theory adjudication among rivals, it is question-begging and *ad hoc* for Searle to assert that these correlations are basic. For the correlations themselves, along with the entities and properties they relate are natural and bear a relevant similarity to other entities, properties, and relations in theism (e.g. God as spirit who can create and causally interact with matter), but are unnatural given the naturalist epistemology, Grand Story, and ontology. As we saw in chapter one, self-reflective naturalists understand this. Thus, Terence Horgan says that "in any metaphysical framework that deserves labels like 'materialism', 'naturalism', or 'physicalism', supervenience facts must be explainable rather than being *sui generis*."[26] And to restate Armstrong's admission:

> I suppose that if the principles involved [in analyzing the single all-embracing spatio-temporal system which is reality] were completely different from the current principles of physics, in particular if they involved appeal to mental entities, such as purposes, we might then count the analysis as a falsification of Naturalism. But the Naturalist need make no more concession than this[27]

Horgan and Armstrong say this precisely because mental entities, the supervenience relation, or a causal correlation between mental and physical entities, simply are not natural given a consistent naturalist paradigm. Nor can they be located in Jackson's sense in the Grand Story. Their reality constitutes a falsification of naturalism for Horgan and Armstrong and, given AC, they provide evidence for theism. It is question-begging and *ad hoc* simply to adjust naturalism, as does Searle, given the presence of AC as a rival explanation.

Naturalists have long criticized Cartesian dualism because the causal relation it posits is so bizarre and its relata so disparate that the relation is virtually unintelligible. Many Cartesian dualists are theists and have sought to rebut this claim by appealing to the alleged clarity of divine miraculous activity in the natural world as a counter example. However, the dialectical situation worsens if the Cartesian is a naturalist for she must now try to render interaction intelligible solely in light of the resources of the Grand Story, and that cannot be done if the interaction relation is taken to be a natural entity at home in the naturalist ontology. It clearly does not bear a relevant similarity to other entities in that ontology. However, this problem is not a function of the ontological category of the relata. Specifically, it is not a problem that arises for naturalism only if the relata are in the category of individual. It applies equally to the category of property. This is why this problem is sometimes called "Descartes' Revenge." Thus, Searle's employment of a supervenience relation—causal or otherwise—between the brain and consciousness is a serious difficulty for his biological naturalism, one he does not adequately address.

Second, Swinburne's version of AC notes that a correlation can be either an accidental generalization or a genuine law (which exhibits at least physical necessity). We can distinguish these two in that laws are (but accidental correlations are not) non-circular correlations that fit naturally into theories that 1) are ontologically simple, 2) have broad explanatory power, and 3) fit with background knowledge from other, closely related scientific theories about the world. By "fit," Swinburne means the degree of naturalness of the correlation and entities correlated in light of both the broader theory of which the correlation is a part and background knowledge. Now Searle admits that mental phenomena are unique compared to all other entities because they "have a special feature not possessed by other natural phenomena, namely, subjectivity."[28] Unfortunately, it is precisely this radical uniqueness that makes mental phenomena unnatural for a naturalist worldview. It also prevents Searle from distinguishing an accidental correlation from a genuine law of nature regarding mental and physical correlations.

So much, then, for Searle's first response to Nagel. His second response is that the apparent necessity of some scientific causal explanations may just be a function of our finding some explanation so convincing that we cannot conceive of certain phenomena behaving differently. Medievals may have thought modern explanations of the emergence of liquidity mysterious and causally contingent. Similarly, our belief that specific mind/brain correlations are causally contingent may simply be due to our ignorance of the brain.

It is hard to see what is supposed to follow from Searle's point here. Just because one can be mistaken in using conceivability as a test for causal necessity, it does not follow that conceivability is never a good test for it. Only a case-by-case study can, in principle, decide the appropriateness of its employment. Now when it comes to things like liquidity or solidity, Nagel is right. Precisely because of what we know about matter, we cannot conceive of certain states of affairs existing and these properties being absent. That Medievals would not be so convinced is beside the point since they were ignorant of the relevant atomic theory. If they possessed the correct theory, their intuitions would be as are ours. However, when it comes to the mental and physical, they are such different entities, and the mental is so unnatural given the rest of the naturalist ontology, that there is no clearly conceivable necessity about their connection. Moreover, this judgment is based, not on what we do not know about the two types of states, but on what we do know.

Moreover, a more detailed correlation in the future will not change the situation one bit. There is no non-circular or non-*ad-hoc* way to formulate such a correlation and we will merely be left with a more detailed dictionary of correlations that will leave intact the same type of problem of causal necessity true of less detailed correlations. Our current lack of belief in such a causal necessity is not due to ignorance of more and more details of the very thing that lacks the necessity in the first place. Rather, it is based on a clear understanding of the nature of the mental and physical, an understanding that Searle himself accepts.

This is why it will not do for naturalists to claim that they are not committed to anything ultimately or utterly brute (like the divine will), just to their being something unexplained at any given time but which can be explained through deeper investigation. No scientific advance in our knowledge of the details of mental/physical correlations will render either the existence of mental entities or their regular correlation with physical ones anything other than utterly brute for the naturalist.

But Searle had another line of defense against Nagel: Even if we grant Nagel's point about the lack of causal necessity in the mental/physical case, nothing follows from this. Why? Because in the water and liquidity case, we can picture the relation between the two in such a way that causal necessity is easily a part of that picture. But since we cannot picture consciousness, we are not able to imagine the same sort of causal necessity. Yet that does not mean it is not there.

Here Searle simply applies his earlier point that, given naturalism, our puzzlement about the emergence of consciousness from unconscious bits of matter is due to our attempt to picture consciousness. Now it seems to me that this point is just false and egregiously so. I, for one, have no temptation to try to picture consciousness. In addition, other naturalists have put their finger on the real difficulty about the emergence of consciousness. D. M. Armstrong states that

> It is not a particularly difficult notion that, when the nervous system reaches a certain level of complexity, it should develop new properties. Nor would there be anything particularly difficult in the notion that when the nervous system reaches a certain level of complexity it should affect something that was already in existence in a new way. But it is a quite different matter to hold that the nervous system should have the power to create something else [mental entities], of a quite different nature from itself, and create it out of no materials.[29]

Along similar lines, Paul Churchland says,

> The important point about the standard evolutionary story is that the human species and all of its features are the wholly physical outcome of a purely physical process. ... If this is the correct account of our

> origins, then there seems neither need, nor room, to fit any nonphysical substances or properties into our theoretical account of ourselves. We are creatures of matter. And we should learn to live with that fact.[30]

Churchland identifies two reasons the naturalist should opt for strong physicalism—there is neither need nor room for anything else. Regarding need, I take it he means that everything we need in order to explain the origin and workings of human beings can be supplied by physicalist causal explanations. Regarding room, entities do not come into existence *ex nihilo* nor do radically different kinds of entities emerge from purely physical components placed in some sort of complex arrangement. This is what Nagel was getting at when he rejected radical emergence. What comes from the physical by means of physical processes will also be physical.

Searle is simply wrong about the problem being the imageability of consciousness. The problem here for naturalism is ontological, not epistemological as most naturalists have seen. What is curious about Searle's *reduction* of an ontological problem to an epistemological one is that his entire work on biological naturalism is replete with criticisms of other naturalists for doing this very thing in other areas of the philosophy of mind. Could it be that Searle's own misidentification of the ontological problem here is "neurotic" in just the sense that he applies to his naturalist colleagues: if one takes the emergence of consciousness as an ontological problem, then biological naturalism will, in fact, give cause for introducing religious concepts and explanations for the mental as expressed in AC?

Searle vs. McGinn on causal necessitation

Searle has one final line of defense against those who place a necessitation requirement on an adequate naturalist explanation for "emergent" properties. Searle seeks to rebut an argument by Colin McGinn to the effect that such a necessitation requirement is both essential for and unavailable to a strictly naturalist account of consciousness.[31] We will investigate the details of McGinn's position in chapter five, but for present purposes, Searle focuses on the following aspects of McGinn's position: Consciousness is a kind of "stuff" that is known by introspection, things known by introspection are non-spatial, an adequate solution to the mind/body problem requires understanding the "link" between matter and consciousness, but given our noetic limitations, it is in principle beyond our ability to know that link and, therefore, there is no naturalist account of consciousness. Searle rebuts McGinn because (1) consciousness is a property not a stuff; (2) introspection is a confused notion and should be abandoned; given (1) and (2), there is no reason to deny that consciousness is spatial; and moreover (3) there is no link between consciousness and the brain anymore than there is a link between liquidity and H_2O.

Setting aside until chapter five the issue of whether or not Searle has adequately rebutted McGinn's particular formulation of this argument, the more important point is whether Searle has rebutted this form of argument if it is stated in more plausible dualist terms. This is a fair approach to Searle's rebuttal because he explicitly takes McGinn's premises to represent broad Cartesian-style commitments (except for McGinn's claim that the link is *in principle* unknowable) and his own rebuttal to be successful against Cartesian dualism in general. Given this broader context, I believe Searle's rebuttal fails. Consider premise (1). I do not know of a single property dualist (Cartesian or otherwise) who would take mental properties to be a sort of stuff that, for example, should be referred to by mass terms. Even with respect to mental substances, a framework of stuff is not usually employed. To be sure, some Cartesian dualists may believe in soul-stuff, but most substance dualists, including me, employ a substance/attribute ontology to characterize a mental substance as an individuated mental essence; they do not use a separable part/whole framework or the notion of stuff.[32] Therefore, Searle is guilty of arguing against a strawman in (1).

What about (2)? Searle's argument against introspection is as follows:[33]

1_I If the standard model is true, then there is a distinction (presumably, not a distinction of reason) between the thing seen and the seeing of it.
2_I The standard model is true.
3_I Therefore, there is a distinction between the thing seen and the seeing of it.
4_I If introspection occurs, then there is no distinction between the thing seen and the seeing of it.
5_I Therefore, introspection does not occur.

There are at least two problems with this argument and they involve (2_I) and (4_I). Let us begin with (4_I). Searle gives no good reason to accept it and, in fact, there are sufficient reasons to reject it. Let us assume, as is standardly granted, that in introspection we have a second-order mental state directed upon a first-order mental state. For example, in introspection the self—whatever it is—is directly aware of a sensation of red or a feeling of pain by directing a second-order mental state onto a first-order one. This is a perfectly intelligible account of introspection and it provides the distinction required to reject (4_I).

If someone rejects this model of introspection, then one can still rebut Searle's argument by rejecting (2_I). That is, one can grant (1_I) for the sake of argument and deny that it applies to introspection because it begs the question. After all, why apply the standard model to introspective acts? Recall that in chapter two I claimed that at least a certain range of mental states relevant to introspection is self-presenting properties. According to a standard characterization of them, a self-presenting property presents to a subject the intentional object of that property (e.g. an apple's surface) and the self-presenting property itself (being-an-appearing-of-red). Such properties present other things to a subject intermediately by means of them, and they present themselves to a subject directly simply in virtue of the fact that he has them. Introspective awareness of being-an-appearing-of-red could be understood as the exemplification of a self-presenting property.

In this case, introspection provides a counter example to the standard model. And while Searle does not mention the self, I see no reason why one cannot be directly aware of oneself. On a certain understanding of intentionality according to which it is a monadic property, when one is aware of oneself (as opposed to a mental state one has), in direct self-awareness, one simply directs one's intentionality onto oneself and the subject and object of awareness stand in the identity relation to each other. Nothing Searle says comes close to undermining such an understanding of self-awareness.

Searle similarly attacks a spatial metaphor associated with "privileged access" that he alleges to go proxy for introspection:[34] When I spatially enter something, there is a distinction among me, the act of entering, and the thing entered. No such distinction obtains in alleged acts of "private access" and, thus, "private access" should be rejected. The appropriate rebuttal analogously follows the lines of response given to the argument against introspection.

This brings us to (3). As we shall see below, liquidity is a bad analogy with conscious properties. Liquidity may be understood as the property of flowing freely, which, in turn, may be characterized in terms of friction, flexibility of bonding angles, degree of spatial compactness, and so forth. In short, liquidity is a structural property and, as such, liquidity constitutively supervenes "upon" a collection of water molecules. There is no causal relation here. Liquidity just is a feature of non-rigid motion constituted by a subvenient base. Thus, it is plausible to deny a "link" between liquidity and a swarm of water molecules. But Searle is clear that conscious properties are simple, *sui generis* emergent properties, and as such, are causally supervenient on the brain. In this case, there is indeed a causal "link" between the brain and consciousness and Searle's analogy employed in (3) is a failure, even in terms of his own views.

I conclude, therefore, that Searle has not succeeded in undermining Nagel: premise (6) of AC (the explanation is not a natural scientific one) is correct and Searle's correlations are not examples of scientific explanation, which count against (6). But what about premise (3) (there is an explanation for these correlations)? Why is it not reasonable to take mental entities and their regular correlations with physical entities to be utterly brute natural facts for which there is no explanation? The answer is provided by the arguments just mentioned about why Searle's correlations are not really scientific explanations. Mental entities are not natural or at home in the naturalist epistemology, etiology, and ontology. Given theism and AC as a rival explanatory paradigm, and given the fact that mental entities and correlations are natural for theism, it is question-begging and *ad hoc* simply to announce that these entities and correlations are natural entities.

Searle could reply that biological naturalism is not question-begging because we already have reason to believe that naturalism is superior to theism prior to our study of the nature of the mental. The only support Searle gives for this claim, apart from a few sociological musings about what it means to be a modern person, is that it is an obvious fact of physics that the world consists *entirely* of physical particles moving in fields of force. It should be clear, however, that this claim is itself question-begging and clearly false. When there is a statement in a physics text about the world in its entirety, it is important to note that this is not a statement of physics. It is a philosophical assertion that does not express any obvious fact of physics. Moreover, it is a question-begging assertion by naturalists prior to a consideration of the evidence and arguments for theism, including AC. If Searle denies this, then he should inform advocates of AC of exactly what obvious fact of physics they deny in their employment of the argument.

Most naturalists have seen this and have opted for strong physicalism in order to avoid abandoning naturalism and legitimizing the introduction of religious concepts and explanations into the picture. It may be "neurotic" to deny consciousness, as Searle points out. But it is far from "neurotic" to be driven to do so in terms of a prior commitment to naturalism, and AC makes clear why this is the case.

Mackie on Locke and thinking matter

But perhaps there is a naturalist rejoinder at this point in the form of a *tu quoque* against theists and AC. J. L. Mackie advanced just such an argument.[35] According to Mackie, theists like John Locke admitted that God could superadd consciousness to systems of matter fitly disposed and, therefore, as a result of Divine intervention, matter may give rise to consciousness after all. Thus, Locke leaves open the possibility that a mere material being might be conscious given theism. Mackie then asks this question: "But if some material structures could be conscious, how can we know *a priori* that material structures cannot *of themselves give rise to* consciousness?"[36] He concludes that this Lockean admission opens the door for the naturalist to assert the emergence of consciousness from fitly disposed matter as a brute fact.

In my view, Mackie's argument carries no force against AC because a main part of AC consists in the recognition that mental/physical correlations exist, they are not explicable within the constraints of scientific naturalism, and they require a personal theistic explanation if they are to be explained at all. In this sense, the idea that, in one way or another, God could "superadd" thinking or other mental states to matter is required for AC to go through.[37]

However, as I have tried to show, it does not follow from this "Lockean admission" that it is a brute, naturalistic fact that material structures of themselves can give rise to consciousness or that adequate naturalistic explanations can be given for this. Indeed, Locke himself constructed detailed arguments to show that mental states like thinkings are not within the natural powers of matter nor could they arise from material structures without an original Mind to create and attach those mental states to matter.[38] Locke's view that God could superadd thinking to a material substance just as easily as to a spiritual substance was a conclusion he drew from the omnipotence of God along with the claim that "thinking matter" is not a contradiction and, thus, possible for God to bring about.

I am not defending Locke's way of arguing that God could superadd thinking to matter. In fact, I do not think it is correct as he formulated it but, clearly, Locke would not have believed that Mackie's naturalistic conclusion could justifiably be drawn from his own (Locke's) admission of the possibility of Divine omnipotence adding a faculty of thought to a material structure.

Mackie cannot simply assert that material structures have the power to give rise to consciousness and also claim to be operating with a naturalistic depiction of matter. According to David Papineau, matter with emergent mental potentiality is not the sort of matter countenanced by naturalists. This is why, when Papineau attempts to characterize the physical in terms of a future ideal physics, he places clear boundaries on the types of changes allowed by naturalism for developments in physical theory. According to Papineau, the naturalist will admit that future physics may change some features of what we believe about matter, but in light of a naturalist commitment and the past few hundred years of development in physics, future physics will not need to be supplemented by psychological or mental categories.[39]

Given theism, we cannot say *a priori* just what capacities or states God will correlate with specific physical states. But given naturalism, and the commitment to the role of physics in naturalism, along with a view of the physical that is required by physics, we can say that mental potentiality is just not part of matter. Thus, it is question-begging and *ad hoc* against AC for Mackie to adjust naturalism to allow that material structures of themselves can give rise to consciousness.

Consciousness, liquidity, solidity and digestion

There is one final issue in Searle's defense of biological naturalism that needs to be addressed, viz., his claim that the emergence of consciousness fits a broad pattern of emergence, e.g. cases of liquidity, solidity, digestion, and, therefore, since the latter present no problem for naturalism, neither does the former. I offer three responses. First, if we take liquidity or solidity to be the degree of rigidity, flexibility, or viscosity of a collection of particles, then these properties are not good analogies to consciousness. Why? Because they turn out to be nothing more than group behavior of particles placed in a relatively compressed, stable, ordered structure for solids or a more viscous, less compact arrangement for liquids. Therefore, there is no problem about emergence here since we can easily understand how liquidity and solidity are related to groups of material particles as they are depicted in physical theory.

Second, when we are dealing with genuinely emergent properties that are categorially different from what physical theory takes to characterize subvenient entities, I think that it could be argued that the naturalist has the same difficulty here as with the emergence of consciousness. Recall Searle's point about the pragmatics of *reduction*: we reduce heat to its causes because we happen to be interested in the objective causes and not the subjective appearances, but in cases of, e.g. pain, we are interested in the painful appearance itself, so we do not reduce pain to its causes. In my view, the decision to reduce heat to its causes is not primarily a scientific matter nor is it a matter of our pragmatic interest. I think it has been a function of two things. First, if we take heat, color, liquidity, or solidity to be identical to the qualia we experience in certain circumstances (e.g. heat is identical to warmth, red is a color not a wavelength, liquidity is wetness), then an ontological puzzle arises analogous to the one about the emergence of mental states: How could warmth emerge in a physical structure as a result of increased atomic agitation?

Second, there was a way of avoiding this question in light of a widely held Lockean view of secondary qualities and sense perception. We can locate these secondary qualities in consciousness and identify them as appearances of the real objective phenomena, viz., the objective causes for our experiences of secondary qualities. John Yolton has shown that during the late seventeenth and early eighteenth centuries debates about materialism, immaterialist philosophers (e.g. Ralph Cudworth) regularly argued against the idea that mental entities could emerge from properly structured matter.[40] A standard rebuttal to this claim was that light and heat were very different from matter but could be generated in material bodies given the right conditions. Therefore, mind could likewise emerge. Cudworth and others responded by asserting that light, heat, and other secondary qualities were not in material bodies, but were sensations in minds and, thus, the problem does not arise as to how they could arise in a material structure devoid of such qualities prior to the right conditions obtaining. It is clear from this debate at the very beginning of the emergence of modern materialism that one philosophical motive for locating secondary qualities in consciousness was to avoid a straightforward metaphysical problem: *ex nihilo nihil fit*.

If I am right about this, then the ontological puzzle is really the driving force behind what Searle calls normal naturalist cases of emergence. The problem is that these cases are not natural any more than the emergence of consciousness and that is why they were located in consciousness. For example, both secondary qualities like redness or warmth and painfulness are dissimilar to the properties that constitute an ideal physics. Jaegwon Kim has argued that in Nagel-type *reductions*, the relevant bridge laws should be taken as biconditionals and not as conditionals, because we need materially equivalent correlations between entities (or terms) in the reduced and base theories in order to assert identities between the entities in question.[41] Moreover, says Kim, the identity of reduced and base entities is preferable to mere correlations because the latter raise potentially embarrassing questions as to why such precise correlations arise in the first place.

Kim's point is not confined to mental and physical correlations. All a naturalist can do with them (if we keep these so-called secondary qualities or other categorially distinct emergent qualities in the external world) is to offer a detailed correlation to describe regular relations between physical structures and emergent entities. No amount of knowledge whatever of subvenient entities would take us one inch toward predicting or picturing why these particular entities regularly emerge in some circumstances and not others. In discussions of emergence over a century ago, it was precisely their unpredictability from knowledge of subvenient entities that was identified as the hallmark of an emergent property.

In more modern terms, it is the inability to either image or understand why warmth emerges regularly here and not somewhere else, or why it emerges at all given our knowledge of molecular agitation. Note carefully that Searle himself seems to accept pictureability as a necessary condition for the acceptance of a claim that one entity emerges from another in the "normal" cases, but pictureability is no more available for heat (warmth) emerging from matter than it is for mental states.[42] Nagel's conceivability test applies here just as it does for mental states.

However, even if I am wrong about this, there is a third response that can be given to Searle. There are two features of mental states that make their emergence disanalogous to the properties of digestion. First, mental states are so unique and different from all other entities in the world that it is far more difficult to see how they could emerge from physical states than it is for the so-called normal cases. Second, mental states are quite natural in a theistic world view and have a higher prior probability given theism over against naturalism even if we agree that, say, the emergence of the properties of digestion are equally natural and probable on both world hypotheses.

In my view, these two features of mental states make them more analogous to value properties than to characteristics of digestion. Mackie argued that the supervenience of moral properties would constitute a refutation of naturalism and evidence for theism: "Moral properties constitute so odd a cluster of properties and relations that they are most unlikely to have arisen in the ordinary course of events without an all-powerful god to create them."[43] Presumably, Mackie's reasons for this claim involve some of the points I have just made above: moral properties have the two features that make them natural for theism but unnatural for naturalism. No matter how far future physics advances our understanding of matter, it will not make the emergence of moral properties the least bit more likely, more pictureable, or more natural.[44] And the same claim could easily be made for mental properties even if features of digestion are granted equally natural for theism and naturalism.

Searle himself admits that of all the entities in the world, mental states are unique and radically different from all the others. And as we saw earlier, Armstrong is willing to accept that more ordinary physical or biological properties could emerge when the nervous system reaches a certain level of complexity. But he could not accept the natural emergence of mental states from matter because mental states are of "a quite different nature" from states accepted by naturalists. The jump from physical states to mental states was too far for Armstrong's naturalism to allow, so he adopted strong physicalism as the only acceptable naturalist solution.

I admit that the problem with my third response to Searle is that it requires one to weigh the difference between acceptable and unacceptable cases of emergence. But to the degree that mental entities are taken as radically unique and very different from all other types of physical or even biological entities, then to that degree the analogy between the emergence of mental states and other cases of emergence is weakened. And to that degree, the emergence of the mental would be radical as Nagel calls it or unnatural as Adams and Swinburne claim.

After all, naturalists have not spent the last fifty years trying to eliminate or reduce solidity or the properties of digestion like they have mental states. This is because the latter are rightly seen as a threat to naturalism even if the former are not. As B. F. Skinner noted just before his death, "Evolutionary theorists have suggested that 'conscious intelligence' is an evolved trait, but they have never shown how a nonphysical variation could arise [in the first place] to be selected by physical contingencies of survival."[45] Indeed. The constraints placed on a naturalist ontology that we discussed in chapters one and two place a severe burden of proof on adding emergent mental properties to that ontology, a burden that Searle has singularly failed to meet.

4 Timothy O'Connor and emergent necessitation

The vast majority of friends and foes of agent causal versions of libertarian freedom agree that it is either inconsistent or not plausibly harmonized with a naturalistic view of the world, including a physicalist depiction of particulars taken to populate the naturalist ontology. Thus, naturalist John Bishop claims that

> the idea of a responsible agent, with the "originative" ability to initiate events in the natural world, does not sit easily with the idea of [an agent as] a natural organism. ... Our scientific understanding of human behavior seems to be in tension with a presupposition of the ethical stance we adopt toward it.[1]

Elsewhere Bishop explains that

> the problem of natural agency is an ontological problem – a problem about whether the existence of actions can be admitted within a natural scientific ontology. ... [A]gent causal-relations do not belong to the ontology of the natural perspective. Naturalism does not essentially employ the concept of a causal relation whose first member is in the category of person or agent (or even, for that matter, in the broader category of continuant or "substance"). All natural causal relations have first members in the category of event or state of affairs.[2]

Moreover, as Robert Kane acknowledges, most people think that agent causation either entails or is best explained by some form of substance dualism:

> Perhaps the most popular traditional libertarian strategy for dealing with free will is to assume some sort of dualism between mind and body, as Descartes did. Many ordinary persons, as well as philosophers, believe the only way to make sense of undetermined free actions is to assume some kind of intervention of mental phenomena ... in the physical order.[3]

In his excellent and penetrating development of an agent causal account of freedom, *Persons & Causes*, Timothy O'Connor acknowledges that this is the case: A great many contemporary philosophers will dismiss [an agent causal account of freedom] as pointless since it blatantly contradicts "the scientific facts."[4] However, O'Connor is actually puzzled by the majority view on this issue, and claims that a robust version of agent causation, including his own, may be very plausibly harmonized with the emerging naturalist picture of the world, including a physicalist view of the agent. O'Connor's puzzlement is odd in light of the considerations we noted in chapters one and two. In any case, for O'Connor, agent causal power is an emergent property. To support this claim, O'Connor defends what I shall call the Harmony Thesis: the emergence of agent causal power may be plausibly located within a widely accepted naturalist ontology, including a physicalist depiction of the agent.

I do not believe that O'Connor has adequately substantiated this claim. In order to explain my reservations, I shall describe features of O'Connor's model relevant to our inquiry and offer three lines of criticism of his position. First, I will expose problems in O'Connor's description of the agent. Second, I will show why a certain model of causation is crucial for O'Connor's project and argue that, given this model, he has provided insufficient reasons for thinking that consciousness in general, and active power in particular, are emergent properties. Third, I will try to show that certain epistemic features that characterize O'Connor's own case for agent causation, if applied consistently, provide adequate grounds for rejecting the Harmony Thesis. Besides problems intrinsic to O'Connor's view, in light of considerations of chapter one and two there is a substantial burden of proof—made precise in those chapters and shown to be far from arbitrary—that he must meet to be successful. I believe it will become obvious that he fails to meet this burden.

I should say at the outset that O'Connor himself is no naturalist. He is a Christian theist and appears to embrace property dualism. Nevertheless, he is concerned to show that agent causation, including active power, may be plausibly located in a widely accepted naturalist ontology, and it this claim that I wish to clarify and dispute.

The logical and epistemic status of O'Connor's thesis

Before we examine the specifics of O'Connor's position, it is helpful to raise issues about the logical and epistemic status of his view. Clearly, O'Connor wants to say that in some sense agent causation, at least some version relevantly similar to his own (hereafter, AGC), is consonant with "the emerging scientific picture of the world", i.e. a widely accepted version of contemporary scientific naturalism, including a physicalist depiction of the agent (hereafter, N). However, the precise nature of "consonant" is not clear.

The harmony thesis and strict logical consistency

In some places, O'Connor's view seems to amount to thesis L:

(L): AGC and N are strictly logically consistent.

L is a strictly logical, conceptual thesis to the effect that there is no logical contradiction in embracing both AGC and N, that is, no proposition that is part of AGC contradicts a proposition that is part of certain aspects of N to be stated shortly. Thus, O'Connor says that it is false to think that

(a) AGC is not *consistent with* N,[5]
(b) AGC *may be realized* by human beings as depicted by N,[6]
(c) AGC is not disallowed by N,[7]
(d) N does not *entail the falsity of* AGC,[8]
(e) embracing naturalism does not *require us to accept things that render AGC impossible,*[9]
(f) an essential component of N—the Causal Unity of Nature Thesis—does not *require* the acceptance of another purported component of N—the Constitution Thesis—that
(g) would render AGC *straightforwardly impossible,*[10] given
(h) N, there is nothing *inconsistent with* the emergence of AGC, and that
(i) the *appearance of incompatibility* between AGC and naturalism is mistaken.[11]

Thesis L is a natural way to interpret these assertions. If L is O'Connor's thesis, then it is a minimalist one indeed, and a critic would shoulder a substantial burden of proof, one that I am not prepared to carry. A critic would have to show that there is a logical contradiction in the two sets of propositions, and that is a difficult task. However, construed as a conceptual thesis, O'Connor's thesis is not very interesting and little of substance would follow from granting his claims.[12] From the fact that "Water is not H_20" is strictly logically possible, it follows neither that water is not H_20 nor that being H_20 is not essential to being water. Similarly, given L, it does not follow that AGC (or active power) is or could be an emergent property exemplified by a physical agent or in some other way adequately harmonized with the ontology of N.

The harmony thesis as hypothesis

In any case, I do not believe that O'Connor is advancing a conceptual thesis about AGC and N, though as far as I can tell, he is not explicit about the matter. However, O'Connor *is* explicit about the status of his view of AGC itself. O'Connor is quite clear that he is uninterested merely in providing a conceptual analysis of our pre-philosophical intuitions about human agency. Instead, he wants to provide an account of human agency as it really is.[13] I assume he intends the same thing regarding the harmony between AGC and N. Thus, his Harmony Thesis is straightforwardly ontological and amounts to the claim that there is no adequate reason to deny that AGC (or, at least the properties central to its elucidation) could emerge in a universe with an ontology accurately captured by N. Moreover, it is most plausible to believe that, given the right physical conditions, active power must emerge in a world accurately described by N.

If this is correct, then there are important implications about the epistemic status of his view and the epistemic requirements of a critique. To see this, consider the claim that water is *de re* necessarily such that it is H_20. In assessing the truth of this claim, a proponent does not need to *prove* there is no possible world that has water but no H_20. Nor does a proponent succeed by showing that the proposition "water is H_20" is strictly logically consistent. An antagonist does not need to show that this proposition is strictly logically impossible or that N requires us to deny that water is essentially H_20. No, debates about the essence of water will be settled because of what we may simply call an inference to the best explanation, and this is so irrespective of the *de re* modal status of the topic in question. Empirical hypotheses and philosophical arguments (e.g. for or against essentialism) will be evaluated and the most plausible position adopted.

Some assertions by O'Connor seem to show that he understands and accepts this depiction of the epistemic status of his Harmony Thesis. Regarding AGC, he says that it is not *likely* that empirical work will undermine it.[14] Regarding the Harmony Thesis, he talks about *the hypothesis of emergence*.[15] While some think that the belief in emergent properties is *much less problematic than it once was*, it still has not been *empirically established* that there are no emergent properties with their own causal powers[16] or that the emergence of consciousness—a crucial fact for the emergence of AGC—is a *good bet*.[17]

Again, according to O'Connor, though it may be difficult to do so, AGC may be reconciled with the Causal Unity of Nature Thesis, but not with the Constitution Thesis:[18]

> The Causal Unity of Nature Thesis: Macro-level phenomena arise through entirely natural microphysical causal processes and the existence of macro-level phenomena continues to depend causally on microphysical processes.
>
> The Constitution Thesis: All macro-level phenomena are constituted by micro-level phenomena.

As we saw in chapter one, most naturalists rightly accept both theses, so they eschew AGC.[19] O'Connor advocates the incorporation of the Causal Unity of Nature Thesis into N, but not the Constitution Thesis. O'Connor seems to think that the burden of proof lies with those who believe that acceptance of the former requires acceptance of the latter. According to O'Connor,[20] those who accept Causal Unity may employ two strategies to show that acceptance of it requires acceptance of the Constitution Thesis: (i) show that the Constitution Thesis follows from the Causal Unity of Nature Thesis. (ii) show that the Constitution Thesis has been empirically established. For present purposes, I focus only on the second option. While it seems unduly stringent to claim, as O'Connor does, that justification of the Constitution Thesis requires that it be empirically *established*, the important thing to note is O'Connor's willingness to let empirical factors play a key role in settling the issue about the ontological status of emergent properties.[21]

Given that O'Connor's Harmony Thesis is an ontological claim with the epistemic status of an hypothesis to be settled by weighing whether N or an alternative model (e.g. substance dualism) is more plausible, I will try to show that AGC, as O'Connor understands it, is not more plausibly integrated with N than with an alternative to N such as substance dualism.[22]

I admit that the notions "best explanation" or "most plausible" are vague and easily twisted in one's own favor. Unfortunately, that is often the way it is when it comes to weighing competing hypotheses. However, there may be a more precise way to characterize the epistemic nature of the following discussion. I believe that in arguing for his view of AGC, O'Connor makes certain claims about the epistemic requirements of his task. I hope to clarify these requirements and apply them to the debate about the Harmony Thesis. Unless there are good reasons to think that the epistemic requirements are different in the two cases—and I know of no such reasons—my approach has two virtues: (1) It takes epistemic requirements that O'Connor himself employs and applies them to his own position. (2) It should facilitate future dialogue by clarifying the nature of the debate beyond that of merely seeking the "best" explanation or "most plausible view" of the agent.

Agent causation (AGC) and the emerging naturalist picture of the world (N)

In order to assess the Harmony Thesis, it is important to get clear on the central features of O'Connor's understanding of AGC and N that are relevant to our present concerns.

Agent causation

Regarding AGC, O'Connor claims that the core of every free act is an ontologically irreducible causal relation between a person and some appropriate internal event that triggers latter elements of the action. O'Connor holds to a realist view of causation according to which the essence of causality is causal production or the bringing about of an effect.

Active power constitutes a special type of causal event that is intrinsically active, that cannot be caused, even by the agent, and that is intrinsically a case of the agent directly causing/controlling his behavior, or at least, the action trigger. Agent causes bring about immediately executive states of intention to act in various ways.[23]

What kind of agent is required for this account of AGC? O'Connor admits that such an agent must have "rather special properties in her constitution."[24] To elaborate, entities that exhibit event causation are such that the capacity to generate a particular effect is exercised as a matter of course: given the right circumstances, the cluster of properties that ground the capacity directly gives rise to the effect. By contrast, having the properties that subserve an agent-causal capacity does not produce the effect; rather, it enables the agent to do so.[25] Such an agent is a "not wholly moved mover,"[26] and an enduring continuant, but not a different kind of substance radically diverse from physical substances.[27] Personal agents are biological entities with irreducible emergent properties, where properties are construed as universals that have essentially their dispositional tendencies.[28] Sometimes O'Connor uses substance talk to describe the agent.[29] However, at other times he describes the agent as a "complex system regulated by dynamic processes"[30] with a structured capacity, structured by tendency-conferring states of having reasons to act in specific ways.[31]

In various places, O'Connor describes the emergent properties essential to AGC. He agrees with Thomas Reid's claim that only entities with more basic attributes can have free will, viz., volition, understanding, practical judgment and the power to believe the act is within one's power.[32] Thus, to be an agent cause the agent must possess conscious awareness.[33] An agent must be able to represent to himself possible courses of action and have belief/desire sets relevant to each.[34] Moreover, given that intentions are both action triggers and internal to the agent, an agent must be able to cause directly an event internal to the agent.[35] In accounting for the role of reasons in AGC, O'Connor claims that an agent directly causes an-action-triggering-intention, the content of which is that an action of a specific sort be performed for certain reasons the agent had at the time. Thus, an agent must have the potentiality to have events intrinsic to his being that exemplify a twofold internal relation of direct reference and of similar content.[36]

Consider an agent coming to have an-action-triggering-intention-to-so-act-here-and-now-to-satisfy-reason R that initiates the relevant ongoing non-basic action the agent carries out to completion. The twofold internal relation exemplified by this intention is that the intention directly refers to the very act of which it is the action trigger and "of similar content." This last locution is a bit unclear to me, but most likely, it means that the complex intention essentially refers to its own propositional content, including the reason for which the action was done, and that concurrent with the ongoing non-basic action, there is the continuation of a similar propositional content (allowing for slight variation over time of that content).

Four relevant aspects of naturalism

So much for O'Connor's account of AGC. What about his view of N? There are four aspects of N relevant to our discussion. First, O'Connor accepts a fairly standard account of reality known as the mereological hierarchy (cf. chapter one). On his view, physics is the basic level of reality and, in the category of individual, all wholes above the fundamental level are systems constituted by parts at lower levels. On this view, the world is fundamentally event causal in nature.[37] I take this to mean two things: (1) All strictly physical entities, most importantly, those at the fundamental level, exhibit event causality. (2) All macro-wholes with or without emergent properties exhibit event causality except for libertarian agents. O'Connor's view of the hierarchy is fairly standard, but it does have an aspect that would be considered controversial among those who accept N, namely, O'Connor rejects the causal closure of the physical.[38]

Second, all particulars are physical objects. More specifically, when discussing N, O'Connor calls the agent "a macrophysical object or system,"[39] and a physical substance.[40] According to O'Connor, N requires substance monism.[41]

Third, O'Connor believes that, in addition to structural properties, there are genuinely emergent properties.[42] For O'Connor, an emergent property has three important traits:

(1) It is a simple, intrinsically characterizeable, new kind of property qualitatively different from and not composed of the parts, properties, relations, and events at the subvenient level;
(2) It is a property which has its own ontologically basic type of causal influence; and
(3) It is a property which is necessitated by and causally grounded in its base.[43]

Trait (3) requires further elaboration. According to O'Connor, the causal powers of properties are essential aspects of those properties and, thus, belong to properties with an absolute, metaphysical necessity. The causal potentialities of a property are part of what constitutes the property's identity.[44] It is in this sense, that in the right circumstances, a subvenient property necessitates an emergent property. By way of application, properties constitutive of consciousness, including the property of active power, are emergent.[45]

Finally, O'Connor embraces the Causal Unity of Nature Thesis but rejects the Constitution Thesis.[46] He recognizes that most naturalists believe that N requires both theses, but he demurs, claiming that N only requires the former. The most plausible way to understand the Constitution Thesis is to take it to allow only for structural macro-properties. In rejecting it, O'Connor wants to allow for emergent properties, as he understands them. According to the typology of chapter one, O'Connor accepts emergence$_{2C}$. And by accepting the Causal Unity Thesis, he believes that he can plausibly harmonize AGC with N.

Problems with O'Connor's description of the agent

There are two serious difficulties with O'Connor's description of the agent: it is hard to see how it is a mere physical particular, and it is hard to see how O'Connor can justify naturalism as opposed to panpsychism as the appropriate ontological framework for locating the agent. Let us consider these in order.

O'Connor's agent is not a purely physical particular

When he speaks of the self qua agent, O'Connor employs what he takes to be justified beliefs about the agent himself, and not merely essential constituents of our common sense concept of the agent, and his view of the agent seems to be dualist in nature. When O'Connor describes the self from the perspective of N, he talks as though it were a physical object.[47] But when he describes the self as an agent cause, it seems that it is essentially mental in nature. Galen Strawson has argued that a necessary condition for free agency is that one have a concept of oneself as single just qua mental, quite independently of whether one also has a concept of oneself as an indissolubly psychophysical thing:

> In some very strong and straightforward sense, we intuitively require that there be a *mental subject* in the case of any free agent, a mental subject that is in some way or other properly distinguishable from all its particular thoughts . . .; a mental subject that is moreover present to itself as such in some way. Whether or not there can correctly be said to *be* such a thing, we require at the very least that any free agent's thought or experience be such that it is overwhelmingly natural for us (and for it) to talk in terms of such a subject.[48]

All that follows from this, says Strawson, is that the concept of the self as a mental particular is a necessary condition for taking the self to be a free agent, not that there actually are mental substances. O'Connor's description of the agent seems to present it as a subject essentially characterized by a range of mental properties necessary for agency. Since O'Connor takes himself to be offering a characterization of agents themselves, and not simply providing an analysis of our common sense concept of agents, O'Connor's agent cause appears to be a mental particular, an essentially mental particular qua agent cause.

It is not clear how he can hold that the agent self is a physical substance necessarily characterized by emergent mental properties. If the agent self is essentially mental, and if we recognize that a particular's actual and potential properties are both relevant for characterizing the kind of entity the particular is, then the agent self would seem to be essentially a mental/physical particular, and not simply a physical particular with emergent mental properties attached to it. When John Locke argued that thinking matter was possible, some of his critics (Edward Stillingfleet, S. G. Gerdil, and Malcolm Flemyng) responded by pointing out that a "material" substance whose essence was constituted in part by mental potentialities was no longer simply a "material" substance.[49] I believe O'Connor's agent is subject to the same criticism.[50]

Perhaps in response to arguments such as these, O'Connor has developed his view of the agent beyond what appeared in *Persons & Causes* and now advances the idea that persons are material substances in a qualified sense.[51] Working within a framework of immanent universals, O'Connor uses these descriptors for the person-as-agent:[52] a biological organism with emergent properties (in his three senses, including top/down active power) that are as basic as the negative charge of an electron; a 3D continuant with a mental life grounded in its physical nature; a cluster of immanent universals with its own unique particularity not reducible to that of the mereological aggregate from which it arises; an emergent biological organism with a new thisness; a new composite that exhibits an objective substantial unity. These descriptors express O'Connor's desire to steer a via media between a mere ordered mereological aggregate on the one hand and a view such as William Hasker's according to which a brand new emergent mental whole exists and is in no way composed of subvenient entities.[53]

To elaborate, O'Connor claims that a standard mereological aggregate is inadequate to ground a genuine enduring continuant, a continuant that is needed to satisfy the requirements for a responsible libertarian causal agent. He also rejects a Haskerian view because only a theistic solution along the lines of AC could account for how a complex physical system could give rise all in one go to a brand new emergent mental entity.[54] O'Connor wants to avoid universalism regarding composite objects, so he attempts to specify conditions under which a new emergent individual arises and he tries to give an ontological account of how such an individual could arise in the first place. Regarding the former, emergent properties are the best candidates for emergent individuals (and the only clear evidence we have for such properties is consciousness). All other macro wholes are merely mereological aggregates. So in the category of individual, O'Connor's ontology includes atomic simples, mereological aggregates, and emergent biological organisms (and as a Christian theist, at least one purely spiritual substance—God).

When it comes to offering an account of all this, O'Connor is not clear about his task, and it is sometimes hard to tell which of these two questions he is answering: (1) How are we to explain ontologically how emergent individuals could come about? (2) When should we judge that an emergent individual has come about? (1) and (2) are ontological and epistemological, respectively, and I shall take (1) to be O'Connor's focus. So understood, he claims that subvenient entities are always trying to bring about the emergent individual, but it is only when an appropriate threshold level of complexity is reached that conditions are right for that base to cause the emergent individual to come into being. When emergent mental properties appear, they constitute holistic mental states—perhaps enduring baseline mental states—and these, in turn, confer on persons their substantial unity as thinking biological substances, presumably by bringing about through top/down causation a new particularity over and above that of the series of subvenient mereological aggregates that are in a constant state of flux. This "composition-conferred-by-holism" view produces an emergent individual that is somehow composed by its composite parts yet has a new thisness all its own.

Why should we believe any of this? There seem to be two reasons. First, according to O'Connor, first-person direct awareness justifies the view that consciousness is emergent in his three senses and this justification overrides any *a posteriori* ascriptions of micro-structure to conscious states. All empirical knowledge, he tells us, presupposes this knowledge. Second, we should limit our account to the constraints provided by the naturalist mereological hierarchy and the grounds we have for accepting it. We should avoid a theistic explanation of emergent individuals, and on the basis of theoretical simplicity, we should adopt a view of the emergent individual that does two things: grounds endurance and agency beyond the flux of change in a mere ordered aggregate and is as close to the mereological aggregate as possible in order to fit the naturalist viewpoint.

What should we make of O'Connor's modified view? I believe the objections raised against his earlier position apply with equal or greater force to the modified view. For example, it is still not clear how a particular with basic mental potentialities is a physical object. To his credit, O'Connor seems to recognize this and, thus, he calls persons material substances "in a qualified form." Moreover, O'Connor's new view is more clearly a version of panpsychism, and in the next chapter, we will see that this is not a legitimate specification of positive naturalism. For example, when he claims that consciousness is just as basic as negative charge, this claim is closer to theism than to naturalism and it will be a hard pill for (positive) naturalists to swallow. This view also renders impossible a strict naturalist explanation of emergence as, for example, in the Causal Unity thesis. Instead, mental potentialities and their causal interaction with physical conditions are required, and this is a long way from (positive) naturalism.

Besides retaining difficulties from the earlier position, the modified view suffers from some new problems not present in the older version. I mention two. First, there are deep metaphysical problems with O'Connor's emergent individuals. For one thing, the framework of immanent universals renders unintelligible the claim that the emergent individual has its own thisness while at the same time being constituted by the relevant mereological complex. The framework of immanent universals depicts property-instances as states of affairs (the so-called thick particular)—in the case of O'Connor's persons, states of affairs that are substantial continuants—with three constituents: the universal, the nexus of exemplification, and an individuator (the thin particular, in my view, a bare particular). Whatever conditions ground the exemplification of the universal are external to (not constituents of) the instance itself. In addition, since the person can endure even though the mereological aggregate is in constant flux, it would seem that the aggregate is accidental to the continuant. To the degree that his emergent individuals provide what is needed (e.g. being enduring continuants), they look strangely like Hasker's emergent mental ego rather than some via media.

Moreover, there is no baseline conscious state constant throughout a person's life and apt for grounding endurance. The property of being conscious cannot provide such a baseline because it is a second order property of mental properties (being a sensation, a thought) that comes-to-be and ceases-to-be exemplified when first order states come and go. *Qua* second order universal, consciousness is not a sufficient ground for endurance. What O'Connor needs is a continuing property-instance of consciousness that remains identical throughout the flux of mental life. But there is no such property-instance. Our mental lives teem with flux just as does the "underlying" aggregate. There seems to be no metaphysical account of the individual that grounds its endurance unless, of course, we treat the individual as a state of affairs constituted by a mental essence, exemplification, and particularity with the aggregate its cause but outside the being of its effect. But, again, this is Hasker's view not O'Connor's. Finally, in criticizing Hasker's view, he claims that unless one appeals to a theistic explanation, one cannot explain how a complex physical system could give rise, all in one go, to a brand new emergent whole. As an advocate of AC, I am cheered by this admission. Unfortunately, this very same argument has been repeatedly raised against emergent properties themselves.

Second, I find O'Connor's composition-conferred-by-holism to be deeply troubling. He apparently accepts the dictum that "thought implies a thinker," or more generally, that consciousness requires a particular to possess it. So far so good. However, it seems to me that this is so because the bearer of consciousness is more basic ontologically that the mental properties it exemplifies or the mental states that obtain within it. But O'Connor's view has this backward. If I understand him correctly, when the mereological aggregate reaches the proper threshold, emergent consciousness arises and this, in turn, causes the conscious individual to come into existence via top/down conferral (by generating a new thisness). Thus, thinkings cause thinkers, but it seems to me that something like the converse is true—the dependence goes the other way.

Additionally, O'Connor claims that emergence is dynamic and causal, not static and formal, that emergent states are caused by temporally prior subvenient states, and, thus, emergence is diachronic and not synchronic.[55] Thus, the following scenario seems to arise: at t_1 subvenient conditions cause emergent conscious state C_1 to obtain at t_2 which, in turn brings about emergent individual I_1 at t_3. Two things seem to follow. First, the very first mental state in one's life (C_1) seems clearly ownerless since at t_2 there is no individual to possess it.

Second, beyond the very first conscious state, the following would seem to hold: for all C_{N+1} (for N greater than zero) at t_{N+2}, the individual I_{N+1} conferred by and, thus, ontologically tied to C_{N+1} exists at t_{N+2}. I see no further relevant ontological relationship between a conscious state and an emergent individual other than the conferral relation. If this is correct, then it is hard to see how a continuing "self" can exist since there just is no single, ongoing "baseline mental state" throughout one's life (e.g. in sleep or surgery). Since conscious states are in flux, so are the instantaneous individuals upon whom they confer existence. In this case, for any time t greater than one, there may be an emergent individual that exists while a particular conscious state obtains, but it is the wrong one. In general, each emergent individual at a time is ontologically associated with a mental state that obtained instantaneously earlier and, thus, is ownerless.

I may have misunderstood O'Connor and he may have already presented materials for an adequate reply to my objections. Fortunately, for my purposes, it is not merely the implausibility of his view of the agent that is my main concern. Rather, it is also that his modified view is even less compatible with naturalism than his earlier view. In light of the ontology-constraining factors that surfaced in chapter one, there is a burden of proof on any ontology that goes beyond these factors. O'Connor has clearly done so (e.g. the mental is as basic as negative charge, the emergence of both active power (emergence_{2c}) and a new individual (emergence_3), the fact that neither emergent entity seems to satisfy the "entry by entailment" condition, top/down causation, epistemic authority given to first-person introspection that trumps *a posteriori* considerations). He also has failed to meet the burden of proof required to claim that his position is a plausible version of naturalism. Moreover, given the presence of AC which O'Connor himself acknowledges, his dismissive attitude towards theistic explanation begs the question at several points and fails to take into account adequately the epistemic impact of AC for his project.

O'Connor and panpsychism

So much for O'Connor's depiction of the agent. Here is the second difficulty with his account: As Colin McGinn points out, in the contemporary setting, a "material" substance such as O'Connor's would properly be characterized according to weak panpsychism.[56] The vast majority of naturalists take panpsychism to be a rival to a naturalist understanding of matter and not a permissible version of N. We will examine this issue in more detail in the next chapter. For present purposes, recall that according to N, the fundamental level of reality is strictly physical and emergent entities "up" the hierarchy depend for their existence, or at least instantiation, on strictly micro-physical entities. However, according to panpsychism, mental properties (either potential or actual properties) are fundamental and *sui generis*, and this conflicts with the naturalist hierarchy according to which the fundamental level is strictly physical.

Of course, O'Connor can simply disagree here that panpsychism is a rival to naturalism. In one place he acknowledges that on his picture it is true that "the presence of agent-causal capacities in select complex entities has always been among the potentialities of the world's primordial building blocks."[57] Elsewhere, he argues that

> [t]he basic properties and relations of our world will be those properties whose instantiation does not even partly consist in the instantiation of distinct properties by the entity *or* its parts. *It is the thesis of emergentism that some basic properties are had by composite individuals.*[58]

Again, "[e]mergent features are as basic as electric charge now appears to be, just more restricted in the circumstances of their manifestation."[59] I suspect that these are hard sayings for most naturalists. In order for O'Connor to justify the claim that this assertion is a permissible version of N, two things seem to be required.

First, he must show that the relevant physical subvenient base causally necessitates the emergence of active power. This would be a necessary condition for him to show that the actual emergence of active power is consistent with the Causal Unity thesis. In the next section, I will argue that O'Connor fails in this regard. If he succeeds in showing that strictly natural microphysical entities are necessary causal conditions for the emergence of active power, this would not be sufficient to justify the claim that his view is an appropriate revision of N and not an abandonment of N in favor of panpsychism as a rival framework. It is not sufficient because O'Connor's view amounts to an abandonment of the Causal Unity thesis. Recall that this thesis states that macro-level phenomena arise through and continue to depend on *entirely* natural microphysical causal processes. On O'Connor's treatment of emergent active power (and consciousness in general), emergence depends on the actualization of non-physical mental potentialities which are not themselves "natural micro*physical* properties," even if strictly natural microphysical entities are necessary causal conditions for such emergence.[60]

Second, he could argue that we have pre-philosophical intuitions, perhaps justified by first-person introspection, for taking mental properties in general, and active power in particular, to be emergent properties in his specific sense of emergence. I shall consider these moves in the following sections.

The harmony thesis, mental properties and the causal grounding condition

Emergent necessitation and contingency

For two reasons, to justify the Harmony Thesis O'Connor needs the "necessitation" of emergent active power by the subvenient base. The best way to clarify "necessitation" is to characterize it in the context of presenting the first reason. To get at that reason, it will be useful to begin by reviewing insights from Frank Jackson that were presented in chapter one.[61]

Jackson contrasts serious metaphysics with a shopping list approach to ontology. According to the latter, metaphysicians adopt a pluralist approach to ontology and seek to provide big descriptive lists of the various kinds of things there are, resting content to add *sui generis* entity to *sui generis* entity. What is missing in such an approach is any attempt to provide a comprehensive, discriminatory account of what is real and how things came to be. According to Jackson, advocates of N should take naturalism to be a piece of serious metaphysics because in so doing, they pattern the epistemic justification of N on that of good scientific theories, and they provide grounds for preferring N to its rivals on the basis of N's superior explanatory power.

Jackson correctly observes that if one takes N to be an expression of serious metaphysics, then one must face the location problem. According to Jackson, given that naturalists are committed to a fairly widely-accepted physical story about how things came-to-be and what they are, the location problem is the task of locating or finding a place for some entity (for example, semantic contents, mind, agency) in that story. The mereological hierarchy is the ontology that results from serious metaphysics and, among other things, it requires one to locate emergent entities up the hierarchy in terms of the basic, subvenient entities at the level of physics.

For Jackson, location amounts to entry by entailment: some entity is located and, therefore, has a place in one's ontology if it is entailed by the basic account. Applied to mental and physical entities, any world that is a minimal physical duplicate of our world is a psychological duplicate of our world.

Because he is concerned to locate certain supervenient structural properties (e.g. broad mental contents), Jackson opts for global supervenience as a way of clarifying his view further: A world which is a minimal physical duplicate of our world is a world that (a) is exactly like our world in every physical respect and (b) contains nothing else (e.g. Cartesian souls) in the sense of nothing more by way of kinds or particulars than it must to satisfy (a).

In the context of O'Connor's thought, since the concern is to locate emergent and not structural properties, a certain version of strong supervenience would be widely accepted by naturalists as adequate for the task. Expressed in terms of physical and psychological properties, N seems to require that in no possible world with the same physical properties and laws as the actual world is there a particular that shares its physical properties with a particular in our world but fails to share its psychological properties. In this way, the physical may be said to "necessitate" the psychological. It is important to keep this framework in mind for what follows.

Though he does not mention it explicitly, O'Connor seems concerned to take N as an expression of serious metaphysics, and he understands this to require the location of emergent properties, including mental properties such as active power, in terms of the understanding of "necessitation" just mentioned. Since he is concerned to show that those who accept N are not thereby given adequate grounds for rejecting AGC, O'Connor must be assuming that AGC may be adequately located in N and, moreover, that AGC does not provide evidence for a rival to N, say theism, along with substance dualism as a component of theism. As O'Connor admits, many—perhaps most—have seen AGC as evidence against N and reject the Harmony Thesis. Thus, O'Connor argues that if one is going to have a scientific understanding of an emergent property, one cannot merely accept a property as emergent without explaining its existence. Rather, one must require that an emergent property be causally grounded in its base properties if it is to be naturalistically explicable.[62]

Elsewhere, O'Connor claims that if an emergent property is depicted in such a way as to be contingently linked to the base properties causing it to emerge, then apart from an appeal to God's contingent choice that things be so, and to God's stable intention that they continue to be so, there will be no explanation for the link itself or its constancy.[63] In short, if the link is contingent, the Harmony Thesis is false and AGC provides evidence for theism, and given theism, there is less need to preserve physicalism in the category of individual.

There is a second reason why O'Connor needs the "necessitation" of emergent active power by the subvenient base: the view of causation that forms the core of O'Connor's depiction of both N and AGC. Recall that for O'Connor, the causal powers of properties are essential aspects of those properties and, thus, belong to properties with an absolute, metaphysical necessity. The causal potentialities of a property are part of what constitutes the property's identity.[64] O'Connor's realist view of causation—event and agent—entails that a cause produces or brings about its effect in virtue of the properties of the cause, and properties are universals that have essentially their causal powers.[65] Since most philosophers identify the supervenience relation with the causal relation in the case of emergent properties, it is in this causal sense that in the right circumstances, the instantiation of a subvenient property necessitates the instantiation of its associated emergent property.

Given this view of causal potentialities, a certain result seems to follow regarding emergent properties. Since an emergent property is simply the actualization of causal potentialities in the right circumstances, the emergent property would seem to be a part of its causal property's identity as well. In this sense, an emergent property would seem to require its base property(s) to exist. Interestingly, in an earlier account of emergence, O'Connor accepted this robust claim about emergent properties.[66] He held this precisely because he took an emergent property to be an expression of the very nature of the subvenient base causing it.

However, in *Persons and Causes* he says that the notion that an emergent property could not exist without its subvenient base is "possibly gratuitous."[67] His concession seems to result from his desire to offer as minimalist an account of emergence as possible to increase its chances of being accepted by critics and, thus, he leaves open the sort of modality (metaphysical, nomological) required for a minimalist account of emergence. But O'Connor himself continues to accept the more robust account of causality, and this would seem to require that he also continue to accept the stronger notion of emergence.[68]

Unfortunately, while the Harmony Thesis requires the relevant physical circumstances to necessitate emergent mental properties, including active power, the link between mental properties and the relevant physical circumstances seems to be utterly contingent. Grounded in strong conceivability, thought experiments proliferate throughout the literature in philosophy of mind, which provide strong justification for this claim. For example, inverted qualia and Chinese Room scenarios seem to be coherent and entirely possible. No strictly physical proposition of N employing solely physical terms for particulars, properties, relations or laws renders these thought experiments broadly logically impossible, even in worlds that resemble ours in every physical respect.

Again, different forms of the well-known Knowledge Argument seem to be quite plausible. Since O'Connor himself accepts a property dualist interpretation of the argument, given this interpretation, no knowledge whatever of merely physical facts gives one any information at all about the presence, absence or nature of mental facts. If this is so, it is difficult to see how one could justify the claim that, say, φ entails Ψ. No amount of information about the former entails anything at all about the latter. φ is consistent with our world and with inverted qualia and zombie worlds that are minimal physical duplicates of our world. If this is so, then the physical/mental link seems contingent indeed.

Further, the modal argument for substance dualism seems to be quite plausible. If so, then at least certain versions of the argument imply that physical entities are not necessary for the instantiation of mental properties. Indeed, theism itself presents (at least) one case in which active power is not dependent upon a physical base. Surely, the existence of God (and of angels) with libertarian power is metaphysically possible, and if so, it is just not clear why the property of active power is causally tied to a physical base.

These various thought experiments have been around a long time and there is no sign that they are going away. They provide evidence against the necessitation claim that is central to the Harmony Thesis. So far as I know, O'Connor does not consider the force of the modal argument. I would be especially interested to see how he would handle cases in which the agent cause is a pure spirit (God and angels, disembodied souls?). If he says that the presence of the relevant physical base necessitates the emergence of active power, but that the latter could obtain without the former, then this would seem to amount to a denial that an emergent property is an essential aspect of the subvenient property whose potentialities actualize it. At the very least, it would imply that the presence of active power is underdetermined by emergence and substance dualism such that there would be no adequate grounds for preferring the former.

Given a functionalist analysis of mental kinds, it may be that a type of mental state could be "realized" in spirits and brains and this fact is consistent with particular brain states in certain circumstances necessitating the realization of a mental state by being sufficient for such a realization. But for two reasons this admission would not provide O'Connor with a rejoinder to my argument from the instantiation of active power in spirits. Given that active power is a simple, intrinsically characterized property that is instantiated, and not a structural property that is realized, O'Connor depicts active power as a disposition of its metaphysical base as a matter of metaphysical necessity, and it is hard to see how this disposition could be actualized without its categorical base.

Further, most naturalists do not cash out emergent supervenience merely as the logical sufficiency of the subvenient base. Rather, they spell out emergence in terms of two other principles that, together with logical sufficiency, constitute minimal physicalism:

(1) The anti-Cartesian principle: There can be no purely mental beings (e. g. substantial souls) because nothing can have a mental property without having a physical property as well.
(2) Mind-body dependence: What mental properties an entity has depend on and are determined by its physical properties.[69]

Naturalists employ (1) and (2) in their analysis of emergence precisely because they want to ensure that emergent properties are located in the naturalist ontology by guaranteeing that such properties require, depend on and are causally determined by their entirely physical subvenient bases. If most naturalists are correct about this requirement for locating an emergent property in the ontology of N, then the actuality or even the metaphysical possibility of the instantiation of active power in a pure spirit is a problem for the Harmony Thesis. It is one thing to reject the existence of God and angels. It is another thing altogether to claim that God or angels are metaphysical impossibilities, even if the modal status of such a claim is limited to possible worlds with the same physical particulars, properties, relations and laws as the actual world.

O'Connor does address the Knowledge Argument and inverted qualia thought experiments. Regarding the former, he opts for a dualist interpretation of the argument and claims that at least two features of many mental phenomena are emergent properties causally necessitated by the appropriate physical bases: the phenomenal feature and subjectivity, which he interprets as the fact that one can come into contact with a conscious property only by having it.[70] What about the apparent contingency of the mental/physical causal link? O'Connor simply denies that all causal necessity must be transparent. He says that there is no good reason to think that when we come to have a scientific understanding of some phenomenon, we will just be able to see that a causal effect had to follow from its cause. In the case of conscious properties, though their causal bases necessitate them, we just cannot see the necessity of the causal connection. Regarding inverted qualia, O'Connor adopts the same dismissive strategy, claiming that inverted qualia thought experiments "implausibly drive a wedge between a phenomenal property's qualitative features and its causal role."[71]

In my opinion, O'Connor's rejoinder to these arguments for causal contingency sounds very much like a mere denial that there is a problem. But the intuitions of contingency that lie behind the various dualist arguments in focus are rooted deep within our pre-philosophical intuitions. Surely, then, there is a burden of proof on O'Connor that is not met by his dismissive strategy.[72]

Four arguments against consciousness as emergent

Besides that, there are four considerations whose cumulative effect undercuts O'Connor's claim that conscious properties are emergent. First, O'Connor himself admits that "there are no widely accepted working theories that are committed to the existence of emergent properties,"[73] and "there is a lack of hard evidence in favor of emergence in areas that are well understood."[74] He does not find this particularly troubling. Rather, he believes that our scientific knowledge is so incomplete that the absence of emergent properties is far from empirically established. However, surely the burden of proof lies in the other direction, and given the state of things, the proper conclusion to draw is that, currently, "the hypothesis of emergence" is yet to be justified.

Second, it is false to claim that "there is convincing evidence"[75] that (at least many) mental properties are emergent. For three reasons, it is difficult and may be impossible to justify their emergence empirically: (1) The emergent hypothesis and substance dualism are empirically equivalent models and there is no empirical evidence that can count in favor of one over the other.[76] (2) In the attempt to correlate mental and physical properties as a first step towards justifying the hypothesis of emergence, one of the two correlates is not available for empirical inspection, and this makes straightforward empirical justification of emergence more difficult. (3) It is only in the case of fairly simple mental states, e.g. specific sorts of pains, that we have any hard evidence of specific mental/physical correlations. There is no evidence whatever that complex mental properties, such as the property thinking-about-the-history-of-skepticism, are correlated with specific base physical properties, much less emergent on them. Part of the problem here is the difficulty of providing criteria for individuating complex mental states in an empirically testable way, a problem that O'Connor himself acknowledges.[77] On a fine-grained theory of properties, this may well be an impossible task, and not just a difficult one. This is why many strong physicalists adopt a course-grained view of mental properties as a response to inverted qualia arguments, but this move requires that mental properties be identified with functional roles, and it is not available to O'Connor.

Third, even if we grant that mental properties are, in some sense, emergent, that does not entail that they are emergent in O'Connor's sense. Recall that for O'Connor, emergent properties have these three features: (1) they are simple, intrinsically characterizable, new kinds of properties, (2) they have their own ontologically basic type of causal influence, and (3) they are causally necessitated by their subvenient physical base.

Roughly, the first two features correspond to what John Searle calls emergent$_1$ and emergent$_2$, respectively.[78] Now Searle is typical of those naturalists who accept emergent properties as merely emergent$_1$ and not emergent$_2$. Since we have seen reasons for this in chapter one (e.g. the claim that N requires the causal closure of the physical), I will not rehearse them here. But one point needs to be emphasized. O'Connor claims that mental properties are the best examples of emergent properties, since they exhibit subjectivity and a phenomenal nature, and he claims that we have "direct evidence" of emergence in the case of consciousness.[79]

I agree that we have direct access to and introspective knowledge by acquaintance of our own mental states, but naturalists such as Searle claim that this "direct evidence" merely justifies conscious properties as emergent$_1$ and not emergent$_2$. As I will argue below, the sort of introspective evidence that might be cited to support the claim that some mental properties, especially active power, have their own causal powers also supports substance dualism and, thus, that evidence provides a defeater for the claim that mental properties are emergent. At the very least, this additional introspective evidence goes beyond the sort of direct evidence O'Connor cites to justify consciousness as emergent$_2$. At best, it merely justifies them as emergent$_1$.

However, even if this "direct evidence" justifies taking active power to be emergent in the first two senses, it utterly fails to justify the third sense.

The vast majority of people agree that in introspection they are completely unaware of anything physical. They have no introspective acquaintance with their brain or any other strictly physical object, or with any subvenient physical properties. When philosophers argue that consciousness is a set of emergent properties, one thing seems clear: they do not appeal to first-person introspection to justify the claim. Indeed, no inspection of the brain or any other candidate for the subvenient physical base from a first or third-person perspective provides "direct evidence" for treating any conscious property as emergent in sense three.

This is an important conclusion that O'Connor apparently fails to see. In a publication subsequent to *Persons & Causes*, O'Connor acknowledges that "[t]he emergentist can and should allow that there is an epistemological presumption against emergentist hypotheses for systems of currently-untested complexity levels *absent special reason to suspect that they are different from run of the mill cases*."[80] So far so good. But right after granting this concession, O'Connor attempts to refute a claim by Brian McLaughlin to the effect that, while emergence is a coherent concept, it is enormously implausible that there are any such properties, and least for those with ostensible scientific sobriety.

O'Connor's response consists in two claims: (1) a person's experiences and other conscious mental states are *sui generis* simple emergent properties and (2) claim (1) is defeasibly justified by direct first-person awareness of conscious states with an epistemic strength that precludes the *a posteriori* ascription to them of hidden micro-structure hidden to introspection. But O'Connor is simply mistaken about this. Direct first-person awareness completely fails to provide any justification whatsoever for his third characterization of emergent properties and this is the sense he needs to justify conscious properties as emergent in the sense needed for his Harmony Thesis.

Finally, given O'Connor's admission that "direct evidence" is involved in justifying the claim that conscious properties are emergent ones, the epistemic grounds for this claim derive from first-person introspection and not from empirical research. As we have just seen, O'Connor insists on this. Given that this evidence provides accurate information about the intrinsic nature of mental properties (his sense one of emergence), and given that we have a fairly good idea of the nature of physical properties, most have seen their connection to be contingent, and that is why naturalists have had such a hard time "locating" them in light of the necessitation condition discussed earlier.

The contingency of the link between mental/physical properties stands in stark contrast to naturalist examples of paradigm cases of located macro-properties. For example, Jackson cites macro-solidity, understood as impenetrability, as something easily construed as necessitated by subvenient base traits, cashed out in terms of intermolecular forces, lattice structures, and so on.[81] Jackson also points out that the pre-scientific notion of macro-solidity as being everywhere dense has been rejected by those who accept N. The reason for this rejection is clear. If real, the latter notion of solidity would be a macro-property only contingently connected to its micro-physical base and, thus, it would not be located in N.

I think most naturalistic philosophers would hold that irreducible mental properties are like the pre-scientific notion of solidity. Since they cannot be located, our dualistic pre-scientific conception of them must be revised according to some strong physicalist strategy. If mental properties are new kinds of properties as O'Connor claims, they fail to resemble paradigm cases of located macro-properties (e.g. solidity as impenetrability), and O'Connor has failed to provide an adequate justification for assimilating them to the paradigm cases. Interestingly, he acknowledges that "[r]eductionism nowadays is much disparaged. Yet by our lights, the most plausible variety of physicalism is *reduction*ist, as it does not require one to make dubious moves in the underlying metaphysics of physical properties."[82] I have been at pains to show that it is no accident that strong physicalism is and ought to be the ontology of naturalism precisely because it does not require one to make dubious moves in the underlying of naturalism. For self-reflective naturalists who claim explanatory superiority for their worldview, the Constitution Thesis is an essential component that fits naturalism like a hand in a glove.

AGC, the harmony thesis, and epistemic features of O'Connor's case

In contending for his views, O'Connor makes implicit or explicit reference to particular epistemic features of his case both for AGC and the Harmony Thesis. I shall focus on two of these features and argue that, if applied consistently, they place a burden of proof on O'Connor's defense of the Harmony Thesis—specifically, the harmony of AGC and a physical agent—that he has failed to meet: the role of pre-philosophical intuitions in his case, and his view of the nature of pre-philosophical intuitions about mental properties.

O'Connor and the role of pre-philosophical intuitions

In arguing for AGC, O'Connor commits himself to two important epistemic requirements for his task:

(i) one's view of agency should be guided by and justified in light of pre-philosophical, common sense intuitions which place a burden of proof on any view that requires abandonment of them; and
(ii) these pre-philosophical intuitions are a source of justified beliefs about the nature of human action itself, and not merely about our concept of human action.[83]

O'Connor uses these intuitions to place a burden of proof on compatibilists and on critics of the Harmony Thesis. Thus, his task in both areas of debate is to rebut and not refute his interlocutors.

Applied to agency, O'Connor claims that incompatibilism is *prima facie* justified by these intuitions, they ground a modal style argument for incompatibilism, and compatibilists fail to overturn the argument based on these *prima facie* justified intuitions. Applied to the Harmony Thesis, given N and the pre-philosophical intuitive justification of AGC, O'Connor says that the burden is on those who reject the Harmony Thesis and accept the Constitution Thesis. Since the latter is neither entailed by the Causal Unity Thesis nor empirically established, then we are not required to accept it. Failure to meet this burden, coupled with positive grounds for emergent properties to be described below, means that there is no good reason to reject the Harmony Thesis.

How does one know when one has solid pre-philosophical intuitions with sufficient justification to do the work required of them in O'Connor's case? I suggest there are at least two features of such intuitions. First, such intuitions should be held widely and deeply by normal folk with no ideological axe to grind. Throughout the literature, friends and foes of incompatibilism acknowledge that it enjoys this sort of intuitive support, and O'Connor makes explicit use of this fact in his case.[84] Second, both sides of a dispute employ concepts derived from or based on those intuitions. John Bishop is typical of many compatibilists when he explicitly employs a libertarian concept of agency to develop his own compatibilist model that falls under that concept "closely enough" to be adequate.[85] Bishop allows a libertarian conception of agency to guide the development of his own account, and to be the legitimate source both of counter arguments in the form of thought experiments and of the sense of adequacy for his responses to those counter arguments. Libertarian intuitions seem pervasive in debates about agency.

Now both of these characteristics seem present for intuitions on behalf of substance dualism and against physicalist views of the self. Friends and foes of dualism widely admit that it is the common sense view, and the vast majority of people throughout history have been dualists about the self in one form or another. Jaegwon Kim acknowledges that "We commonly think that we, as persons, have a mental and bodily dimension. . . . Something like this dualism of personhood, I believe, is common lore shared across most cultures and religious traditions."[86] Along similar lines, Frank Jackson says that "our folk conception of personal identity is Cartesian in character."[87]

Pre-philosophical intuitions in support of a substantial, immaterial self are widely and deeply held, and they ground the modal argument for substance dualism.[88] Moreover, these intuitions seem expressed in the concepts and arguments used by dualists and physicalists. The intelligibility of NDE's (Near Death Experiences), arguments from the unity of one's conscious field, thought experiments about personal identity to the effect that the person is merely contingently related to his body or psychological traits, and responses to these thought experiments (e.g. various causal chain analyses of personal identity) seem to employ a substantial, immaterial conception of the self.

O'Connor could respond that in the case of substance dualism, grounds for N justify a rejection of these pre-philosophical intuitions, but in light of his own employment of similar pre-philosophical intuitions for AGC and the Harmony thesis, this response seems arbitrary. After all, most naturalists employ N to justify a rejection of the intuitions in support of AGC, a fact that O'Connor acknowledges. Most naturalists agree that pre-philosophical intuitions are on the side of AGC and substance dualism, but they adopt a consistent attitude—rejection—towards both sets of intuitions. While strictly consistent with the grounds for N, most naturalists believe that AGC and substance dualism are not as plausible as compatibilism (or non causal versions of incompatibilism) and physicalism in light of those grounds.

Moreover, just as the Causal Unity Thesis fails to entail the Constitution Thesis and the latter has not been empirically established, so the empirical grounds for N fail to entail or empirically establish a physical agent. If O'Connor thinks otherwise, he is invited to cite the empirical evidence that accomplishes this feat. In the absence of such evidence and in light of his own epistemic characterization of the requirements placed on those who would reject the Harmony Thesis, it is hard to see what O'Connor would say to the same claim made by substance dualists about the epistemic status of physicalism, given the presence of pre-philosophical intuitions for substance dualism.

O'Connor and the nature of pre-philosophical intuitions

In addition to the role of pre-philosophical intuitions in O'Connor's case for AGC and the Harmony Thesis, the nature of those intuitions is also of crucial importance. Philosophers differ about the nature of intuitions, e.g. some hold that they are merely dispositions to believe certain things. However, the traditional view of intuitions takes them to be cases of (perhaps, defeasible) first-person direct awareness of a relevant intentional object. So understood, they are reported by way of the phenomenological use of "seems" or "appears."

O'Connor seems to agree with this view of intuitions. He claims that intuitions in support of AGC are the way things "seem" to people.[89] In arguing that consciousness is an emergent property, he claims that people have "direct evidence" of the nature of conscious properties themselves. Here, he seems to take it that one has direct first-person access to one's own mental states and, indeed, if this is so, such access seems to provide non-doxastic justification for pre-philosophical beliefs about/concepts of mental properties, including the nature of active power. He also claims to experience himself directly bringing about the formation of an intention.[90] If one accepts this account of intuitions, then one has the resources to explain why certain beliefs are so widely and deeply held.

But dualists, regarding intuitions about the self, often make the same claim. For example, Stewart Goetz has argued that we are directly aware of ourselves (e.g. of our own simplicity) and, on this basis, we are justified in believing substance dualism.[91] It is on the basis of such first-person self-awareness, that people have the pre-philosophical dualist beliefs they do, and this is why these beliefs (or, at least, dualist concepts) play such a regulative role in philosophical arguments about personal identity and related topics.

Of course, it is fashionable today to claim that people have direct access to their mental states but not to their selves. From the time of Hume, the major strategy employed to justify this assertion is the claim that, in fact, people just are never aware of themselves. I believe that dualists have provided adequate responses to this strategy, but that is beside the present point, because I do not believe that O'Connor can avail himself of this strategy. To see why, we need to examine his response to an epistemological objection raised against his version of AGC. The objection is that we could not, in principle, ever know whether any events are produced in the manner that AGC postulates since agent caused events would be indistinguishable from ones that were essentially random.[92]

O'Connor points out that this Humean-type objection would be equally telling against his realist version of event causation (event causes produce or bring about their effects). The Humean skeptic will say that all we have direct evidence for is the pattern of relations among types of events, not of the causal event bringing about its effect. In reply, O'Connor says that in at least some cases we seem to observe directly the causal connectedness between cause and effect. He illustrates this by pointing out that we do not merely observe the movement of the hammer followed by the movement of the nail; rather, we see the hammer moving the nail.

Now it is not clear how one can directly see the hammer moving the nail without directly seeing the hammer. Similarly, it is hard to see how one could directly be aware of one's own self-producing an intention to act without being directly aware of one's own self. Indeed, O'Connor acknowledges that "in the deliberate formation of an intention, the coming to be of my intention doesn't seem to me merely to occur at the conclusion of my deliberation; I seem to experience myself directly bringing it about."[93] This would seem to imply that people are able to be directly aware of their own selves. If so, and given that pre-philosophical intuitions are widely acknowledged to be of a substance dualist sort, the very nature of intuitions as first-person forms of direct access seems to offer defeasible justified beliefs of a substance dualist sort.

It may be that O'Connor has other reasons for rejecting the use of first-person direct awareness of the self as grounds for substance dualism. To my knowledge, he has not addressed the topic in writing, but I could be wrong about this. If he does, there would seem to be two requirements for any such response. First, without begging the question, he is going to have to provide sufficient grounds for rejecting first-person awareness of the self and the role such awareness plays in justifying substance dualism in such a way that he does not undermine his own use of first-person awarenesses as a source of justification for AGC. For example, he cannot simply assert that naturalism makes substance dualism implausible, so we must reject the force of this dualist argument, because the same thing is widely said about the epistemic impact of naturalism on the justification of AGC.

Second, he would need to offer an explanation of the origin and justification of the various dualist intuitions that are a part of O'Connor's own characterization of the agent. I am not disagreeing with that characterization. I am simply asking where it came from and why we should believe it. I believe there is a good answer to these questions—first-person awareness of the self—but these questions would need to be answered in a way that avoids lending support to substance dualism. For example, it seems implausible to suggest that we have first-person awareness of ourselves as physical substances. If we are physical substances, yet we lack first-person awarenesses that this is so and, in fact, seem to have awarenesses that support substance dualism, we would need to know the source of and justification for dualist intuitions that form an essential part of the self qua agent.

The simple fact is that it does not seem to most folk that they are macro-level objects. On the contrary, it seems to most people from the first-person perspective—the perspective upon which O'Connor draws to justify agent causation—that we are mental subjects who fail to be aware of exemplifying any physical properties. The issue then becomes whether there is any good reason to think we are physical objects, though we are not aware of being such. As far as I know, O'Connor never gives us any reason to think we are physical objects, and he must provide such an argument. When he does, he runs the danger of bringing forth considerations of a kind (e.g. from the third-person perspective) that, if persuasive, could also be brought forth to undermine our conviction that we have libertarian freedom. If he simply breaks rank with most people and says that he is, in fact, aware of being a material object by first-person introspection, then this would at best justify locating his view within panpsychism and not within naturalism.

In sum, I agree with most of O'Connor's model of agent causation. But I do not believe he has provided sufficient grounds for accepting the Harmony Thesis and I have tried to say why I cannot follow him in this regard.

5 Colin McGinn and mysterian "naturalism"

Unsatisfied with strong physicalism on the one hand and the various extant naturalist solutions for the origin of consciousness on the other hand, Colin McGinn has offered the most radical "naturalist" alternative to date.[1] It is so bizarre that it is fair to question whether, even if successful, it is a naturalist position in any meaningful sense of the term. In this chapter, I shall describe and seek to rebut McGinn's position.

McGinn's mysterian "naturalism"

According to McGinn, there is a radical difference between mind and matter. Furthermore, because of our epistemic limitations inherited from evolution, there is *in principle* no knowable naturalistic solution to the origin of consciousness or its regular correlation with matter that stays within the widely accepted naturalist epistemology and ontology. Nor is there a plausible non-natural alternative. What is needed is a solution radically different in kind from anything previously offered, one that must meet two conditions: (i) It must be a naturalistic solution. (ii) It must depict the emergence of consciousness and its regular correlation with matter as necessary and not contingent facts. More specifically, there must be three kinds of unknowable natural properties that solve the problem. We can unpack McGinn's position by examining four different aspects of his view.

McGinn and property/event dualism

First, McGinn is committed to property/event dualism. He defines consciousness by giving first-person, introspective, ostensive definitions of particular phenomenal states. He also believes that a fairly simple form of the Knowledge Argument is conclusive. I think McGinn is correct about this, but more importantly, since we are granting premise (1) of AC, I shall simply accept McGinn's characterization and defense of property/event dualism.

McGinn on standard naturalist solutions

Second, he rejects all the standard naturalist solutions for many of the reasons mentioned in chapter one: the uniformity of nature; the inadequacy of Darwinian explanations; the centrality for naturalism and inadequacy of combinatorial modes of explanation along with the bottom/up combinatorial processes constitutive of the Grand Story; the acceptance of a necessitation requirement for an adequate naturalist account. Since I have elaborated on these themes already, let us also grant these points to McGinn.

McGinn on anti-naturalist solutions

Third, various anti-naturalist solutions must be rejected. He evaluates and rejects three of them: theistic dualism and AC, hyperdualism and panpsychism. I shall set aside until chapter six a discussion of panpsychism. For now, let us examine McGinn's treatment of the other two positions beginning with theistic dualism and AC.

McGinn agrees that AC is a plausible argument and, indeed, that there is no plausible rival explanation for a naturalist outside of his own. But for six reasons, AC is a bad argument. For one thing, if we appeal to a conscious God to explain finite consciousness, we generate a vicious infinite regress for we will have to explain why God Himself is conscious. Moreover, if we stop the regress with an unexplainable conscious God, we could just as easily do the same thing by taking finite consciousness as an unexplainable brute fact.

Second, the God hypothesis dignifies consciousness with the word "soul" as an independent thing that uses the body, and thereby generates unanswerable questions that undercut AC: Do rats have souls? Why does God give souls to rats and not worms? Third, theists exaggerate the gap between minds and brains. Mind depends on brain. Why would this be so if mind depends on God?

Fourth, the existence of causally powerful substantial souls that are in some sense dependent upon brains to which they are contingently connected leads to the zombie problem. Such a view renders zombie worlds possible, namely, a world just like the actual one in which minds and consciousness are absent. Now, such a world seems *prima facie* possible, says McGinn, but on further inspection, it faces an insurmountable difficulty. It means that consciousness is epiphenomenal and any view that entails epiphenomenalism must be rejected. Epiphenomenalism ensues because if a zombie world is possible if follows that the physical will chug along just the same regardless of whether or not consciousness obtains. McGinn's employment of an (alleged) association of epiphenomenalism and the possibility of zombie worlds to deny the latter is far from idiosyncratic. For example, John Perry claims that zombies are possible if and only if epiphenomenalism is true; it is a matter of commonsense that epiphenomenalism is false, so zombie worlds are impossible. Zombies are conceivable only in the sense that it is conceivable that Clemens is not Twain, and this sort of reflexive conceivability is clearly consistent with identity.[2]

Fifth, we do not know how God produces consciousness, so at best AC is a stalemate vis-à-vis naturalism. Finally, AC gets off the ground only if we grant that consciousness is a mystery for which we need an explanation. However McGinn claims that his account provides a deflationary explanation for why consciousness is a mystery and, in so doing, it becomes obvious that the sort of mystery involved is not of the right kind needed to justify AC.

What about hyperdualism? On this view, there are two realms of reality—the physical world and an undifferentiated, homogeneous sea of conscious entities that are the constituents of consciousness—that causally interact with each other. When brains evolve to an appropriate level of complexity, a hole is punched through to the mental realm and interactions begin to take place. McGinn gives two reasons for rejecting hyperdualism: It violates physical causal closure and its fatal flaw lies in the notion of causality it employs: How could disembodied consciousness cause anything? How could physical sequences in one realm be disrupted by what is happening in a parallel universe? Physical causation in the physical universe involves energy transfer. But can we really use energy transfer for such a bizarre notion of causality, which is entailed by hyperdualism? Once we raise these questions, it becomes obvious that hyperdualism is inadequate and too outlandish to be taken seriously.

McGinn's solution

Finally, McGinn offers his own "solution" to the problem. He begins by claiming that while evolutionary processes formed noetic faculties in us apt for doing science, it did not develop faculties capable of doing philosophy. Thus, we have cognitive closure regarding philosophical topics, where an organism has cognitive closure with respect to some domain of knowledge just in case that domain is beyond the organism's faculties to grasp. An area of inquiry in which there is no progress is a good sign of cognitive closure, and philosophy in general, and the mind/body problem in particular, are cognitively closed to human faculties due to their limitations that follow from the evolutionary processes that generated them. Thus, the mystery of consciousness would be no mystery at all if we did not have the cognitive limitations we do.

What we can do, however, is characterize the kinds of conditions that must be true of any solution that would be adequate. According to McGinn, there must be some order underlying the heterogeneous appearances of mind and matter because nature abhors a miracle. Moreover, as I mentioned above, McGinn further claims that (i) It must be a naturalistic solution. (ii) It must depict the emergence of consciousness and its regular correlation with matter as necessary and not contingent facts. More specifically, there must be three kinds of unknowable natural properties that solve the problem. First, there must be some general properties of matter that enter into the production of consciousness when assembled into a brain. Thus, all matter has the potentiality to underlie consciousness. Second, there must be some natural property of the brain he calls C* that unleashes these general properties under the right conditions. Third, just as the brain must have a hidden unknowable structure that allows consciousness to emerge from it, so consciousness must have a hidden unknowable essence that allows it to be embedded in the brain.

There is one final aspect to McGinn's position that provides a naturalistic solution to the apparent non-spatiality of the mental. According to McGinn, ours is a spatial world yet conscious states have neither spatial extension nor location. This raises a problem: If the brain is spatial but conscious states are not, how could the brain cause consciousness? This seems like a rupture in the natural order. The non-spatiality of consciousness raises serious problems for emergence and causal interaction. McGinn proffers two solutions to this problem. First, he argues that the Big Bang had to have a cause, this cause "operated" in a state of reality temporally prior to the creation of matter and space, and this reality existed in a non-spatial mode. Therefore, the cause of the Big Bang was not spatial or material, yet it obeyed some laws in the prior state. At the Big Bang, we have a transformation from non-spatial to spatial reality, and at the appearance of consciousness, we have a converse transformation. The non-spatial dimension continued to exist in matter after the Big Bang, lurking behind the scene until brains evolved at which time this dimension showed itself again.

McGinn's second solution focuses on our concept of space. Typically, we think we are correct to depict space as a three-dimensional manifold containing extended objects. But perhaps this depiction is wrong. Maybe its not that consciousness is non-spatial; perhaps it is spatial according to the real nature of space that is quite different from the commonsense view. If we define "space" as "whatever is out there as a containing medium of all things," then it may be that the real nature of space allows it to contain consciousness and matter in a natural way. Here the Big Bang was a transformation of space itself and not a transition from non-space to space.

Critique

I do not believe that McGinn's position will be widely accepted and that for good reason. In this section I will criticize his evaluation of theistic dualism and AC, surface an inconsistency with his rebuttal of hyperdualism and show how McGinn's aversion to hyperdualism is relevant to the relationship between naturalism and abstract objects, and rebut his own solution. Let us begin with McGinn's arguments against theistic dualism and AC. I shall reserve discussion of McGinn's view of the mystery of consciousness for latter when I examine his positive solution.

Theistic dualism and AC

McGinn argues that by appealing to God to explain finite consciousness, one generates a vicious infinite regress and if the regress is stopped with Divine consciousness as a brute fact, then one could just as easily stop with finite consciousness. This sort of argument has been around a long time and McGinn appears to be ignorant of what many believe is a long-standing, successful rebuttal to it. Let us consider the first horn of McGinn's dilemma. McGinn seems to think that if we acknowledge there is a problem with cases of finite consciousness that must be solved by appealing to other finite consciousness, then this problem generalizes and applies equally to a conscious God. Unfortunately, McGinn is wrong about this and fails to appreciate what motivates the relevant regress and the sort of regress it is.

For one thing, the infinity of the regress is impossible because it involves traversing an actual infinite and, arguably, that cannot be done. To illustrate, one cannot count from one to $\aleph_0$ for no matter how far one has counted, he will still have an infinite number of items to count. Such a task can begin, but it cannot be completed. Moreover, trying to count from $-\aleph_0$ to 0 can neither be completed (it involves the same number of tasks as going from one to $\aleph_0$) nor begun for the following reason: Trying to reach any number in the past will itself require an infinite traversal as a preliminary step. Now in a per se regress (see below), the transitivity of the relation ordering the regress implies that the dependence among members runs from the earlier to latter members. Thus, such regresses are precisely like traversing from $\aleph$ to 0. Space considerations forbid me to discuss this line of argument further, but in philosophy of religion it is part of what is called the Kalam cosmological argument. I believe the argument is sound, and I refer the reader to some relevant sources that provide a more thorough evaluation of it than can be done here.[3]

If this is correct, the regress must be finite, and this requires there to be a first member. Below I shall describe some necessary conditions that must be satisfied if one is to select an adequate first member. For now, I merely note that it is not an arbitrary decision to stop the regress because it is vicious, indeed.

The first problem with the existence of an infinite regress of the sort McGinn mentions is, as it were, its *length*—it involves traversing an actual infinite series of members. Besides, with the problem of traversing an actual infinite, there is another problem with the regress that McGinn fails to note: by its very *nature* it is vicious. To see this, let us ask how should "vicious" be characterized here? At least four characterizations have been offered. Roderick Chisholm says that "One is confronted with a vicious infinite regress when one attempts a task of the following sort: Every step needed to begin the task requires a preliminary step."[4] For example, if the only way to tie together any two things whatever is to connect them with a rope, then one would have to use two ropes to tie the two things to the initial connecting ropes, and use additional ropes to tie them to these subsequent ropes, and so on. According to Chisholm, this is a vicious infinite regress because the task cannot be accomplished.

D. M. Armstrong claims that when a reductive analysis of something contains a covert appeal to the very thing being analyzed, it generates a vicious infinite regress because the analysis does not solve anything, but merely postpones a solution.[5] No advance has been made. He says that this is like a man without funds who writes checks from an empty account to cover his debts, and so on, forever.

Chisholm and Armstrong's analyses are helpful. But by far, the most sophisticated treatment of regresses, including vicious ones, was provided by Thomas Aquinas and Duns Scotus. According to Thomas Aquinas a vicious regress is a per se regress which exhibits two key features:[6] 1) It is not just a list of members, but an ordering of members in the sequence. 2) The relationship among the members of the series is transitive. If a stands in R to b and b in R to c, then a stands in R to c, and so on. According to Aquinas, if there is no first member in the series that simply has the relevant feature in itself, no other member of the series will have that feature since each subsequent member can only "pass on" that feature if it first receives it.

As an analogy, consider a chain of people borrowing a typewriter. Whether or not the chain is vicious depends on one's view of the correct description of entities at each stage in the chain. Suppose *a* goes to *b* to borrow a typewriter and *b* complies, claiming to have just what *a* needs. If asked how *b* has a typewriter to loan, he claims to have borrowed it from *c* who, having already borrowed one from *d*, has one to give to *b*. Allegedly, at each stage in the chain, the relevant entity can be described as "a possessor of a typewriter who can loan it to another." Thus, it is alleged, the regress is not vicious.

But it is incomplete to describe each person as "a possessor of a typewriter who can loan it to another." Rather, each person is "a possessor of a typewriter who can loan it to another who first had to borrow it from another." At each stage, the person *qua* lender is such only because he is also a borrower from another, and this means that, given the nature of the series, each stage cannot be adequately described without reference to the earlier stage. Because each member is a borrowing lender, no one will ever get a typewriter unless the regress stops with someone who differs from all the other members of the series in being a lender who just has a typewriter without having to borrow it.

The analogy with finite conscious beings should be apparent. Because they are contingent, then in Chisholm's terms, before each such being can give what it has (consciousness) to another, it must first undergo the preliminary step of receiving finite conscious being first. In Armstrong's terms, each member of the chain exhibits the same problematic feature, namely, being a lender of consciousness who must himself "borrow" consciousness from another. In Aquinas' terms, the members of the regress qua conscious lenders stand in a transitive relationship to the relevant other members in the chain, so without a member who just has consciousness without lending it, there would be no consciousness.

Finally, Duns Scotus offered detailed analyses of various regresses some of which is relevant for present purposes.[7] According to Scotus, there are two very different sorts of ordered sequences involving causal or other sorts of dependence relations: An essentially ordered or per se regress and an accidentally ordered or per accidens regress. The former are irreflexive (if reflexive, then Scotus says one will have self-causation which is absurd), asymmetrical (if symmetrical, then a member will be both a cause and an effect of the same member in the series), and, most importantly, transitive. In some essentially ordered regresses, an earlier member actually causes a latter member to cause: either *a* causes effects in *b* sufficient for *b* to cause the relevant effect in *c* (*a* effects *b*) or *a* causes *b*'s causing *c* (*a* affects *b*). In various sorts of per se dependency chains, the ordering of dependency is (at least) an ordering of necessary dependency conditions from earlier to latter members in the chain.

Scotus identifies three essentially ordered regresses relevant to our discussion: existence, getting the power to operate, and exercising the power to operate. Scotus' main argument against the infinity of such regresses is crafted to avoid a fallacy of composition (e.g. since each member of the series is dependent, the whole must be dependent). His argument is that there is something in the final effect, the last member of the chain about which we are puzzling and seeking an adequate explanation (existence, causal power, consciousness), which is missing in all the other members precisely as essentially ordered with respect to each other, and that requires a first member that is (1) not a part of the chain and (2) simply has the feature of the final effect in itself without having to get it elsewhere.

But why must we stop with God and not some particular finite conscious being? This brings us to the other horn of McGinn's dilemma. The decision to stop with God and not some finite conscious being is not arbitrary but, rather, justified for the following reason. The sort of regress we are considering is one such that in the respect relevant to the ordering of the regress's members, the stopping place must be unique and different from all others. In the typewriter case, the relevant respect is that each member does not simply have a typewriter; he is himself one who must borrow before he lends. The proper stopping place is with a "first-mover" who simply has a typewriter with no need to borrow one before lending it.

Now, each finite conscious being is contingent in two senses: with respect to its existence and with respect to the fact that consciousness was actualized in it. These types of contingency disqualify finite conscious beings from being the proper first mover. Being a necessary being in both senses, God is such a proper First-Mover.

This kind of dialectic occurs frequently in philosophy. To see this, consider the development of agent-causal theories of human freedom. An advocate of agent causation begins with certain concerns about human action and responsibility, formulates a set of arguments for regarding agent causation as the best view of action and responsibility, and confronts a problem with that view, viz., what does the agent do to bring about an action? Partly in response to this question and out of a desire to avoid a vicious infinite regress, the advocate of agent causation arrives at the view that an agent cause is a first-cause, a first-mover, an entity that may bring about a change without having to change first or be changed to do so. In this sense, agent causes are *sui generis* compared with ordinary event causes in that the latter are changed changers characterized by passive liabilities; and agents, being characterized by *sui generis* active power, cannot be caused to act freely.

In epistemology, foundational beliefs are discovered to be such that they provide justification for non-foundational beliefs without having to receive their entire justification from their relationship with other beliefs. In one way or another, foundationalists stop the epistemic regress with an epistemic first-mover, e.g. a non-doxastic self-presenting property. In ontology, discussions of relations and Bradley's famous regress lead to the notion that relations are discovered to be able to relate relata without having themselves to stand in a different relation to those relata. They are unrelatable relaters. AC is an argument form relevantly analogous to these.

McGinn's second critique of theistic dualism and AC is the claim that it uses "soul" to dignify consciousness and this generates serious difficulties (do rats have souls and, if so, why rats and not worms?). As it stands, this is not much of an argument. For one thing, it is simply false. AC does not quantify over souls in any of its premises, and premise (1) launches AC because of the existence of consciousness or its law-like correlations with the brain.

Second, the question "Why do rats have souls and not worms?" is an ambiguous question. If it is the question "Why would God, if He exists, give souls to rats and not worms?" presumably, the answer would be along the lines of why I painted my dining room walls and not the bathroom yellow: I wanted to. What is so problematic about that? If He exists, presumably, God wanted to create certain things and give them certain accidental attributes, and He did not wish to do so for other possible beings He refrained from creating or giving certain accidental attributes. If, instead, the question is about why some things are conscious and others are not, one could say that this is just part of the nature of different things. It is part of the nature of a rat to be conscious and not part of the nature of, say, a tree or rock. Obviously, such an answer involves a commitment to some form of essentialism. But whether or not essentialism is a plausible metaphysical framework is not specifically a theistic concern. This theistic response could employ "nature" in a variety of ways and still be successful.

Finally, focusing on consciousness and not souls, McGinn may be claiming that there is a sort of arbitrariness about theistic dualism such that it entails that at some point, God rather arbitrarily decided to create beings with consciousness and others without it. In response, the sort of "arbitrariness" that seems to underlie this claim is precisely what one would expect if property dualism is true. On a widely accepted dualist understanding of the knowledge of other minds, one starts with first-person acquaintance of one's own mental states and is justified in attributing to other minds whatever mental states are needed to explain the organism's behavior. Ontologically, an organism either is or is not conscious; it either does or does not have some specific mental state. However, epistemologically, as organisms become increasingly disanalogous to humans, one is less and less justified in attributing specific mental states or consciousness itself to the organism. Thus, one is increasingly less justified in such attributions applied to another normal human, a dog, a rat, or a worm. As with other cases involving degreed properties (in this case, "being justified to such and such a degree"), sorites-style difficulties surface about drawing precise lines among the relevant ordered entities. However, far from being a problem, this is precisely what one would expect from a dualist perspective and McGinn is mistaken if he thinks otherwise.

McGinn also criticizes theistic dualism and AC because, if true, it entails that consciousness depends entirely on God's will but this is not true since consciousness clearly depends on the brain. Again, McGinn's objection is ambiguous. I can see two interpretations each of which is fairly easy to rebut. First, his question may be interpreted as assuming that if something depends entirely upon God, then it will not depend on something else in any sense of the word. However, this is a bizarre view of Divine providence and God's continual act of sustaining contingent beings in existence. No matter what the precise theistic formulation of these matters is, theists agree that there is a relevant distinction between primary and secondary causality. For example, just because God created and continually sustains the physical universe and its laws, and is in this sense that upon which they "depend entirely," it hardly follows that lightning does not causally depend on certain antecedent conditions within the cosmos. Various causal relations and dependencies within the created order are consistent with the view that if God had not created and does not continually sustain the universe (or some feature within it), then the universe (or some feature within it) would not exist. Clearly, there is no problem here.

Alternatively, the question may be interpreted as asking why, if the creation of consciousness is a contingent act of God, there is a co-varying dependence among life forms according to which as brains become less and less complex, consciousness does so as well. Note carefully the sort of question this is. It is a theological question about why God would arrange things in this way. So understood, the question is not a request for a scientific answer or even a distinctively philosophical one. It is a question whose answer requires reference to God's possible intentions and motives for arranging things in this way. As I see it, the question is part of a larger one about why there are bodies in the first place.

What are the adequacy requirements for a theological answer to this question? In my view, we have a situation parallel to the difference between a theodicy and defense regarding the problem of evil for theism. A theodicy aims at providing an account of why God actually permits evil in the world. By contrast, a defense offers no such account but seeks merely to show that atheists have failed to carry their case that evil is inconsistent with the existence of God. A defense seeks to undercut the atheist's argument by providing a possible solution because there is a substantial burden of proof on the atheist for which a defense is adequate.

By way of application, it is hard to see that this problem has much force to it. McGinn would need to give reasons for thinking that the dependency of mind on the brain in the manner specified above (and the dependency goes in both directions) is such that there is no reason God would have for creating such a situation. To be successful, McGinn would have to assume that there is no possible reason for God to make things this way. But it is hard to see why this would be the case. The theist could easily hold that God has reasons for doing things this way and even if the details of those reasons are not available to us, the mere fact that God could easily have them is sufficient to undercut this objection.

Moreover, according to a theology of the body that I favor, God created bodies to provide a source of power for living things so they could act in ways independent of God's own exercise of efficient causal power. Bodies provide power for action in the created world. Further, the more complicated an animal's consciousness is, the more complex and finely tuned the body would need to be in order to be responsive to the fine-graded mental states in causal interaction with it. Consider a form of consciousness with a complexity sufficient to engage in a variety of quite specific actions associated with precise nuances in thought, believe, emotion, desire and so forth. On this view, if such a consciousness were causally connected to a material object without the physical complexity needed to register in the physical world the appropriate mental complexity, that mental complexity would be wasted. Such a theology of the body is clearly a possible reason God could have for making things the way he has, and it is sufficient for the purposes of defense required to undercut McGinn's objection.

McGinn's fourth criticism of theistic dualism is that, if true, it entails the possibility of zombie worlds that, in turn, entails an implausible epiphenomenalism regarding conscious states. But the latter entailment is not the case. One could consistently embrace a form of dualism that entails the possibility of zombie worlds, and also believe that causal interaction between consciousness and matter in the actual world is contingent. From this, it follows that an epiphenomenal world is, indeed, a possible world, but it does not follow that the actual world is an epiphenomenal one. One could go on to unpack "brings about" in "mental state M brings about brain state B" in terms of causal necessitation, viz., "M brings about B in all interactionist worlds relevantly similar to the actual world." All this is clearly consistent with the ontological possibility of zombie worlds. The theistic dualism can cheerfully grant that such worlds are distant ones indeed, since her argument goes through quite irrespective of considerations about the remoteness factor.

I am among those dualists who believe that the causal relation (and any other relevant relations, e.g. the emergent supervenient relation construed in non-causal terms) between consciousness and matter is a contingent one. If God wished, he could have created an epiphenomenal world. Inverted qualia worlds, zombie worlds, the metaphysical possibility of body switches or disembodied existence are part of the case for the contingency of the relevant mind/matter relations. Since McGinn's objection assumes that dualism entails such contingency, I need not defend it in the present dialectic. Rather, I am arguing that if we grant this contingency and the possibility of both zombie and epiphenomenal worlds, it does not follow that our word is an epiphenomenal one. The dualist will hold that as a matter of contingent fact we live in a world of causal interaction and nothing McGinn says threatens this claim.

McGinn's fifth objection to theistic dualism and AC is the claim that the theistic solution does not solve anything because it does not tell us *how* God created consciousness. Without providing such a mechanism, the God hypothesis is vacuous and fails to be an advance over a naturalistic explanation, which likewise fails to answer the how, question.

There are two things to be said in response to this argument. First, McGinn's claim simply fails to understand the logic of personal explanation. I will not repeat here our discussion in chapter two of the nature of personal explanation. I make one simple point: A personal explanation can be epistemically successful without referring to a mechanism or other means by which the hypothesized agent brought about the state of affairs in the explanandum. I can explain the existence and precise nature of a certain arrangement of objects on our dinner table by saying that my wife brought it about so we could have an Italian dinner with the Isslers. That explanation is informative (I can tell its Italian food we're having, that we are having the Isslers over and not the Duncans, that my wife did this and not my daughter, that natural processes are inadequate). In addition, the adequacy of such a personal explanation is quite independent of whether or not I know exactly how my wife did it.

Many sciences essentially involve formulating justificatory criteria for inferring intelligent agent causes to explain certain phenomena and for refraining from inferring such causes. And in these sciences, such an inference is usually both epistemically justified and explanatorily significant completely independently of knowledge as to how the agent brought about the phenomena. In forensic science, SETI, psychology, sociology, and archeology, a scientist can know that an intelligent agent is the best explanation of a sequence involving the first twenty prime numbers in a row, or that something is an intelligently designed artifact used in a culture's religious sacrifices, without having so much as a clue as to how the sequence or artifact was made.

Furthermore, an appeal to a particular epistemic value, in this case to the requirement that a necessary condition for successful explanation is that a theory explains how a certain phenomenon was produced, is question-begging against AC and represents a naive understanding of the role various epistemic values play in adjudicating between rival explanations of some phenomenon.

For one thing, two rivals may solve a problem differently depending on the way each theory depicts the phenomenon to be solved. Copernicus solved the motion of the planets by placing the sun in the center of the universe. Ptolemy solved that motion by a complicated set of orbitals with smaller orbitals (epicycles) contained within larger ones. Each solution was quite different in the epistemic value to which it appealed. Copernicans appealed to simplicity and those who sided with Ptolemy claimed that empirical accuracy was on their side. Thus, the epistemic values for assessing one theory may differ substantially from those relevant to its rival.

I am not saying that rivals are incommensurable. I am simply pointing out that it is often more complicated to compare rivals than McGinn's objection seems to assume. It is possible for two rivals to rank the relative merits of epistemic virtues in different ways or even give the same virtue a different meaning or application. Rivals can differ radically about the nature, application, and relative importance of a particular epistemic virtue. Thus, it is question-begging to claim that a criterion P set by one hypothesis should be most important for its rival such that if it fails to satisfy P it is explanatorily inferior.

Finally, sometimes one rival will consider a phenomenon basic and not in need of a solution, empirical or otherwise. It may, therefore, disallow questions about how or why that phenomenon occurs and, thus, can hardly be faulted for not being fruitful in suggesting lines of empirical research for mechanisms whose existence is not postulated by the theory. As Nicholas Rescher has pointed out:

> One way in which a body of knowledge S can deal with a question is, of course, by *answering* it. Yet another, importantly different, way in which S can deal with a question is by disallowing it. S *disallows* [Q] when there is some presupposition of Q that S does not countenance: given S, we are simply not in a position to raise Q.[8]

For example, motion was not natural in Aristotle's picture of the universe and, thus, examples of motion posed problems in need of explanation. But on Newton's picture of the universe, uniform, linear motion is natural and only changes in motion pose problems in need of solution. Thus, suppose a Newtonian and an Aristotelean are trying to solve the observational problem of how and why a particular body is moving in uniform linear motion. The Aristotelean must tell how or why the body is moving to solve the problem. But the Newtonian can disallow the need for a solution by labeling the phenomenon as a basic given for which no solution in terms of a how question utilizing a more basic mechanism is possible.

By way of application, theistic dualism could easily take God's action of creating the existence of consciousness and its precise causal correlation with the brain to be a basic action for which there just is no further "how" question to be asked. Moreover, the theistic dualist can also claim that, given the nature of personal explanation, the epistemic value of citing a mechanism in answer to a "how" question is not as important as other epistemic values and, thus, failure to answer such a question is not a particularly significant issue in light of its own inner logic. But the same cannot be said for naturalism, and given the way physical explanation works, the importance of answering "how" questions by citing a mechanism is, indeed, quite high. Thus, the naturalist's failure to answer this question is a serious one but the same cannot be said for theistic dualism.

Hyperdualism

So much for McGinn's criticism of theistic dualism and AC. What about his response to hyperdualism? You may recall that according to McGinn the central reason why hyperdualism must be rejected lies in the notion of causality it employs: How could disembodied consciousness cause anything? How could physical sequences in one realm be disrupted by what is happening in a parallel universe? Physical causation in the physical universe involves energy transfer. But can we really use energy transfer for such a bizarre notion of causality entailed by hyperdualism? These questions make it obvious that hyperdualism is inadequate and too outlandish to be taken seriously.

Since I do not have a dog in this fight, I have no interest in defending hyperdualism. However, I do think that McGinn's argument against it backfires in such a way that it reintroduces a range of defeaters for naturalism that we are not considering in this book.

To see this, it is important to note that McGinn claims that as long as the naturalist gives an account of the instantiation of all properties in terms of the instantiation of physical properties taken as straightforward physical facts(s), he is free to take properties themselves as non-physical, abstract entities.[9] Presumably, on either a constituent or relational ontology, this would mean that the nexus of exemplification is at the very least a queer entity and, most likely, an abstract object in its own right. In fact, the admission of abstract objects—e.g. properties and relations, including exemplification—and their instantiation is sufficient for naturalist philosophers who are sensitive to matters in general ontology such as D. M. Armstrong, Keith Campbell and Wilfred Sellars to justify a rejection of naturalism.[10] For example, Wilfrid Sellars claimed that "a naturalist ontology must be a nominalist ontology."[11] Elsewhere, Sellars argued that a nominalist analysis of predication is the "very foundation of a naturalist ontology."[12]

I have defended these claims elsewhere, and shall not develop them here.[13] However, here is a summary of two key issues:

(1) Traditional properties and spatio-temporal location: Some have offered a sort of "argument from queerness" against traditional realist properties construed as abstract objects to the effect that they are entities of a very strange sort, utterly different from anything else in the universe as depicted by the strong naturalist. Some have developed this argument by focusing on a special class of universals (e.g. propositions, axiological properties), others have claimed that no physicalist or naturalist non-reductive account of deep, metaphysical modality is possible and, thus, realist properties and their relations to each other are utterly different from the rest of the naturalist ontology.

(2) Traditional properties and predication: Traditional realism is a classic example of a "two world" ontology and, as such, it becomes difficult to explain in naturalist terms how there could be any kind of connection between abstract objects on the one hand and the spatio-temporal world of particulars and events on the other. Moreover, because the predication relation (i.e. nexus) 1) is non-spatio-temporal; 2) connects entities from different "worlds" (How could physical sequences in one realm be disrupted by what is happening in the abstract realm?) and 3) does not involve energy transfer, it is hard to see how the relation itself bears a relevant similarity to strictly physical entities. In this regard, the predication relation presents the same sorts of problems to global naturalists that Cartesian interaction and emergent/supervenient relations do to weak naturalists (e.g. Where does Cartesian interaction take place and where is the predication relation exemplified?).

Naturalists who are persuaded by McGinn's critique of hyperdualism, must face the fact that this very sort of argument has been forcefully employed by major naturalist figures to justify a rejection of abstract objects. At the very least, McGinn owes us an explanation as to how he can advance his argument against hyperdualism while accepting the conjunction of naturalism and the exemplification of abstract objects. At the end of the day, there may be a much closer relationship between naturalism and rejection of abstract objects than many realize, and McGinn's argument provides a nice place to raise this problem.

Four problems with mysterian "naturalism"

We come to an evaluation of McGinn's own position—mysterian "naturalism." For at least four reasons, it must be judged a failure. First, given McGinn's agnosticism about the properties that link mind and matter, how can he confidently assert some of their features? How does he know they are non-sensory, pre-spatial or spatial in an unknowable way? How can he confidently assert that we are naturally constituted from smoothly meshing materials, as seamless as anything else in nature? How does he know some of these properties underlie all matter? Indeed, what possible justification can he give for their reality?

The only one he proffers is that we must provide a naturalistic solution and all ordinary naturalistic ones either deny consciousness or fail to solve the problem. However, given the presence of AC, McGinn's claims are simply question-begging and *ad hoc* according to criteria developed in chapter two. Indeed, his agnosticism seems to be a convenient way of hiding behind naturalism and avoiding a theistic explanation. Given that theism enjoys a positive degree of justification prior to the problem of consciousness, he should avail himself of the explanatory resources of theism.

In a related fashion, it is sometimes argued, and not without some justification, that attempts to draw a line between what we can and cannot know requires that one must first cross the line to draw it. McGinn comes perilously close to doing the very thing he claims cannot be done. Whether or not one accepts this claim about drawing lines, it seems that McGinn's view is self-refuting. He tells us that we did not evolve with faculties apt for doing philosophy, that when confronted with a lack of progress we should draw the conclusion that we are cognitively closed to the subject matter in question, and so on. Yet McGinn's entire book is a species of philosophical argument and he explicitly states that his purpose is to develop and defend his viewpoint over against rivals. He also derives philosophical theses (e.g. skeptical theses in areas for which we have cognitive closure) by philosophically studying the history of philosophy, he gives an analysis of the nature of human knowledge, he offers philosophical—not scientific—arguments against positions that rival naturalism. I may be missing something here, but it is hard to avoid the conclusion that McGinn's own project is refuted, or at least undercut by his own views that constitute the core of that very project.

Second, it is not clear that his solution is a version of naturalism, except in name only. In contrast to other entities in the naturalist ontology, McGinn's three hypothesized properties cannot be known by employment of the naturalist epistemology, nor are they relevantly similar to the rest of the naturalist ontology. For the sake of argument, I grant that McGinn may appropriately call these "naturalistic" properties in the sense that they are 1) not created by God and 2) are regularly involved in giving rise to consciousness in organisms. However, it is vacuous to call these properties "naturalistic" in the only sense relevant to theistic dualism and AC, namely, as entities whose nature, existence and activity can be located in a natural ontology and given a naturalistic explanation. Given that naturalism is a worldview that claims superior explanatory power to its rivals, these are bizarre, *sui generis* brute facts on a naturalist view. Indeed, McGinn's ontology is so bizarre that it may be taken as a *reductio* against naturalism if McGinn is correct that no other naturalist solution is available. In fact, McGinn's solution is actually closer to an agnostic form of panpsychism than to naturalism. In the next chapter, we shall evaluate panpsychism and discuss whether it can be taken as a version of naturalism. For now, I note that McGinn is clear on the matter: panpsychism is a rival to and not a legitimate specification of naturalism.

Third, McGinn does not solve the problem of consciousness; he merely relocates it. Rather than having two radically different entities, he offers us three unknowable properties with radically different aspects, e.g. his links contain the potentiality for ordinary spatiality and non-spatiality, for ordinary materiality and mentality. Moreover, these radically different aspects of the linking properties are just as contingently related as they seem to be without a linking intermediary. The contingency comes from the nature of mind and matter as naturalists conceive it. It does not remove the contingency to relocate it as two aspects of unknowable intermediaries with both.

Finally, there are serious difficulties with McGinn's solution to the problem of the non-spatiality of mental states. According to his first option the Big Bang had to have a cause, this cause "operated" in a state of reality temporally prior to the creation of matter and space, this reality existed in a non-spatial mode, and while the cause of the Big Bang was neither spatial nor material, it still obeyed some laws in the prior state.

There is much in this solution that brings a smile to the theist: the Big Bang had to have a cause, presumably because either events per se or those in which something comes-to-be must have causes, the cause is not spatial nor is it material. This cause shares important features with the God of classic theism. At the very least, it is hard to see how the hypothesized state of affairs satisfies the conditions for location in a naturalist ontology specified in chapter one. The presence of temporality is not sufficient to claim this is a naturalistic state of affairs because based on strong conceivability there are possible worlds in which angels alone exist temporally. As Kant argued, finite consciousness entails temporality, so such worlds are temporal but hardly apt for appropriation by a naturalist.

Nor is the presence of law sufficient. In his discussion of constituent/whole relations, Edmund Husserl described a host of (*a priori*) laws of being that he claimed governed the nature of various entities, their coming-to-be and perishing, and different changes that take place among them.[14] However, these laws are not in any sense physical laws of nature. Even if

Husserl is wrong, his ontology and many others like it demonstrate that the mere presence of laws that govern change in some purported ontological model is far from sufficient to claim that the model is a naturalistic one. Moreover, it seems reasonable to hold that the nature of a relation is constituted by the nature of its relata—spatial, musical, odor, logical relations are such because they can relate certain kinds of entities and not others. If this is right, it is hard to see how the laws envisaged by McGinn are natural laws.

Finally, McGinn seems unfamiliar with the Kalam cosmological argument and the literature surrounding it, a literature of central importance for evaluating his proposal. The argument has generated a lot of attention in the last fifteen years or so and it has no small number of defenders. It is safe to say that the argument is sufficiently robust to require inclusion in any discussion of the beginning of the spatio-temporal physical universe. The Kalam cosmological argument involves a defense of these three propositions:

(1) The universe had a beginning.
(2) The beginning of the universe was caused.
(3) The cause of the beginning of the universe was personal.

Two different philosophical arguments are typically offered on behalf of (1).

Argument A

(A1) An actual infinite number of things cannot exist.
(A2) A beginningless temporal series of events is an actual infinite number of things.
(A3) Therefore, a beginningless temporal series of events cannot exist.
(A4) Either the present moment was preceded by a beginningless temporal series of prior events or there was a first event.
(A5) Therefore, there was a first event.

Argument B

(B1) It is impossible to traverse an actual infinite by successive addition.
(B2) The temporal series of past events has been formed by successive addition.
(B3) Therefore, the temporal series of past events cannot be actually infinite.
(B4) Either the temporal series of past events is actually infinite or finite.
(B5) Therefore, the temporal series of past events is finite.
(B6) If the temporal series of past events is finite, there was a first event.
(B7) Therefore, there was a first event.

It is not my purpose to defend the argument here, but it should be pointed out that, if successful, it justifies the claim that time itself had a beginning that was caused by something that can exist without time. And on the assumption that laws of nature govern temporal processes and, thus, require events to be instantiated, it becomes clear that a law of nature did not govern the cause of the first event. At the very least, McGinn's speculations regarding his first option are grossly incomplete and they open the door for considerations quite favorable to theism.

What about McGinn's second option: We are wrong to think of space as a three-dimensional manifold containing extended objects. Perhaps the real nature of space is "whatever is out there as a containing medium of all things." If this is correct, then the real nature of space allows it to contain consciousness and matter in a natural way.

I do not have a knock-down argument against this option, but I do find it highly counter-intuitive and, in fact, unintelligible. It may be useful to say why. I begin with an observation about the difference between formal concepts and certain material concepts. I recognize that my remarks to follow are controversial and inadequately developed. Still, I want to get some ideas on the table that I take to be relevant to McGinn's second option, even if they are expressed in précis form.

In my view, formal concepts are capable of being expressed adequately by way of definite descriptions. To illustrate, the formal concept of a substance is "whatever is an essentially characterized continuant;" the formal concept of justice is "whatever outcome is fair and accords with the maxim 'treat equals equally and unequals unequally'." Functional concepts are good examples of formal concepts. By contrast, material concepts, at least those defined by ostensive definition, are defined by rigid designation. If we limit ourselves to sense perceptible entities with which we may be acquainted, then "red," "sour," "middle C" may be taken as expressing material concepts.

Now I take the notion of extension to be such a material concept. If I am right, then the only intelligible notion of a spatial dimension is the material concept of "extended one-directional magnitude" which must be defined ostensively. Along similar lines, "space" is a material concept defined by acquaintance as "extended three-directional magnitude." I, for one, have no idea what it means to use spatial language to speak of multi-dimensionality in the way McGinn does. When a scientist claims that a three-dimensional object can be "*spatially* rotated" into other spatial dimensions, I can give no material content to the claim and, thus, I cannot understand what is being said. Likewise, when McGinn tell us that space is "whatever is *out there* as a *containing medium* of all things," the terms "out there," "containing," "medium," are either used in the ordinary way characterized above, in which case the definition is circular and seems to require ostensive definition to give these terms intelligible content, or else they are used equivocally in which case they are unintelligible, at least to me.

I recognize that physicists talk about a multitude of spatial dimensions. In my view, the scientific notion of an extra dimension of space is a mere mathematical devise, a formal definition with no material content that can intelligibly be ascribed to reality, and theories that employ such language should be understood in anti-realist terms. When scientists speak of multi-dimensionality with respect to space, they say things like the following: there are millions of dimensions of space, there could be an infinitely small volume, mass and space are literally interchangeable, triangles can be identical to circles, that a one dimensional line (a string) could literally have clockwise vibrations in ten dimensions of space and counterclockwise vibrations in twenty-six space dimensions.[15] I find such language unintelligible, and while the problem may be my lack of imagination, I suspect that others may agree with me.

In any case, I have tried to show that McGinn's position is not as plausible as AC and is not a legitimate version of naturalism. Long ago, Thomas Kuhn taught us that there are certain telltale signs of a paradigm in crisis among which are the proliferation of epicycles, of rival specifications of the paradigm formulated to preserve that paradigm in the face of stubborn, recalcitrant facts. Especially significant are specifications so bizarre that it is hard to recognize them as specifications of the paradigm. I take McGinn's mysterian "naturalism" to be an indication that naturalism is in serious crisis with respect to consciousness. Kuhn also taught us that as bizarre and *ad hoc* as some of the specifications may be, if there is no rival paradigm, then an advocate of the degenerative paradigm must simply do the best he or she can with the recalcitrant facts and leave it at that. But if there is a plausible rival, a paradigm shift may well be in order. In my view, McGinn's position, coupled with theism and AC as a rival, serve as evidence that such a paradigm shift away from naturalism towards theism is past due.

6 David Skrbina and panpsychism

Most contemporary philosophers do not consider panpsychism to be a plausible position, though it is safe to say that the failure of strong physicalism and the growing adoption of property/event dualism will most likely restore panpsychism as a viewpoint to be taken seriously. Indeed, there is some evidence that this is already taking place, even among tough-minded analytic philosophers.[1]

However, irrespective of its current popularity, the longevity and perennial endurance of panpsychism reflect the genuineness of a serious metaphysical problem for which there are a limited number of solutions. The problem, of course, is the appearance of mind, sentience, inner psychic reality, consciousness in the history of the cosmos. The plausible explanatory options seem to be these:

(1) Accept a strong physicalist version of naturalism and reject irreducible, uneliminable consciousness. In this book, we are setting aside this option.
(2) Accept emergent naturalism according to which at some point in cosmic history, matter reached a suitable state of complexity and consciousness appeared for the first time from materials, which were neither actually conscious nor contained irreducibly conscious potentialities. Consciousnesses just showed up all at one go "out of nothing," that is, out of pure, brute matter exhaustively characterizable by physics and chemistry. Searle's biological naturalism may be construed as a form of this option.
(3) Accept some mysterian view and call it a version of naturalism. Colin McGinn's view is the paradigm case of this position, and with certain qualifications, so is Philip Clayton's (see chapter seven).
(4) Accept some version of panpsychism. We will investigate this option below, but arguably, Timothy O'Connor's view is a version of panpsychism. It is a further question as to whether this is a legitimate form of naturalism or a rival to it.
(5) Accept a theistic explanation. This is the position for which I am arguing.

What exactly is panpsychism? It is possible to give it a topic neutral definition such that it is consistent with every option in philosophy of mind, including strong physicalism.[2] But this is not how the viewpoint has been characterized since the Pre-Socratics and it is not a definition that is of interest to me. Therefore, I will follow historical precedent and current usage by its advocates and characterize panpsychism along dualist lines. So understood, there are a handful of definitions in the literature: All objects in the universe have an inner or psychological nature. Physical reality is composed of individuals each of which is to some degree sentient. Mind is a fundamental feature of the world that exists throughout the universe. Everything is conscious. Everything has a mind. Clearly, these definitions are different, yet they overlap and revolve around a core that is admittedly hard to specify if one is trying to speak for all panpsychists.

For present purposes, I shall follow David Skrbina's characterization: All things have a mind or a mind-like quality. Skrbina unpacks this definition by describing three essential characteristics of panpsychism:[3] (1) Objects have experiences for themselves; that is, the mind-like quality is something internal to or inherent in the object. (2) This experience is singular and unified. (3) Any configuration or system of mass/energy counts as such an object. Thus, says Skrbina, panpsychism may also be understood as the claim that "All objects, or systems of objects, possess a singular inner experience of the world around them."[4]

One may distinguish two forms of panpsychism. According to the strong version, all objects or systems of objects possess an actualized singular inner experience of the world around them. According to the weak form, all objects or systems of objects possess a singular inner experience of the world around them in a degraded, attenuated way in the form of "proto-mental states," i.e. in the form of real mental dispositions/potentialities that, under the right circumstances, become actualized.

Historically, panpsychism has been seen as a rival to naturalistic materialism. However, its relationship with theism is less clear. Clearly, construed as an overarching worldview, panpsychism is a rival to traditional monotheism, but advocates of process theology and panentheism on the one hand and Mormonism on the other hand clearly embraces a form of panpsychism.[5]

In the remainder of the chapter, I shall do three things: present an exposition of the most important contemporary defense of panpsychism—David Skrbina's; criticize panpsychism on its own merits and argue that it is inferior to theism and AC; argue that is it a rival to and not an appropriate specification of naturalism. To achieve my dialectical aims, I am going to present a mostly negative critique of his view. This should not be taken as an indication of my assessment of his work. There is much in *Panpsychism in the West* with which I agree and I have learned much from Skrbina. Indeed, I believe his view (and even more so, Philip Clayton's) is preferable to strong naturalism.

The panpsychism of David Skrbina

Précis of Skrbina's view

In my opinion, David Skrbina's *Panpsychism in the West* is the most authoritative account and defense of panpsychism in several years. I have already presented Skrbina's characterization of panpsychism.[6] According to Skrbina, two things follow from panpsychism so conceived. First, there are degrees of consciousness ("proto-mentality," "low-grade awareness,") and weak panpsychism (all things have at least psychic potentiality, latent consciousness, universal inert mental potentiality) is a legitimate form of panpsychism.[7] Second, panpsychism implies a world-soul (the cosmos as a whole has a mind or at least a mind-like quality all its own) and is consistent with the emergence of a finite god, e.g. as construed in panentheism.[8]

Eleven arguments for panpsychism

Skrbina presents eleven arguments for panpsychism.[9] Here they are in his own words:

(1) Argument by Indwelling Powers—All objects exhibit certain powers or abilities that can plausibly be linked to noetic qualities.
(2) Argument by Continuity—A common principle or substance exists in all things; in humans, it accounts for our soul or mind, and thus by extrapolation it infers mind in all things. Also expressed as a rejection of the problem of "drawing a line" somewhere, non-arbitrarily, between enminded and supposedly mindless objects.
(3) Argument from First Principles—mind is posited as a fundamental and universal quality, present individually in all things; this is a kind of "panpsychism by definition."
(4) Argument by Design—The ordered, complex, and/or persistent nature of physical things suggests the presence of an inherent mentality.
(5) Argument from Non-Emergence—It is inconceivable that mind should emerge from a world in which no mind existed; therefore mind always existed, in even the simplest of structures. Also expressed as "nothing in the effect that is not in the cause." Sometimes called the "genetic" argument.
(6) Theological Argument—God is mind and spirit, and God is omnipresent, therefore mind and spirit are present in all things. Or, all things participate in God and thus have a share in spirit.
(7) Evolutionary Argument—A particular combination of Continuity and Non-Emergence arguments. Claims that certain objects (e.g. plants, the Earth) share a common dynamic or physiological structure with human beings, and thus possess a mind; and, points to the continuity of composition between organic and inorganic substances (i.e. anti-vitalism).

(8) Argument from Dynamic Sensitivity—The ability of living systems to feel and to experience derives from their dynamic sensitivity to their environment; this holds true for humans and, empirically, down to the simplest one-celled creatures. By extension, we know that all physical systems are dynamic and interactive, and therefore all, to a corresponding degree, may be said to experience and feel. Additionally, other aspects of dynamical systems theory supports the panpsychist view (a combination of the Indwelling powers, Continuity, and Non-Emergence arguments.)

(9) Argument from Authority—Not a formal argument, but a potentially convincing claim nonetheless. Writers as diverse as Bruno, Clifford, Paulsen, and Hartshorne have cited the large number of major intellectuals who expressed intuitive or rational belief in some form of panpsychism. And in fact the whole of the present work [Skrbina's] makes this claim.

(10) Panpsychism "truly naturalizes mind," because it deeply integrates mind into the natural order of the world. Furthermore, it does so in a way that no other theory does. Though this basic feeling has been expressed by others, it has not been presented as a core argument. I [Skrbina] will designate this as the Naturalized Mind Argument.

(11) In light of "the 'terminal' failure of the approaches built on the Cartesian intuition about matter," panpsychism stands as the most viable alternative. This is an important point, and one that has been neglected in the past. If intensive critical inquiry of dualism and materialism over the past, say, few hundred years has failed to produce a consensus theory of mind, then it stands to reason that a third alternative like panpsychism, in some positive formulation should gain in viability. This "negative argument" for panpsychism may be called, for want of a better name, the Last Man Standing Argument.

Skrbina develops some of these arguments a bit more, but when he does, it usually involves illustrating them and not providing additional considerations besides those above. Though brief, this description of the eleven arguments is an adequate presentation of Skrbina's case for panpsychism.

Evaluation of Skrbina's panpsychism

Panpsychism and AC

It seems clear that some of these arguments are better than others and I shall shortly look at each one, albeit somewhat briefly in certain cases. For now, I want to offer one overarching observation about the arguments. It may well be that some of them exhibit varying degrees of success against strong naturalism. Indeed, argument (5) from Non-Emergence has been a major component of my own critique of naturalist explanations of consciousness and my defense of AC. So let us grant for the sake of argument that some of Skrbina's arguments are successful against naturalism. The same does not hold for classical theism and, sadly, Skrbina's book almost exclusively advocates panpsychism vis-à-vis naturalism and not theism.

As a theist, there are important points in Skrbina's book with which I agree. But given the success of those arguments against naturalism, panpsychism follows only if classic theism is also ruled out and Skrbina fails to carry out such a project. Thus, it seems to me that some of his arguments provide equal justification for panpsychism and classic theism, and others relative to classic theism and others support classic theism better than they do panpsychism. Moreover, it is highly likely that the case for classic theism is quite superior to that of panpsychism on grounds independent of these eleven arguments. If that is correct, then the evidence for panpsychism relative to classic theism from these eleven arguments must be high indeed, if the former is to enjoy greater overall epistemic status than the latter. Therefore, the dialectical situation seems to be this: When the total epistemic impact of these arguments is considered, they support classic theism better than panpsychism. Moreover, when additional factors are considered, classic theism is better justified than panpsychism in light of those factors. Thus, classic theism is to be preferred to panpsychism. Moreover, panpsychist arguments provide additional evidence against naturalism and, thus, for classic theism.

Setting strong naturalism aside, let us consider the arguments in light of panpsychism vs. classic theism in this order: those I take to be equally supportive of the two views or slightly more supportive of classic theism, those that are, in my view, simply unconvincing arguments, and those that clearly support classic theism.

Arguments on a parity with or slightly in favor of classic theism

It seems to me that (1), (2a) ((2) has two parts), (3) (on one interpretation), (7c) ((7) has three parts) and (10) are equally supportive of both views (10 may be slightly more favorable to panpsychism.) As formulated above, (1) is no better than a wash for panpsychism relative to classic theism because the claim that certain powers and abilities of all objects "can plausibly be linked to noetic qualities" can easily be interpreted to imply a creative, designing Mind behind such objects at least as plausibly as implying noetic qualities within the objects themselves. Elsewhere, Skrbina unpacks "linked" as follows:[10] objects have the power of motion, they exhibit forces of attraction, repulsion and so forth, and there is a rational order to all things. While these may provide material content for "linked," unfortunately, they actually provide grounds for thinking that the best explanation for "linked" is classic theism and not panpsychism (setting aside other worldviews). I believe this will become evident below when I discuss (4). For now, I make two observations.

First, more scientists have followed Newton than Skrbina in the sense that Newton saw the rational order of things and gravity as grounded in the mind and constant will of a transcendent God, respectively. Recall that Newton distinguished offering a mathematical description of gravity from offering an ontological analysis of what it is. Clearly, the theistic option is at least as, if not more attractive here. Second, when inert corpuscularianism was replaced by dynamic corpuscularianism, forces were located in objects themselves.[11] But for two reasons, this move did not provide justification for panpsychism. For one thing, many thinkers continued to hold that the forces themselves were actually the result of the constant exercise of power by God, and this view "saved the appearances" as well as alternative ontological analyses of the forces. For another, granting that forces are actually in particular things, is it easy to interpret them as passive liabilities created by God and bequeathed to various powerful particulars.

What about (2a)? Argument (2) has two components. (a) A common principle or substance exists in all things and it accounts for soul or mind in humans. (b) If we extrapolate to other sorts of things, then clearly some organisms have mind, and if that is granted, it becomes impossible to draw a non-arbitrary line between enminded and supposedly mindless objects. I shall focus on (2b) below. Regarding (2a), it seems clear that a theistic explanation employing AC is at least as plausible as a panpsychist one. A theist will reject the claim that a common principle or substance exists in all things and defend the notion that a common creator/designer exists behind all (finite contingent) things. Both worldviews provide an explanation of consciousness in humans (and certain other entities). Further, I will argue against (2b) below. If I am successful, then AC is superior to panpsychism because the latter fails to employ (2) as adequate grounds for the ubiquity of mind.

(3) is capable of two interpretations. First, one may construe the First Principles argument as the brute posit of panpsychism for which there is nothing more basic that could support it. In this sense, one reasons from panpsychism but not for it. Panpsychism is, as Skrbina puts it, a definitional truth. So understood, this is a very weak "argument." It is clearly up to one simply to take panpsychism as a mere analytic truth that has nothing to do with reality. In addition, I see no reason why a theist cannot be equally justified in positing the existence of God. While I am not among them, there is a branch of Christian scholarship that adopts what is called "presuppositionalism," viz., the existence of God is taken as a fundamental presupposition from which all further argument derive, though they do not take "God exists" as a mere analytic truth. Alternatively, (3) may be construed as the claim that panpsychism is a "basic" posit justified by other factors, e.g. the intuitive awareness of mind in all things, and its explanatory power. So understood, I shall postpone discussion of (3) until later.

(7) contains three parts. (a) is the claim that humans (and other higher animals) clearly have consciousness, and consciousness cannot emerge

from dead, naturalistically described matter by way of mechanical processes. (b) It is impossible to draw a line between enminded and allegedly mindless entities, so there must be mind in all things. (c) Moreover, the continuity of composition of all things (e.g. all things have "chemical affinity") best explains the presence of consciousness in humans, viz., it is to some degree in everything (e.g. "affinity" is equivalent to some sort of feeling.) I shall look at (a) and (b) below when I examine (5) and (2b), respectively. That leaves (c). I have already provided a theistic response to (c) in my discussion of (1). One need not construe "affinity" as feeling, or treat other "continuous compositional features" in mental terms. For example, one can treat forces such as "affinity" in anti-realist terms or one can unpack them as purely physical passive liabilities such that "affinity" is purely a metaphorical anthropomorphic expression. Thus, there is no clear way to take (7c) as supporting panpsychism over classic theism.

This brings us to (10). *Prima facie*, (10) is unclear in its claim that panpsychism "truly naturalizes mind," that it "deeply integrates mind" into the natural order of the world. However, based on Skrbina's discussion of (10) in places other than his summary of the eleven arguments as stated above, it is plausible to understand it as follows: Panpsychism avoids a supernatural explanation of consciousness by showing that if construed along panpsychist lines, the "natural" world has latent within it all the resources needed to ground the existence of consciousness in humans and higher animals.[12] It may be that (10) provides some evidence for panpsychism over classic theism. Since I am at pains to show that 1) the combined weight of all eleven arguments supports theism over panpsychism, or 2) setting consciousness aside, the prior probability of theism over panpsychism is sufficiently large to justify the claim that the former is to be preferred to the latter even if the evidence from these eleven arguments is a draw or slightly in favor of panpsychism, this admission does not amount to much. If the first claim is correct, then the support of (1) is offset by the evidence for theism from the other arguments taken together. If this second claim is correct, then given that panpsychism is not a legitimate form of strong naturalism, it follows that consciousness provides evidence for theism and panpsychism over against naturalism, and the choice between these non-naturalist alternatives must be made on other grounds.

That said, I make two additional points about (10). First, a good bit of the sociological, if not intellectual preference for a "natural" over a supernatural explanation for some phenomenon derives from the widespread acceptance of strong naturalism. Granting merely for the sake of argument that if we limit the rivals to strong naturalism and classic theism, then some argue that there is always a burden of proof on a supernatural explanation. But it does not follow from this that the same burden obtains if our rivals are panpsychism and classic theism. It is far from clear that most thinkers would rightly prefer to explain various features of the cosmos (its origin in light of a finite past; its contingency, the presence of beauty, order, information, specified complexity, religious experience, objective morality, alleged miracles), including human consciousness considered alone, in light of panpsychism, and not classic theism.

This leads to my second point. I am among those who believe that theism is better justified than strong naturalism or panpsychism and, given theism, that there is sufficient evidence to justify New Testament miracles, including the resurrection of Jesus, and additional miracles done in the name of Jesus throughout church history. Clearly, space considerations and the limited scope of our inquiry prevent me from developing arguments for these claims.[13] The disadvantage of a supernatural vs. a panpsychic explanation for human consciousness must be defended in light of the overall evidence for theism vs. panpsychism, including the evidence for miracles.

Arguments of no value in supporting panpsychism

I turn to those arguments I take to be of no value in supporting panpsychism: (2b) and (7b) taken together, (6), (8), and (11).

(2b) (which is also employed as (7b)) argues for the ubiquity of mind because it is impossible to "'[draw] a line' somewhere, non-arbitrarily, between enminded and supposedly mindless objects." There are at least two reasons why this argument fails. First, it is an example of a sorites-style argument, and it is widely accepted that these sorts of arguments do not work.[14] Though the refutation of sorites-style arguments may not require the adoption of Chisholmian particularism, the latter provides the resources for generating counter-examples to sorites-style arguments. According to Chisholmian particularism, one can know paradigm cases of some item in dispute without having to know how one knows them or without having to provide a criterion for such knowledge as a necessary condition for having it.

Chisholm formulated his version of particularism in light of general issues between the cognitivist and skeptic. His particularism was not limited to providing a solution to sorites cases though it does have application to them. To see this, consider any range of phenomena that is degreed in the relevant way: degreed transitions from having hair to being bald, from being orange to being red, and other alleged cases of ontological vagueness. Let us grant that it is impossible to draw a line at the exact place where, say, in the transition from orange to red objects a shade first appears that is more red than orange. It does not follow from this that it is not the case that some objects are red and not orange and some are orange and not red, nor does it follow that one cannot recognize paradigm cases of red and orange objects. The same may be said for "enminded" and mindless objects.

Second, a favored strategy for treating alleged cases of ontological vagueness is to reduce them to epistemic vagueness. This strategy gains force when we are dealing with mental properties as intrinsically characterized attributes of which one is directly aware from the first-person perspective.

And that is what I am granting in this book. So construed, mental properties are as the dualist claims. Now it is a typical aspect of property (or substance) dualism to unpack knowledge of one's own mind and other minds by starting with the first-person case and moving to the third-person. Whether or not this approach is further analyzed in Plantingian externalist terms, treated as an inference to the best explanation, an argument by analogy, or in some related way, the first-to-third-person approach implies that while something either is or is not conscious, one is increasingly less justified in ascribing consciousness to another entity as it becomes less analogous in behavior, composition, etc. to one's own case. Now this is precisely what is claimed in (2b) (and (7b)). Given that epistemic vagueness is all one needs to account for problems of "drawing a line," there is no justification for following Skrbina and ontologizing the situation. Moreover, the epistemic approach avoids the panpsychist mess of trying to clarify the notion of "proto-mentality" or "attenuated awareness" construed as actual and not merely dispositional states.

(6) involves a very serious misunderstanding of the classic theistic view of omnipresence. There are two different understandings of omnipresence. Some reduce it to causality and knowledge, viz., to say that God is omnipresent is to say that he has immediate awareness of and causal access to all spatial locations. Thus, God is not literally spatially in each such location. Alternatively, to say that God is omnipresent is to say that he is "fully present" everywhere in space. "Fully present" can be understood spatially in which case God is conceived as being entirely present in all places at once and, thus, God does not conform to the so-called axiom of localization: No entity whatsoever can exist at different spatial locations at once or at interrupted time intervals.

"Fully present" may also be understood in a primitive non-spatial sense of "being in" such that God is non-spatially in each spatial location. An analogy may be of help here. Let us adopt a constituent ontology along with a view of universals as abstract objects. Let us also grant "the victory of particularity," viz., when a universal is instantiated by a particular, the resulting state of affairs—the-particular's-having-the-universal—is itself particular. Under these assumptions above, the universal is literally in the being of its instances in a primitive non-spatial sense. This primitive is not identical to but merely provides an analogy for "being in" construed as a non-spatial primitive in the case of divine omnipresence.

Now what notion of omnipresence is affirmed by (6)? Clearly, it is not a classic theistic form. To avoid equivocation, (6) must equate "omnipresent" with the panpsychist notion of "being present in all things." Elsewhere, Skrbina provides an example of the employment of (6) by the philosopher Fechner who affirms that in traditional theology God is everywhere and if one concedes such divine omnipresence, one has already conceded "the universal animation of the world by God."[15] I take this to be what it means for "all things to participate in God and thus have a share in spirit."

Earlier, Skrbina asserts that all things have their own minds; each particle of matter has its own individual intelligence and, thus, all such particles have experiences for themselves.[16] Perhaps this entails that God is a sort of scattered object such that each particle of matter has its own "chip off the Old Block." Perhaps this is to be construed as emergent theism according to which God emerges as a new individual when particles of spirit/matter reach a certain level of complexity. Some panpsychists do, in fact, opt for this view. Perhaps it is a form of polytheism according to which each particle of matter has its own divine mind and the universe as a whole has its own World-Soul. This may be what Mormonism teaches because it is arguably a version of polytheistic panpsychism.[17]

However, one thing is clear: The panpsychist and classic theist ontology of omnipresence are very different. At the very least, (6) seems to imply that one can move from the former to the latter, but so far as I can discover, no argument is given for this claim. Moreover, (6) seems in some sense to equate the two versions of omnipresence, and that is simply false.

Argument (8) fails for at least two reasons that result from problems with "derives from" and "dynamic sensitivity." First, the claim that "the ability of living systems to feel and to experience derives from their dynamic sensitivity to their environment" is terribly ambiguous. The problem lies in "derives from" which seems capable of three interpretations. It may mean, "is ontologically grounded in and supervenient upon" in which case (8) asserts that the existence of feeling/experience in living systems and by extension, all physical systems, obtains in virtue of their dynamic sensitivity (causal interaction with their environment). But this interpretation is more consistent with emergent physicalism than with panpsychism since the latter takes the presence of mind/feeling/experience to be basic, indeed, just as basic as matter.

Alternatively, it may mean, "is epistemically justified on the basis of" in which case (8) asserts that our epistemic justification for attributing mentality to systems is their dynamic sensitivity. Elsewhere, Skrbina cites approvingly precisely this argument offered by C. S. Peirce. Peirce claimed that the dynamic sensitivity of protoplasm cannot be accounted for by mechanistic laws and, thus, we are forced to admit that physical events are but degraded or undeveloped forms of psychic events.[18] I will consider the epistemic grounds for this claim below.

That leaves us with interpretation three: "derives from" is to be understood as "is caused by" according to which there is a sort of causal interaction between physical inputs into a system and mental states caused by those inputs. Earlier, Skrbina seems to affirm some form of modal necessity in this interaction: "The dynamic sensitivity of protoplasm necessarily results in an enhanced capability for feeling."[19] Unfortunately, the causal interaction between mental and physical events (which is arguably contingent and not even physically necessary much less *de re* metaphysically necessary) neither explains why there is an interacting mental entity there in the first place nor does it alone justify claiming that it is there.

The second problem with (8) involves difficulties in clarifying dynamic sensitivity in a way needed for the argument to go through and in the exaggerated claims made about dynamic sensitivity. Let us construe "dynamic sensitivity" minimally as various sorts of efficient causal interactions—by contact, by forces—between one paradigm case physical particular and another. I think there is a point to (8) if its target is a version of strong physicalism that adopts a functionalist approach to mental kinds with only physical realizers and that provides efficient causal *reductions* of both intentionality and teleological behavior. In this case, the well-known problem of ascribing a mental life to a thermometer arises and does, I think, generalize. The problem is quite simply that efficient causal law-like relations obtain across the board and it is easy to adopt an intentional stance towards or to employ functional language for practically every physical particular in its environment.

However, if the rival is theistic dualism with irreducible intentionality, agent causation and genuinely purposive teleological behavior, then (8) fails. Why? Because on this view, there is a clear difference between full-blown mental subjects and purely physical objects, and this difference is adequate to bring in a dualist first-person argument for ascribing mental states to increasingly different subjects. To see this difference, consider Skrbina's discussion of (8) as employed by Whitehead.[20] According to Whitehead, there are "structured societies" which have dominant and sub-ordinate sub-societies. In such cases, the overall structure provides a protected environment that guards and sustains the sub-societies. As examples, Whitehead cites molecules, crystals, rocks, and the solar system as structured societies. The "dynamic sensitivity" of such structured societies consists at least in part in their developing such protective environments for the sake of guarding the sub-societies within them. All of this requires sentience.

As a theistic dualist, I must confess that it is hard to take this seriously. It is one thing for a group of people each with intentional concepts *of* danger, warfare, protection, building blueprints and so on, consciously, purposively, and with freely chosen cooperation to build a castle. It is quite another thing for a group of molecules under the right circumstances to form a crystal. Mechanistic explanations are fully adequate for the latter and quite inadequate for the former. I'm afraid it will take more than a few illustrations along with panpsychic assertions to convince me otherwise. And I suspect most others will be so inclined.

This leaves (11), the claim that a consensus has not been reached for hundreds of years because of serious problems with a Cartesian view of matter, and panpsychism gains viability by this failure. I have three things to say in response. First, if consensus is a necessary condition for "viability" in philosophy, we are all in trouble. Moreover, given the fact that panpsychist views have been around for at least twenty-five hundred years and throughout that period it has hardly been a consensus viewpoint, the viability test undermines panpsychism more than it does naturalism or classic theism.

Second, the main problem for dualism has been causal interaction, but in my view, this is the most exaggerated problem in the history of philosophy. Skrbina notwithstanding, traditional formulations of the problem have been adequately rebutted within both a Cartesian and non-Cartesian framework,[21] and more recent formulations of the problem (e.g. Kim's causal-pairing objection) have also been adequately addressed.[22] So Skrbina has misrepresented the actual dialectical situation.

Finally, given that panpsychism entails that all particulars have a physical and mental nature, and given that these natures are described in pretty standard terms that a naturalist and theistic dualist would recognize, panpsychism has the same problem of interaction that theistic dualists do. Panpsychism is merely a label for and not an explanation of the phenomena to be explained. As Geoffrey Madell notes, "the sense that the mental and the physical are just inexplicably and gratuitously slapped together is hardly allayed by adopting … a pan-psychist … view of the mind, for [it does not] have an explanation to offer as to why or how mental properties cohere with physical."[23]

Two arguments strongly in favor of classic theism

So much for the arguments I consider inadequate. We are left with two arguments I think are clearly in favor of classic theism over against panpsychism: (4) and (9). Let us look at them in reverse order. (9) asserts that a large number of major intellectuals have taken panpsychism to be intuitive or rational and this provides potentially convincing grounds for the view. Now I do not believe Skrbina is employing a bare-bones appeal to authority in (9). In fact, there is some plausibility for (9) if his assertion is charitably interpreted. If a large number of respected craftsmen in some field find a certain view to be rational or intuitive, this does carry some weight though it is admittedly hard to assess precisely how much. After all, there does appear to be such a thing as tacit knowledge or something closely akin to it, and counting noses need not be a mere sociological exercise.

So let us grant this point to Skrbina. The problem is that throughout the history of western philosophy (and other fields as well) from the Pre-Socratics to the present, classic theism has been dominant, and compared to "the large number of major intellectuals" who have found theism to be "rational and intuitive" panpsychists are as rare as hen's teeth. So if we employ (9) charitably understood, it supports classic theism.

That leaves us with (4)—a design argument according to which the ordered, complex, persistent nature of physical things suggests the presence of inherent mentality. It is not my purpose to defend the design argument *tout court*. Given that we are limiting our evaluation of (1)–(11) to the support they provide for panpsychism and classic theism, since both sides use their own form of the design argument, we may assume its effectiveness. Here is the question: Do the various sorts of design we find in the cosmos provide more support for inherent mentality or an external designer as its cause? Let us look at two cases: simple law-like order and other examples.

We may cite as examples of the former any system or sequence of events that is governed by regular law, e.g. the relationship among pressure, volume, and temperature in a gas or the formation of a water molecule when oxygen and hydrogen are combined. It may be that such cases may equally be explained by the two paradigms. I have a reservation, however. If such law-like behavior is due to inherent mentality, then it is hard to see why the inherent minds of each particle would not have freewill and the power of spontaneous action such that law-like behavior would not be predicted. This is no theoretical problem. As I mentioned above, Mormonism is a panpsychist view and certain Mormon thinkers such as Orsen Pratt tried to resolve this problem by simply asserting as a matter of brute fact that the plethora of minds just always choose to behave together in law-like ways.[24] Perhaps the resources of quantum theory could help the panpsychist here (minds at the quantum level exercise freedom but only in a way that is within quantum probabilities). But in any case, this is my reservation about calling it a draw.

However, when it comes to other cases of data apt for inferring design, it is clear that classic theism is better justified than inherent mentality. I have in mind two sorts of cases. The first is beauty. The second is harder to classify but, historically, it included the existence of wholes composed of heterogenous parts that mutually interact for the sake of an end relevant to the whole. In recent days, the category has included the existence of information and/or the existence of specified or irreducible complexity (the combination of low probability and independent specifiability).[25]

In non-question-begging cases where we observe the origin of phenomena within this category, it is the result of an external designer and not inherent mentality. The various works of art, the origin of books, machines and a host of entities that exhibit beauty, information or specified/irreducible complexity clearly come from an external designer. Indeed, a host of sciences requires this assumption along with criteria for inferring external intelligent causes from non-intelligent ones: forensic science, SETI, archeology, sociology, linguistics, psychology. These sciences and the observable phenomena cited above provide solid grounds for inferring an external designer and not inherent mentality for the beauty in the cosmos and for the fine-tuning of the universe, the information in biological systems, and the plethora of irreducibly complex structures in the world. I conclude, then, that (4) supports classic theism more than it does panpsychism.

Defeaters for Skrbina's defeaters of six arguments against panpsychism

We turn now to an examination of the arguments that have been raised against panpsychism. Skrbina lists six such arguments:[26]

(12) Inconclusive Analogy—The purported analogical basis between humans and other objects is groundless.
(13) Not Testable—There are no "new facts" or empirical basis on which to evaluate the panpsychist claim. Also known as the No Signs objection. This includes the assumption that non-verifiable theories are invalid in some fundamental sense.
(14) Physical Emergence—Emergence is in fact possible because we see it in other realms of the physical world; mind is not ontologically unique; hence, emergence of mind is conceivable.
(15) Combination Problem—Sub-minds, such as those of atoms, cannot be conceived to combine or sum into complex, unified minds such as humans have. Hence, panpsychism is not an adequate account of mind.
(16) Implausibility—Panpsychism is so implausible and counter-intuitive that it cannot be true. Also known as the *reductio ad absurdum* objection.
(17) Eternal Mystery—The mind-body problem is unsolvable in principle, and hence panpsychism, which purports to offer a solution, must be false.

I have already provided support for (12) in conjunction with my response to (1) (Indwelling Powers), (2) (Continuity), (4) (Design), and (8) (Dynamic Sensitivity) and will not rehearse those point here. Suffice it to say here that I agree with (12). And I have provided grounds for rejecting (17) in my treatment of (11) (Last Man Standing), so I set it aside as well. I shall address (14) (which is the other side of (5) (Non-Emergence)) and (7a) (consciousness cannot evolve from dead matter naturalistically described) below. That leaves (13), (15) and (16).

If (13) is understood as an expression of some sort of empiricism or scientism (e.g. verificationism) according to which ontology must be done within these epistemic constraints, then (13) if far less plausible today than thirty years ago. In that time, we have witnessed a remarkable revival in metaphysics, and philosophers seldom labor any longer within these constraints. Moreover, in chapter eight I shall argue for the Principles of Authority and Autonomy, roughly, the claims that in important cases, the claims of philosophy are authoritative with respect to or simply independent of the claims of science or those of more extreme versions of empiricism.

On the other hand, if we evaluate panpsychist claims about electrons, atoms, rocks, and other particulars at the other end of the scale of analogy from humans, I must confess that it is hard to see what sorts of evidence could be given that would justify panpsychist assertions over against materialistic ones. In making this claim, I take it that (13) limits the sort of evidence relevant to its assessment to those of the behavior, activity, forces of attraction/repulsion, combinatorial activities, requirements for moving or being at rest, and so on. The evidence from other arguments for panpsychism, e.g. Non-Emergence, is not relevant. Under these limitations, we face a sort of Turing Test problem for these sorts of entities. So (13) seems to me to carry some force.

(16) is the assertion that panpsychism is so implausible and counter-intuitive that it cannot be true. Now I grant that such judgments can be influenced by factors in the sociology of knowledge. When this occurs, it does blunt the normative epistemic force of appeals to plausibility judgments. But I do not think this acknowledgment captures why I and, I suspect, many others agree with (16). For one thing, I think it is so obvious that at least phenomenal consciousness is not physical, and that mind cannot emerge from naturalistically described matter according to the processes that constitute the naturalist Grand Story (see chapter one), that arguments (5) and (7a) provide strong grounds for rejecting strong naturalism. But for reasons already given, I do not believe there are adequate arguments to support panpsychism, and as I will note below, before the attempt to explain the origin of consciousness, the prior probability of classic theism vs. panpsychism is so superior, that there is a severe burden of proof on the latter. And relative to this disadvantage for panpsychism, it seems bizarre, incredible and ontologically bloated to claim, for example, that when atoms join to form molecules, or various parts join to form crystals, that this somehow involves consciously creating a protective, guarding environment for the relevant sub-systems.

We are left with (15)—the Combination Problem and the unity of the self for (at least some) macro-objects. I take this to be the Achilles' heel of panpsychism. There are different ways of stating the problem. For example, if each particle of matter has its own unified point of view, how do they combine to form the same sort of unity when they interact to form larger wholes, a unity that appears to be unanalyzable and primitive? How do low-order experiences of ultimate atomic simples combine to form a single, unified field of consciousness or a unified self in larger wholes? Some panpsychists hold that all composed objects above the level of atomic simples have their own unified consciousness while others distinguish mere mereological aggregates without such a unity from "true individuals" that have it. Those who make such a distinction face two additional problems: How does one characterize the difference between the two? How could "true individuals" arise from processes that are combinatorial?

As far as I can tell, panpsychists fall into two groups with respect to "true individuals" that genuinely have a unified point of view or even a unified self. First, there are those who reject such individuals and opt for a sort of pseudo-unity for humans and other macro-objects. For example, according to Skrbina, Charles Strong held that mind-stuff with innumerable feelings fuses to create higher-level psychological states that lack the ability to differentiate many feelings. Thus, the genuine unity of the higher state is not real; it is an illusion due to the inability to perceive the multiplicity of individual experiences. It is far from clear what it is that has this illusion, but in any case, that is the view. Orson Pratt held that the unity of consciousness, free will and so forth of humans is really the collective agreement of one's atomic simples to act or move into the same sentient state simultaneously. Somehow, each simple interacts and communicates with all the others and, as a result, change in unison.[27]

Others believe in such individuals with "genuine unity" and have solved the unification problem in a number of ways:

(a) somehow a dominant monad arises;
(b) such unity obtains when a certain compactness and intensity of attraction is reached;
(c) mind-stuff with actual or potential mentality just fuses in the right circumstances;
(d) the latent soul/spiritual substance in each atomic simple unite to become a fully animated unity when absorbed into the body of an animal or plant;
(e) the quantum principle of superposition.

Interestingly, Skrbina points out that William Seager—one of the today's leading panpsychists—takes the Combination Problem to be a real "show-stopper" for panpsychism, but Seager and Skrbina hold that superposition and related quantum notions is the way forward towards a solution.[28]

It is hard to know how to respond to these "solutions." But as a start, it is important to note that the Combination Problem has been around since Democritus, it is a very serious metaphysical conundrum, and Aristotle's distinction between a metaphysical treatment of mere aggregates and genuine substances may well be the best sort of solution we have to the problem. Unfortunately, such a solution entails that if one is limited to combinatorial processes governing atomic simples (whether physical or psycho-physical), various systems up the hierarchy will not exhibit genuine substantial unity.

The problem is in trying to conceive just how it could be that the mere spatial arrangement of parts to form a different spatial ordering could be sufficient to generate a new kind of primitive unity. This difficulty seems almost self-evident to me and I do not know how to argue for it in terms that are more basic. However, the longevity of the Combination Problem bears witness to the fact that for centuries, many thinkers have acknowledged the severity of this issue and the correctness of this conceptual insight.

If this is correct, then a panpsychist ought to opt for a "pseudo-unity" position. Unfortunately, it is difficult to take the unity of consciousness or the self to be unreal. In fact, it is hard to see how anything could be more epistemically basic than our knowledge of such unity. And as I said above, it is difficult to see how the illusion of unity could arise? Surely, the individual members of one's combinatorial group do not suffer such delusion, and if there just is no unified consciousness or self, it is hard to see what has the illusion.

Alternatively, if one opts for "true individuals," then, curiously, the panpsychist account of their coming-to-be is in bed with the mechanistic view of the ontology and generation of purely physical macro-wholes: both resort to combinatorial solutions, external relational connections, and atomic parts that have (actually or potentially) the stuff characteristic of the whole. Again, the problem here is that we clearly understand the combinatorial story, and all it can do is provide an account of "the generation of conjunction from disjunction," that is, the appearance of mereological aggregates without a primitive, *sui generis* unity characteristic of this panpsychist option. Moreover, the alleged panpsychist "accounts" listed above are either question-begging assertions or misleading proposals.

In my view, (a)–(d) above are question-begging and amount to little more than hand-waving magic (without a Magician!). The superposition alternative that is alleged to be so promising is actually misleading. In its basic form, the quantum principle of superposition is just the claim that when waves meet their amplitudes add. Thus, two waves "combine" to form one wave in the mere sense that at every point the new wave's amplitude is the sum of those of the two waves. Superposition is merely additive summation, precisely the sort of combination that forms mereological aggregates. This not the sort of unification needed to generate a "true individual" and it is misleading to claim otherwise.

Before I leave this topic, I should say that the Combination Problem is not limited to the category of individual. Just as problems of causal interaction (that allegedly arise for Cartesian minds and bodies) are equally problematic for the emergence of *sui generis* properties, so combinatorial difficulties surface with emergent properties. There is a two-fold source of trouble for *sui generis* emergent properties: they are non-structural, simple and unique (e.g. normative properties, secondary qualities, consciousness); their origin must be explained by purely natural, combinatorial processes without the aid of Divine action, processes that are suitable only for structural properties.

There are three major views of the generation of emergent properties relevant to our discussion. First, micro-base entities and the laws governing their interaction lack the actuality of or potentiality for the emergent property; nevertheless, under the right circumstances the emergent property just appears. Second, each micro-particular with its micro-properties has the potentiality for the emergent property and under the right combinatorial circumstances, they jointly bring about the exemplification of the emergent property. Third, each micro-particular with its micro-properties is always actually striving, as it were, to bring about the exemplification of the emergent property, but their joint activity becomes effective only under the right combinatorial circumstances.

I have argued already that if one is going to operate within the constraints of a legitimate and plausible version of naturalism, the first alternative must be adopted if one is going to quantify over emergent properties. But option one faces the "getting-something-from-nothing" problem. Limiting our discussion to emergent mental properties, the problem may be put this way: Let P's and M's stand for purely physical and mental properties, respectively. Given that micro-particulars, micro-properties, micro-processes and micro-laws are characterized by and only by P's, effects of such and only such processes will also be characterized by and only by P's. If some entity appears that must be characterized by one or more of the M's, then this entity is not an effect solely of the micro-particulars, micro-properties, micro-processes and micro-laws characterized by and only by P's.

Solutions two and three are attempts to avoid this difficulty. But they face two objections. First, they are no longer naturalist positions. I have argued for this claim repeatedly, and at the close of this chapter I will reinforce this assertion by showing that panpsychism is not a version of naturalism. Second, they still face the Combination Problem, but now in the category of property. Recall that in chapter four, according to Timothy O'Connor, if an emergent property is depicted as contingently linked to the base properties causing it to emerge, then apart from an appeal to God's contingent choice that things be so and to God's stable intention that they continue to be so, there will be no explanation for the link itself or its constancy.

I agree with O'Connor, but I think a similar point applies to the Combination Problem: If a *sui generis* emergent property or a new "true individual" is acknowledged and its appearance is correlated with a certain set of circumstances formed by combinatorial processes acting on myriads and myriads of subvenient entities, then apart from an appeal to God's contingent choice that things be so and to God's stable intention that they continue to be so, there will be no explanation—naturalistic, panpsychist, or otherwise—for its appearance or constancy.

So far I have contended that the combined weight of the arguments for panpsychism actually provide more support for classic theism and that there are good arguments against panpsychism that justify rejecting it if classic theism is the only rival in view. Before we leave Skrbina's presentation of panpsychism, I want to make three concluding points. First, the enduring presence of panpsychism provides evidence that there is a legitimate philosophical problem for which it is a plausible solution. That problem is captured by (5), (7a) and (14) all of which center on the problem of emergent consciousness given strong naturalism. This entire book is an attempt to show that consciousness cannot emerge from matter and material processes as they are depicted by strong naturalism. Thus, the presence of, say, human consciousness supports both classic theism and panpsychism and provides a defeater for strong naturalism. Second, as I just noted above, if we limit ourselves to the arguments for and against panpsychism, finite consciousness provides more evidence for classic theism than for panpsychism. Finally, even if the arguments regarding consciousness were equally supportive of classic theism and panpsychism, I believe that all things considered, there is more evidence for the former than for the latter.

It is beyond the scope of this book to provide anything even approximating a defense of this last assertion. I have already provided sources for such a defense.[29] Here I make two observations. For one thing, the phenomena employed in arguments for the theistic God go far beyond those in support of panpsychism, e.g. the origin and contingency of the cosmos, design, various aspects of the moral life, religious experience, miracles, and so forth. Panpsychism is primarily an attempt to explain consciousness and classic theism does this and much more. Moreover, when one ventures beyond this to include the phenomena of design, dynamic sensitivity, indwelling powers, and so forth, I have argued that classic theism is superior in these areas.

Secondly, I think classic theism is vastly superior to panpsychism as the different candidates for the ultimate stopping place, the system's brute fact. If I understand panpsychism correctly, the psycho-physical cosmos is the system's brute fact. But for three reasons, this appears to be a contingent brute fact. For one thing, based on a) the most plausible interpretation of the Big Bang; b) the second law of thermodynamics applied to the cosmos; c) arguments for the impossibility of traversing an actually infinite series of events; and d) arguments for the impossibility of an actually infinite set of members such as temporal events that are finite and contingent; it follows that the cosmos came into existence, and whatever comes into existence is contingent.[30]

Moreover, the actual world is clearly only one of many possible worlds. Worlds that are minimal physical duplicates of our world are a small range of all possible worlds. For example, compared to the necessary laws of logic, mathematics, and general ontology, physical laws are contingent, indeed.

Finally, the existence of finite consciousness in the cosmos along with its specific connection to particular physical entities seems contingent (e.g. in light of zombie worlds, inverted qualia worlds, modal arguments from the possibility of disembodied existence, arguments from the insufficiency of physical conditions to determine alternative possibilities that follow from the exercise or refraining from the exercise of agent causal power).

Setting aside issues surrounding the precise formulation and defense of the Principle(s) of Sufficient Reason, it just seems to be a bad idea to have a contingent brute fact. It also is a problem in light of the transitivity of *per se* regresses as we saw in chapter five. There is one exception to this rule, and that is the actions of a libertarian agent. Theism provides a brilliant solution to the need for a necessary being as the appropriate brute fact and the need for a contingent explanation for the three aspects of contingency cited above. The God of classic theism is (at least) a *de re* necessary being, and his acts of bringing the cosmos into being, sustaining it, and causing the existence of finite consciousness along with the precise mental/physical correlations that obtain in the cosmos are all libertarian acts. Thus, they provide a contingent explanation for these contingent facts. I believe that in this way, classic theism provides a better account of bruteness than does panpsychism.

Panpsychism as a version of naturalism

I think that the days of strict physicalism are drawing to a close. For sixty years or so, we have been through several epicycles of strong naturalism—behaviorism, type identity physicalism, anomalous monism (construed anti-realistically), eliminative materialism, a cottage industry of versions of functionalism (with only physical realizers), and so on. These have all failed and more and more philosophers are embracing (at least emergent) property dualism for (at least) phenomenal consciousness.

In my view, the enduring appeal of panpsychism and of AC bears witness to the fact that consciousness is real, irreducibly mental, and completely incapable of explanation within a naturalist framework. Thus, the move to property dualism represents the falsification of naturalism and not merely an appropriate revision of it. Since naturalists claim superiority for their worldview on the grounds of its comportment with empirical data, the movement towards property dualism is an inappropriate *ad hoc* adjustment of naturalism that heads in the direction of unfalsifiability. This is to shift towards lessening naturalism's empirical content and, thus, towards weakening its claim to hegemony.

If a naturalist posits mental properties or potentialities as basic, then in light of the background issues discussed in chapters one and two, he has opted for a version of panpsychism and abandoned naturalism. Historically speaking, whether weak or strong, panpsychism has always been taken as a rival to a positive form of naturalism. Positive naturalism is not content with the mere negative denial of God's existence. It also seeks to provide a positive vision of what is real and how things came to be. Such a form of naturalism has always been combinatorial, mechanistic, and physicalistic. Thus, Skrbina notes that "throughout history, panpsychism has, at almost every point, served as an antipode" to a naturalistic, mechanistic view of reality.[31]

For example, even though the earliest atomists—Democritus and Leucippus—may have retained the notion of a soul-like entity for spherical atoms (being soul-like, spherical atoms were self-movers and capable of explaining motion itself), by carefully distinguishing spherical from other atoms and describing the latter in purely mechanistic terms, they made very clear the atomistic, dead, mechanistic nature of purely physical atoms. During the rise of the mechanical philosophy in the seventeenth and eighteenth centuries, whether it was inert corpuscularianism, dynamic corpuscularianism, or the point-particles of Boscovich, strong naturalists were careful to distinguish their views of matter from those of the panpsychists.

Thus, throughout history, positive naturalism and panpsychism have been rivals, and advocates of the former went to great lengths to characterize physical particles and forces in ways that avoided the slightest hint of panpsychism. Regarding physical particles, they have been characterized as dead, insensitive, lifeless, inert (not-self movers) stuff exhaustively describable in third-person language, and subject to laws expressed in mathematical form. Completely absent is any hint of mental properties or potentialities. Regarding forces, they have been characterized to avoid non-metaphorical mental description, irreducible entelechies, substantial forms, and causal powers beyond passive liabilities, specifically, active agent-causal power. Thus, these forces are "blind," efficiently causal and law-like. When we talk in terms of chemical *affinity*, or forces of *attraction* and *repulsion*, we do not speak literally. Historically, one of the intellectual motivating factors for avoiding action at a distance was to preserve the purely physical nature of material forces.

Finally, since the earliest days of panpsychism, there has been an intellectual tendency towards postulating either a world-soul or some version of finite theism. This tendency is hard to avoid. Once you quantify over mental potentialities or actual properties, as long as you set aside the Combination Problem, there is no *a priori* way to draw a line as to where the emergence of new individuals must stop. And given a number of factors, e.g. religious experience, some form of emergent deity is quite plausible. Most naturalists seem unaware of the fact that if one allows the camel's nose under the tent in the form of (at least) basic mental potentialities that ground emergent mental properties, it is hard to stop the inevitable slide toward emergent theism. It seems, then, that solving the problem of emergence by opting for basic mental potentialities amounts to a rejecting of naturalism and not an appropriate adjustment to it.

7 Philip Clayton and pluralistic emergentist monism

In recent years, Philip Clayton has established himself as the leading thinker on behalf of a view that tries to steer a *via media* between strong physicalism and theistic substance dualism. Beside AC, of all the positions considered thus far, his is the most plausible. Nevertheless, after laying out his position, I shall argue that it is not a version of serious, explanatory naturalism, highlight its difficulties, and show that theism and AC are preferable to it.[1]

Clayton's pluralistic emergentist monism

Précis of Clayton's view

Clayton is dissatisfied with substance dualism and reductive physicalism because the former has been rendered implausible by the increasingly precise correlations between states of the central nervous system and mental states, and the latter leaves out our first-person experience of being conscious agents in the world.[2] In their place, he defends "the thesis that mind—causally efficacious mental properties—emerges from the natural world, as a further step in the process of evolution."[3] More generally, Clayton is committed to a pluralistic version of emergentist monism.[4] According to Clayton's view, reality consists of one basic kind of stuff, of which descriptions in physics are not fundamental or sufficient, and from which a plethora of *sui generis* emergent properties arise through entirely natural processes[5] that are incapable of explanation in physics.[6]

For Clayton, mental properties emerge from a substrate that is neither mental nor physical[7] and this implies that we should not assume that "the entities postulated by physics complete the inventory of what exists."[8] By proffering pluralistic emergentist monism, Clayton means to reject strong physicalism along with the primacy of physics,[9] the unity of science,[10] substance dualism,[11] panpsychism,[12] the causal closure of physics[13] and weak and strong property supervenience when associated with a rejection of top/down causation.[14]

Six central features of pluralistic emergentist monism

We may grasp more thoroughly Clayton's pluralistic emergentist monism by elaborating on six aspects of his position. To begin with, Clayton claims that "emergentists should be monists but not physicalists"[15] because, "the one 'stuff' of the world actually plays a greater diversity of causal roles in the world than old-time materialists thought (and, sadly, still think)."[16] Moreover, "the one 'stuff' of the world takes a wide variety of forms and manifests some amazing features."[17] Along with the descriptions of the previous paragraph, this gives the precise sense in which Clayton is a monist.

Regarding emergence, although Clayton sometimes defines emergentism in terms of new, distinct laws and causal forces,[18] he usually characterizes his position primarily in terms of emergent properties, and I shall accept this characterization as the correct depiction of his position. Clayton admits that weak emergence (emergent properties are epiphenomenal) is the default position, and strong emergentism (emergent properties have new top/down causal powers) sustains a burden of proof relative to weak emergentism "which is the position to beat."[19] Nevertheless, he defends strong emergentism[20] along with downward causation, which amounts to "*the process whereby some whole has an active non-additive causal influence on its parts.*"[21] "*Emergence just is that pattern that recurs across a wide range of scientific (and non-scientific) fields.*"[22] Emergent properties are irreducible to and completely unpredictable from their subvenient base.[23]

Clayton accepts the standard mereological hierarchy and claims that emergent properties/laws/causal powers appear at various levels in the hierarchy. In this way, he is an ontological pluralist according to which there are many different levels—perhaps as many as two dozen or more—which exhibit not only radically different sorts of emergent properties, but also radically different sorts of emergence. Thus, "emergence" should be viewed as a term of family resemblance.[24] Still, Clayton offers the following as a characterization of broad similarities shared in common by most instances of emergence in natural history:[25] For any two levels, L_1 and L_2 where L_2 emerges from L_1:

(a) L_1 is prior in natural history.
(b) L_2 depends on L_1, such that if the states in L_1 did not exist, the qualities in L_2 would not exist.
(c) L_2 is the result of a sufficient degree of complexity in L_1. In many cases one can even identify a particular level of criticality which, when reached, will cause the system to begin manifesting new emergent properties.
(d) One can sometimes predict the emergence of some new or emergent qualities based on what one knows about L_1. But using L_1 alone, one will not be able to predict (i) the precise nature of those qualities, (ii) the rules that govern their interaction (or their phenomenological patterns),

or (iii) the sorts of emergent levels to which they in turn may give rise in due course.

(e) L_2 is not reducible to L_1 in any of the standard senses of "*reduction*" in the philosophy of science literature: causal, explanatory, metaphysical, or ontological *reduction*.

According to Clayton, there may be as many as twenty-eight distinct levels of emergence, but for his version of emergentism to be true, there must be at least three such levels[26] or else the view collapses into dualism or panpsychism which, allegedly, believe in only two different sorts of properties and causes—mental and physical. Thus, the plurality of emergent properties is among the features of Clayton's position that make it different from dualism and panpsychism. It is clear that Clayton's emergentism is a paradigm case of a shopping-list ontology (see chapter one).

Third, evolution plays a critical role in Clayton's emergentism. Partly to offset the starkness of the appearance of consciousness, Clayton argues that emergent properties have arisen often in the evolutionary history of the world. Thus, "consciousness is in one sense 'just another emergent level', emergence theory is not dualism in disguise."[27] In fact, evolution is so central to Clayton's position that he incorporates it into the characterization of strong emergence: "Strong emergentists maintain that evolution in the cosmos produces new, ontologically distinct levels, which are characterized by their own laws or regularities or causal forces."[28] Again, "Emergence is a repeating pattern that connects the various levels of evolution in the cosmos."[29] Elsewhere, Clayton states that "It is not possible to engage in reflection on the relationship of mind and brain without considering the evolutionary history that produced brains in the first place."[30] Finally,

> Explaining the supervenience of the mental on the physical, understood as an example of evolutionary emergence, therefore requires a diachronic as well as a synchronic perspective. Mental properties depend upon the entire natural history that caused increasingly complex brains and central nervous systems to evolve … This evolutionary dependency is neither logical nor metaphysical. … Rather, the assertion of both a diachronic and a synchronic dependence of mental properties is our best reconstruction of the highly contingent natural history that produced organisms like *homo sapiens*. Therefore we might best label the resulting position as *emergentist supervenience*.[31]

Fourth, Clayton's view is consistent with and embraces emergent theism. At the very least, pluralistic emergentist monism is consistent with the employment of divine predicates with respect to the one "natural" world.[32] This may be understood in pantheistic, panentheistic, e.g. dipolar, or World-Soul terms. Clayton is clear that the phenomena of religious experience do not require such a higher level of emergence, but religious experience and other phenomena point to and open the door for some sort of emergent deity.[33] However, if we use certain metaphysical arguments that justify belief in a God who is the ultimate ground and support of the universe, this move supports theistic dualism and not an emergent deity since such a divine being exists independently of the cosmos and, thus, is more like the God of classic theism than some emergent being.

According to Clayton, if we use "spirit" to stand for a new kind of substantial entity beyond human culture and mind, then emergentism does not provide justification for such a being. Emergentism merely supports the extension of emergence to a higher-level beyond the human level, and the use of "deity" to refer to a quality that the universe progressively instantiates. Since emergence is in the category of property and not substance, emergentism provides analogous support for this latter notion of deity and not the idea of a substantial spirit or mind.[34] Emergentism supports the increasing deification of the universe but not the existence of an independent substantial God.

Clayton concludes that the success of the sciences of emergence provides some justification for such deification,[35] but he also considers the question of whether such success is capable of a different metaphysical interpretation ranging from different non-naturalist worldviews to classic theism. If the answer to these questions is "yes," says Clayton, then emergentism provides grounds for placing limits on scientific explanation and, thereby, it provides further justification for employing additional arguments to support a metaphysic that is even further away from naturalism than is a deified universe. In this case, there may be additional facts about the cosmos that a non-naturalist metaphysic explains and a naturalist worldview does not.

Clayton suggests that there are at least four non-deflationary sorts of questions that naturalism fails to answer adequately and which provide evidence for theistic dualism (classic theism): (1) Why is there anything at all[36] and what caused the Big Bang?[37] (2) How can there be objective ethical obligation and irreducible "oughts" given the inadequacy of a purely naturalist ontology to account for such things? (3) How can we account for the ubiquity and temporally pervasive existence of powerful religious experiences? (4) How are we to explain and satisfactorily provide a response to the human longing for meaning and purpose in life? How are we to explain the adequacy of our sensory and cognitive faculties for gaining truth about reality?

Given the long history of solid philosophical arguments against naturalism, given that emergent pluralism justifies rejection of strong naturalism, and given that these four areas cannot be adequately addressed within naturalism but are adequately explained by theistic dualism (roughly, classic theism), Clayton rejects naturalism in favor of theistic dualism.[38] According to Clayton, emergent pluralism plays an important role in supporting theistic dualism because it weakens the explanatory power of strong naturalism and reductive physicalism and provides grounds for considering these broader questions that justify theistic dualism.[39]

The fifth and sixth aspects of Clayton's position involve his methodology and theory of existence and they may be stated briefly. Regarding methodology, Clayton believes that the sciences are authoritative within their proper domains, that there are limits on science, and that debates regarding the reality and origin of consciousness involve both scientific and philosophical considerations. At the very center of Clayton's methodology is a radical shopping-list approach to ontology. This is clear in his fervent rejection of strong naturalism in favor of a number of levels at which there are *sui generis* properties, laws, causal powers, types of emergence and scientific methods appropriate for studying entities at those various levels.[40] Regarding existence, Clayton adopts a causal theory of existence according to which something exists if and only if it has causal powers.[41]

Pluralistic emergentist monism as a rival to strong naturalism

Clayton and minimalist naturalism

To put the matter forthrightly: Clayton's ontology is so bloated that virtually all serious naturalists—those who take naturalism to be superior precisely because of its explanatory power derived from methodological and epistemic considerations in physics and chemistry and the combinatorial processes that drive the Grand Story—will see it as a non-naturalist view and not a legitimate version of a naturalism. Moreover, as we shall see below, there is no scientific evidence at all for emergent properties construed as Clayton does, and without such evidence, not even his attenuated naturalism is epistemically obligatory. Clayton's naturalism is clearly not of the strong sort and I think that he fails to see the centrality of reductive physicalism for justifying the explanatory superiority of naturalism. And since Clayton is a theist, he is not a naturalist in this sense either.

So exactly why does Clayton think his position is a naturalist one? His naturalism is minimalist: Emergent properties are naturally produced by processes of nature alone;[42] the natural world alone accounts for emergence[43] and, in this sense, biologists should say they are naturalists and not physicalists;[44] emergence theory is to be defended on the basis of contemporary science which points to the natural world alone as the source of emergent properties;[45] emergence theory implies that the causal history of the appearance of all entities in the natural world is knowable by science, and without this implication science itself could not be practiced.[46]

Problems with Clayton's methodology

Clayton's methodology and ontology will prevent serious or strong naturalists from accepting his views as naturalistic. Regarding methodology,

Clayton's emergentism is an extreme form of a shopping-list approach to ontology that rests content to pile up numerous cases of *sui generis* properties, forms of emergence, and law-like contingent correlations all the while resting content to label them as brute facts. Clayton opines that there may be as many as twenty-eight different levels of emergence and dozens of different sorts of emergence. This shopping-list approach fails to grasp the centrality of ontological simplicity, reductive physicalism (whether Nagelian as support for property identities or functional realization *reduction* with only physical realizers), the adequacy of third-person knowledge,[47] causal closure, mechanistic modes of explanation, and combinatorial processes for justifying naturalism's claim to explanatory and epistemic superiority.

It is worth recalling Timothy O'Connor's insight once more: If an emergent property is depicted in such a way as to be contingently linked to the base properties causing it to emerge, then apart from an appeal to God's contingent choice that things be so and to God's stable intention that they continue to be so, there will be no explanation for the link itself or its constancy. Otherwise, you end up with a mere shopping list of facts that need to be explained.

Correlations in science, especially those involving an emergent property, are merely contingently linked phenomena as such, and, thus, they are the things that need to be explained. The correlation between pressure and temperature in the ideal gas equation is not an explanation of the sort needed to justify a naturalist worldview. The atomic model of gases provides what is needed. The model transforms what appear to be contingent correlations into real explanations that show why pressure *must* be such-and-such given that the temperature (and volume) is thus and so. However, given the complete unpredictability of emergent properties from exhaustive knowledge of their subvenient bases, such explanations will not be forthcoming, and one has an ontology with a lot of contingent, unique brute facts, a situation that can be solved by a theistic explanation but not a naturalist one.

Clayton also misunderstands the methodological and explanatory resources of evolutionary theory. While he acknowledges that the evolutionary dependence of emergent properties such as mental ones are not metaphysically or logically dependent upon their evolutionary histories, he still claims in several places that "Strong emergentists maintain that evolution in the cosmos produces new, ontologically distinct levels, which are characterized by their own laws or regularities or causal forces."[48] Again, "It is not possible to engage in reflection on the relationship of mind and brain without considering the evolutionary history that produced brains in the first place."[49]

Unfortunately, Clayton's employment of evolution fails to grasp the central problematic for such employment, a problematic that is correctly stated by Colin McGinn (see chapter five). It is not hard to see how an evolutionary account with its combinatorial processes could be given for new and increasingly complex physical structures that constitute different organisms. However, organisms are black boxes as far as evolution is concerned. As long as an organism, when receiving certain inputs, generates the correct behavioral outputs under the demands of fighting, fleeing, reproducing and feeding, the organism will survive. What goes on inside the organism is irrelevant and only becomes significant for the processes of evolution when an output is produced. Strictly speaking, it is the output, not what caused it, which bears on the struggle for reproductive advantage. Moreover, the functions that organisms carry out consciously *could just as well have been done unconsciously*. Thus, both the sheer existence of conscious states and the precise mental content that constitutes them is outside the limits of evolutionary explanation.

Given consciousness and its causal powers, one could give an evolutionary explanation of why certain mental states would be selected over others in the struggle for reproductive advantage. What cannot be explained is why consciousness exists in the first place. Evolution in particular, and combinatorial processes in general are simply inadequate to explain the hard problem of consciousness and, more generally, any *sui generis*, simple, emergent property.[50] Moreover, given the combinatorial processes involved in the Grand Story, such processes are apt for explaining the origin of combinatorial structures constituted by external relations. What they cannot explain is the appearance of a new, *simple* property.

Clayton employs the term "combinatorial novelty"[51] to express the idea that when suitable combinatorial complexity obtains, an emergent property arises, but this is just a label for the problem and not an explanation. If fact, "suitable complexity" is an *ad hoc* notion that is far from enlightening. Given Clayton's view of the complete unpredictability of emergent properties from exhaustive knowledge of the correlated subvenient base, the only way to identity "suitable complexity" is to register the complexity after discovering the emergent property. "Suitable complexity" is a definite description that means, "whatever the complexity is that is associated with the relevant emergent property" and, as such, is hardly enlightening. The real question is why the emergent property arises in the first place, and naturalism is silent about that question. Clayton's "explanatory pluralism" fails to explain anything and merely amounts to providing labels for a wide variety of *sui generis* entities.

It is ironic that Clayton proffers emergent pluralism as having explanatory superiority to theistic dualism which Clayton characterizes as entailing two theses: substance as well as property dualism, and a rejection of emergent pluralism in favor of the view that mental and physical properties are the only sorts there are.[52] While the latter claim may apply to very narrow Cartesians, there is nothing about property or substance dualism that entails a rejection of a plurality of properties, and Clayton is wrong if he things otherwise. I, for one, am among those substance dualists who accept a plurality of sorts of properties besides physical and mental.

Now it is the former claim (emergent pluralism has greater explanatory power than theistic dualism and AC) that represents a serious error in Clayton's attempt to wed pluralism and naturalism together. Clayton argues that if there are not a number of levels of emergence in the natural world and consciousness is the only clear case, then this would support a dualist ontology and, indeed, a theistic dualist explanation of the origin of consciousness. Why? This one case would be so novel that it would be question-begging and implausible to claim to have a naturalistic explanation of consciousness. What Clayton fails to see, however, is that by quantifying over numerous cases of emergent properties and forms of emergence, he is actually providing further cases of radical novelty and such cases provide additional grounds for a theistic explanation. What makes them radical is not their number but their uniqueness coupled with the inadequacy of naturalism to account for them.

This is clearly grasped by tough-minded naturalists. As I have noted earlier, Frank Jackson correctly sees that if naturalism is to be embraced, it must give reductive or eliminative treatments of all *sui generis* emergent properties, and he explicitly does this for consciousness, secondary qualities and various "normative" properties.[53] By multiplying cases of emergence, Clayton may provide fodder for people to be psychologically used to novel properties, and in this sense, the origin of consciousness may not be psychologically surprising. But McGinn's insight that the origin of consciousness cannot be explained by scientific naturalism (Given the Grand Story, why do *any* physical structures give rise to consciousness?) applies with equal force to normative properties, secondary qualities and the two dozen or so cases of emergent properties and sorts of emergence mentioned by Clayton. By multiplying cases of emergence, Clayton actually provides multiple cases of phenomena suitable for theistic explanations beyond consciousness.

It is important to recall that the unpredictability of emergent properties—something that Clayton accepts—is an ontological and not merely an epistemological principle. Properly understood, it is the claim that emergent properties really are *sui generis*, and no matter what we learn in the future, no reductive analysis of them will be forthcoming. This straightforward ontological claim is sometimes expressed in terms of unpredictability in the God's-eye sense. That is, given exhaustive knowledge of the ontological nature of particulars, properties, relations, processes and laws at the subvenient level, nothing follows about the presence or absence of the emergent entity.

Relative to the subvenient ontology, it is genuinely different and new, and the ontological difference means that subvenient processes by themselves cannot give rise to the emergent entity. And if one postulates an emergent potentiality at the subvenient level, neither the potential property nor the fact that it is actualized by subvenient processes can be predicted or known from an exhaustive description of the rest of the subvenient base, or given any naturalistic explanation whatsoever. All a naturalist can do with emergent properties is provide contingent correlations between the emergent entity and subvenient factors. No real explanation can be offered. In the case of emergent properties, epistemic unpredictability translates into ontological contingency. Curiously, Clayton admits this in one place: "At most one will be able to establish a series of *correlations* between brain states and phenomenal experiences as reported by subjects."[54] And by embracing ontological pluralism, he multiplies the problem.

Problems with Clayton's ontology

So much for Clayton's methodology. There are also aspects of his ontology that rule it out as a viable naturalist one, and we have already ventured into discussing some of them in our investigation of his methodology. Several aspects of Clayton's ontology cannot be incorporated into a naturalist ontology in light of considerations we saw in chapters one and two:

(a) a rejection of a physicalist in favor of a monist description of the fundamental stuff;
(b) an unwieldy pluralism that defies mechanistic, physicalist, combinatorial explanation and, thus, cannot be located in the Grand Story;
(c) all sorts of top/down causation along with a rejection of the causal closure of the physical (i.e. the physics-al); acceptance of cultural causation;[55]
(d) the idea that the causal processes of evolution have been superseded by dynamic causal processes of cultural evolution, according to which, ideas, institutions, language, and art forms have unique causal powers that contribute to the flow of human history in a distinctively non-physical way;
(e) the possibility of an emergent deity in a pantheist, panentheist or World-Soul sort of way; and
(f) certain facts about the world that transcend the limits of scientific explanation and provide grounds for theism.

Further difficulties for Clayton's pluralistic emergentist monism

There are at least three further problematic areas for Clayton's position: a misrepresentation of dualism; problems with his characterization and employment of emergence; and difficulties with the mereological hierarchy in the category of individual.

Misrepresentation of dualism

Regarding dualism, when one is going to reject a philosophical position, one should present the strongest and not a weaker version of that position, and one should not generalize that weaker version as representative of all who hold the targeted viewpoint. But this is exactly what Clayton does.

Clayton presents dualism as entailing two theses:

(1) the cosmos is characterized by two and only two different sorts of properties—mental and physical—and there is an absolute dividing line between them;
(2) the mind is not a property but, rather, an immaterial, non-physical, substantial object that is outside space and time, independent of matter and is not composed of parts[56]

Now certain extreme forms of Cartesianism may satisfy Clayton's characterization, but I do not know of a single contemporary Cartesian dualism that would identify with this description. And there have been and are other forms of dualism, e.g. Thomistic, that quantify over substantial souls and a pluralistic ontology quite contrary to (1).[57]

Moreover, if "absolute dividing line" is interpreted to mean that mental and physical properties are quite different ontologically speaking, then dualists do accept "the absolute dividing line" between them, but so does Clayton.[58] If the definite description is interpreted to mean "so different that the mental cannot emerge from the physical," then Clayton's description amounts to a false and question-begging assertion. William Hasker's substance dualism entails that a substantial mind emerges from a certain level of complexity that actualizes the mental potentiality for that substantial mind, and Hasker does not believe there is an adequate naturalistic explanation for that potentiality or its emergence.[59] But he is still an emergentist of a sort. It would be question-begging for Clayton simply to dig his heels in and say that Hasker is not a real emergentist. After all, Clayton acknowledges that emergence is a family resemblance, and Hasker's is a non-naturalistic member of that family.

Finally, Clayton's representation of a mental substance is false on four counts:

(1) no one holds that finite substantial minds exist outside of time;
(2) many dualists hold that while not spatially extended, the mind is spatially located (and some, e.g. Hasker, hold that the mind is extended);
(3) the mind is not composed of separable parts, but it is composed of inseparable parts (a distinction with which Clayton is apparently unfamiliar); and
(4) the mind is not independent of the brain/body in the sense that there is no deep, holistic, functional/causal interaction from mind to body and conversely.

Incredibly, Clayton asserts that the increasingly precise correlations between mental and neurological phenomena provide defeasible yet strong evidence against dualism, but this is a wildly inaccurate strawman. Clayton is invited to cite one contemporary dualism that would have the slightest objection against the correlations we have discovered.

Clayton's strawman presentation of dualism is not tangential to his views. Indeed, he is able to "establish" the mereological hierarchy and emergentism only if he can both distinguish his views from dualism and show dualism to be out of touch with advances in science. But when dualism is correctly presented, it is every bit as much in harmony with the sciences as emergentism. There is more on this below.

Three problems with Clayton's employment of emergence

Regarding emergence, three difficulties undermine Clayton's attempt to provide a position that is superior to theistic dualism and AC. First, there is a growing consensus among philosophers of mind that "emergence" (the point is often made regarding supervenience) is nothing but a name for the problem and not a genuine solution. Given that Clayton's description of mental properties is the one property dualists employ, and given that he accepts the so-called hard problem of consciousness, it is hard to see how Clayton can avoid this objection. In fact, since his pluralist ontology quantifies over a multiplicity of novel, simple emergent properties incapable of combinatorial explanation and completely unpredictable from an exhaustive knowledge of their subvenient bases, Clayton's view entails a multitude of hard problems.

In my opinion, emergentists, Clayton included, have been slow to acknowledge this problem because the regular observation of the relevant correlations provides a psychological expectation of and an ability to predict future instances of the correlations, but unless one is willing to accept a Humean view of causation, this stops far short of providing an explanation of the correlations. I may be wrong about this, but I believe something like a lack of psychological surprise at the emergence of consciousness relative to pluralistic emergence compared to Clayton's depiction of dualism blinds Clayton to the fact that plural emergence makes the explanatory problem worse and not better.

Second, there are problems with Clayton's characterization of emergence. Recall that according to Clayton, for any two levels, L_1 and L_2 where L_2 emerges from L_1:

(a) L_1 is prior in natural history.
(b) L_2 depends on L_1, such that if the states in L_1 did not exist, the qualities in L_2 would not exist.
(c) L_2 is the result of a sufficient degree of complexity in L_1. In many cases one can even identify a particular level of criticality which, when reached, will cause the system to begin manifesting new emergent properties.

(d) One can sometimes predict the emergence of some new or emergent qualities based on what one knows about L_1. But using L_1 alone, one will not be able to predict (i) the precise nature of those qualities, (ii) the rules that govern their interaction (or their phenomenological patterns), or (iii) the sorts of emergent levels to which they in turn may give rise in due course.

(e) L_2 is not reducible to L_1 in any of the standard senses of "*reduction*" in the philosophy of science literature: causal, explanatory, metaphysical, or ontological *reduction*.

I am in basic agreement with (d) and (e), but I will mention below that they actually count against Clayton's overall position, specifically against (b) and (c). If I am right about this, it follows that there is no scientific evidence for emergence, that Clayton's own position contains philosophical commitments that undermine philosophical evidence for emergence, and, in any case, emergence is simply false when it comes to mental properties. That leaves (a) through (c).

Principle (a) suffers from two defeaters: It is clearly not a necessary condition for emergence, and if true, it entails that one cannot recognize the presence of an emergent property from inspecting the mereological aggregate that exemplifies it. (a) is not necessary as can be seen from the famous (or infamous!) Swamp Man thought experiment: While walking through a swamp, Joe, a *homo sapien*, who has resulted from the long process of evolutionary development, passes a tree stump at the precise moment a bolt of lightening hits it. Incredibly, the stump turns into an exact, completely indistinguishable, duplicate we shall call Smoe. Joe and Smoe are exact doubles with respect to all their constituents, including their mental states. It seems clear that each has a mental state identically emergent on his brain state, but Clayton's position wrongly entails that only Joe has an emergent property. Moreover, no amount of inspection of Joe or Smoe, and more generally, no inspection of any emergent property and its respective whole will allow anyone to know whether the property is emergent, since the presence or absence of an evolutionary history is cognitively opaque.

Principle (b) is false when applied to mental properties. If we tighten up (b) so that it ranges throughout all possible worlds that are minimal physical duplicates of our world, then inverted qualia, zombie, and modal (disembodied) thought experiments present undercutting if not rebutting defeaters for (b). In fact, while I think these thought experiments succeed against strong physicalism, Clayton seems even more vulnerable to them. Principles (d) (which, I suspect, allows for only the sort of prediction that follows after the fact from repeated observations of regular correlations and not from knowledge of the subvenient base) and (e) (which contains the claim that emergent properties resist *explanatory reduction* which I take to mean that there is in principle no explanation of emergence from exhaustive knowledge of the subvenient base) imply the following: Knowledge of the complete physical description of all minimal physical duplicates of our world provides no evidence whatsoever about what does and does not obtain mentally or about what can and cannot obtain mentally. Absent such knowledge, and it is hard to see what evidence could be employed to rebut these thought experiments.

But we have more evidence that (b) is false than mere thought experiments, and that evidence comes from two sources inexcusably absent from most discussions of the issues with which we are currently preoccupied. These sources may be avoided for sociological or psychological reasons, and in chapter nine I will argue for spiritual reasons, but as far as I can tell, there are no rational considerations that justify their exclusion. I have in mind the widespread and convincing evidence for a disembodied substantial mind/soul that in no way depends for its existence on subvenient conditions from Near Death Experiences (NDE's) and from cases of demon possession not plausibly explained within naturalistic resources.

For example, an especially interesting NDE case was reported by pediatrician Melvin Morse, who resuscitated a young girl who had nearly drowned while swimming in a pool, being under water for about nineteen minutes. Even though she had fixed and dilated pupils during that time, she was able to describe minutely what her parents and family were doing back at her home, including the clothes they were wearing, what her brother and sister were doing, and the specifics of the meal that her mother was preparing. Soon after her resuscitation by Morse and another physician, she also gave a highly detailed account of the doctors' procedures and the contents of the emergency room.[60]

In addition to the little girl who nearly drowned, there are documented accounts where NDErs see items and hear conversations both in and out of the room where they are located, sometimes including blind patients and those who were without heart or brain activity.[61]

Besides NDEs, there is powerful, pervasive evidence for the existence of demons and the reality of demonization. Only people in the Ivory Tower could dispute this evidence because they know in advance of sifting the evidence that such things cannot be true. But the vast majority of people around the world, including even educated people, have encountered demonic phenomena. Moreover, there is more than sufficient evidence, for those with an open mind, to show that much of these phenomena cannot be adequately explained naturalistically and, by contrast, can be distinguished from mere psychological phenomena.

There is a vast literature in support of the reality of demons, and criteria have been developed for distinguishing demonization from mere psychological trauma.[62] Three such criteria are: (1) the universal presence of certain symptoms, including satisfaction of biblical criteria, along with responsiveness to the name of Jesus, all of which take place uniformly throughout the world, including cultures that know nothing about the Bible or Jesus;

(2) the presence of supernatural power evidenced by such phenomena as moving material objects; (3) the revelation by the demon of precise, detailed, private and embarrassing information in front of others about the exorcist that no human person could have known.

These phenomena occur frequently and widely. In fact, in a recent alumni publication of the university at which I teach, the cover story featured faculty members—intellectually sophisticated professors with doctorates from the same institutions that most of us attended—who had experienced such demonic phenomena.[63] During an exorcism, one professor saw metal objects fly across the room. I know a professor at another institution who has seen this very sort of phenomena in his own condominium in conjunction with a demonized person moving into the home right next to the professor's dwelling place. During another exorcism, a different professor experienced the sort of embarrassment mentioned above. A demon accused him in front of the entire prayer team of specific sins that were detailed, including time and location. I know of others who have seen the same thing.

Of course, naturalists do not need to look at the evidence, because they already "know" that such things do not happen. In this way, they evince an anti-empirical attitude. But for those with an open mind, there is more than enough evidence to justify belief in disembodied existence for human selves in NDE's and for demons in cases of demonization. Note carefully, that whether or not these things are happening is a function of factors such as the quality of eyewitness testimony, the satisfaction of certain criteria, e.g., the plausibility of alternative psychological explanations. What is entirely irrelevant, however, is a description of the laws of physics and chemistry. Let φ stand for an exhaustive, God's eye description of the physical features of the actual world and all minimal physical duplicates of it. φ is simply irrelevant to evaluating these data. At the very least, this shows how contingently related the mental world is to the physical world. Given that mental phenomena represent L_2, (b) and (c) are false.

Finally, Clayton's emergentism boils down to an egregious *post hoc ergo propter hoc* fallacy. Indeed, for at least three reasons, there is no scientific evidence whatsoever for genuinely emergent properties. For one thing, the in-principle unpredictability of emergent properties from exhaustive knowledge of their alleged emergent bases entails that there is no empirical evidence for emergence. And the fact that there are no criteria for identifying a "sufficient degree of complexity" apart from slapping the label on whatever was present when the emergent property appeared in an *ad hoc*, after-the-fact manner, implies that there is no straightforward scientific evidence for emergence. This may be why Clayton equivocates on the nature of the subvenient base, sometimes claiming that emergence is "out of matter"[64] and most often asserting that it arises out of neutral monistic stuff.[65] He also claims that emergent properties arise from the complex interactions among the parts of subvenient structures.[66] None of these statements can be given one iota of empirical support.

Second, as Jaegwon Kim has convincingly shown, the appearance of emergent mental properties is consistent with numerous positions on the mind/body problem, e.g. substance dualism, type physicalism, epiphenomenalism, double-aspect theories (e.g. personalism)[67] Thus, the scientific evidence is underdetermined with respect to these options, including emergentism.

Moreover, it is far from clear that the philosophical arguments for emergentism vs. substance dualism are in support of the former. Emergentists will hold that epistemic simplicity is in their favor, but it must be remembered that this epistemic value applies only if the options are considered equal on other grounds. And this is what the substance dualist will argue. She will claim that issues regarding the unity of the self at and through time, the irreducibility of the first-person indexical, the reality of agent causality and a number of other arguments favor a substantial self. I have presented these arguments elsewhere and my purpose here is not to defend them.[68] I note simply that it is far from clear that emergentists get the better of this argument. Remember, Clayton cannot appeal to science to make his case, and the general presumption in favor of emergentist as opposed to substance dualism is, in my view, without adequate justification.

Problems with the mereological hierarchy in the category of individual

Our discussion of emergentist and substance dualist theories provides a fitting transition to my final objection to Clayton's emergentism: He fails to provide reasons for preferring ordered aggregates and the mereological hierarchical treatment of individuals as opposed to a plurality of unique (Aristotelian/Thomistic) substances.

For one thing, Kim has argued, conclusively in my view, that the mereological hierarchy itself generates the problem of top/down causation. Clayton seems to be confused about this point because he thinks that the argument against top/down causation derives from a reductive physicalist depiction of science. Given this understanding, Clayton's rejoinder is merely to define top/down causation and claim that an emergentist approach to science is open to the discovery of cases that satisfy the definition. Clayton's confusion is evidenced by the fact that he actually claims to provide an *argument* for top/down causation by merely offering a *definition* of levels that include by fiat the notion of top/down causation.[69] Unfortunately, this sort of "argumentation" is what Bertrand Russell called philosophy by theft, not honest toil.

The problem remains for Clayton: Given the nature of the hierarchy, there is no room for top/down causation. Kim's argument for this point may be flawed, though I am persuaded by it. But Clayton does not enjoin it adequately, and by affirming the hierarchy, he is left with no adequate solution for top/down causation. And defining it into existence hardly solves the problem.

Clearly, a substance ontology does not face the problem of top/down causation because it quantifies over a plurality of powerful particulars each of which has its own irreducible causal powers and which does not depend upon separable parts for its existence. Aristotelian substances do not ride upon anything, so there is no "down" that generates the problem.

Clayton baulks at a substance dualist approach to top/down causation because: (1) It postulates a causally powerful entity that is "ontologically of a qualitatively different kind" that exerts top/down causation. But, he asserts, this notion is ambiguous, strange and inadequate for justifying top/down causation because (1) "an eel or elephant seems qualitatively different from an electron, yet one does not have to be a dualist to say that an elephant's movements can affect the motion of the electrons that are a part of it";[70] and (2) It involves a "strange new addition of energy into the natural world."[71]

Neither conjunct is persuasive. Regarding (1), the same argument has been leveled at emergentism and Clayton's ontology postulates a plurality of "qualitatively different" kinds of entities. Clayton's pluralism may imply that emergent properties are psychologically less strange than his (inadequate) depiction of dualism, which postulates only one different kind of entity, but, ontologically speaking, all simple, genuinely emergent properties are qualitatively different from matter as it is described by physics. And Clayton's counter-examples of qualitatively different properties do not work, because the strong naturalist will treat "being an eel" and "being an elephant" as structurally and not emergently supervenient properties, and mental properties are not structural.

Regarding (2), Clayton speculates that "downward causation for emergentists might involve transduction, the transformation of energy into forms of energy (say, mental energy) not well understood by contemporary science."[72] From my perspective, this does not appear to be any less "strange" than his depiction of the dualist alternative, given the mereological hierarchy and the exclusion argument against top/down causation.

Secondly, scientific data does not favor one ontology over another. Though a minority, there are philosophers who have developed a view of chemical change as substantial change that includes but cannot be reduced to a mere re-arrangement of parts to form new mereological aggregates.[73] Similarly, there are those who have developed ontologies of living organisms such that they, too, are substances and not ordered aggregates. Interestingly, such models invariably include the notion that DNA is not the fundamental unit of morphogenesis; rather, the individual organism taken as a substantial unit is. Clayton accepts this position.[74] While he tries to flesh it out within a framework of relational structures/systems, he emphasizes the irreducible unity of biological wholes, information and systems biology, and top/down causation. By adopting such a stance, Clayton's view becomes much less distinguishable from a substance model than he apparently realizes. After all, the view of an individual as an essentially characterized particular was developed by Aristotle precisely to distinguish ordered aggregates with a *per accidens* unity from genuine substances with a *per se* unity, and it is the latter that Clayton is clearly after.

In response, Clayton claims that the quantity of separable parts (he calls them particles) and the (apparently quantitative) *degree* of complexity suffices to explain emergence[75] and, more specifically, it allows one to avoid a substance ontology in favor of the mereological hierarchy.[76] Moreover, Clayton acknowledges that to make sense of his emergentist view of the hierarchy, there must be a new *kind* of relation at new levels, such that there is a new integral entity *in virtue of* a new kind of relatedness within.[77] This ontology of relations, along with epistemological simplicity, says Clayton, allows one to avoid a pluralist ontology of unique substances.[78]

Clayton's response is inadequate for at least two reasons. First, he fails to see that in order to get the sort of integrated wholeness he seeks, the new kind of relation must be an internal relation. In this case, the integrated wholes are constituted by internal relations among the parts of the whole and the whole itself, and the parts turn out to be inseparable parts. Unfortunately, the sort of combinatorial processes to which Clayton appeals to explain the emergence of such relations is inadequate. Those processes are, one and all, constituted by external relations among separable parts. It is substantial change, not a re-arrangement of externally related separable parts that adequately provides the ontological resources for a new kind of relation and a new, integral whole.

Moreover, neither approach is simpler than the other. Both involve a shopping-list of unique entities. Clayton's view involves a new category of relation—internal relations—and the view that the unity of emergent wholes takes place *in virtue of* those relations. The substance view involves new essences in the category of individual and the view that the internal relatedness of certain parts takes place *in virtue of* the new whole. To avoid an eliminativist treatment of new wholes, Clayton would seem to have to postulate at least new surfaces/boundaries in addition to internal relations, but the substance ontologist does not need to be committed one way or another to such an entity.

It is far from clear that Clayton's view is "more scientific" or epistemically simpler. And without these, his view comes perilously close to the substance position, a fact that he himself acknowledges. At the end of the day, he fails to realize that his own emergentist analysis of the hierarchy prevents him from having the resources consistently to avoid the substance alternative.

We saw something similar to this in chapter four regarding O'Connor. As most naturalists see, the epistemic commitments and the sorts of processes that constitute the Grand Story (see chapter one) justify a unified view of the mereological hierarchy in the categories of property and individual: structural and only structural properties, and mereological aggregates treated in eliminativist or minimalist (e.g. surfaces only and no unifying essences) ways. O'Connor sought to smuggle emergent properties, especially active power, in the category of property, but the reasons for expanding the ontology in that category also justified the adoption of a substantial self in the category of individual. Similarly, by opting for pluralistic emergence in the category of property, Clayton starts down a path that prevents him from limiting ontological expansion to that category. After all, the hierarchy itself was justified by the explanatory power of mechanistic physicalism, and mechanistic physicalism works with respect to changes in external relations in both categories. By admitting exceptions in the category of property, it is hard to limit exceptions to that category.

Third, not only does Clayton fail to provide adequate reasons for preferring mereological aggregates and the hierarchy to a plurality of unique substances, there is one aspect of this thought that actually provides ground for favoring the latter: his adoption of theistic dualism coupled with his acceptance of an analogy between God and human persons. Clayton believes that there are limits to science and naturalistic explanation and that there are grounds for believing in God's existence. By "God", Clayton means a suprapersonal mind or spirit who is a source of agency,[79] that God is an infinite, transcendent, substantial mind non-emergent from and quite independent of the cosmos.[80] Thus, Clayton explicitly embraces theistic dualism, and with it, at least one unique substance (besides atomic simples if such there be) that is not a mereological aggregate.

Further, Clayton correctly notes that one must avoid equivocation in talking about God as a conscious personal agent and human persons as such. Indeed, Clayton believes there is an important analogy between the two. But I think Clayton misunderstands the proper implications of this. He starts with a non-dualistic, emergentist theory of human persons and moves to a dualistically conceived God. But I believe that this is wrongheaded. In the order of knowing, it is appropriate to move from us to God. But in the ontological order, things go in the other direction. Now if we start with an emergentist view of human persons, and for certain reasons move to what we take as the justified belief in a dualistic God qua conscious personal agent, we have a defeater for the emergentist view of human persons. Why? Because we have a Paradigm Case of what a conscious personal agent is, and we accept an ontological, and not merely an epistemological analogy with us.

Think of it this way. Whatever else may be different between us and God, Clayton's own argument presents God as the paradigm case of a conscious personal agent, and, as such, the paradigm case grounds the class of conscious personal agents precisely as such in that each member bears the relevant similarities with the paradigm case. It is hard to see what these analogy-grounding similarities would be if not a self-conscious, substantial agent-self.

Clayton's failure to come to terms with this problem may be due, in part, to what I think is his confused notion of what it means for a human person to be a conscious personal agent. Clayton clearly wants to understand this in terms of agent causation,[81] but he then claims that to regard human persons as self-conscious agents is to commit one to accepting that mental states have causal force.[82] Now this is not sufficient for agent causation, which implies that it is the agent-self-qua-mental-substance, not mental properties/states that is the mental cause.

Clayton is aware of this problem, but avoids this move towards a substantial agent-self by merely asserting that the emergentist position is simpler and more in harmony with the natural sciences. But this is a false, groundless assertion as I have tried to show above. Moreover, Clayton fails to include in his methodological approach the implication of the importance of classic theism for justifying the assumptions of science. Fortunately, for my purposes, I do not need to justify such importance because Clayton himself argues for such.[83]

Granting, as he does, that this is the case, we have the following epistemic approach to knowledge or justified belief about the world. Epistemically prior to the employment of natural science, we must justify the assumptions of science, and to do that we must postulate the existence of God. Now God is a dualistically conceived substance qua conscious, self-aware agent. This means that prior to exploring the world through natural science, we already have a dualist ontology and we are under no pressure from simplicity considerations to favor a mereological-aggregate view of individuals, since we already have the category of "mental individual" filled. And when we discover other self-aware, conscious agent-causes, we should treat them as dualistically conceived agent-causes unless there are overriding reasons to the contrary.

This is much different from opting for naturalistic assumptions regarding atomic simples and combinatorial processes, which would justify a mereological view of various aggregate wholes and a relational view of the unity of such wholes. But the naturalist view actually undermines the assumptions of science as Clayton acknowledges, and it fails to have the resources to explain radically new kinds of wholes constituted by internal and not external relations. When this radically new sort of relational structure is combined with a pluralist view of emergent properties, I see no reason to think that it is in any sense simpler to a substance ontology. But given a theistic framework justified in the fashion just mentioned, such methodological pressure to employ relations as unifiers is gone.

Moreover, once we have a substance ontology for understanding the sort of unity God and human persons exhibit, we have a metaphysical framework for understanding similar sorts of unities. If certain entities exhibit certain sorts of unity, e.g. chemical elements and molecules, then we are justified in treating them as substances. If they do not, we should treat them as mereological aggregates. I have explained elsewhere the differences regarding unity between substances and mereological aggregates, and shall not repeat my explanation here.[84] I merely note that the decision to go one way or another will be grounded where it ought to be—in unity considerations, and not in irrelevant appeals to scientific parsimony. A substance ontology quantifies over Aristotelian/Thomistic substances, and mereological aggregates and so does Clayton's emergentist ontology. This, I believe, makes inscrutable his appeals to parsimony to justify his ontology relative to mine. And apart from emotional hostility to such a substance ontology, it is empirically equivalent to Clayton's and there are no non-question-begging criteria that give an edge to the latter.

Theism, AC, and Clayton's position

In this chapter, I have been at pains to show that Clayton's pluralistic emergentist monism is not an appropriate version of a positive naturalism that does not rest content in denying theism, but which seeks to justify its claim of explanatory superiority relative to rival worldviews. I have also argued that there are serious difficulties with Clayton's views that justify a rejection of his emergentist monism, and more specifically, its claim to superiority over a theistic dualism that embraces substantial minds regarding human persons and also employs the classic notion of substance in the category of individual when unity considerations justify it. The merits of the mereological hierarchy relative to such a substance ontology are vastly over-rated and regularly over-stated.

Given this background and the fact that Clayton is a theistic dualist, it is hard to see why his views of emergence are superior to those of theistic dualism coupled with AC. Three brief points should be noted: First, Clayton acknowledges that

> much of the suspicion about emergence within the scientific community stems from the sense that emergence is sometimes used as a "magic pill." That is, scientists complain that in certain treatments emergence seems to represent a strange mystical power within evolution that constantly works to lift the universe to new levels of reality.[85]

Scientists and, more generally, naturalists have been correct in this concern, because it is obvious that neither evolution nor the other processes constitutive of the Grand Story can plausibly give rise to simple emergent properties. All science can do is to label emergent phenomena as such, and leave them as brute facts.

So as far as natural processes are concerned, there must indeed be a "strange mystical power" responsible for them, strange and mystical in that it is not a natural entity and for which there is no evidence whatever that the cause of emergence is within the natural order. It must be kept in mind that AC does not require special creation of each emergent at the time it appears. Indeed, Howard van Till has argued that a theistic perspective best explains emergent phenomena and he holds that at the beginning of creation God placed within the stuff he made all the potentialities tl would eventually emerge.[86] It is the inadequacy of strong naturalism or the other approaches mentioned in this book, including Clayton's, that justify a theistic explanation for the existence of such (contingent) potentialities in minimal physical duplicates of our world and the fact that they are (contingently) actualized at the time certain physical phenomena obtain.

There is no naturalistic explanation—Clayton's or otherwise—for the reality and constancy of these phenomena. Moreover, it seems implausible that the Big Bang created matter such that when myriads upon myriads of small atomic simples come to stand in certain external relations with each other, some sort of striving potentiality within each member is finally brought to a critical mass and, presto, a new simple property emerges. Naturalism "explains" such data only by committing the *post hoc ergo propter hoc* fallacy. Certainly, Clayton's emergentism does not solve the problem of emergence; it merely labels it. G. K. Chesterton once noted that magic requires a Magician, and Clayton's "solution" amounts to embracing a shopping list ontology without a Shopper, accepting magical emergence without a Magician.

Clayton's "solution" is quite curious in light of two further points. For one thing, he acknowledges that there really is no adequate naturalistic account for the emergence of consciousness or its regular correlation with neurological states.[87] For another, Clayton actually argues that the existence of objective "oughts" and ethical obligation cannot be made sense of within the constraints of naturalistic explanation and, thus, he opts for a theistic explanation of such. Surely, Clayton knows that there are moral realists who have advanced naturalistic emergentist arguments for the appearance of intrinsic value-making properties quite similar to his emergentist approach to consciousness and other areas of "emergence."[88]

It is hard to see how he can have it both ways. By accepting an emergentist line in other areas, including consciousness, how can Clayton avoid embracing a similar strategy regarding moral realism and emergent value? It is more consistent to employ AC in all areas of genuine emergence rather than choose according to one's liking. By quantifying over a plurality of emergent properties, Clayton actually provides more data for arguments for God's existence than those who merely accept consciousness and AC.

8 Science and strong physicalism

In the first seven chapters, I have argued for several crucial points:

(1) Naturalism cannot adequately account for the origin of mental states given the ontological constraints that follow if naturalism is taken as an explanatorily superior worldview. So understood, naturalists ought to be strong physicalists.
(2) The presence of theism and AC combine with the inner logic of naturalism to place a severe burden of proof on any version of naturalism that countenances property/event dualism.
(3) Paradigm-case representatives of the most plausible versions of naturalism that accept property/event dualism (contingent correlation, emergent necessitation, mysterianism) suffer from damaging criticisms and fail to meet this burden of proof.
(4) Panpsychism and pluralistic emergentist monism are rivals to and not versions of naturalism, and they are less preferable to theism and AC.

My argument can be taken as supporting a conditional: If mental events/properties exist and are characterized along the lines of property dualism, then they provide evidence for the existence of God. The strength of this evidence was variously characterized in chapter two. And while I have not provided much justification for the antecedent, I did offer some general considerations in favor of it in chapter two. In fact, I take it to be obvious because of direct first-person awareness that property/event dualism is correct. I also take the degree of such justification to be strong enough to be an overriding defeater for the various arguments that have been raised against property/event dualism.

In my view, the philosophical arguments—issues regarding causal interaction, problems with soul stuff, pairing problems, the problem of other minds, private language difficulties—are really quite weak, and I believe that most physicalists take strong physicalism to be justified largely on the basis of scientific and not philosophical considerations. Thus, Daniel Dennett speaks for most physicalists when he says that "the fundamentally anti-scientific stance of dualism is, to my mind, its most disqualifying feature and [why] dualism is to be avoided *at all costs*."[1] So while I will not develop a detailed case for property/event dualism in this book, it is important for my project that I weigh in on the impact of modern science on philosophy of mind. I hope to show that the hard sciences have almost no bearing at all on the nature of consciousness (or the self); more specifically, that findings in the hard sciences provide virtually no evidence at all for strong physicalism and, thus, for strong naturalism. If I am right about this, then given the weakness of the philosophical arguments against dualism, we are justified in taking the antecedent of my conditional to be true.

Most philosophers agree that the vast majority of people throughout history have been substance and property dualists. Some form of dualism appears to be the natural response to what we seem to know about ourselves through introspection and in other ways. In this regard, Jaegwon Kim's concession may be taken as representative: "We commonly think that we, as persons, have a mental and bodily dimension. . . . Something like this dualism of personhood, I believe, is common lore shared across most cultures and religious traditions."[2] People don't have to be taught to be dualists like they must if they are to be physicalists.

However, as I mentioned above, today it is widely held in the academic community that, while broadly logically possible, dualism is no longer plausible in light of the advances of modern science. Thus, John Searle says that it is an obvious fact of physics that "the world consists entirely of physical particles in fields of force."[3] He goes on to say that much of the justification for the various forms of physicalism that dominate philosophy of mind is the assumption that

> they represent the only scientifically acceptable alternatives to the antiscientism that went with traditional dualism, the belief in the immortality of the soul, spiritualism, and so on. Acceptance of the current views is motivated not so much by an independent conviction of their truth as by a terror of what are apparently the only alternatives. That is, the choice we are tacitly presented with is between a "scientific" approach, as represented by one or another of the current versions of "materialism" and an "antiscientific" approach, as represented by Cartesianism or some other traditional religious conception of the mind.[4]

Nancey Murphy claims that physicalism is not primarily a philosophical thesis, but the hard core of a scientific research program for which there is ample evidence. This evidence consists in the fact that "biology, neuroscience, and cognitive science have provided accounts of the dependence on physical processes of *specific* faculties once attributed to the soul."[5] Dualism cannot be *proven* false—a dualist can always appeal to correlations or functional relations between soul and brain/body—but advances in science make it a view with little justification. According to Murphy, "science has provided a massive amount of evidence suggesting that we need not postulate the existence of an entity such as a soul or mind in order to explain life and consciousness."[6]

I find myself among the dissenters of this view of the impact of modern science on issues in philosophy of mind. My thesis is that *once we get clear on the central first and second order issues in philosophy of mind, it becomes evident that stating and resolving those issues is basically a (theological and) philosophical matter for which discoveries in the hard sciences are largely irrelevant*. Put differently, *these philosophical issues are, with rare exceptions, autonomous from (and authoritative with respect to) the so-called deliverances of the hard sciences*.

My main purpose is to clarify and defend this thesis. In what follows, I shall 1) clarify certain preliminary notions; 2) defend my central thesis by focusing on select paradigm cases that are representative of the actual dialectic in the literature in philosophy of mind; 3) respond to two defeaters of my thesis.

Clarification of important preliminaries relevant to the autonomy thesis

Two preliminaries need clarification in light of the arguments to follow: identification of the central first and second order issues in philosophy of mind and the nature of the Autonomy and Authority Theses.

Central issues in philosophy of mind

I doubt that any list of the proper issues within a sub-branch of philosophy would be complete. Still, it is possible to provide a reasonably adequate characterization of the central first-order topics that are ubiquitous in the literature in philosophy of mind. Those topics tend to revolve around three interrelated families of issues constituted by the following kinds of representative questions:[7]

(1) Ontological Questions: To what is a mental or physical property identical? To what is a mental or physical event identical? To what is the owner of mental properties/events identical? What is a human person? How are mental properties related to mental events (e.g. Do the latter exemplify or realize the former?)? Are there (Aristotelian or Leibnizian) essences and, if so, what is the essence of a mental event or of a human person?

(2) Epistemological Questions: How do we come to have knowledge or justified beliefs about other minds and about our own minds? Is there a proper epistemic order to first-person knowledge of one's own mind and third-person knowledge of other minds? How reliable is first-person introspection and what is its nature (e.g. a non-doxastic seeming or a disposition to believe)? If reliable, should first-person introspection

be limited to providing knowledge about mental states or should it be extended to include knowledge about one's own ego?

(3) Semantic Questions: What is a meaning? What is a linguistic entity and how is it related to a meaning? Is thought reducible to or a necessary condition for language use? How do the terms in our common-sense psychological vocabulary get their meaning? How are meaning and intentional objects "in" the mind?

The main second-order topics in philosophy of mind are these:

(4) Methodological Questions: How should one proceed in analyzing and resolving the first-order issues that constitute the philosophy of mind? What is the proper order between philosophy and science? Should we adopt some form of philosophical naturalism, set aside so-called first philosophy, and engage topics in philosophy of mind within a framework of our empirically best-attested theories relevant to those topics? What is the role of thought experiments in philosophy of mind and how does the "first-person point of view" factor into generating the materials for formulating those thought experiments?

The Autonomy and Authority Theses

These are the sorts of questions that form the warp and weft of philosophy of mind. In order to clarify the Autonomy and Authority Theses, I can do no better than cite advocate George Bealer's statement of them:

> I wish to recommend two theses.
>
> [1] The Autonomy of Philosophy: Among the central questions of philosophy that can be answered by one standard theoretical means or another, most can in principle be answered by philosophical investigation and argument without relying substantively on the sciences.
>
> [2] The Authority of Philosophy: Insofar as science and philosophy purport to answer the same central philosophical questions, in most cases the support that science could in principle provide for those answers is not as strong as that which philosophy could in principle provide for its answers. So, should there be conflicts, the authority of philosophy in most cases can be greater in principle.[8]

In their massive work *Philosophical Foundations of Neuroscience*, M. R. Bennett and P. M. S. Hacker argue, correctly in my view, for both theses with respect to philosophy of mind.[9] They claim that empirical questions about the nervous system are the province of neuroscience, but underlying issues about the nature of consciousness, self-consciousness, mind, thought, and the general nature of the relationship between mind and brain are the proper province of philosophy. Moreover, these two logically different kinds of inquiries relate in such a way that the relevant philosophical issues are not amenable to scientific theorizing, investigation, or experimentation and, indeed, the former are presupposed by the later. When the Autonomy and Authority Theses are not acknowledged, they claim, serious confusions arise such as the (on their view) incoherent ascription of psychological attributes to the brain.

Of the two, the Autonomy Thesis is less controversial and, in my view, clearly correct, at least in certain areas outside philosophy of mind. Debates about universals, the status of the identity of indiscernibles, the merits of foundationalism, the ontological status of possible worlds, the appropriateness of various normative ethical theories, and so forth are carried out with virtually no regard whatever for the latest findings in chemistry, physics. Most of the first and second order topics in philosophy of mind are similarly autonomous, or so I shall shortly argue.

The Principle of Authority is more controversial, but in my opinion, not for the reason that may first come to mind. At first glance, ambivalence towards or rejection of the principle may arise from the idea that science is, in general, a superior guide to joint areas of exploration. I think this idea is wrong. In my view, the controversial nature of the Authority Principle derives from the fact that, in those cases where philosophical considerations carry more weight than scientific ones, it is usually open to someone to adopt an anti-realist depiction of the relevant scientific view, operationalize the relevant terms that constitute it, and avoid epistemic conflict by resorting to an autonomy depiction of the philosophical and scientific aspects of the disputed area.

As an illustration, consider debates about the nature of time. It seems to be widely accepted, perhaps because of simplicity considerations, that the scientific factors are best captured by a B-series view of time. For the sake of argument, let us grant that this is correct. Let us also grant that there are powerful, overriding, uniquely philosophical considerations (e.g. from certain considerations about temporal indexicals) for an A-series view of time. In this case, one may hold that the Authority Thesis has been satisfied. However, it is also possible to advert to the Autonomy Thesis by claiming that science is merely interested in empirical or measured time, but philosophy is interested in the essence of time itself. Thus, it is tricky to make an authority claim stick, and I shall not attempt to do so here. Instead, my purpose is to defend the Autonomy Thesis as stated by Bealer and as applied to the central first and second order issues in philosophy of mind.

First-philosophy and Cartesian foundationalism

The Authority or Autonomy Thesis are aspects of what has come to be called first-philosophy and the question can be raised as to why one ought to accept these theses or first-philosophy which they entail. A fairly standard answer is given to this question and I believe it is a strawman that is easy to refute. This strawman characterization of the intellectual motivation for embracing one or both of these theses may serve the dialectical interests of naturalists, but it is a gross misrepresentation of the current status of philosophical discourse.

According to the strawman characterization, acceptance of first-philosophy is due to a commitment to Cartesian foundationalism along with its quest for incorrigible foundations to knowledge, foundations needed to refute the skeptic and save knowledge, especially scientific knowledge. Thus, embracing a version of philosophical naturalism that entails the rejection of first-philosophy, David Papineau asserts without argument that

> Traditionalists will counter that we are not *entitled* to any empirically based assumptions until we have somehow established the legitimacy of empirical knowledge by independent means ...
>
> This argument depends on the assumption that knowledge needs to be *certain* in the sense that it should derive from methods that necessarily deliver truths ...
>
> So the dialectical situation is as follows. If you hold that knowledge requires certainty, then you will hold that philosophy needs to come before science. If you reject this demand, ... then you will have reason to regard philosophy as continuous with science.[10]

Along the same lines, Patricia Churchland opines that all of our "convictions about what it is to acquire knowledge and about the nature of explanation, justification, and confirmation—about the nature of the scientific enterprise itself—are subject to revision and to correction."[11]

> It is in this sense that there is no *first* philosophy. There is no corpus of philosophical doctrine concerning science and epistemology such that we can be sure it is the Truth to which all science must conform. There is, as Quine remarks, no Archimedean point outside all science from which we can pronounce upon the acceptability of scientific theories.[12]

Elsewhere she says that "Empirical foundations of science and knowledge generally are not absolute and forever fixed; rather, they are foundations only relative to a particular encompassing network."[13] As a result, "Naturalism follows hard upon the heels of the understanding that there is no first philosophy."[14] Applied to philosophy of mind, Churchland claims that there is no purely *a priori* knowledge, in particular, no introspective knowledge that is epistemologically privileged.[15]

There may have been a grain of truth to these assertions in the nineteenth and first half of the twentieth century, though even in this period philosophers who practiced "first-philosophy" did so because of the nature of the issues with which they dealt, and not simply because of Cartesian anxiety. But with the renaissance of philosophy of religion, hard-core metaphysics, and the widespread rejection of naturalized epistemology (along with the proliferation of versions of modest foundationalism), claims such as these from Papineau and Churchland are not only false, but also intellectually irresponsible. All one has to do to do to see this is to pick up the relevant literature and examine it.

The practice of first-philosophy, specifically the Autonomy and Authority Theses, is done because of a fairly simple insight: If we examine the nature of claims P and Q, along with the alternative claims and the argument for and against each, and if we discover that the issues regarding P are essentially relevant to resolving the issues regarding Q but not conversely, then P is authoritative with respect to Q. And if we simply discover that the relevant issues regarding Q are in an area of argument unrelated to those surrounding P, then P is autonomous with respect to Q.

Because of this insight, advocates of first-philosophy enjoin us to examine carefully the details of specific issues in philosophy, and decide on a case-by-case basis whether that issue is authoritative or autonomous with respect to the so-called "deliverances of the hard sciences." If I am right about this, then the devil is in the details, and I shall proceed in what follows to show that the details surrounding issues in philosophy of mind render them autonomous with respect to the hard sciences. And I assure you that I have no Cartesian anxiety fueling the dialectic to follow.

Two paradigm case studies on behalf of the Autonomy Thesis

Perhaps I am naïve, but I think that once we get before us the four families of questions listed above, it becomes evident that scientific discoveries play virtually no role at all in formulating or resolving those issues. In any case, I have selected, almost at random, two paradigm case debates in philosophy-of-mind literature to serve as illustrations of the Autonomy Thesis.

Paul Churchland on semantic and epistemic issues

Case one involves Paul Churchland's treatment of two different approaches to closely related semantic and epistemic issues.[16] According to Churchland, a popular physicalist approach to these issues—one that he favors—is the network theory of meaning for the terms in our psychological vocabulary. On this approach, one looks not for an ontological analysis of meaning itself, but rather for a theory about how psychological terms get meaning. On this view, the best way to embark on this quest is to start with a third-person perspective and focus on publicly accessible language to see how terms in folk psychology get their usage. These terms primarily function in a theory as theoretical terms used to explain/predict other people's behavior. Moreover, says Churchland, as theoretical terms, they get their meaning by their relations to laws, principles and other terms in the entire theory in which they are embedded.

For Churchland, the epistemic approach most suited to this semantic theory is one that starts with third-person questions about knowledge of other minds and assimilates first-person to third-person knowledge. We are justified in applying a mental term to another creature just in case this provides the best explanation for and prediction of the creature's behavior. Churchland claims that one's justification here need owe nothing at all to one's examination of one's own case. According to Churchland, it follows that one could justifiably apply a mental term such as "pain" to a creature and, thus, know its meaning, even if one had never had the relevant experience himself.

Regarding self-consciousness and knowledge of one's own mind, Churchland characterizes self-consciousness as the ability to use a linguistic network to judge that one's various mental states satisfy the interlocking network of folk psychology. Thus, self-consciousness is largely something that is learned. Moreover, according to Churchland, all perception is theory-laden, including self "perception," and self-consciousness is essentially linguistic behavior of a certain sort.

Space considerations prevent me from presenting Churchland's largely accurate depiction of a dualist approach to these questions, but it involves a commitment to such things as irreducible self-presenting properties, first-person introspection and ostensive definition, epistemic movement from the first to the third-person, non-doxastic mental states as temporally and epistemically prior to concepts and judgments, and meanings that are not essentially linguistic.

Who is right in this debate and what factors are relevant to this question? The answer is, of course, complicated and the dialog involves thought experiments that, in my view, derive their force from first-person introspection, debates about private languages, analyses of the relationship between thought and language, and so on. What is less complicated is that factual information in the hard sciences is virtually irrelevant to these issues. Almost no book in philosophy of mind where these issues are discussed contains any detailed scientific information that plays a role in the discussion. Curiously, while Churchland himself is a physicalist and an advocate of naturalism as a second-order methodological thesis, and while he does include scientific information in *Matter and Consciousness*, that scientific information comes in the second half of the book and it plays absolutely no role whatsoever in presenting the core philosophical issues and arguments in the first half of the book. Thus, his actual practice underscores the Autonomy Thesis.

Jaegwon Kim and type identity physicalism

For my second paradigm case, I select Jaegwon Kim's discussion of type identity physicalism.[17] According to Kim, advocates of type identity physicalism are committed to at least three theses:

T_1: Law-like mental type/physical type correlations exist.
T_2: Mental type/physical type identity statements are contingent, empirical, theoretical identity statements with non-synonymous yet co-referring expressions.
T_3: A property exemplification view of events, or something very close to it, is correct.

According to Kim, T_1 is justified because of empirical evidence. Since my purpose here is not to evaluate directly type identity physicalism, to forestall objections to it from multiple realization, we may relativize the correlations it expresses to species or individual organisms or we may just grant it for the sake of argument. The important question for our purposes is this: Do scientific considerations play a role in assessing type identity physicalism and, if so, how important is that role relative to the one philosophical considerations play?

It seems to me that scientific considerations play little or no role at all in assessing T_1–T_3. Due to space considerations, I shall limit my remarks to T_1 and T_2. The hard sciences do, indeed, play an important role in establishing the correlations in question, and it may well be that future discoveries will make them increasingly precise. Even here, however, we must not overstate the role of the hard sciences. I cannot enter here a debate about methodology in the hard sciences, but that methodology seems essentially to employ a third-person approach to the relevant objects of study.[18] Since the correlations expressed in T_1 rely on first-person introspective reports, they are not as straightforwardly empirical as, say, the correlations between temperature and pressure in a gas. Moreover, establishing these correlations for complex mental states, such as one's view of modernist epistemology, is virtually impossible and will require, among other things, a decision about the proper criterion for property identity (e.g. a coarse or fine-grained criterion).[19] Still, the hard sciences are crucially involved in establishing the data for which type identity physicalism is an explanation.

What about T_2? For three reasons, scientific considerations are virtually irrelevant for its assessment. First, it is far from clear that the alleged theoretical identities to which mental/physical type correlations are assimilated, for example, color and wavelength, are identities and not correlations. Crucial considerations in that discussion are those relevant to assessing the nature and mind independence of secondary qualities, and the nature of intentionality is at the core of that debate. And even if these are taken as identities, Kripkean considerations (e.g. with color there is a difference between appearance and reality not present in, say, pain) are relevant to attempts to take them as proper analogies for mental/physical type identities.

Second, there are various ways to analyze the correlations and these are not rival scientific paradigms nor are the central issues that divide them scientific. Kim himself lists seven empirically equivalent views:[20] causal 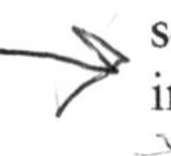 interactionism, preestablished harmony, occasionalism, the double-aspect view, epiphenomenalism, emergentism, and type identity physicalism. No matter where one comes down on this debate, the reasons for one's choice will be philosophical, not scientific.

Third, what about the role of theoretical simplicity in this dispute? Kim claims that theoretical simplicity is a mark of a good theory and type identity physicalists assert that application of simplicity to this debate decides it in their favor. Since my purpose is to assess the Autonomy Thesis and not type identity physicalism, the question before us is whether the introduction of simplicity into the debate turns it into one in which scientific considerations are the relevant factors in resolving it. For two reasons, a negative answer must be given to this question. For one thing, most dualists do not take their views to be primarily theories; rather, they see dualism as a report about what is known about mental properties/events and the self through first-person awareness. So simplicity is irrelevant to most dualist claims, and arguments about the role of simplicity will be distinctively philosophical ones.

Second, there are several epistemic virtues that a good theory should exhibit: factual accuracy, predictive success, internal clarity, simplicity, ability to handle external conceptual problems, comportment with proper methodological rules, and so on. Often, debates between advocates of rival theories are debates about the relative merits of different epistemic virtues and, generally speaking, these debates are not scientific in nature. This is especially true of the debate about type identity physicalism. To see this, consider the following claim by Roderick Chisholm:

> Let us consider some particular psychophysical identity statement – the statement, say, that thinking about unicorns is the same thing as to have Q fibres that vibrate in manner N. One cannot *understand* such a statement, of course, unless one can grasp or conceive the property or properties that are referred to. . . . To the extent that we *can* understand the statement in question, we can *see* that the two properties referred to are not the same property – just as we can *see* that the property of believing that all men are mortal is different from that of wondering whether there is life in outer space. It has been held, not implausibly, that to deny the validity of such rational insights is to undermine the possibility of every type of reasoning.[21]

Underlying Chisholm's argument is an epistemic priority given to first-person introspective knowledge of the intrinsic features of mental properties over third-person knowledge of facts about other people. Now, just exactly what consideration from the hard sciences and for which scientists are the appropriate experts is the relevant one for assessing the strength of Chisholm's argument relative to the use of simplicity to justify type identity physicalism? It is hard to see what it could be. The issue is not science vs. first-philosophy. Rather, it is between philosophers who employ distinctively philosophical arguments to support philosophical naturalism and those who are unpersuaded by those arguments. This debate is between two philosophical positions, not between a scientific and philosophical viewpoint. With regard to evaluating Chisholm's statement, among other things, one must weigh the epistemic value of first-person direct awareness of one's mental states and descriptive reports that ensue vs. theoretical simplicity considerations. Science is simply irrelevant to this debate.

In a way, the dualist is in a dialectical disadvantage because he/she takes his/her view to be obvious in light of first-person introspection. Thus, many dualist arguments, e.g. the Knowledge Argument or the Simple Argument, involve thought experiments that point to our direct knowledge of mental entities, and the dualist invites others to attend to what he or she believes is a matter of commonsense knowledge.[22] The dualist will be inclined to agree with Searle's remark that if one is unwilling to admit that one is conscious, one needs therapy not an argument.[23]

In a similar manner, an advocate of the Autonomy Thesis is at a dialectical disadvantage. He/she takes the thesis to be fairly obvious and invites others to attend to the actual dialogical issues as they pepper the pages of literature in philosophy of mind, believing that one will simply be able to see that those issues are largely philosophical and not scientific.

This is precisely what I have tried to do in this section. If my claims on behalf of the Autonomy Thesis are persuasive, then it will not do for philosophers, such as David Papineau, to adopt philosophical naturalism prior to entering the debate in philosophy of mind as a way of limiting the relevant considerations to those in the empirical sciences and of shifting a substantial burden of proof onto dualists.[24] The simple fact is that those relevant issues are not scientific. Moreover, second-order arguments for or against philosophical naturalism are not themselves scientific. It is not science that says the world consists entirely of aggregates of particles standing in fields of force. It is philosophical naturalists who are making claims about the limits of ontology and epistemology, and those claims are themselves philosophical, not scientific.

In my opinion, there is no straightforward scientific evidence for philosophical naturalism or mind/body physicalism and, *a fortiori*, no such evidence for naturalism's employment to set the terms of debate in philosophy of mind. If someone thinks I am wrong about this, he or she is invited to state the scientific evidence that a theist or dualist could not accommodate easily into his or her views.

Response to two counterarguments

Science makes substance dualism implausible

There are two counterarguments to the Autonomy Thesis I want to consider. Both of them have been stated nicely by Nancey Murphy. First,

Murphy claims that while substance dualism cannot be proven false, nevertheless, "biology, neuroscience, and cognitive science have provided accounts of the dependence on physical processes of *specific* faculties once attributed to the soul."[25] According to Murphy, "science has provided a massive amount of evidence suggesting that we need not postulate the existence of an entity such as a soul or mind in order to explain life and consciousness."[26] Thus, since advances in science have provided detailed accounts of mental/physical dependencies that make postulation of the soul otiose, the Autonomy Thesis is false, at least in this case.

I have three responses to this argument. First, many substance dualists do not believe in a substantial ego primarily because it is a theoretical postulate with superior explanatory power. Rather, they take the ego to be something of which people are directly aware. The point is not that they are right about people's awareness of the self. Given this dualist approach, the point is that advances in our knowledge of mental/physical dependencies are simply beside the point. And the further debate about which approach is the fundamental one for defending substance dualism is not something for which advances in scientific knowledge are relevant.

Second, in those cases where substance dualism *is* postulated as the best explanation for a range of purported facts, typically, those facts are not the scientific ones Murphy mentions, but rather, distinctively philosophical ones, usually surfaced from commonsense beliefs based in first-person non-doxastic seemings. Arguments from the unity of consciousness, the possibility of disembodied survival or body switches, the best view of an agent to support agent causation, the metaphysical implications from the use of the indexical "I" are typical of arguments offered by substance dualists, and the facts Murphy mentions are not particularly relevant for assessing these arguments. Those scientific facts or others lurking in the neighborhood (e.g. split brain phenomena) may provide difficulties for certain versions of substance dualism, but they are not decisive—dualists have provided reasonable responses to them—and, in any case, they are less important than the philosophical issues mentioned above.

Finally, contrary to what Murphy claims, the discovery of "the dependence on physical processes of *specific* faculties once attributed to the soul" does not provide sufficient grounds for attributing those faculties to the brain rather than to the soul. (After all, are dualists supposed to think that mental/physical correlations or causal relations are vague and unwieldy and not specific and regular?) To see this it is important to get clear on the use of "faculty" as the term has been historically used in discussions of substances in general and the soul in particular.[27] Roughly, a faculty of some particular substance is a natural grouping of resembling capacities or potentialities possessed by that thing. For example, the various capacities to hear sounds would constitute a person's auditory faculty. Moreover, a capacity gets its identity and proper metaphysical categorization from the type of property it actualizes. The nature of a capacity-to-exemplify-F is properly characterized by F itself. Thus, the capacity to reflect light is properly considered a physical, optical capacity. This fact about the proper categorization of a capacity is one reason why some philosophers, perhaps in reliance on simplicity considerations, have sought to reduce or eliminate dispositions to rid them from their ontology in favor of their associated categorical properties. According to property dualists, the capacities for various mental states are mental and not physical capacities. Thus, the faculties that are constituted by those capacities are mental and not physical faculties.

Now, arguably, a particular is the kind of thing it is in virtue of the actual and potential properties/faculties essential and intrinsic to it. Thus, a description of the faculties of a thing provides accurate information about the kind of particular that has those faculties. For example, a description of the (irreducible) dispositions of gold provide us with information about the sort of thing gold is.

It seems to me that a description of a particular's capacities/faculties is a more accurate source of information about what kind of thing that particular is than is an analysis of the causal/functional conditions relevant for the particular to act in various ways. This is because the causal/functional conditions relevant to a particular's actions can either be clues to the intrinsic nature of that particular or else information about some other entity that the particular relates to in exhibiting a particular causal action. For example, if Smith needs to use a magnet to pick up certain unreachable iron filings, information about the precise nature of the magnet and its role in Smith's action does not tell us much about the nature of Smith (except that he is dependent in his functional abilities on other things, e.g. the magnet). We surely would not conclude that the actual and potential properties of a magnet are clues to Smith's inner nature. Similarly, a description of the intrinsic features of a chemical compound is more relevant for getting at its essential nature than is a description of the features of a catalyst upon which that compound depends for causal interaction with other compounds.

In the same way, functional dependence on/causal relations to the brain are of much less value in telling us what kind of thing a human person is than is a careful description of the kind-defining mental capacities, i.e. faculties, human persons as such possess. In this case, various forms of non-reductive physicalism and substance dualism are empirically equivalent theses and, in fact, there is no non-question begging theoretical virtue (e.g. simplicity, fruitfulness) that can settle the debate if it is limited to being a scientific debate. But it should not be so limited and, indeed, paradigm case substance dualists such as F. R. Tennant approached the subject of the nature of the self and its relationship to faculties from a distinctively first-person introspective point of view. The choice to side with Murphy over against Tennant cannot be made based on detailed scientific correlations. Rather, it must be made based on factors such as one's evaluation of the strength of first-person awareness of the self and its conscious life.[28]

Physicalism as the hard core of a scientific research program

Murphy's second counterargument is that we should take physicalism not merely as a philosophical thesis, but primarily as the hard core of a scientific research program. According to Murphy, if we look at physicalism—in her case, a specific version of non-reductive physicalism—not as a philosophical thesis but as a scientific theory, then there is ample scientific evidence for it.[29]

If one follows Murphy's advice, then the Autonomy Thesis will have to be set aside. But for at least two reasons, I think Murphy's recommendation is ill-advised and, in fact, question-begging. For one thing, not all neuroscientists adopt physicalism as a research heuristic. For example, U.C.L.A. neuroscientist Jeffrey Schwartz is a leading researcher in obsessive-compulsive disorders. Schwartz explicitly employs a substance dualist view of the person, coupled with a libertarian account of freedom in his research and he claims that this heuristic has generated accurate predictions, provided explanations for various data, and lead to cures that could not have been found on the basis of a physicalist heuristic.[30] Schwartz may be in the minority, but even if this is so, it is just a sociological fact about the community of neuroscientists, not a view about the necessary conditions for a scientifically appropriate heuristic for research programs.

For another thing, it is entirely unclear as to how physicalism in any of its forms is actually used as the "hard core of a scientific research program" in a way relevant to debates in philosophy of mind. To see this, it will be helpful to get before us some important points made by Alvin Plantinga and Bas C. van Fraasen.

Plantinga contrasts Duhemian and Augustinian science derived, respectively, from the ideas of Pierre Duhem and St. Augustine.[31] According to Duhem, religious and, more importantly, metaphysical doctrines have often entered into physical theory. Many physical scientists have seen their job as explaining the phenomena, the appearances, in terms of underlying material causes. A proffered characterization of those causes often employs divisive metaphysical commitments as when Aristotelians, Cartesians and atomists gave disparate accounts of the phenomenon of magnetism.

If the aim of physical theory is to explain phenomena in terms of the ultimate nature of their causes, says Duhem, then physical science becomes subordinate to metaphysics, and is no longer an autonomous science. In this case, estimates of the worth of a physical theory will depend upon the metaphysics one adopts. When practitioners of an area of physical science embrace different metaphysical schemes, progress is impeded because there is a compromise in the cooperation needed for progress. Successful science, if it is to be common to all, should not employ religious or metaphysical commitments only acceptable to some, including theism or physicalist naturalism.

For Duhem, it is not the absence of metaphysics as such that serves the prudential interests of science, but of metaphysical views that divide us. According to Plantinga, Augustinian science stands in contrast to Duhemian science. Roughly, an Augustinian approach to science eschews methodological naturalism, and employs religious or metaphysical commitments specific to a group of practitioners not widely shared throughout the scientific community. Among other things, Augustinian science sanctions the use of scientific data to justify a religious or metaphysical proposition specific to a group of practitioners, at least in principle.

According to Plantinga, Duhemian science will not "employ assumptions like those, for example, that seem to underlie much cognitive science. For example, it could not properly assume that mind-body dualism is false, or that human beings are material objects; these are metaphysical assumptions that divide us."[32] More generally, in my view, that there is a distinction between Duhemian and Augustinian science, and that the former can be practiced at all, seems to justify the Autonomy Thesis. For it shows that the progress of and data derived in accordance with Duhemian science are not of fundamental importance for resolving the deeper metaphysical issues that divide practitioners into different Augustinian camps, at least in many cases.

For different reasons, some aspects of van Fraasen's philosophy of science lead to a similar conclusion. While one need not be an anti-realist to appreciate the point, van Fraasen has argued that the theoretical postulates of a scientific theory typically go beyond the observational evidence and, strictly speaking, several different metaphysical characterizations are empirically equivalent.[33] Moreover, says van Fraasen, the primary goal of a scientific theory is to be empirically adequate, and acceptance of the unobservable metaphysical postulates of a theory is merely a pragmatic stance taken by advocates of a research program to continue searching for greater and greater empirical adequacy.

It seems clear that this is what is actually going on when scientists employ physicalism as the hard core of a scientific research program. They are simply proffering either physically detectable operational definitions of mental states or are straightforwardly searching for physical correlates/causal relations for those mental states. There is not a single discovery in neuroscience (or cognitive science) that requires or even provides adequate justification for abandoning property or substance dualism, since the main issues in neuroscience and philosophy of mind conform to the Autonomy Thesis.

In Plantingian terms, the actual success of, say, neuroscience is strictly due to its Duhemian nature. This is why in the last few decades' three Nobel Prize winners in neuroscience or related fields were a substance dualist (John C. Eccles), an emergent property dualist (Roger Sperry), and a strict physicalist (Francis Crick). What divided them was not a difference of opinion about a range of scientific facts. Their differences were philosophical in nature.

In fact, in a recent article on consciousness and neuroscience, Crick and Christof Koch acknowledge that one of the main attitudes among neuroscientists is that the nature of consciousness is "a philosophical problem, and so best left to philosophers."[34] This posture comports perfectly with Duhemian science. Elsewhere, they claim that "scientists should concentrate on questions that can be experimentally resolved and leave metaphysical speculations to 'late-night conversations over beer'."[35] Methodologically, Crick and Koch choose to set aside philosophical questions about the nature of consciousness, qualia, meaning and so forth, and study the neural correlates of consciousness and the causal/functional role of conscious states. If this is all it means to say that physicalism is "the hard core of a scientific research program," a dualist will heartily agree and, in any case, such a Duhemian appropriation of physicalism underscores and does not provide a counterargument to the Autonomy Thesis.

The mistaken notion that progress in neuroscience requires an Augustinian commitment to physicalism as an essential component of that progress derives not from the actual physical facts of neuroscience or the actual way neuroscience is practiced as evidenced by the Duhemian approach of Crick and Koch. Rather, it is from the sociological fact that many contemporary neuroscientists just happen to be physicalists, and many people, including some philosophers, seem overly impressed with the cultural authority of science.

Second, when scientists study the causal correlates/functional relations between conscious states or the self and the brain, they must rely on first-person reports about those states themselves. To see this, consider the binding problem delineated by John Searle:

> I need to say something about what neurobiologists call "the binding problem." We know that the visual system has cells and indeed regions that are especially responsive to particular features of objects such as color, shape, movement, lines, angles, etc. But when we see an object, we have a unified experience of a single object. How does the brain bind all of these different stimuli into a single, unified experience of an object? The problem extends across the different modes of perception. All of my experiences at present are part of one big unified conscious experience (Kant, with his usual gift for catchy phrases, called this "the transcendental unity of apperception").[36]

Scientists are seeking to find a region of the brain that "unifies" all the different stimuli that activate various parts of the brain. But exactly why would anyone think that such unification should be sought? Certainly not from an empirical investigation of the brain itself. Rather, we know from first-person introspection—in my view, of our own substantial selves and our conscious states—that all of our experiences are unified into one field of consciousness and, in fact, are possessed by one unified I, and it is because of this knowledge that the scientific research program is justified and motivated. Moreover, William Hasker has argued that the phenomena that underlie this research are best explained by (emergent) substance dualism.[37] Whether Hasker is right or not is itself a philosophical matter that illustrates the Autonomy Thesis.

Given that (1) substance and property dualism are widely acknowledged to be the commonsense position based on first-person introspection; (2) the task of arguing for or against dualism so grounded is a philosophical one; and (3) neuroscientific research must rely on first-person introspective reports, the Autonomy Thesis seems to capture adequately the role of pre-philosophical intuitions and distinctively philosophical issues in neuroscience. The debate between dualists and physicalists is not about scientific facts. It is about things such as the status of first-person introspection as a source of justification for commonsense beliefs about the self and consciousness, the status of philosophical knowledge, and the proper philosophical interpretation of the role of physicalism in scientific research.

I think that the truth of the Autonomy Thesis is what philosophers should have expected all along, and it constitutes philosophical self-understanding throughout the history of philosophy up to and including the present. In his 1868 lectures on the limitations of scientific materialism, John Tyndall claimed that "The chasm between the two classes of phenomena" is of such a nature that we might establish empirical association between them, but it

> would still remain intellectually impassable. Let the consciousness of love, for example, be associated with a right-handed spiral motion of the molecules in the brain, and the consciousness of hate with a left-handed spiral motion. We should then know when we love that the motion is in one direction, and when we hate that the motion is in the other; but the "WHY" would remain as unanswerable as before.[38]

Nothing substantial has changed since Tyndall made this remark. Specifically, no advance in knowledge of the specificity of detail regarding the correlations between mental and physical states provides any evidence against dualism or, more importantly, against the Autonomy Thesis. When philosophers write about or teach topics in philosophy of mind, they do not avail themselves of specific information in the hard sciences because it is not relevant to their issues. In evaluating functionalism, it does not matter if one claims that a functional state is realized by brain state alpha or by a more detailed description of the relevant brain state.

If one reads the literature in philosophy of mind, one will find that scientific data plays virtually no role at all in the analysis or arguments. In fact, it is rare for a philosophical text in philosophy of mind to include any scientific information. As was mentioned above, a notable exception to this rule is Paul Churchland's *Matter and Consciousness*.

The same cannot be said, however, of scientific discussions of topics in these areas. To cite one illustration, after claiming to set aside philosophical issues in order to focus on the more important empirical issues, Crick and Koch's discussion of consciousness and neuroscience is literally teeming with philosophical claims about topics philosophical and with which they qua scientists are inadequately equipped to deal. For example, they claim that "Philosophers, in their carefree way, have invented a creature they call a 'zombie,' who is supposed to act just as normal people do but to be completely *un*conscious. This seems to us to be an untenable scientific idea."[39]

Relatedly, in considering whether two people in a similar brain state would experience the same quale, they say that

> One is therefore tempted to use the philosopher's favorite tool, the thought experiment. Unfortunately, this enterprise is fraught with hazards, since it inevitably makes assumptions about how brains behave, and most of these assumptions have so little experimental support that conclusions based on them are valueless.[40]

Crick and Koch seem to have a poor grasp of the role of thought experiments in philosophical argumentation (Does the Knowledge Argument advocate make assumptions about how brains works in the actual world?). But in any case, when compared to philosophical treatments of topics in philosophy of mind, the discussion by Crick and Koch illustrates an asymmetry between neuroscience and philosophy of mind and, therefore, the Autonomy Thesis: scientists cannot adequately discuss the central topics in philosophy of mind without making substantive philosophical claims, but philosophers need not discuss scientific data to treat adequately these same philosophical issues. This is true currently and throughout the history of philosophy, and it is what one would expect if the Autonomy Thesis were true.

Does the Autonomy Thesis mean that science plays no role in philosophical discussion? No, it does not. Science is especially important when it concerns details about the causal relations between mind and body. When philosophers have erred in the past, they have done so when they have used philosophical theses to answer empirical, causal questions (e.g. using vitalism or animal spirits in an attempt to answer efficient causal questions about the precise nature of mind/body interaction). Again, on a certain view of agent causation according to which a libertarian act creates a small amount of energy, scientific investigation could, in principle, confirm or falsify this view, though I have argued elsewhere that the scientific role in this case is not as straightforward as one might think.[41] But the areas where science is relevant are not central to the main first and second order philosophical issues listed at the beginning of this chapter.

If I am right about all this, then if someone is going to be a mind/body physicalist, he or she cannot appeal to science to justify that commitment. It may well be that in first-person introspection one discovers one to be constituted by animality, or there may be overriding philosophical and theological arguments for physicalism, though I suspect that these concessions will be a hard sell to many of us. Explaining why I have these suspicions must be left for another occasion, but one thing seems clear. Whenever and wherever that dialog takes place, it will be a nice illustration of the Autonomy Thesis.

9 AC, dualism and the fear of God

I have argued that if property/event dualism is true, it provides evidence for the existence of God. Recall the distinction between a C-inductive (one in which the premises add to the probability and, in this sense, confirms the conclusion) and a P-inductive (one in which the premises make the conclusion more probable than not) argument. I have argued that AC is at least a correct C-inductive argument, though as a part of a cumulative case, consciousness contributes to a P-inductive theistic argument.

In chapter two, I provided a précis of some evidence for the antecedent of the conditional, though it was not, nor is it now within my objectives to make a case for property/event dualism. In my view, property/event and substance dualism are so obviously true, that it is hard to see why there is so much contemporary hostility to dualism in its various incarnations. At the very least, there are reasons to believe that the rejection of dualism is not primarily a result of the poor intellectual credentials of dualism or the unproblematic nature of strong physicalism. Consider the following pronouncement by Barry Stroud:

> "Naturalism" seems to me … rather like "World Peace." Almost everyone swears allegiance to it, and is willing to march under its banner. But disputes can still break out about what it is appropriate or acceptable to do in the name of that slogan. And like world peace, once you start specifying concretely exactly what it involves and how to achieve it, it becomes increasingly difficult to reach and to sustain a consistent and exclusive "naturalism." There is pressure on the one hand to include more and more within your conception of "nature," so it loses its definiteness and restrictiveness. Or, if the conception is kept fixed and restrictive, there is pressure on the other hand to distort or even to deny the very phenomena that a naturalistic study—and especially a naturalistic study of human beings—is supposed to explain.[1]

In chapters one through eight, I have been at pains to show why naturalism is so hard to define. As we have seen, the answer is related to the two-sided pressure to which Stroud refers. If we think of versions of naturalism along a continuum, then at one end we have robust positive naturalism: naturalism whose claim to worldview superiority resides in its certification by the epistemology/methods of the hard sciences and the Grand Story's ability to explain how everything has come-to-be. Robust positive naturalism is correctly seen as entailing strict physicalism, but its ontology is hard to defend. For this reason, versions of naturalism are formulated at other points along the spectrum, with those at the other end resting content to quantify over a large shopping list of *sui generis*, recalcitrant entities or degenerating into the merely negative thesis that God does not exist. The increasing price to be paid for residence along the spectrum whose distance from robust positive naturalism widens is a growing loss of explanatory power and comportment with the ontology, epistemology, and methodology of the hard sciences. In short, the robust positive naturalist response to restrictive pressure retains (in principle) the potential for naturalist explanatory and epistemic superiority, but also renders it a distorted, false picture of reality. Naturalist responses that seek to be more inclusive increasingly render naturalism less definite, more *ad hoc* and question-begging, and weaken its claim to explanatory/epistemic superiority.

In this closing chapter, I want to step back from specific issues and alternatives central to explaining the origin of consciousness and focus on the psychological, sociological, and even spiritual climate within which topics in philosophy of mind are currently being discussed. I believe such an exercise is quite revealing and, moreover, very relevant to all who want to get at the truth surrounding the nature of consciousness, the self, and the best explanation for their appearance in cosmic history. In what follows, I shall identify and clarify a psychological, sociological and spiritual phenomenon, viz., the fear of God, which I believe explains the reactionary attitude towards, loathing of, and widespread rejection of dualism. These attitudes are held more strongly and widely than can be justified by strictly intellectual argumentation, and as a result, there is considerable social pressure on younger philosophers to be physicalists. After I have identified and clarified the fear of God, I shall provide three pieces of evidence that it is the fear of God that drives the current and confident acceptance of strong physicalism and naturalism and rejection of dualism. It will become clear, I believe, that AC is a part of the background of this rejection. I shall close by offering a way to turn my observations into an argument against strong physicalism and naturalism.

The fear of God

Hylomania and pneumatophobia

On one occasion, John Locke bemoaned the fact that the idea of soul, especially when compared to the idea of matter, was regarded as obscure by many in his day. Locke thought that this judgment followed from people being preoccupied with the study of material substances compared to immaterial ones: "I know that People, whose Thoughts are immersed in Matter, and have so subjected their Minds to their Senses that they seldom reflect on anything beyond them."[2]

In this judgment, Locke was probably correct. Around two decades before the publication of *An Essay Concerning Human Understanding*, Ralph Cudworth had noted a growing number of thinkers "possessed with a certain Kind of Madness, that may be called pneumatophobia, that makes them have an irrational, but desperate abhorrence from spirits or incorporeal substances." According to Cudworth, this attitude went along with hylomania "whereby they madly dote upon Matter."[3]

In my view, there are reasons to think that the current hylomania characteristic of naturalists is due in large measure to pneumatophobia or, more specifically, to a fear of God. Even if philosophers do not believe dualism provides evidence for the existence of God, nevertheless, dualism is often associated with theism, usually Christian theism. Naturalist William Lyons notes that

> [physicalism] seem[s] to be in tune with the scientific materialism of the twentieth century because it [is] a harmonic of the general theme that all there is in the universe is matter and energy and motion and that humans are a product of the evolution of species just as much as buffaloes and beavers are. Evolution is a seamless garment with no holes wherein souls might be inserted from above.[4]

His expression "a seamless garment with no holes wherein souls might be inserted from above" clearly refers to the fact that the appearance of souls cannot be adequately explained by naturalistic evolution and the best account of their appearance would be a miraculous intervention by a transcendent Creator.

Religion and neurotic physicalism

Along similar lines, John Searle has some pretty harsh things to say about the last fifty years or so of work in the philosophy of mind.[5] Specifically, he says that the field has contained numerous assertions that are obviously false and absurd and has cycled neurotically through various positions precisely because of the dominance of strong physicalism as the only live option for a naturalist. Searle's statement of the reason for this neurotic behavior is revealing:

> How is it that so many philosophers and cognitive scientists can say so many things that, to me at least, seem obviously false? . . . I believe one of the unstated assumptions behind the current batch of views

> is that they represent the only scientifically acceptable alternatives to the antiscientism that went with traditional dualism, the belief in the immortality of the soul, spiritualism, and so on. Acceptance of the current views is motivated not so much by an independent conviction of their truth as by a terror of what are apparently the only alternatives. That is, the choice we are tacitly presented with is between a "scientific" approach, as represented by one or another of the current versions of "materialism," and an "unscientific" approach, as represented by Cartesianism or some other traditional religious conception of the mind.[6]

In other words, philosophy of mind has been dominated by scientific naturalism for fifty years and scientific naturalists have advanced different versions of strong physicalism, however implausible they may be in light of what is obviously known by us about consciousness, because strong physicalism was seen as a crucial implication of taking the naturalistic turn. For these naturalists, if one abandons strong physicalism one has rejected a scientific naturalist approach to the mind/body problem and opened himself up to the intrusion of religious concepts and arguments about the mental.

The cosmic authority problem

Perhaps the clearest expression of the role that the fear of God plays in sustaining strong naturalism and the avoidance of dualism has been stated by Thomas Nagel. In the context of discussing a view that takes irreducible, rational mind and its relationship to the world as something fundamental, in a rare moment of candor, Nagel says that this view

> makes many people in this day and age nervous. I believe that this is one manifestation of a fear of religion which has large and often pernicious consequences for modern intellectual life.
>
> In speaking of the fear of religion, I don't mean to refer to the entirely reasonable hostility toward certain established religions and religious institutions, in virtue of their objectionable moral doctrines, social policies, and political influence. Nor am I referring to the association of many religious beliefs with superstition and the acceptance of evident empirical falsehoods. I am talking about something much deeper—namely, the fear of religion itself. I speak from experience, being strongly subject to this fear myself: I want atheism to be true and am made uneasy by the fact that some of the most intelligent and well-informed people I know are religious believers. It isn't just that I don't believe in God and, naturally, hope that I'm right in my belief. It's that I hope there is no God! I don't want there to be a God; I don't want the universe to be like that.

> My guess is that this cosmic authority problem is not a rare condition and that it is responsible for much of the scientism and reductionism of our time. One of the tendencies it supports is the ludicrous overuse of evolutionary biology to explain everything about life, including everything about the human mind. Darwin enabled modern secular culture to heave a great collective sigh of relief, by apparently providing a way to eliminate purpose, meaning, and design as fundamental features of the world.[7]

This Pneumatophobia provides the psychological, sociological and spiritual background that I believe sustains a commitment to strong physicalism/naturalism far beyond the intellectual considerations that can be marshaled on its behalf. And this fear of God is also what sustains the rejection and loathing of dualism far beyond the meager quality of the intellectual considerations against it. By including a chapter on this subject, I am not referring to the fear of God as a substitute for argumentation. Dualists and theists provide arguments for their views, and I have tried to defend AC in the preceding chapters. In fact, I will argue later that there is a way to turn these psychological, sociological and spiritual factors into an argument for dualism. Irrespective of this, however, for those philosophers and, indeed, those in the broader intellectual community who are still interested in truth, it would be foolish not to consider the role such fear plays in shaping the dialog in philosophy of mind in its current setting.

Three lines of evidence that the fear of God sustains strong naturalism

I believe that there are three lines of evidence in the literature of the philosophy of mind that justifies the idea that it is not primarily intellectual considerations that explain the widespread acceptance of strong physicalism/naturalism. Rather, it is Pneumatophobia and the fear of God.

Argumentation and dualism

First, there is the low quality of argumentation when it comes to evaluating substance dualism (or theism) when it is related to philosophy of mind. Most strong naturalists are exceptionally capable philosophers and the quality of their argumentation is evident when they defend a certain version of physicalism or criticize alternatives. But when it comes to stating and criticizing substance dualism, the quality dips considerably. This consideration is a bit subjective, I admit. About all I can do to defend the claim is to provide some examples and invite the reader to examine the literature.

We saw in chapter five that Colin McGinn's critique of theism in *The Mysterious Flame* is completely out of touch with the explosion—now at least two decades old—of sophisticated defenses of theism and dualism.

This is not characteristic of McGinn. But his dismissal of theism is unworthy of a philosopher of his stature. He seems out of touch with the last twenty years or so of work in philosophy of religion. He does not list one relevant source in his footnotes and he seems to lack awareness of detailed distinctions regarding different infinite regresses, distinctions that have been around a long time and which are required material for an intellectually responsible treatment of God and infinite regresses, a treatment that McGinn purports to offer.

The main arguments for substance dualism are these:

> *Argument 1*: In acts of introspection, I am aware of 1) my self as an unextended center of consciousness; 2) various capacities of thought, sensation, belief, desire, and volition which I exercise and which are essential, internal aspects of the kind of thing I am; 3) my sensations, e.g. this very pain, as being necessarily such that there is no possible world in which they could exist and not be mine. If we grant that my sensations are either modes of my self or events externally related to some physical particular, then my sensations are modes because modes are internally related to their substances but there are possible worlds in which a specific mental event is externally related to a different physical particular.[8]

What I am calling argument one is actually three arguments that draw their force from what substance dualists claim we know about ourselves from attending to ourselves and our conscious states. Put more formally, these three variants of an argument from introspection look like this:

Variant One:

(1) I am an unextended center of consciousness (justified by introspection).
(2) No physical object is an unextended center of consciousness.
(3) Therefore, I am not a physical object.
(4) Either I am a physical object or an immaterial substance.
(5) Therefore, I am an immaterial substance.

Variant Two:

(1) My various capacities for conscious states are essential to me and when actualized, the properties of consciousness that constitute those states are predicatively internal to me and characterize the type of thing I am. They do not stand to me by way of some external relation.
(2) If I am a physical object, then there is a possible world in which I exist without the capacities for consciousness (justified by strong conceivability) and, thus, those capacities are not essential to me. Moreover, when actualized, the properties of consciousness that constitute those states are externally related to me.

(3) Thus I am not a physical object.
(4) Either I am a physical object or an immaterial substance.
(5) Therefore, I am an immaterial substance.

Variant Three:

(1) My sensations (and other states of consciousness) are either externally or internally related to me.
(2) If I am a physical object, then my sensations are externally related to me such that there is a possible world in which those sensations exist and are not so related to me.
(3) There is no possible world in which my sensations exist without being mind.
(4) Therefore, I am not a physical object and my sensations are internally related to me.
(5) If a sensation is internally related to me, then it is a mode of my self, where a mode is an inseparable, dependent part of the thing it modifies and, as such, it is modally distinct from and internally related to that thing and it provides information about the nature of the thing of which it is a mode.
(6) Therefore, I am a thing whose nature is to have sensations (and other states of consciousness).

While my purpose is not to defend these arguments, it may be useful to clarify certain notions central to them, e.g. "being predicatively internal" or "internally related to me", "an external relation". To begin with, let us take as primitive the notion of a constituent/whole relation. A constituent/whole relation takes place between two entities just in case one entity is in the other as a constituent. So understood, there are two main types of constituent/whole relations: the standard separable part/whole relation of mereology and the accidental or essential predication relation. When a whole has a part or an accidental or essential property, the part or property is a constituent in the whole. In the sense used here, when one entity is a constituent of a whole, it is internally related to that whole. By contrast, "an external relation" in this context is one which relates one entity to another without the former becoming a constituent of the latter. Thus, "to the left of" is an external relation in my sense as is "being causally emergent upon."

Next, I need to clarify the notion of a mode. Here is a sufficient condition of some entity being a mode of another entity. If, for some substance S and Property P, S exemplifies P, then the state of affairs—S's exemplifying P (call it A)—is a mode of S. As such, the mode is a dependent part of S internally related to S. There is no possible world where A exists and S does not.

Moreover, if at some time T, S has A (S exemplifies P), then at all times prior to T, S had the (first or higher order) potentiality to have A. And part of what makes S the kind of substance it is, is its potentialities.

Now the substance dualist takes sensations (and other mental states) to be modes of the substantial self according to the different variants of argument one above. In current debates about physicalism, if supervenience is taken as a relation causal or otherwise, the relevant mental properties or tokens are externally connected to the brain or other relevant physical object (e.g. a physical simple in the brain). One reason for this is the possibility (justified on the basis of strong conceivability) of zombie worlds without the relevant properties or tokens and disembodied worlds with those properties or tokens.

Stewart Goetz and Geoffrey Madell have advanced versions of argument one.[9]

> *Argument 2*: Personal identity at and through time is primitive and absolute. Moreover, counter examples exist which show that the various body or psychological (e.g. memory) views of personal identity are neither necessary nor sufficient. Put linguistically, talk about persons is not analyzable into talk about their connected mental lives. This fact is not innocuous but, rather, has important metaphysical implications. Substance dualism, in which the soul is taken as a substance with an essence constituted by the potential for thought, belief, desire, sensation and volition, is the best explanation of these facts.

This argument has been advanced by Richard Swinburne.[10]

> *Argument 3*: The indexicality of thought provides evidence for the truth of substance dualism and the nature of the substantial self. A complete, third-person physical description of the world will fail to capture the fact expressed in "I am J. P. Moreland." No amount of information non-indexically expressed captures the content conveyed by this assertion. The first-person indexical "I" is irreducible and uneliminable and this feature of "I" is not innocuous, but rather, is explained by claiming that "I" refers to a nonphysical entity—the substantial self. Moreover, if we add mental predicates to our third-person descriptive language, we still will not be able to capture the state of affairs expressed by statements like "I am thinking that P" or "I am being appeared to redly." Finally, the system of indexical reference (e.g. "I", "here", "there", "this", "that") must have a unifying center that underlies it.[11] This unifying center is the same entity referred to by "I" in expressions like "I am thinking that P", namely, the conscious substantial subject taken as a self conscious, self referring particular.[12] We may state the argument this way:

(1) Statements using the first-person indexical "I" express facts about persons that cannot be expressed in statements without the first-person indexical.

(2) If I am a physical object, then all the facts about me can be expressed in statements without the first-person indexical.
(3) Therefore, I am not a physical object.
(4) The facts mentioned in (1) are best explained by substance dualism.

Geoffrey Madell and H. D. Lewis have advocated this type of argument.[13]

> *Argument 4*: Some have argued for substance dualism because libertarian freedom is true and either a necessary condition for libertarian freedom is substance dualism or the latter is the best explanation for the former. The argument may be put this way (using only the form in which substance dualism is a necessary condition for libertarian freedom):

(1) If human beings exercise libertarian agency, then (i) they have the power to initiate change as a first mover; (ii) they have the power to refrain from exercising their power to initiate change; and (iii) they act for the sake of reasons as irreducible, teleological ends for the sake of which they act.
(2) Human beings exercise libertarian agency.
(3) No material object (one which is such that all of its properties, parts, and capacities are at least and only physical) can exercise libertarian agency.
(4) Therefore, human beings are not material objects.[14]
(5) Human beings are either material objects or immaterial substances.
(6) Therefore, they are immaterial substances.

Substance dualist John Foster has employed this sort of argument.[15]

> *Argument 5*: Thought experiments have rightly been central to debates about personal identity and dualism. For example, we are often invited to consider a situation in which two persons switch bodies, brains, or personality traits or in which a person exists disembodied. In these thought experiments, someone argues in the following way: Because a certain state of affairs S (e.g. Smith existing disembodied) is conceivable, this provides justification for thinking that S is metaphysically possible. Now if S is possible, then certain implications follow about what is/is not essential to personal identity (e.g. Smith is not essentially a body).

Some have criticized the use of conceivability as a test for possibility because the notion of conceiving is vague and used in a variety of different ways.[16] I agree that "to conceive" does not mean "to image" (we can conceive of things, e.g. God, without imaging them) or "to understand" (we can understand impossible states of affairs, e.g. that there are square circles). What exactly do I mean by "to conceive"? In my view, what is conceived is "what seems to be coherently supposed."

There are two forms of conceiving relevant to personal identity—weak and strong conceiving.[17] Something is weakly conceivable for a person when he reflects on it and sees no reason to believe it to be impossible. Something is strongly conceivable for a person when he judges that it is possible based on a more positive grasp of the properties involved and of the compatibility of what he is conceiving with what he already knows. If something is weakly conceivable, one sees no reason for thinking it is impossible. If something is strongly conceivable, one sees good reason for thinking it is possible.

We all use conceiving as a test for possibility/impossibility throughout our lives.[18] I know that life on other planets is possible because I can conceive it to be so. I am aware of what it is to be living and to be on earth and I conceive no necessary connections between these two properties. I know square circles are impossible because it is inconceivable given my knowledge of being square and being circular. To be sure, judgments that a state of affairs is possible/impossible grounded in conceivability are not infallible. They can be wrong. Still, they provide strong evidence for genuine possibility/impossibility. In light of this, I offer the following criterion:

> For any entities x and y, if I have grounds for believing I can conceive of x existing without y or vice versa, then I have good grounds for believing x is not essential or identical to y or vice versa.

Let us apply these insights about conceivability and possibility to the modal argument for substance dualism. The argument has been advanced by Keith Yandell and Charles Taliaferro, and while it comes in many forms, it may be fairly stated as follows:[19]

(1) The law of identity: If x is identical to y, then whatever is true of x is true of y and vice versa.
(2) I can strongly conceive of myself as existing disembodied or, indeed, without any physical particular existing.
(3) If I can strongly conceive of some state of affairs S that S possibly obtains, then I have good grounds for believing of S that S is possible.
(4) Therefore, I have good grounds for believing of myself that it is possible for me to exist and be disembodied.
(5) If some entity x is such that it is possible for x to exist without y, then (i) x is not identical to y and (ii) y is not essential to x.
(6) My physical body is not such that it is possible to exist disembodied or without any physical particular existing.
(7) Therefore, I have good grounds for believing of myself that I am not identical to a physical particular, including my physical body and that no physical particular, including my physical body is essential to me.

A parallel argument can be developed to show that possessing the ultimate capacities of sensation, thought, belief, desire, and volition are essential to me.

My purpose in mentioning these arguments is not to defend them or even present them in a thorough way. Rather, I have listed and elaborated on these arguments with enough detail to make it evident that there is a serious lack of interaction with these arguments in physicalist writings where it would be appropriate to do so. Thus, Paul Churchland's otherwise excellent work *Matter and Consciousness*[20] suffers a clear lack of quality when substance dualism is discussed. These arguments are not mentioned, much less enjoined. Instead, we have *ad hominem* remarks about religion, the mandatory mention of the Vatican's treatment of Galileo, and so on. In fact, Churchland actually mentions with mockery how supermarket tabloids try to prove life after death ("TOP DOCS PROVE LIFE AFTER DEATH!!!") while confidently asserting that there is no empirical evidence for these claims even though he does not interact with one single credible NDE case or source.[21]

Likewise, even though Jaegwon Kim has been concerned about mental causation, you will search in vain in his major works to find any attempt at all to examine the case for agent causation and the implications it may have for philosophy of mind. It is as though Kim keeps his philosophy of mind and action entirely separate from each other. But substance dualists have advanced technical arguments for their view from libertarian agency and agent causation, and Kim should interact with them when he treats the topic of mental causation.

Moreover, in the 1996 edition of his *Philosophy of Mind* text Kim's discussion of substance dualism is incredibly weak when compared to the excellent treatment of other topics in the book. In Churchland's case, it takes a mere fourteen pages to dismiss substance and property dualism (about half of which describes and sets aside substance dualism), and the rest of the book consists largely though not exclusively in evaluating the various physicalist philosophies of mind. In Kim's case, substance dualism is presented in a scant three pages after which the rest of the book is devoted to physicalist theories.

Happily, the 2006 revised edition of *Philosophy of Mind* contains a chapter on substance dualism with a fair representation of the arguments for it. However, Kim (and most others, including Churchland) continues to present only Cartesian dualism. This is a serious omission, especially in Kim's case, because Thomistic dualism contains a solution to his version of the pairing problem he takes to be decisive against Cartesianism. I cannot imagine Kim treating another topic without interacting with a major viewpoint that claims to rebut one of his main arguments. Yet this is precisely what Kim does regarding causal pairing. It is as though he simply is not aware of the Thomistic view or its solution to causal pairing. How could a philosopher of Kim's stature claim to be taking dualism seriously when he fails to interact even briefly with a major, relevant version of dualism?[22]

I cite one more example, which may be the most egregious one so far. In *Beyond Evolution: Human Nature and the limits of Evolutionary*

Explanation, Anthony O'Hear provides a detailed, convincing case that there are a number of features of human beings that lie entirely outside naturalistic, including evolutionary explanation.[23] So far so good. But O'Hear offers no plausible explanation whatever as to how human beings so construed could ever have arisen. Clearly, the context of his book cries out for interaction with sophisticated Christian theistic accounts of the origin and nature of human beings, even if they are mentioned for the express purpose of refuting them. However, inexplicably, he does not interact with any theistic literature at all, and in his bibliography, he does not include one theistic source that informs his topic. This is intellectually irresponsible because the thesis of his book is precisely what one would predict, given Christian theism and the doctrine of the image of God, viz., that several aspects of human beings would be recalcitrant facts for alternative worldviews, especially for naturalism.

I am not trying to be mean-spirited here. I am simply pointing out that when it comes to presenting the best arguments for theism or dualism and rebutting them, strong naturalists who deal with philosophy of mind do not sustain the level of excellence in treating these topics that are characteristic of their careful analyses of physicalist issues and options. At the very least, this is curious, and it may be a sign of the fact that dualism and AC are largely dismissed for non-intellectual reasons. Thus, it is not taken seriously and that explains the lack of quality to which I am referring.

Failure to enjoin dualist literature

Second, physicalists do not interact with leading dualists, particularly substance dualists, in their writings, endnotes, or bibliographies. In fact, there is usually no mention at all of key defenses of dualism, and when they are listed in a bibliography, they are hardly enjoined. Leading dualists (some of whom lean more towards some form of idealism) include Robert Adams, George Bealer, Francis Beckwith, Mark Bedau, Roderick Chisholm, John Foster, Stewart Goetz, W. D. Hart, William Hasker, Brian Leftow, Geoffrey Madell, Paul Mosser, Alvin Plantinga, Howard Robinson, Jeffrey Schwartz, Eleanore Stump, Richard Swinburne, Charles Taliaferro, Dallas Willard, Dean Zimmerman. It is too often the case that naturalistic treatments of philosophy of mind do not mention or interact with the arguments presented by these and other leading dualists.

Dualism and dismissive rhetorical moves

Finally, there are various rhetorical devices used to dismiss dualism, AC or theism that are not worthy of those who employ them. Searle points out four of them, which I have also observed:[24]

(1) The use of technical jargon to cover up the implausibility of one's view: the sheer implausibility of such [physicalist] theories [e.g. they imply

that consciousness does not really exist] is disguised by the apparently technical character of the arguments bandied back and forth.[25]

(2) Authors [usually physicalists for Searle] who are about to say something that sounds silly very seldom come right out and say it. Usually a set of rhetorical or stylistic devices is employed to avoid having to say it in words of one syllable. The most obvious of these devices is to beat around the bush with a lot of evasive prose. I think it is obvious in the writings of several authors, for example, that they think we really don't have mental states, such as beliefs, desires, fears, etc. But it is hard to find passages where they actually say this straight out. Often they want to keep the commonsense vocabulary, while denying that it actually stands for anything in the real world.[26]

(3) Another rhetorical devise for disguising the implausible is to give the commonsense view a name and then deny it by name and not by content. Thus, it is very hard even in the present era to come right out and say, "No human being has ever been conscious." Rather, the sophisticated philosopher gives the view that people are sometimes conscious a name, for example, "the Cartesian intuition," then he or she sets about challenging, questioning, denying something described as "the Cartesian intuition." ... And just to give this maneuver a name, I will call it the "give-it-a-name" maneuver.[27]

(4) Another maneuver, the most favored of all, I will call the "heroic-age-of-science" maneuver. When an author gets in deep trouble, he or she tries to make an analogy with his or her own claim and some great scientific discovery of the past. Does the view seem silly? Well, the great scientific geniuses of the past seemed silly to their ignorant, dogmatic, and prejudiced contemporaries. Galileo is the favorite historical analogy. Rhetorically speaking, the idea is to make you, the skeptical reader, feel that if you don't believe the view being advanced, you are playing Cardinal Ballarmine to the author's Galileo.[28]

Unfortunately, Searle is guilty of his own rhetorical ploys and egregiously so. He assures us that it is an "obvious fact of physics—that the world consists entirely of physical particles in fields of force"[29] Obvious? A fact of physics? I would like to have the journal reference in a physics journal where this fact was discovered and by whom. The truth is that physics has no view of being at all and, thus, no view qua physics of what the world does or does not consist in. This is obvious, not Searle's overstatement.

Again, regarding Cartesian souls that can survive death, Searle opines that "nowadays, as far as I can tell, no one believes in the existence of immortal spiritual substances except on religious grounds. To my knowledge, there are no purely philosophical or scientific motivations for accepting the existence of immortal mental substances."[30] We will see below why this remark is intellectually irresponsible. However, rhetorically, its dismissive function is to associate substance dualism with the excess baggage of immortality—and the two are quite independent—and to paint a picture of dualists as a band of cowering fundamentalists heroically trying to cling to their doctrine in spite of an avalanche of evidence against them.[31]

Finally, in the context of claiming that the naturalist worldview consisting of the atomic theory of matter and evolutionary biology is the only view a contemporary well-educated person can believe, Searle says,

> Our problem is not that somehow we have failed to come up with a convincing proof of the existence of God or that the hypothesis of an afterlife remains in serious doubt, it is rather that in our deepest reflections we cannot take such opinions seriously. When we encounter people who claim to believe such things, we may envy them the comfort and security they claim to derive from such beliefs, but at bottom we remain convinced that either they have not heard the news or they are in the grip of faith. We remain convinced that somehow they must separate their minds into separate compartments to believe such things.[32]

Searle published these remarks in 1992, but his book continues to be reprinted without revision, so I assume he still holds them. His statements are so incredible and outlandish, that I must conclude that it is he who has not heard the news. And I would not be surprised to learn that his own version of naturalistic faith is something that provides him "comfort and security" in the face of the cosmic authority problem. One wonders how a philosopher of Searle's stature can get away with saying things like this. In the last forty years, there has been a dramatic revolution in Anglo-American philosophy. Since the late 1960s, Christian philosophers have openly identified themselves as believing Christians and defending the truth of a Christian worldview with philosophically sophisticated arguments in the finest scholarly journals and professional societies. And the face of Anglo-American philosophy has been transformed as a result.

In a recent article lamenting "the desecularization of academia that evolved in philosophy departments since the late 1960s," Quentin Smith, a prominent atheist philosopher, observes that "in philosophy, it became, almost overnight, 'academically respectable' to argue for theism, making philosophy a favored field of entry for the most intelligent and talented theists entering academia today."[33] He complains that "Naturalists passively watched as realist versions of theism … began to sweep through the philosophical community, until today perhaps one-quarter or one-third of philosophy professors are theists, with most being orthodox Christians."[34] He concludes, "God is not 'dead' in academia; he returned to life in the late 1960s and is now alive and well in his last academic stronghold, philosophy departments."[35] Smith continues:

> The current practice, ignoring theism, has proven to be a disastrous failure. More fully, naturalist philosophers' pursuit of the cultural goal of mainstream secularization in a philosophically governed way has failed both philosophically (in regards to the philosophical aspects of this philosophically governed pursuit of the cultural goal) and culturally. The philosophical failure has led to a cultural failure. We have the following situation: A hand waving dismissal of theism, such as is manifested in the following passage from [John] Searle's *The Rediscovery of the Mind*, has been like trying to halt a tidal wave with a hand-held sieve. Searle responds to about one-third of contemporary philosophers with this brush-off: Talking about the scientific and naturalist world-view, he writes: "this world view is not an option. It is not simply up for grabs along with a lot of competing world views. Our problem is not that somehow we have failed to come up with a convincing proof of the existence of God or that the hypothesis of afterlife remains in serious doubt, it is rather than in our deepest reflections we cannot take such opinions seriously. When we encounter people who claim to believe such things, we may envy them the comfort and security they claim to derive from these beliefs, but at bottom we remained convinced that either they have not heard the news or they are in the grip of faith." Searle does not have an area of specialization in the philosophy of religion and, if he did, he might, in the face of the erudite brilliance of theistic philosophizing today, say something more similar to the non-theist Richard Gale (who does have an area of specialization in the philosophy of religion), whose conclusion of a 422 page book criticizing contemporary philosophical arguments for God's existence (as well as dealing with other matters in the philosophy of religion), reads "no definite conclusion can be drawn regarding the rationality of faith"[36] (if only for the reason, Gale says, that his book does not examine the inductive arguments for God's existence). If each naturalist who does not specialize in the philosophy of religion (i.e. over ninety-nine percent of naturalists) were locked in a room with theists who do specialize in the philosophy of religion, and if the ensuing debates were refereed by a naturalist who had a specialization in the philosophy of religion, the naturalist referee could at most hope the outcome would be that "no definite conclusion can be drawn regarding the rationality of faith," although I expect the most probable outcome is that the naturalist, wanting to be a fair and objective referee, would have to conclude that the theists definitely had the upper hand in every single argument or debate.[37]

In light of these matters that Smith chronicles, the following statement by Searle is hard to understand. When asked if he had a belief in the supernatural, Searle responded:

> None. But you see, there's something else that is, in a way, more important in this issue of the supernatural. Intellectuals in our culture have become so secularized, there's a sense in which the existence of the supernatural wouldn't matter in the way that it mattered a hundred years ago. Suppose we discovered that we're wrong, that there really is this divine force in the universe. Well then, most intellectuals would say, okay, that's a fact of physics like any other—instead of just four forces in the universe, we have a fifth force. In this sense, our attitude about the existence of God wouldn't be as important because the world has already become demystified for us. Essentially our worldview would remain even if we discovered that we had been wrong, that God did exist.[38]

Searle is clearly not speaking for hundreds, indeed, thousands of philosophers or for the tens of thousands of university professors who are classic theists. Thus, it is rhetorically misleading at best and intellectually irresponsible at worst for Searle to paint with such a big brush. And I don't know of any serious philosopher of religion who would use "God" and "a divine force" which is "a fifth force" interchangeably without at least some justification. But more importantly, it is hard to see how one would argue for theism in general, or substance dualism and AC in particular with someone whose views are as indefeasible as Searle's. When statements like these are made, there is usually something more happening than mere intellectual viewpoints, and the cosmic authority problem is a good candidate for that "something more."

I do not wish to continue with this section except to say that I could provide numerous examples of each line of evidence. But I do not think that is necessary. I can only appeal to the reader to look at the relevant literature and see if what I am saying is true. Let us suppose for the sake of argument that it is. What follows from this? For one thing, I believe naturalists need to be more self-reflective about what is driving them and how it is affecting the quality of their work in this area. But I believe that there is another implication of the ubiquitous fear of God that these three lines of evidence support and expose.

Turning the fear of God into an argument

Epistemic externalists and internalists can agree that having properly functioning faculties is relevant to knowledge and justified belief, though they will spell out the details of this agreement differently. Still, the agreement is not without significance. In March of 1984, the philosophy department at the University of Mississippi sponsored two debates between Kai Neilsen and me on the existence of God that were subsequently published.[39] During both debates, we each presented arguments for our position and sought to defeat the others.

At one point, I introduced a consideration (that I carefully distinguished from a genetic fallacy) which introduced a second-order debate.[40] I pointed out that we each had presented evidence for our side and against the other viewpoint, and we each believed our case was the better one. In this case, I suggested, we each could claim that the other was not seeing the evidence clearly or adequately appreciating its dialogical force. In order to prevent this from becoming a shouting match, I introduced the following claim: Atheists fit a tighter control group than theists in that the class of atheists are more homogenous, viz., there is a strong, if not universal trait among atheists according to which they have had difficulties with their father figure—he was harsh, stern and critical, or he was passive and embarrassing. I pointed to studies that supported my assertion.[41]

By contrast, I claimed that theism was the ordinary response of the human person to creation; it did not need to be taught to people (though culture could influence the direction it took), but atheism did. Moreover, the class of theists was so diverse that no single factor could be identified that unified the class, e.g. some were intelligent, others not, some emotional, some not, some wanted theism to be true, others not, and so forth. Thus, I could identify a factor that was, arguably, the faculty distorter that caused atheists to fail to see the evidence clearly and adequately appreciate its force, but no such factor could be identified for theists. Since I could identify a plausible psychological, sociological or spiritual distorting factor while Nielsen could not, then in addition to the presentation of my first-order evidence for theism, I had an objective, factual second-order argument against the atheist's treatment of the first-order evidence.

More generally, if the issue of faculty reliability or proper function is epistemically relevant, then it is hard to see why this observation should be left there. It would seem to be epistemically relevant if one could actually make a case that a particular faculty relevant to a specific area of debate was not reliable or functioning properly. Whether or not such a case is persuasive in a particular instance, it is still correct to say that one who makes such a case is advancing an *argument*.

I believe the same thing is going on with respect to dualism and AC. Almost everyone agrees that dualism is the common sense view that virtually all cultures throughout history have embraced. Jaegwon Kim's acknowledgement is typical: "We commonly think that we, as persons, have a mental and bodily dimension ... Something like this dualism of personhood, I believe, is common lore shared across most cultures and religious traditions."[42] Along similar lines, Frank Jackson says,

> I take it that our folk concept of personal identity is Cartesian in character—in particular, we regard the question of whether *I* will be tortured tomorrow as separable from the question of whether someone with *any* amount of continuity—psychological, bodily, neurophysiological, and so on and so forth—with me today will be tortured tomorrow.[43]

Moreover, this advice from Joshua Hoffman and Gary S. Rosenkrantz seems both wise and applicable to the issue of dualism: "If entities of a certain kind belong to folk ontology [the ontological presuppositions of our common sense conceptual scheme], then there is a *prima facie* presumption in favor of their reality. … [T]hose who deny their existence assume the burden of proof."[44]

Whether or not one accept the *prima facie* justification of folk ontology, it seems plausible that the fear of God, the cosmic authority problem supports the current popularity of strong physicalism and influences its treatment of dualism in a way that a parallel motivation does not inflict dualism. Dualism is pretty much commonsense. The same cannot be said for physicalism. And even if one believes that at the end of the day, some version of strong physicalism is the best option in philosophy of mind, the fear of God could still have plenty of explanatory work to do. I believe that such a person, if he or she honestly examines the literature in philosophy of mind, will find that the lines of evidence listed in this chapter provide grounds for believing that the fear of God is what enables strong physicalism to enjoy such widespread and unflinching acceptance far beyond what the evidence for it will sustain.

Conclusion

Strong naturalism/physicalism has been in a period of Kuhnian paradigm crisis for a long time, and physicalist epicycles have multiplied like rabbits in the last two decades. Moreover, the various versions of physicalism are in a period of stalemate. No progress seems evident. In spite of dismissive rhetoric to the contrary, I believe that some form of substance and property dualism represent the most plausible view of the constitution of human persons. Admittedly, I have not been able to argue for this claim directly in this book with anything approaching the thoroughness such a task would require. But I have been at pains in this chapter to show that the widespread preference for physicalism coupled with the loathing of dualism can be significantly explained because of the fear of God.

The truth is that naturalism has no plausible way to explain the appearance of irreducible, genuinely mental properties/events in the cosmos, nor do mysterian, panpsychic or emergentistic monist explanations when compared to the rich explanatory resources of theism and AC. Ned Block confesses that we have no idea how consciousness could have emerged from nonconscious matter: "we have nothing—zilch—worthy of being called a research programme. … Researchers are stumped."[45] John Searle says this is a "leading problem in the biological sciences."[46] Colin McGinn observes that consciousness seems like "a radical novelty in the universe";[47] he wonders how our "technicolour" awareness can "arise from soggy grey matter."[48] David Chalmers asserts that "No explanation given wholly in physical terms can ever account for the emergence of conscious experience."[49]

Responding to the question of why consciousness (construed dualistically) emerges, David Papineau acknowledges: "to this question physicalists 'theories of consciousness' seem to provide no answer."[50] Papineau's solution is to deny the reality of consciousness as a genuinely mental phenomenon.[51] He correctly sees that strong physicalism is the only real alternative for a naturalist.

The inexplicability of consciousness for physicalist naturalism has been noted for a long time. As Leibniz argued:

> It must be confessed, moreover, that *perception*, and that which depends on it *are inexplicable by mechanical causes*, that is, by figures and motions. And, supposing there were a machine so constructed as to think, feel and have perception, we could conceive of it as enlarged and yet preserving the same proportions, so that we might enter it as a mill. And this granted, we should only find on visiting it, pieces which push one against another, but never anything by which to explain a perception. This must be sought for, therefore, in the simple substance and not in the composite or in the machine.[52]

While our conception of matter has changed in certain ways beyond the mechanistic depiction of Leibniz's day, his assertion is as applicable today as it was then. If naturalism is construed as a worldview and a naturalist so inclined embraces genuinely emergent mental properties, then he or she has really admitted defeat as Frank Jackson acknowledges: "Our primary concern is with physicalism as a doctrine of the *kind of world* we are in. From this perspective, attribute dualism is not more physicalistically acceptable than is substance dualism."[53] Supervenience in general, and emergentism in particular are only names for a problem to be solved and not solutions, they are also consistent with substance dualism, double-aspect theory, certain forms of personalism, and epiphenomenalism. This is not a result most naturalists will want to accept.

He or she also risks being professionally ostracized. U.C.L.A. neuroscientist Jeffrey Schwartz bemoans the fact that there is so much social and professional pressure to conform to the naturalist, physicalist culture of the academy:

> that to suggest humbly that there might be more to mental life than action potentials zipping along axons is to risk being branded a scientific naïf. Even worse, it is to be branded nonscientific. When in 1997, I made just this suggestion over dinner to a former president of the Society for Neuroscience, he exclaimed, "Well, then you are not a scientist." Questioning whether consciousness, emotions, thoughts, the subjective feeling of pain, and the spark of creativity arise from nothing but the electrochemical activity of large collections of neuronal circuits is a good way to get dismissed as a hopeless dualist. Ah, that dreaded label.[54]

Jaegwon Kim notes our “seeming inability” to understand consciousness in an “essentially physical” world.[55] He also observes that “if a whole system of phenomena that are *prima facie* not among basic physical phenomena resists physical explanation, and especially if we don’t even know where or how to begin, it would be time to reexamine one’s physicalist commitments.”[56] For Kim, genuinely non-physical mental entities are the paradigm case of such a system of phenomena. Not long ago, Kim’s advice to fellow naturalists was that they must simply admit the irreality of the mental and recognize that naturalism exacts a steep price and cannot be had on the cheap.[57] If feigning anesthesia—denying that consciousness construed along commonsense lines is real—is the price to be paid to retain naturalism, then the price is too high. Fortunately, the theistic argument from consciousness reminds us that it is a price that does not need to be paid.

Notes

1 The epistemic backdrop for locating consciousness in a naturalist ontology

1 Leibniz, "Monadology" 17, in *Leibniz Selections*, ed. Philip Weiner (N. Y.: Charles Scribner's Sons, 1951), 536.

2 Geoffrey Madell, *Mind and Materialism* (Edinburgh: Edinburgh University Press, 1988), 141.

3 Colin McGinn, *The Mysterious Flame* (N.Y.: Basic Books, 1999), 13–14. See G. K. Chesterton's claim that the regular correlation between diverse entities in the world is magic that requires a Magician to explain it. See *Orthodoxy* (John Lane Company, 1908; repr., San Francisco: Ignatius Press, 1950), chapter five.

4 Crispin Wright, "The Conceivability of Naturalism," in *Conceivability and Possibility*, ed. by Tamar Szabo Gendler and John Hawthorne (Oxford: Clarendon, 2002), 401 (the article is from 401–39).

5 William Lyons, "Introduction," in *Modern Philosophy of Mind*, ed. by William Lyons, (London: Everyman, 1995), lv. In context, Lyons remark is specifically about the identity thesis, but he clearly intends it to cover physicalism in general. Similarly, while he explicitly mentions an entity in the category of individual—the soul—the context of his remark makes clear that he includes mental properties and events among the entities out of step with scientific materialism.

6 Cf. Alex Rosenberg, "A Field Guide to Recent Species of Naturalism," *British Journal for the Philosophy of Science* 47 (1996): 1–29; J. P. Moreland, "The Argument from Consciousness," in *The Routledge Companion to Philosophy of Religion*, ed. by Paul Copan, Chad Meister (London: Routledge, 2006), 204–20; J. P. Moreland and William Lane Craig, eds, *Naturalism: A Critical Analysis* (London: Routledge, 2000); Steven Wagner and Richard Warner, eds, *Naturalism: A Critical Appraisal* (Notre Dame, Indiana: University of Notre Dame Press, 1993); Michael Rea, *World Without Design* (Oxford: Clarendon, 2002).

7 David Papineau, *Philosophical Naturalism* (Oxford: Blackwell, 1993), 3.

8 Wilfrid Sellars, *Science, Perception, and Reality* (London: Routledge & Kegan Paul, 1963), 173.

9 Steven J. Wagner and Richard Warner, *Naturalism: A Critical Appraisal* (Notre Dame: University of Notre Dame Press, 1993), 1.

10 Roy Bhaskar, *The Possibility of Naturalism* (New Jersey: Humanities Press, 1979), 3.

11 John Searle, *The Rediscovery of the Mind* (Cambridge, Mass.: MIT Press, 1992), 11.

12 I am assuming here a realist construal of explanation according to which we seek explanations that carve the world at the joints, that quantify over real entities, and/or that provide at least approximately true causal accounts of phenomena. I

set aside anti-realist notions of explanation, e.g. adopting an intentional stance whose function merely is to provide accurate predictions of behavior.

13 David Papineau, *Philosophical Naturalism*, 3.

14 Paul Churchland, *Matter and Consciousness* (Cambridge, Mass.: MIT Press, 1984), 67–81, especially 71.

15 Keith Campbell, "Abstract Particulars and the Philosophy of Mind," *Australasian Journal of Philosophy* 61 (1983): 129–41; *Abstract Particulars* (Oxford: Blackwell, 1990), 43–45.

16 Papineau, *Philosophical Naturalism*, 1–5; 29–32.

17 Colin McGinn, *The Mysterious Flame*, 55–56. Cf. 54–62, 90, 95.

18 John Searle, *The Rediscovery of the Mind*, 83–93.

19 I will continue to talk in terms of particles and not fields because much of the literature in philosophy of mind does so, e.g. debates about atomic simples and constitution, but I do not think anything important hangs on this. Cf. Robert Clifton and Hans Halverson, "No place for particles in relativistic quantum theories?" *Philosophy of Science* 69 (2002): 1–28.

20 Bruce Aune, *Metaphysics: The Elements* (Minneapolis: University of Minnesota Press, 1985), 35.

21 D. M. Armstrong, "Naturalism, Materialism, and First Philosophy," *Philosophia* 8 (1978): 263. Cf. *Universals and Scientific Realism Volume I: Nominalism & Realism* (Cambridge: Cambridge University Press, 1978), 126–35. Subsequently, Armstrong has modified and weakened this formulation of his criterion of being: "Everything that exists makes a difference to the causal powers of something." See *A World of States of Affairs* (Cambridge: Cambridge University Press, 1997), 41–43.

22 Daniel Dennett, *Elbow Room* (Cambridge, Mass.: MIT Press, 1984), 76.

23 Keith Campbell, *Abstract Particulars* (Oxford: Basil Blackwell, 1990), 172.

24 Jaegwon Kim, "Mental Causation and Two Conceptions of Mental Properties," unpublished paper delivered at the American Philosophical Association Eastern Division Meeting, Atlanta, Georgia, December 27–30, 1993, 23.

25 See J. P. Moreland, "Naturalism and the Ontological Status of Properties," in *Naturalism: A Critical Analysis,* edited by J. P. Moreland and William Lane Craig (London: Routledge, 2000), 67–109; J. P. Moreland, *Universals* (Canada: McGill-Queen's University Press, 2001), 121–29.

26 Frank Jackson, *From Metaphysics to Ethics* (Oxford: Clarendon Press, 1998), 1–5.

27 Ibid., 13.

28 Ibid., 14.

29 Ibid., 25.

30 For a treatment of and bibliography for Brentano's treatment of parts and wholes, see R. M. Chisholm, *Brentano and Intrinsic Value* (Cambridge: Cambridge University Press, 1986); for a treatment of and bibliography for Husserl's treatment of parts and wholes, see Barry Smith, ed., *Parts and Moments: Studies in Logic and Formal Ontology* (Munchen: Philosophia Verlag, 1982); J. P. Moreland, "Naturalism, Nominalism, and Husserlian Moments," *The Modern Schoolman* 79 (January/March 2002): 199–216.

31 See Peter van Inwagen, *Material Beings* (Ithaca, N. Y.: Cornell University Press, 1990); Trenton Merricks, *Objects and Persons* (N. Y.: Oxford: Clarendon, 2001).

32 J. P. Moreland, *Universals* (Bucks, Great Britain: Acumen Press; Canada: McGill-Queen's University Press, 2001); "Theories of Individuation: A Reconsideration of Bare Particulars," *Pacific Philosophical Quarterly* 79 (1998): 251–63; "Issues and Options in Individuation," *Grazer Philosophische Studien* 60 (Winter 2000): 31–54.

33 Boundaries or surfaces also provide a way of avoiding Aristotelian universalism. Not all "collections" of objects standing in various relations have surfaces or boundaries and, thus, are not genuine wholes.
34 Jackson, *From Metaphysics to Ethics*, 18.
35 Jaegwon Kim, *Mind in a Physical World* (Cambridge, Massachusetts: MIT Press, 1998), 40.
36 See John Haldane, "The Mystery of Emergence," *Proceedings of the Aristotelian Society* 96 (1996): 263.
37 See Kim, *Mind in a Physical World*, 29–56; *Physicalism, or Something Near Enough* (Princeton, N. J.: Princeton University Press, 2005), 8–22, 32–69; *Philosophy of Mind* (Boulder, Colorado: Westview Press, 2nd. ed., 2006), 173–204.
38 Cf. Theodore Sider, "What's So Bad About Overdetermination?" *Philosophy and Phenomenological Research* 67 (November 2003): 719–26. Sider's target is the part/whole overdetermination that figures into Trenton Merricks book *Objects and Persons* (Oxford: Clarendon, 2001). But Sider does include other sorts of overdetermination in his discussion among which is (alleged) mental/physical overdetermination. In my view, however effective his critique is against Merricks' form of overdetermination, it fails as a rebuttal to those who eschew mental/physical overdetermination. Two areas of Sider's discussion are what he calls the metaphysical and coincidence objections. A central aspect of the former amounts to the claim that overdetermination is metaphysically incoherent because it is precluded by the correct theory of causation. Sider attempts to rebut this claim with respect to various theories of causation. For example, he claims that on a counterfactual analysis of causation, the shattering of the glass is counterfactually dependent on the baseball and its parts and an effect could counterfactually depend on the instantiation of mental and physical properties. But if mental properties are contingently related to physical ones, such dependence is too bizarre to count as an analysis of causation: It does not range throughout possible worlds where the effect is produced by the physical cause alone (worlds without mental states), the mental cause alone (worlds without physical antecedents to physical actions), or inverted worlds with mental/physical properties instantiated but in which the mental is unrelated to the physical cause or the effect. Moreover, the counterfactual analysis would violate the (admittedly controversial) principle of the conditional excluded middle from mental states to either brain states or physical actions. Nor could one count on the generation of stabilizing nested counterfactuals across relevantly close worlds. And Sider begs the question and merely asserts that on a primitive causal analysis, an effect can be primitively related to both a mental and physical cause. Perhaps he believes his assertion is *prima facie* justified because he also asserts that it does not *seem* wrong to say that human actions have both physical and mental causes. On the contrary, this does seem wrong. Rather, what seems to be true is that human actions have both physical and mental causal conditions that are jointly sufficient. Regarding the coincidence objection (overdetermination is tantamount to postulating unexplained coincidences on a massive scale—one might as well postulate that every person killed by a bullet is really killed by two bullets that just happen to hit at the same time), Sider replies that (1) the joint causal activity of mental and physical events is a function of the realization relation connecting them and, thus, no coincidence and (2) there are necessary truths that govern the correlation between mental and physical events. Regarding (1) the realization relation applies only if we functionalize the mental event, and we are assuming that mental events are genuinely emergent (and contingently related to physical events) in which case the exemplification and not the realization relation is relevant. Further, we could create a thought experiment in which a shadow (functionally) realizes its associated object, but it would

be the object's impact on a second object that was causally responsible for the second object and its shadow moving, not the first object's shadow. Regarding (2), the connection between the mental and physical is contingent, so there are no such necessary truths.

39 Roger Sperry, "In Defense of Mentalism and Emergent Interaction," *Journal of Mind and Behaviour* 12 (Spring 1991): 221–45.
40 Ibid, 230; emphasis is Sperry's.
41 See Kim, *Mind in a Physical World*, chapter 3.
42 See J. P. Moreland, *Universals*.
43 Nick Herbert, *Quantum Reality* (Garden City, N. Y.: Doubleday, 1985), 15–29.
44 Cf. J. P. Moreland, "Should a Naturalist Be a Supervenient Physicalist?" *Metaphilosophy* 29 (January/April 1998): 35–57.
45 D. M. Armstrong, *Universals and Scientific Realism Volume I: Nominalism & Realism*, (1978), 130.
46 D. M. Armstrong, "Naturalism: Materialism and First Philosophy," *Philosophia* 8 (1978): 262.
47 D. M. Armstrong, *The Mind-Body Problem: An Opinionated Introduction* (Boulder, Colorado: Westview Press, 1999), 2–5, 10–11, 47–48.
48 Ibid., 124.
49 D. M. Armstrong, "Can A Naturalist Believe in Universals?" in *Science in Reflection*, ed. by Edna Ullmann-Margalit (Boston: Kluwer Academic Publishers, 1988), 111–12; *Universals & Scientific Realism Volume II: A Theory of Universals* (Cambridge: Cambridge University Press, 1978), 84–88.
50 Cf. Roderick Chisholm, *Theory of Knowledge* (Englewood Cliffs, N. J.: Prentice Hall, 3rd. ed., 1989); *On Metaphysics* (Minneapolis: University of Minnesota Press, 1989), especially 162–68.
51 Kim, *Philosophy of Mind*, 2nd edition (2006), 91. Cf. 89.
52 See Jaegwon Kim, *Physicalism or Something Near Enough* (Princeton, N. J.: Princeton University Press, 2005), especially chapter six. Cf. his *Mind in a Physical World*, chapter four.
53 See Jackson, *From Metaphysics to Ethics*, 24–27. By "entails" here Jackson means the ordinary truth-functional connective. Jackson actually thinks physicalism *a priori* entails the psychological and that this is a necessary truth. If physicalism φ is true, then of necessity the psychological truths ψ follow *a priori*. Jackson employs a version of two-dimensional semantics to defend the claim that instances of φ→ψ are *priori* necessary. But this is a stronger claim and many naturalists, e.g. those of a Kripkean persuasion, would not follow him in this, so I shall employ the weaker truth-functional version in what follows. I am indebted to Shaun McNaughton for pointing this out to me.
54 Roderick Chisholm, *Theory of Knowledge* (Englewood Cliffs, N.J.: Prentice-Hall, 3rd. ed., 1989), 16.
55 Timothy O'Connor, *Persons & Causes* (N. Y.: Oxford University Press, 2000), 112.
56 Ibid., 70–71, fn. 8.

2 The argument from consciousness

1 For example, suppose theory S explains phenomena in terms of discrete corpuscles and actions by contact, while R uses continuous waves to explain phenomena. If some phenomenon x was best explained in corpuscularian categories, it would be *ad hoc* and question-begging for advocates of R simply to adjust their entities to take on particle properties in the case of x. Such properties would not bear a relevant similarity to other entities in R and would be more natural and at home in S.

2 For example, suppose that R is Neo-Darwinism and S is a version of punctuated equilibrium theory. Simply for the sake of illustration, suppose further, that R depicts evolutionary transitions from one species to another to involve running through a series of incrementally different transitional forms except for some specific transition e which is taken as a basic phenomenon, say, the discrete jump from amphibians to reptiles. S pictures evolutionary transitions in general, including e, as evolutionary jumps to be explained in certain ways that constitute S. In this case, given the presence of S, it would be hard for advocates of R to claim that their treatment of e is adequate against S. Phenomenon e clearly counts in favor of S over against R.

3 Evan Fales, Naturalism and Physicalism, in *The Cambridge Companion to Atheism*, ed. by Michael Martin (Cambridge: Cambridge University Press, 2007), 120. In presenting alternative naturalist ontologies ranging from what he calls sparse to liberal, Fales does not do an adequate job of relating the naturalist epistemology and Grand Story to the role they should play in placing constraints on a naturalist ontology for those naturalists who claim to have a worldview with explanatory superiority to theism. As a result, besides being *ad hoc* and begging the question against theism, some of the (more liberal) ontologies presented by Fales run amuck in light of considerations noted in chapter one.

4 Jaegwon Kim, *The Philosophy of Mind* (Boulder, Colorado: Westview Press, 2006), 233.

5 Angus Menuge, *Agents Under Fire* (Lanham, Maryland: Rowman & Littlefield, 2004).

6 See Robert Adams, "Flavors, Colors, and God," reprinted in *Contemporary Perspectives on Religious Epistemology*, ed. by R. Douglas Geivett, Brendan Sweetman (N.Y.: Oxford University Press, 1992), 225–40.

7 Richard Swinburne, *The Existence of God* (Oxford: Clarendon, 1979), chapter 9; *The Evolution of the Soul* (Oxford: Clarendon, 1986), 183–96; *Is there a God?* (Oxford: Oxford University Press, 1996), 69–94; "The Origin of Consciousness," in *Cosmic Beginnings and Human Ends*, ed. by Clifford N. Matthews, Roy Abraham Varghese (Chicago and La Salle, Illinois: Open Court, 1995), 355–78.

8 See Richard Swinburne, *The Existence of God* (Oxford: Clarendon, 1979), 6–8, 16–19.

9 In chapters six and seven, we will examine, respectively, panpsychism and pluralistic emergentist monism. I will conclude that each is not, in fact, a version of but, rather, a rival to naturalism. To simplify our present discussion, let us disregard this claim until chapters six and seven and consider panpsychism and pluralistic emergentist monism as versions of naturalism.

10 Quentin Smith, "The Metaphilosophy of Naturalism," *Philo* (2001).

11 Timothy O'Connor and Hong Yu Wong, "The Metaphysics of Emergence," *Nous* 39 (2005): 665–66.

12 I am indebted to Thomas Crisp for pointing this out to me.

13 David Papineau, *Philosophical Naturalism* (Oxford: Blackwell, 1993), 119, 120.

14 Cf. D. M. Armstrong, "Naturalism: Materialism and First Philosophy," *Philosophia* 8 (1978): 262.

15 Cf. Paul Churchland, *Matter and Consciousness* (Cambridge, Massachusetts: MIT Press, rev. ed., 1988), 21–22.

16 Cf. Terence Horgan, "Nonreductive Materialism and the Explanatory Autonomy of Psychology," in *Naturalism*, ed. by Steven J. Wagner, Richard Warner (Notre Dame: University of Notre Dame Press, 1993), 313–14.

17 Richard Swinburne, *The Evolution of the Soul*, revised edition (Oxford: Clarendon, 1997), 183–96.

18 Ibid.

19 John Bishop, *Natural Agency* (Cambridge: Cambridge University Press, 1989), 36–44, 74–76. Selmer Bringsjord rejects Swinburne's version of AC because it focuses on the regular correlations of specific types of mental and physical events. But Bringsjord thinks that a version of AC that starts with agent causation is likely to be successful. See "Swinburne's Argument from Consciousness," *Philosophy of Religion* 19 (1986): 140–41.

20 See Alvin Plantinga, *Warrant and Proper Function* (N.Y.: Oxford University Press, 1993), 194–237. Cf. James Beilby, ed., *Naturalism Defeated? Essays on Plantinga's Evolutionary Argument Against Naturalism* (Ithaca, N. Y.: Cornell University Press, 2002).

21 Swinburne, *Evolution of the Soul*, 191–95.

22 See Roderick Chisholm, *Theory of Knowledge* (Englewood Cliff, N. J.: Prentice-Hall, 2d. ed., 1977), 20–22; *Theory of Knowledge* (Englewood Cliff, N. J.: Prentice-Hall, 3d. ed., 1989), 18–25; *The First Person* (Minneapolis: University of Minnesota Press, 1981), 79–83.

23 Chisholm, *Theory of Knowledge* (Englewood Cliff, N. J.: Prentice-Hall, 3d. ed., 1989), 19.

24 See Roderick Chisholm, *On Metaphysics* (Minneapolis: University of Minnesota Press, 1989), 143–45; cf. *A Realist Theory of Categories* (Cambridge: Cambridge University Press, 1996), 11–21.

25 Elsewhere, I have argued that propositions of this sort cannot be reduced to or replaced by sentences that do not employ "red," "color," "green," and "yellow" as abstract singular terms. See J. P. Moreland, *Universals* (Great Britain: Acumen Press; Canada: McGill-Queen's University Press, 2001), 40–49, 71–73; "Nominalism And Abstract Reference," *American Philosophical Quarterly* 27 (October 1990): 325–34.

26 Cf. Peter Ludlow, Yujin Nagasawa, and Daniel Stoljar, eds., *There's Something About Mary* (Cambridge, Massachusetts: MIT Press, 2004).

27 Searle makes a similar point but it is in the context of phenomenal consciousness. See his *The Mystery of Consciousness* (N.Y: The New York Review of Books, 1997), 30–31.

28 Howard Robinson has argued persuasively that attempts by Arthur Peacocke and Donald Davidson to embrace physicalism but avoid *reduction*ism actually fail because of a confusion about the nature of *reduction*. See Howard Robinson, *Matter and Sense* (Cambridge: Cambridge University Press, 1982), 22–34. Such accounts do avoid analytic *reduction*, claims Robinson, but they entail a topic neutral *reduction* of persons to complexly organized physical entities combined with a token physical analysis of mental events. For an argument that shows that the holism of the mental does not entail a denial of strong psycho-physical laws, see John Foster, "A Defense of Dualism," in *The Case For Dualism*, ed. by John R. Smythies, John Beloff (Charlottesville: University of Virginia Press, 1989), 15–17.

29 For a careful naturalist defense of this claim, see David Papineau, *Philosophical Naturalism* (Oxford: Blackwell, 1993), 9–51, especially 36–43.

30 Bishop, *Natural Agency*, 58, 72, 69, 95–96, 103–4, 110–11, 114, 126–27, 140–41, 144. Bishop also admits that a causal analysis of agency requires a physicalist view of the mental if the account is to satisfy the constraints that are part of a naturalist theory of agency. See 8, 43, 103.

31 John Bishop, *Natural Agency*, 8, 43, 103.

32 See J.P. Moreland and Scott Rae, *Body & Soul* (Downers Grove, Illinois: InterVarsity Press, 2000), 122–46, especially 135–44.

33 Samuel Alexander, *Space, Time and Deity: The Gifford Lectures at Glasgow, 1916–1918*, vol. 2 (New York: Dover Publications, 1920, 1966), 47.

34 Jaegwon Kim, *Philosophy of Mind* (Boulder, Colorado: Westview Press, 1996), 54.

35 Thomas Nagel, *The View From Nowhere* (N. Y.: Oxford, 1986), 49–53.

36 For a critique of panpsychism in the process of defending AC, see Stephen R. L. Clark, *From Athens to Jerusalem* (Oxford: Clarendon, 1984), 121–57.
37 Geoffrey Madell, *Mind and Materialism* (Edinburgh, The University Press, 1988), 3.
38 Nagel, *View from Nowhere*, 49. Note that Nagel claims that this argument is "given more fully" in chapter 13 of his *Mortal Questions* (New York: Cambridge University Press, 1979, 1991).
39 Nagel, *View from Nowhere*, 110–37.
40 There is some debate about whether each of these basic actions requires its own intending. Richard Swinburne argues that in performing actions which take a long time (writing a chapter), we do not exercise a separate volition for each intentional action (e.g. willing to write the first sentence) that is part of the long term act. Rather, we just intend to bring about the long term effect by bringing about a generally conceived series of events and the body unconsciously selects a particular routine to accomplish that effect. See Richard Swinburne, *The Evolution of the Soul* (Oxford: Clarendon Press, 1986), 94–95. I leave the matter open except to note that to the degree that a non-basic action contains sub-acts of a discontinuous nature (picking up keys, getting into a car vs. a series of steps in taking an hour long walk), then it is more likely that sub-intentions are required to characterize adequately those sub-acts.
41 Thus, we see that there are at least three kinds of intentional actions: Basic actions with a basic intent (simply intentionally moving my finger), basic actions with non-basic intents (ultimate intents that have other intents as means, e.g. intentionally squeezing my finger to fire a gun to kill Smith), and non-basic actions (those that contain sub-acts—sub endeavorings and intendings—as parts, e.g., going to the store to buy bread).
42 Cf. Michael Martin, *Atheism: A Philosophical Justification* (Philadelphia: Temple University Press, 1990), 220.
43 Roderick Chisholm, *Theory of Knowledge* (Englewood Cliffs, N.J.: Prentice-Hall, 3d. ed., 1989), 10–17.

3 John Searle and contingent correlation

1 John Searle, *The Mystery of Consciousness* (N.Y.: The New York Review of Books, 1997), 195–201. Cf. J. P. Moreland, "Searle's Biological Naturalism and the Argument from Consciousness," *Faith and Philosophy* 15 (January 1998): 68–91.
2 John Searle, *The Rediscovery of the Mind* (Cambridge, Massachusetts: MIT Press, 1992), 89, 100–104.
3 Searle, *The Mystery of Consciousness*, 197–98.
4 Searle, *The Rediscovery of the Mind*, 100–104.
5 Searle, *The Rediscovery of the Mind*, chapters 1 and 2. Cf. Tyler Burge, "Philosophy of Language and Mind: 1950–90," *The Philosophical Review* 101 (January 1992): 3–51, especially 29–5. Since the publication of *The Rediscovery of the Mind* Searle has restated his views on these topics, but he continues to cite this earlier work as his most thorough treatment on the topic from which he has not deviated. See his *The Mystery of Consciousness*, 194; *Mind: A Brief Introduction* (Oxford: Oxford University Press, 2004), 2. Thus, I will rely on *The Rediscovery of the Mind* in explicating Searle's views and supplement them when needed. Cf. J. P. Moreland, "Searle's Biological Naturalism and the Argument from Consciousness," *Faith and Philosophy* 15 (January 1998): 68–91.
6 Searle, *The Rediscovery of the Mind*, 3–4. Cf..31.
7 Ibid. 28.
8 Ibid. 85–91.
9 Ibid. 3, 13–16.
10 Ibid. 90–91.

11 Ibid. xii, 13–19, 25–28, 85–93.
12 Ibid. 13, 16. See also Searle's "Why I am not a Property Dualist," *Journal of Consciousness Studies* 9:12 (2002), 57–64.
13 Ibid. 13, 126.
14 Ibid. 2–4, 13–16.
15 Cf. J. P. Moreland, "Humanness, Personhood, and the Right to Die," *Faith and Philosophy* 12 (January 1995): 95–112; J. P. Moreland and Stan Wallace, "Aquinas vs. Descartes and Locke on the Human Person and End-of-Life Ethics," *International Philosophical Quarterly* 35 (September 1995): 319–30; J. P. Moreland and Scott Rae, *Body & Soul* (Downers Grove, Illinois: InterVarsity Press, 2000), chapter six.
16 Cf. Richard Swinburne, *The Evolution of the Soul* (Oxford: Clarendon, 1986), especially chapter 8.
17 Jaegwon Kim, "Mental Causation and Two Conceptions of Mental Properties," unpublished paper delivered at the American Philosophical Association Eastern Division Meeting, Atlanta, Georgia, December 27–30, 1993, 21.
18 Ibid. 23.
19 David Papineau, *Philosophical Naturalism* (Oxford: Blackwell, 1993), 9–32.
20 Searle, *The Rediscovery of the Mind*, 55. Cf. 32, 56–57 where Searle considers and rejects as incoherent a closely related question formulated in terms of intelligence and intelligent behavior and not consciousness. If intelligence and intelligent behavior are interpreted from a third-person perspective in behavioristic terms (e.g. as regular and predictable behavior), then it is false that bits of matter are not intelligent. If first-person subjective criteria are formulated for intelligence, then the question reduces to the one asked in terms of consciousness. So this is the correct question to ask on Searle's view.
21 Ibid. 95.
22 Cf. Peter van Inwagen, *Metaphysics* (Boulder, Colorado: Westview Press, 2nd ed., 2002), 176–78.
23 Ibid. 118–24.
24 Ibid. 89, 100–104.
25 Ibid. 101–4.
26 Terence Horgan, "Nonreductive Materialism and the Explanatory Autonomy of Psychology," in *Naturalism*, ed. by Steven J. Wagner, Richard Warner (Notre Dame: University of Notre Dame Press, 1993), 313–14.
27 D. M. Armstrong, "Naturalism: Materialism, and First Philosophy," *Philosophia* 8 (1978): 262.
28 Searle, *The Rediscovery of the Mind*, 93.
29 D. M. Armstrong, *A Materialist Theory of Mind* (London: Routledge & Kegan Paul, 1968), 30.
30 Paul Churchland, *Matter and Consciousness*, revised edition (Cambridge, Mass.: MIT Press, 1988), 21. Cf. Arthur Peacocke and Grant Gillett, eds., *Persons and Personality* (Oxford: Basil Blackwell, 1987), 55.
31 Searle, *The Rediscovery of the Mind*, 104–5.
32 See E.J. Lowe, *An Introduction to the Philosophy of Mind* (Cambridge: Cambridge University Press, 2000), 9–10; 13–21.
33 Searle, *The Rediscovery of the Mind*, 96–97, 143–44, 149.
34 Ibid., 98.
35 J. L. Mackie, *The Miracle of Theism* (Oxford: Clarendon Press, 1982), 120–21. See also, Clifford Williams, "Christian Materialism and the Parity Thesis," *International Journal for Philosophy of Religion* 39 (February 1996): 1–14. Cf. J. P. Moreland, "Locke's Parity Thesis about Thinking Matter: A Response to Williams," *Religious Studies* 34 (September 1998): 253–59; "Christian Materialism and the Parity Thesis Revisited," *International Philosophical Quarterly* 40

(December 2000): 423–40; "Topic Neutrality and the Parity Thesis: A Surrejoinder to Williams," *Religious Studies* 37 (March 2001): 93–101.

36 J. L. Mackie, *The Miracle of Theism.*, 121.

37 Locke's point about God superadding thinking to matter can be understood as an argument against substance dualism. So understood, Locke is not claiming that thinkings themselves are material or that God is not required to explain their correlation with material states. Rather, he is asserting that there is a parity between material and spiritual substances as fitting candidates to contain the faculty of thought. For an exposition of this understanding of Locke, see Williams, "Christian materialism and the Parity Thesis." I do not agree with this rendition of the parity thesis. For it seems to require a topic neutral account of consciousness and thinking. Moreover, it fails to take into account the fact that the immateriality of the self is known both by first-person acquaintance and by reasoning to the precise type of immateriality that constitutes the essence of a substantial soul from the immaterial effects that express its capacities. Fortunately, this rendition is not relevant to AC per se since property/event dualism is all AC needs to make its case.

38 John Locke, *An Essay Concerning Human Understanding*, 4.10.10–17 (313–19 of the 1959 Dover edition).

39 Papineau, *Philosophical Naturalism*, 29–32.

40 John W. Yolton, *Thinking Matter: Materialism in Eighteenth-Century Britain* (Minneapolis: University of Minnesota Press, 1983), 4–13, especially 6–7.

41 Jaegwon Kim, *Philosophy of Mind* (Boulder, Colorado: Westview Press, 1996), 214–15. See G. K. Chesterton's claim that the regular correlation between diverse entities in the world is magic that requires a Magician to explain it. See *Orthodoxy* (John Lane Company, 1908; repr., San Francisco: Ignatius Press, 1950), chapter five.

42 Searle, *The Rediscovery of the Mind*, 102–3.

43 J. L. Mackie, *The Miracle of Theism*, 115. Cf. J. P. Moreland and Kai Nielsen, *Does God Exist?* (Buffalo, N. Y.: Prometheus, 1993), chapters 8–10. Mackie found it easy to deny the objectivity of moral properties and opted for a form of moral subjectivism. But he could not bring himself to deny the mental nature of qualia. So he adopted a solution for qualia similar to Searle's. I shall not look at Mackie's case because Searle's is more forceful and better developed.

44 It could be argued that the supervenience of moral properties does not imply theism and, thus, they are of no help to AC. I offer two responses to this claim. First, the supervenience of such properties (as depicted by Mackie) would at least entail some form of ethical non-naturalism, e. g. Platonism, and this would count against naturalism. Given that non-theistic and theistic versions of non-naturalism are the remaining live options, each would receive some degree of confirmation from the falsity of a rival paradigm (naturalism), and the debate would be moved to what I take to be an intramural discussion between the other paradigms. Elsewhere, I have argued that theistic non-naturalism gets the better of this dialog. See J. P. Moreland, Kai Nielsen, *Does God Exist?* 123. Second, in the reference just cited, I use the existence of moral properties as part of an inference to the best explanation, so even if their existence does not *entail* theism, they may still lend support to it, especially vis-à-vis naturalism.

45 B. F. Skinner, "Can Psychology Be A Science of Mind?" *American Psychologist* 45 (November 1990): 1207.

4 Timothy O'Connor and emergent necessitation

1 John Bishop, *Natural Agency* (Cambridge: Cambridge University Press, 1989), 1. Bishop's own solution eschews libertarian agency in favor of a compatibilist version of the causal theory of action.

2 John Bishop, *Natural Agency*, 40.

3 Robert Kane, *The Significance of Free Will* (N. Y.: Oxford University Press, 1996), 118. Kane himself develops a particular version of libertarian indeterminism that he takes to avoid the need for substance dualism. By contrast, Stewart Goetz argues that even non-agent-causal accounts of libertarian freedom require substance dualism. See his "Naturalism and Libertarian Agency," in *Naturalism: A Critical Analysis*, ed. by William Lane Craig and J. P. Moreland (London: Routledge, 2000), 156–86. Central to Goetz's case is the claim that reasons function as irreducibly teleological ends and this is inconsistent with a material agent.

4 Timothy O'Connor, *Persons & Causes* (N.Y.: Oxford University Press, 2000), 108. Hereafter, for O'Connor citations I will be mainly using *Persons & Causes*. Cf. J. P. Moreland, "Naturalism and Libertarian Agency," *Philosophy and Theology* 10 (1997): 351–81; "Timothy O'Connor and the Harmony Thesis: A Critique," *Metaphysica* 3 No. 2 (2002): 5–40.

5 O'Connor, *Persons & Causes*, xv, 108.

6 Ibid., 107.

7 Ibid., 108.

8 Ibid., xv, 121.

9 Ibid., 109–10.

10 Ibid.

11 Ibid., 125.

12 In *Natural Agency*, John Bishop accepts L, but claims to develop a compatibilist view of agency that (1) is "at home" in N and (2) adequate to fall under a libertarian concept of agency. If Bishop is correct, then L, indeed, is a minimalist thesis that allows for compatibilism to satisfy it.

13 O'Connor, *Persons & Causes*, xii.

14 Ibid., xii.

15 Ibid., 116.

16 Ibid., 115.

17 Ibid., 121.

18 Ibid., 109.

19 See David Papineau, *Philosophical Naturalism* (Oxford: Blackwell, 1993), 1–13; Paul Churchland, *Matter and Consciousness* (Cambridge, Massachusetts, rev. ed., 1988), 18–21; John Bishop, *Natural Agency*, 10–48; Jaegwon Kim, *Mind in a Physical World* Cambridge, Massachusetts: MIT Press, 1998).

20 O'Connor, *Persons & Causes*, 110.

21 Cf. Timothy O'Connor, "Causality, Mind, and Free Will," in *Soul, Body and Survival*, ed. by Kevin Corcoran (Ithaca, N. Y.: Cornell University Press, 2001), 56–58.

22 O'Connor does not explicitly address the question of whether the Harmony Thesis should be assessed by, among other things, weighing its plausibility against a rival hypothesis such as substance dualism. But for three reasons, I believe that this is implicit in his account and, in any case, it is what he must do to justify the Harmony Thesis. I have been at pains to show the first reason: Given that the Harmony Thesis is an hypothesis with the epistemic status I have described, its acceptance or rejection should be adopted by viewing the Harmony Thesis as an inference to the best explanation. When a hypothesis is justified by way of an inference to the best explanation, one crucial factor for assessing it is how it compares with its chief rivals, and substance dualism is the chief rival to the Harmony Thesis as O'Connor himself admits. Even if O'Connor's explicit project is the attempt to show that AGC could emerge in a naturalistic universe or that, given the right physical conditions, active power must emerge in a naturalistic universe, since he takes the Harmony Thesis to be an

hypothesis, it should be assessed in light of its chief rival, irrespective of the modal status of the Harmony Thesis itself. My second reason will be developed more fully in section six. There I will try to show that the precise role of pre-philosophical intuitions in O'Connor's case for AGC makes it difficult for him to reject the same role of pre-philosophical intuitions in justifying substance dualism. If I am right about this, then his attempt to justify the Harmony Thesis without explicitly assessing substance dualism as a rival viewpoint is, at best, seriously incomplete. In this case, my chapter may be understood, minimally, as an attempt to challenge O'Connor to fill out his account of the Harmony Thesis by explicitly addressing issues that I claim are already implicit in his account. Third, O'Connor states that he is not interested in merely defending a libertarian conception of free agency; rather, he is after a true account of free agency. This goal is important for O'Connor's project of developing an account of agency. Why? Because it deflects a compatibilist rebuttal to his case, viz., that while our *notion* of free agency may be libertarian, there is no *inconsistency* in thinking that actual agents merely possess compatibilist freedom of a sort sufficiently developed to count as falling under the libertarian concept, at least throughout those possible worlds that are minimal physical duplicates of the actual world. O'Connor rightly thinks that such an approach is deflationary, and by developing an account of agency in keeping with pre-philosophical intuitions, O'Connor takes himself to be providing an account of agency as it really is. Now this same point can be said about the Harmony Thesis. It is relatively uninteresting to develop the *notion* of an agent that is merely consistent with N. We should want a true account of ourselves as libertarian agents. In section six, I will show the role that pre-philosophical intuitions play in developing that account. The reader may not agree with that role, but consistency would seem to imply that O'Connor should.

23 There are two desiderata for an adequate theory of human action: (1) explain agent control and (2) account for the role of reasons in human action. I set aside (2) because it is beyond the scope of my present concern. O'Connor's account employs a strategy which avoids an irreducible teleological role for reasons in free action by incorporating reasons into complex hyphenated action-triggering-intentions. See *Persons and Causes* chapter five, especially 85–86, 98–99. Stewart Goetz has argued, correctly in my view, that reasons are, in fact, irreducibly teleological ends and not efficient causal components of action, and therefore, that irrespective of the presence or absence of emergent properties, a physical particular—including an agent—cannot exhibit libertarian freedom because it does not behave in irreducibly teleological ways. See his "Naturalism and Libertarian Agency."

24 O'Connor, *Persons and Causes*, 49.

25 Ibid., xiv, 75.

26 Ibid., 67.

27 Ibid., 73.

28 Ibid.

29 Ibid.

30 Ibid., 95.

31 Ibid., 97–98.

32 Ibid., 45–46.

33 Ibid., 122.

34 Ibid., 72.

35 Ibid.

36 Ibid., xiv, 85–86.

37 Ibid., 107.

38 Ibid., 79.

39 Ibid., 95, 109, 111, 118.
40 Ibid., 73.
41 Ibid., 121.
42 Cf. Timothy O'Connor, "Emergent Properties," *American Philosophical Quarterly* 31 (April 1994): 91–104.
43 O'Connor, *Persons & Causes*, 70, 110–15, 117–18.
44 Ibid., 70–71, 117–18.
45 Ibid., 115–23.
46 Ibid., 108–10.
47 See O'Connor, "Causality, Mind, and Free Will," 51.
48 Galen Strawson, *Freedom and Belief* (Oxford: Oxford University Press, 1986), 161–62; cf. 146–69, 323–29.
49 See John W. Yolton, *Thinking Matter: Materialism in Eighteenth-Century Britain* (Minneapolis: University of Minnesota Press, 1983). For more on this in the context of Locke's claims about thinking matter, see Clifford Williams, "Christian Materialism and the Parity Thesis," *International Journal for Philosophy of Religion* 39 (February 1996): 1–14; J. P. Moreland, "Locke's Parity Thesis about Thinking Matter: A Response to Williams," *Religious Studies* 34 (September 1998): 253–59; Clifford Williams, "Topic Neutrality and the Mind-Body Problem," *Religious Studies* 36 (2000): 203–7; J. P. Moreland, "Christian Materialism and the Parity Thesis Revisited," *International Philosophical Quarterly* 40 (December 2000): 423–40; and idem, "Topic Neutrality and the Parity Thesis: A Surrejoinder to Williams," *Religious Studies* 37 (March 2001): 93–101.
50 In order to establish that human persons are essentially mental substances, or at least mental/physical substances, I would need the premise that human persons are essentially entities with at least the ultimate potentiality for agency. If, solely for the sake of argument, we accept some sort of emergence requirement for our account, it would seem that the emergence of active power would require the emergence of an agent (or human person essentially possessing the potentiality for agency) that was a mental or mental/physical substance. Thus, my argument (granting emergence) provides grounds for preferring an account such as the one offered by William Hasker over O'Connor's. See William Hasker, *The Emergent Self* (Ithaca, N. Y.: Cornell University Press, 1999).
51 Timothy O'Connor and Jonathan D. Jacobs, "Emergent Individuals," *The Philosophical Quarterly* 53 (October 2003): 540–55; Timothy O'Connor and Hong Yu Wong, "The Metaphysics of Emergence," *Nous* 39:4 (2005): 659–79.
52 This is not quite accurate. O'Connor considers four ontological approaches to properties: transcendent universals, kind-Aristotelianism, immanent universals and tropes. He rejects the first two, allows for the possibility of a very specific version of trope nominalism, but clearly favors immanent universals which is the only framework in which he really develops his doctrine of emergence. I have subjected trope nominalism to severe criticism elsewhere and I believe it is not only false but unintelligible. So I shall not consider it further. See J. P. Moreland, "Keith Campbell and the Trope View of Predication," *Australasian Journal of Philosophy* 67 (December 1989): 379–93; "A Critique of Campbell's Refurbished Nominalism," *The Southern Journal of Philosophy* 35 (Summer 1997): 225–46. I agree with O'Connor's rejection of kind-Aristotelianism, including his main argument against it—that there is no second relatum to which to connect the nexus of exemplification besides the kind-universal. However, O'Connor fails to see that kind-universals are not really universals, but totalities like sets absent extensional identity conditions, and he fails to see that the problem of the absent second relatum follows from the blob ontology of kind-instances, a problem that undermines trope nominalism and, if noticed, would have saved O'Connor from having to consider the trope view. See J. P. Moreland,

"How to Be a Nominalist in Realist Clothing," *Grazer Philosophische Studien* 39 (Summer, 1991): 75–101. Finally, O'Connor's treatment of transcendent universals is seriously misleading. Setting aside questions about the historical Plato and Aristotle, the debate about transcendent universals is often framed as a debate between Platonists and Aristotelians. So understood, the debate is about three questions: (1) Are there uninstantiated universals—universals not exemplified by a particular—or does the existence of a universal depend on at least one particular instantiating it? (2) Do universals remain outside or are they in the being of the things that have them? (3) Do universals remain outside the things that have them in some spatial location, a Platonic heaven, or are they spatially in the being of the things that have them? He fails to treat adequately a view widely held today that embraces uninstantiated universals but also holds that when instantiated, they are non-spatially in their instances in keeping with a constituent ontology and not a relational one. His main objection to a view close to this (which he calls the "participation" position) rests on an equivocation regarding the nature of an internal relation. A relation that does not leave the universal outside the being of its instance but, rather, locates the universal in the very being of its instances vs. a relation that holds in virtue of the intrinsic features of the relata. The second characterization is part of a classic treatment of an internal relation and it is the version O'Connor criticizes—there must be something in the concrete particular that is logically prior to its instantiation of a property and this moves the transcendent view towards immanent universals. But this criticism misses the nature of an internal relation classically construed. O'Connor seems to think that this logically prior "something" pushes the view towards immanent universals in that it requires an individuator to be this something. But it has always been held that it is a property or properties of the "something" that is logically prior to an internal relation, not an individuator. More importantly, this second sense of "internal relation" is irrelevant to transcendent universals as I and many others employ that notion. On this view, transcendent universals commits one to internal relations in O'Connor's first sense and not the second one, so the latter's inadequacy is irrelevant as a criticism of transcendent universals. See J. P. Moreland, *Universals* (Canada: McGill-Queen's University Press, 2001), 129–34.

53 See Hasker, *The Emergent Self*.

54 O'Connor rejects this move because, among other things, it suffers from the causal pairing problem and the most plausible solution to that problem—singular causation—is bogus. O'Connor seems quite unfamiliar with Thomistic dualist solutions to this problem. See J. P. Moreland and Stanley Wallace, "Aquinas vs. Descartes and Locke on the Human Person and End-of-Life Ethics," *International Philosophical Quarterly* 35 (September 1995): 319–30.

55 See O'Connor and Wong, "The Metaphysics of Emergence": 665–69.

56 Colin McGinn, *The Mysterious Flame* (N. Y.: Basic Books, 1999), 95–101. As McGinn shows, a view such as O'Connor's is a version of weak panpsychism and not of naturalism precisely because it accords to matter irreducibly mental potentialities. Thus, it will not do simply to assert that O'Connor's agent is a unique kind of physical particular, e.g. a composite physical particular with ontologically emergent mental properties, that is properly called a physical particular and plausibly located within N. If an emergent mental property is an actualization of an irreducibly mental potentiality that characterizes some particular, then that potentiality is part of what gives the particular its ontological character. I believe that part of the confusion about this point comes from conflating metaphysics as a descriptive discipline with metaphysics as an explanatory discipline. For a good example of this confusion, see Frank Jackson, *From Metaphysics to Ethics* (Oxford: Clarendon, 1998), 1–27. As a descriptive

discipline, one task of metaphysics is to give an ontological analysis of the parts, properties (actual and potential), and relations that constitute an entity so the nature and ontological classification of the entity can be vouchsafed. Explanatory metaphysics attempts to show how the presence of one feature of an entity may be explained in terms of other features of the entity. Usually, the latter is irrelevant to the former. For example, necessarily, some particular is colored only if it is extended, so an analysis of the factors necessary to account for a particular's being colored would include its being extended. But this is not relevant if the question is to give an ontological description of the sorts of properties that constitute that particular. Our question is what sort of thing is an agent with essentially mental potentialities, it is not what are the explanatory conditions under which mental potentialities are actualized.

57 O'Connor, "Causality, Mind, and Free Will," 58.

58 Timothy O'Connor and Hong Yu Wong, "The Metaphysics of Emergence": 665.

59 Timothy O'Connor and Jonathan D. Jacobs, "Emergent Individuals": 541.

60 It could be argued that on O'Connor's picture, everything that occurs at the macro level rests on the total potentialities of the microphysical properties, including the potentiality to produce mental properties. But this will not do. Descriptively, a mental potentiality is a *mental*, not a physical potentiality. Strictly physical properties do not have the power to produce mental properties if the particular in question does not have a mental potentiality. At best, physical properties may have the power to actualize an already present mental potentiality that is not itself physical.

61 Frank Jackson, *From Metaphysics to Ethics*, 1–27.

62 O'Connor, *Persons & Causes*, 111–12.

63 Ibid., 70–71.

64 Ibid., 70–71, 117–18.

65 Ibid., 73.

66 See Timothy O'Connor, "Emergent Properties."

67 O'Connor, *Persons & Causes*, 112.

68 If I am correct about this, then O'Connor cannot simply argue that the emergence of active power is merely metaphysically co-possible with N. Rather, the existence of active power would seem to require N. Thus, the existence of substance dualism as a rival position is a crucial aspect of evaluating the Harmony Thesis since the presence of substance dualism as a coherent rival counts against this stronger claim.

69 Cf. Jaegwon Kim, *Philosophy of Mind* (Boulder, Colorado: Westview Press, 1996), 9–13.

70 O'Connor, *Persons & Causes*, 116.

71 Ibid., 120.

72 The contingency of the link is part of the thought experiments themselves, e.g. inverted qualia thought experiments. While I admit this is anecdotal, I have taught philosophy of mind to hundreds of college students and lay people, and there is almost unanimous agreement that these thought experiments are coherent and the states of affairs involved are possible. For more on the asymmetry between emergent mental properties and paradigm cases of emergence (e.g. solidity), see chapter three.

73 O'Connor, *Persons & Causes*, 114.

74 Ibid., 115.

75 Ibid., 116.

76 Consider clause (b) of Jackson's depiction of a minimal physical duplicate of the actual world. It may well be that empirical evidence could be provided for the presence of non-physical particulars (e.g. from miracles), but it is hard to see how empirical evidence could justify the claim that there are no such non-physical

particulars. Thus, (b) is not entailed by the Grand Story and should be eliminated.

77 O'Connor, *Persons & Causes*, 118.
78 John Searle, *The Rediscovery of the Mind* (Cambridge, Massachusetts: MIT Press, 1992), 111–12.
79 O'Connor, *Persons and Causes*, 114.
80 Timothy O'Connor and Hong Yu Wong, "The Metaphysics of Emergence," 674.
81 Jackson, 1998, 3–4.
82 O'Connor and Hong Yu Wong, "The Metaphysics of Emergence,": 661.
83 O'Connor, *Persons & Causes*, xii–xiii, 3–5, 42.
84 O'Connor, *Persons & Causes*, 4–5. For statements of this sort, see John Foster, *The Immaterial Self* (London: Routledge, 1991), 267; Robert Kane, *The Significance of Free Will* (N. Y.: Oxford, 1996), 4; J. A. Cover and John O'Leary-Hawthorne, "Free Agency and Materialism," in *Faith, Freedom, and Rationality*, ed. by Jeff Jordon and Daniel Howard-Snyder (Lanham, Md.: Rowman & Littlefield, 1996), 51.
85 See Bishop, *Natural Agency*, 58, 69, 72, 95–97, 103–4, 114, 120, 126–27, 137, 140–41, 144, 177–80.
86 Jaegwon Kim, "Lonely Souls: Causality and Substance Dualism," in *Soul, Body and Survival* ed. by Kevin Corcoran (Ithaca, N. Y.: Cornell University Press, 2001), 30.
87 Jackson, *From Metaphysics to Ethics*, 45.
88 It could be objected that these intuitions do not entail substance dualism or other claims that entail substance dualism. But even if this objection is correct, it does not undercut my argument. The evidence that water is de re necessarily H_2O does not entail this conclusion, and the pre-philosophical intuitions O'Connor employs to argue for agent causation do not entail that conclusion. Still, in both cases, the respective evidence does ground the conclusion and contributes to a burden of proof on dissenters, and that is all I am claiming for pre-philosophical dualist intuitions.
89 O'Connor, *Persons & Causes*, 4.
90 Ibid., 124.
91 See Stewart Goetz, "Modal Dualism: A Critique," in *Soul, Body and Survival*, ed. by Kevin Corcoran (Ithaca, N. Y.: Cornell University Press, 2001), 89–104.
92 O'Connor, *Persons & Causes*, 123–24.
93 Ibid., 124.

5 Colin McGinn and mysterian "naturalism"

1 Colin McGinn, *The Mysterious Flame* (N.Y.: Basic Books, 1999). Unless otherwise noted, my description of McGinn's position is taken from this source. McGinn first thought of his mysterian naturalism in the late 1980s [see his *The Problem of Consciousness* (Oxford: Blackwell, 1991), vii; cf. chapters 1–4], and his view has remained largely unchanged until the present [see his *Consciousness and its Objects* (Oxford: Oxford University Press, 2004, reprinted unchanged in 2006), 1]. I focus on *The Mysterious Flame* because it is the clearest exposition of McGinn's position relevant to developing AC.
2 John Perry, *Knowledge, Possibility, and Consciousness* (Cambridge, Massachusetts: MIT Press, 2001), 71–92.
3 Cf. William Lane Craig *Reasonable Faith* (Wheaton, Illinois: Crossway Books, 1994); William Lane Craig and Quentin Smith *Theism, Atheism, and Big Bang Cosmology* (Oxford: Clarendon Press, 1993). See also, J. P. Moreland, "A Response to a Platonistic and Set-theoretic Objection to the Kalam Cosmological Argument," *Religious Studies* 39 (2004): 373–90; "Agent Causation and the

Craig/Grünbaum Debate about Theistic Explanation of the Initial Singularity," *American Catholic Philosophical Quarterly*, 71 (Autumn 1997), 539–54; "Resemblance Extreme Nominalism and Infinite Regress Arguments," *The Modern Schoolman* 80 (January 2003): 85–98.

4 Roderick Chisholm, *A Realistic Theory of the Categories* (Cambridge: Cambridge University Press, 1996), 53.

5 D. M. Armstrong, *Universals & Scientific Realism Vol. I: Nominalism & Realism* (Cambridge: Cambridge University Press, 1978), 19–21.

6 Thomas Aquinas, *Summa Theologica* I, 1981, Q. 46, Art. 2, Reply Obj. 7; cf. *Summa Contra Gentiles* I, Chapter xiii. See Patterson Brown, "Infinite Causal Regression," in *Aquinas: A Collection of Essays* edited by Anthony Kenny (Notre Dame: University of Notre Dame Press, 1976), 214–36.

7 For an overview of Scotus' treatment of causality and regresses, including a list of primary sources, see Richard Cross, *Duns Scotus on God* (Hants, England: Ashgate Publishing Limited, 2005), 17–28).

8 Nicholas Rescher, *The Limits of Science* (Berkeley: University of California Press, 1984), 22.

9 Colin McGinn, *Mental Content* (Oxford: Basil Blackwell, 1989), 13. Cf. Jeffrey Poland, *Physicalism* (Oxford: Clarendon, 1994), especially 10–44, 226–32, 307–12.

10 See J. P. Moreland, "Naturalism and the Ontological Status of Properties," in *Naturalism: A Critical Analysis,* edited by William Lane Craig and J. P. Moreland (London: Routledge, 2000), 67–109; J. P. Moreland, *Universals* (Canada: McGill-Queen's University Press, 2001), 121–29.

11 Wilfrid Sellars, *Naturalism and Ontology* (Atascadero, CA: Ridgeview Pub. Co., 1979), 109.

12 Sellars, *Naturalism and Ontology*, 47. Cf. Wilfrid Sellars, "Towards a Theory of Predication," in *How Things Are*, ed. by James Bogen, James E. McGuire (Dordrecht: D. Reidel, 1985), 285–322.

13 See the sources cited in note 10.

14 For a discussion of this topic along with a bibliography, see J. P. Moreland, "Naturalism, Nominalism, and Husserlian Moments," *The Modern Schoolman* 79 (January/March 2002): 199–216.

15 See Hugh Ross, *Beyond the Cosmos* (Colorado Springs, CO: NavPress, 1996).

6 David Skrbina and panpsychism

1 See references to Timothy O'Connor's panpsychist tendencies in chapter four. Cf. Thomas Nagel, *The View From Nowhere* (N. Y.: Oxford, 1986), 49–53. David J. Chalmers, *The Conscious Mind* (N. Y.: Oxford, 1997), 293–301.

2 David Skrbina, *Panpsychism in the West* (Cambridge, Mass.: MIT Press, 2005), 2.

3 Ibid. 37.

4 Ibid. 16.

5 For an exposition and critique of Mormon panpsychism, see J. P. Moreland, "The Absurdities of Mormon Materialism: A Reply to the Neglected Orson Pratt," in *The New Mormon Challenge* ed. by Francis Beckwith, Carl Mosser, and Paul Owen (Grand Rapids: Zondervan, 2002), 243–70.

6 Skrbina, *Panpsychism in the West*, 2, 11, 15–17, 249.

7 Ibid., 18, 37, 209, 237–38.

8 Ibid., 39, 209, 166.

9 Ibid., 250–52.

10 Ibid., 26, 107.

11 John Yolton, *Thinking Matter: Materialism in Eighteenth-Century Britain* (Minneapolis: University of Minnesota Press, 1983).

12 Skrbina, *Panpsychism in the West*, 13, 102, 106–7.

13 For a summary of the case for Christian theism, see Paul Copan and Paul Moser, eds, *Rationality of Theism* (London: Routledge, 2003); William Lane Craig, ed., *Philosophy of Religion: A Contemporary Reader*, (Edinburgh: Edinburgh University Press; N. Y.: Rutgers University Press, 2002); J. P. Moreland and Kai Nielsen, *Does God Exist?: The Debate Between Atheists and Theists* (Buffalo: Prometheus Books, 1993); J. P. Moreland and Michael Wilkins, eds, *Jesus Under Fire: Modern Scholarship Reinvents the Historical Jesus* (Grand Rapids: Zondervan, 1995); Larry W. Hurtado, *Lord Jesus Christ* (Grand Rapids, Michigan: Eerdmans, 2003); N. T. Wright, *The Resurrection of the Son of God* (Minneapolis: Fortress Press, 2003). See also, Richard Casdorph, *Real Miracles* (Gainesville, Florida: Bridge-Logos, 2003).

14 See Hud Hudson, *A Materialist Metaphysics of the Human Person*. (Ithaca, New York: Cornell University Press, 2001), chapter three. Cf. J. P. Moreland, "Hud Hudson's 4DPartism and Human Persons," *Philosophia Christi* 5 (2003): 545–54.

15 Skrbina, *Panpsychism in the West*, 126.

16 Ibid., 16; cf. 108–08, 211.

17 See the work cited in note five above.

18 Skrbina, *Panpsychism in the West*, 153–54.

19 Ibid., 154.

20 Ibid., 211–13.

21 For a Cartesian response, see See Mark Bedau, "Cartesian Interactionism," in *Midwest Studies in Philosophy X: Studies in the Philosophy of Mind*, ed. by Peter A. French, Theodore E. Uehling, Jr., and Howard K. Wettstein (Minnesota: University of Minnesota Press, 1986), 483–502; see also John Foster, "In Defense of Dualism," in *The Case For Dualism*, ed. by John R. Smythies and John Beloff (Charlottesville: University Press of Virginia, 1989), 1–25; Keith Yandell, "A Defense of Dualism," *Faith and Philosophy* 12 (1995). Skrbina's chapter four in *Panpsychism in the West* provides a non-Cartesian response. Also see J. P. Moreland and Stan Wallace, "Aquinas vs. Descartes and Locke on the Human Person and End-of-Life Ethics," *International Philosophical Quarterly* 35 (September 1995): 319–30.

22 See Jaegwon Kim, *Physicalism, or Something Near Enough* (Princeton: Princeton University Press, 2005), chapter three; J. P. Moreland, "If You Can't Reduce, You Must Eliminate: Why Kim's Version of Physicalism Isn't Close Enough," *Philosophia Christi* 7 (Spring 2005): 463–73; Timothy O'Connor, "Causality, Mind, and Free Will," in *Soul, Body, and Survival* (Ithaca, N. Y.: Cornell University Press, 2001), 44–58.

23 Geoffrey Madell, *Mind and Materialism Mind and Materialism* (Edinburgh: Edinburgh University Press, 1988), 3.

24 See note five above.

25 For an exposition of independent specifiability, see William Dembski, *Intelligent Design* (Downers Grove, Illinois: InterVarsity Press, 1999). For an exposition of irreducible complexity, see Michael Behe, *Darwin's Black Box* (N. Y.: The Free Press, 1996).

26 Skrbina, *Panpsychism in the West*, 264–65.

27 See references to Pratt's work and a response in the book cited in note five above.

28 Skrbina, *Panpsychism in the West*, 243.

29 See the sources in note eight above.

30 See William Lane Craig, *Reasonable Faith* (Wheaton, Illinois: Crossway, 1994), chapter three; J. P. Moreland, *Scaling the Secular City* (Grand Rapids, Michigan: Baker, 1986), chapter one; "A Response to a Platonistic and Set-theoretic

Objection to the Kalam Cosmological Argument," *Religious Studies* 39 (2004): 373–90.

31 Skrbina, *Panpsychism in the West*, 4.

7 Philip Clayton and pluralistic emergentist monism

1 The most extensive statement of Clayton's position is his *Mind & Emergence* (Oxford: Oxford University Press, 2004). Therefore, most Clayton page citations in chapter seven refer to this text.
2 Ibid., vi.
3 Ibid.
4 Ibid., 128.
5 Ibid., 4, 11.
6 Ibid., 4.
7 Ibid., 158.
8 Ibid., 4.
9 Ibid., 65, 158, 201.
10 Ibid., 58.
11 Ibid., v, 1, 49, 50, 53.
12 Ibid., 4, 123–24, 130, 201.
13 Ibid., 56.
14 Ibid., 124–28.
15 Ibid., 4; cf. 60.
16 Ibid., 54.
17 Ibid., 198.
18 Ibid., 9.
19 Ibid., 31–32.
20 Ibid., 31.
21 Ibid., 49.
22 Ibid.
23 Ibid., 4.
24 Ibid., 61.
25 Ibid.
26 Ibid., 156.
27 Ibid., vi.
28 Ibid., 9.
29 Ibid., 49.
30 Ibid., 107; cf. 158.
31 Ibid., 127.
32 Ibid., cf. 28–29.
33 Ibid., 59–60.
34 Ibid., 166–69.
35 Ibid., 169.
36 Ibid., 172.
37 Ibid., 205.
38 Ibid., 172–79.
39 Ibid., 184–87.
40 Ibid., 3, 42, 44, 45, 108, 112, 156, 171–74, 193.
41 Ibid., 30, 62, 107–8, 111, 123.
42 Ibid., vi.
43 Ibid., 65.
44 Ibid., 66.
45 Ibid., 156.
46 Ibid., 163.

47 Ibid., cf. 120.
48 Ibid., 9.
49 Ibid., 107; cf. 158.
50 For an analysis of a number of aspects of human beings that are outside the limits of evolutionary explanation, see Anthony O'Hear, *Beyond Evolution: Human Nature and the limits of Evolutionary Explanation* (Oxford: Clarendon, 1997). Curiously, O'Hear offers no plausible account of how human beings could have appeared with these constitutional features. And he does not interact with theistic explanations, yet the thesis of his book is precisely what one would predict, given Christian theism and the doctrine of the image of God, viz., that several aspects of human beings would be recalcitrant facts for alternative worldviews, especially for naturalism.
51 Clayton, *Mind & Emergence*, 84; cf. 89.
52 Ibid., vi, 50, 53, 60, 107, 111, 128–29, 164.
53 Frank Jackson, *From Metaphysics to Ethics* (Oxford: Clarendon, 1998).
54 Clayton, *Mind & Emergence*, 120.
55 Ibid., 157, 171–72.
56 Ibid., v, 10, 12, 40, 49–50, 53, 60, 98, 107, 111, 128, 129, 158, 164.
57 Dennis Des Chene, *Life's Form: Late Aristotelian Conceptions of the Soul* (Ithaca, N. Y.: Cornell University Press, 2000). Cf. J. P. Moreland and Scott Rae, *Body & Soul* (Downers Grove, Illinois: InterVarsity Press, 2000).
58 Clayton, *Mind & Emergence*, 164.
59 William Hasker, *The Emergent Self* (Ithaca, N. Y.: Cornell University Press, 1999).
60 Melvin Morse, MD, with Paul Perry, *Closer to the Light: Learning from the Near-Death Experiences of Children* (N.Y.: Random House [Villard Books], 1990), 3–9.
61 I am indebted to Gary R. Habermas for providing these insights to me. For more of his research on NDE's see Gary R. Habermas and J. P. Moreland, *Beyond Death* (Wheaton, Illinois: Crossway, 1998), chapters 7–9. See also, Peter Shockey, *Reflections of Heaven* (N. Y.: Doubleday, 1999).
62 See C. Fred Dickason, *Demon Possession & the Christian* (Wheaton, Illinois: Crossway, 1987); Felicitas D. Goodman, *How About Demons?* (Bloomington, Indiana: Indiana University Press, 1988); Charles Kraft, *Defeating Dark Angels* (Ann Arbor, Michigan: Servant, 1992); Francis McNutt, *Deliverance from Evil Spirits* (Grand Rapids, Michigan: Baker, 1995); George Otis, Jr., *The Twilight Labyrinth* (Grand Rapids, Michigan: Baker, 1997); Scott Peck, *People of the Lie* (New York, New York: Touchtone, 2nd. ed., 1998); Jane Rumph, *Signs and Wonders in America Today* (Ann Arbor, Michigan: Servant, 2003); Peter S. Williams, *The Case for Angels* (Carlisle, UK: Paternoster Press, 2002); Colin Wilson, *The Occult* (London: Watkins Publishing, 2003).
63 Holly Pivec, "Exorcizing Our Demons," *Biola Connections* (Winter 2006): 10–17.
64 Clayton, *Mind & Emergence*, v.
65 Ibid., 4.
66 Ibid., vi.
67 Jaegwon Kim, *Mind in a Physical World* (Cambridge, Mass.: MIT Press, 1998), 9–15
68 See J. P. Moreland, "Christian Materialism and the Parity Thesis Revisited," *International Philosophical Quarterly* 40 (December 2000): 423–40.
69 Clayton, *Mind & Emergence*, 52–53, 57.
70 Ibid., 50.
71 Ibid., 51.
72 Ibid., 51.
73 Richard Connell, *Substance and Modern Science* (Houston, Texas: Center for Thomistic Studies, 1988); cf. Enrico Cantori, *Atomic Order* (Cambridge, Mass.:

MIT Press, 1969). Cantori's work should be read in light of the careful metaphysical distinctions made by Connell.

74 Clayton, *Mind & Emergence*, 95; cf. 84–96.

75 Ibid., 6.

76 Ibid., 16.

77 Ibid.

78 Ibid., 16–17.

79 Ibid., 182.

80 Ibid., 186–87.

81 Ibid., 140–42.

82 Ibid., 142, 175.

83 Ibid., see 174, 176–79.

84 J. P. Moreland, Scott Rae, *Body and Soul*, chapters two and three.

85 Clayton, *Mind & Emergence*, 47.

86 Howard J. van Till, "Basil and Augustine Revisited: The Survival of Functional Integrity," *Origins & Design* 19:1 (Summer 1998): 1–12; "Special Creationism in Designer Clothing: A Response to *The Creation Hypothesis*," *Perspectives on Science and Christian Faith* (June 1995): 124–27; "Basil, Augustine, and the Doctrine of Creation's Functional Integrity," *Science and Christian Belief*, Vol. 8, No. 1 (April 1996): 21–38.

87 Ibid., 112.

88 See Russ Shafer-Landau, *Moral Realism: A Defense* (New York: Oxford University Press, 2005).

8 Science and strong physicalism

1 Daniel Dennett, *Explaining Consciousness* (Boston: Little, Brown and Co., 1991), 37.

2 Jaegwon Kim, "Lonely Souls: Causality and Substance Dualism," in *Soul, Body and Survival* ed. by Kevin Corcoran (Ithaca, N. Y.: Cornell University Press, 2001), 30. Cf. J. P. Moreland, "A Christian Perspective on the Impact of Modern Science on Philosophy of Mind," *Perspectives on Science and Christian Faith* 55 (March 2003): 2–12.

3 John Searle, *The Rediscovery of the Mind* (Cambridge, Massachusetts: MIT Press, 1992), xii.

4 Ibid, 3–4.

5 Nancey Murphy, "Human Nature: Historical, Scientific, and Religious Issues," in Warren S. Brown, Nancey Murphy and H. Newton Malony, *Whatever Happened to the Soul?* (Minneapolis: Fortress Press, 1998), 17. Cf. 13, 27, 139–43.

6 Ibid, 18.

7 Paul Churchland orders the first half of his book *Matter and Consciousness* (Cambridge, Massachusetts: MIT Press, rev. ed., 1988) around these families of issues.

8 George Bealer, "On the Possibility of Philosophical Knowledge," in *Philosophical Perspectives 10: Metaphysics, 1996*, ed. by James E. Tomberlin (Cambridge, MA: Blackwell, 1996), 1.

9 M. R. Bennett and P. M. S. Hacker, *Philosophical Foundations to Neuroscience* (Oxford: Blackwell, 2003).

10 David Papineau, *Philosophical Naturalism* (Oxford: Blackwell, 1993), 3, 4.

11 Patricia Churchland, *Neurophilosophy* (Cambridge, Massachusetts: MIT Press, 1986), 265.

12 Ibid.

13 Ibid, 270.

14 Ibid, 277.
15 Ibid, 248–49.
16 Paul Churchland, *Matter and Consciousness* (revised edition, 1988), chapters three and four.
17 Jaegwon Kim, *Philosophy of Mind* (Boulder, Colorado: Westview Press, 1996), chapter three.
18 The point is not limited to the hard sciences. The history of experimental psychology from the last third of the nineteenth century until the middle of the twentieth century is essentially the replacement of first-person introspection for third-person measurements as central to psychological method. See William Lyons, *Matters of the Mind* (N. Y.: Routledge, 2001), chapter one.
19 For more on criteria for property identity, see J. P. Moreland, *Universals* (Montreal & Kingston: McGill-Queen's University Press, 2001), 116–20.
20 Kim, *Philosophy of Mind* (1996), 49–53.
21 Roderick Chisholm, "Mind," in *Handbook of Metaphysics and Ontology*, ed. by Hans Burkhardt and Barry Smith (Munich: Philosophia Verlag, 1991): II, 556.
22 For a recent discussion of the Knowledge Argument, see J. P. Moreland, "The Knowledge Argument Revisited," *International Philosophical Quarterly* 43 (2003): 219–228. For an exposition and defense of the Simple Argument, see Stewart Goetz, "Modal Dualism: A Critique," in *Soul, Body & Survival*, ed. by Kevin Corcoran (Ithaca, N. Y.: Cornell University Press, 2001), 89–104.
23 Searle, *The Rediscovery of the Mind*, 8–9.
24 David Papineau, *Philosophical Naturalism* (Oxford: Blackwell, 1993), 1–5.
25 Nancey Murphy, "Human Nature: Historical, Scientific, and Religious Issues," in Warren S. Brown, Nancey Murphy and H. Newton Malony, *Whatever Happened to the Soul?* (Minneapolis: Fortress Press, 1998), 17. Cf. 13, 27, 139–43.
26 Ibid, 18.
27 For example, see F. R. Tennant, *Philosophical Theology I: The Soul and Its Faculties* (Cambridge: Cambridge University Press, 1956), 1–138, especially 33–43.
28 The Autonomy Thesis and the epistemic authority of first-person introspective knowledge relative to scientific claims is powerfully woven into Edmund Husserl's practice of bracketing the world and proffering phenomenological descriptions of various intentional objects as experienced and of the intrinsic features of the various mental acts directed upon those objects. For a detailed description of a paradigm case of Husserl in this regard, see J. P. Moreland, "Naturalism, Nominalism, and Husserlian Moments," *The Modern Schoolman* 79 (January/March 2002): 199–216.
29 Nancey Murphy, "Nonreductive Physicalism: Philosophical Issues," in *Whatever Happened to the Soul* (1998):127–48.
30 See Jeffrey Schwartz and Sharon Begley, *The Mind and The Brain* (N.Y.: HarperCollins, 2002).
31 Alvin Plantinga, "Methodological Naturalism," in *Facets of Faith and Science Vol. 1: Historiography and Modes of Interaction*, ed. by Jitse M. vander Meer (Lanham, Maryland: University Press of America, 1996), 177–221.
32 Ibid., 209–10.
33 Bas C. van Fraasen, *The Scientific Image* (Oxford: Oxford University Press, 1980); "To Save the Phenomena," in *Scientific Realism*, ed. by Jarrett Leplin (Berkeley: University of California Press, 1984), 250–59.
34 Francis Crick and Christof Koch, "Consciousness and Neuroscience," *Cerebral Cortex* 8 (1998): 97–107.
35 Cf. John Horgan, "Can Science Explain Consciousness?" *Scientific American* (July 1994): 91.
36 John Searle, "The Mystery of Consciousness: Part I," *The New York Review of Books*, November 1995, 60–66. The quote is from page 64.

37 See William Hasker, *The Emergent Self* (Ithaca, N. Y.: Cornell University Press, 1999), 122–46, 171–203.
38 John Tyndall, "Scientific Materialism," in his *Fragments of Science Vol. II* (New York: P. F. Collier & Son, 1900), 95.
39 Francis Crick and Christof Koch, "Consciousness and Neuroscience," 98.
40 Ibid, 104.
41 J. P. Moreland, "Reply to Fales," *Philosophia Christi* NS 3, No. 1 (2001): 48–49.

9 AC, dualism and the fear of God

1 Barry Stroud, "The Charm of Naturalism," Proceedings and Addresses of the American Philosophical Association, November 1996, 43–55. Reprinted in M. DeCaro and M. Macarthur (ed.), *Naturalism in Question*, Cambridge University Press, 2004, 21–35, The quote is from page 22. Cf. Michael Rea, *World Without Design* (Oxford: Clarendon Press, 2002), especially chapter three.
2 John Locke, *An Essay Concerning Human Understanding* (Dover, 1959), Book II, Ch. XXIII, sec. 22, 308.
3 Ralph Cudworth and Johann Lorenz Mosheim, *The True Intellectual System of the Universe: wherein all the reason and philosophy of atheism is confuted, and its impossibility demonstrated*, John Harrison, trans. vol. 1 (London: Thomas Tegg, 1845), 200. For further discussion on Cudworth, see John Yolton, *Thinking Matter: Materialism in Eighteenth-Century Britain* (Minneapolis: University of Minnesota Press, 1983), 4–13, 64, 126, 191, 202, 204.
4 William Lyons, Introduction, in *Modern Philosophy of Mind*, ed. by William Lyons, (London: Everyman, 1995), lv.
5 John Searle, *The Rediscovery of the Mind* (Cambridge, Mass.: MIT Press, 1992), chapters 1 and 2. Cf. Tyler Burge, "Philosophy of Language and Mind: 1950–90," *The Philosophical Review* 101 (January 1992): 3–51, especially 29–51.
6 Ibid., 3–4. Cf. 31.
7 Thomas Nagel, *The Last Word* (N. Y.: Oxford, 1997), 130–31. Nagel's "solution" concerning how there could be such a thing as universal, normative, objective reason is simply to say that it is self-defeating to seek a justification beyond reason for reason itself. Rather, reason is its own authority and its validity is universal, so reason is its own justification. To seek a further justification for it is a confusion. Unfortunately, Nagel fails to distinguish the first-order question when asked in the context of skepticism and subjectivism: "Is reason objective?" from the second-order question: "How could there be such a thing as objective reason?" Nagel's "solution" works for the first but not for the second question. As it stands, Nagel's "solution" is consistent with a Kantian transcendental stance according to which from within the rational point of view, we must act *as if* reason were objective and valid, but this does not entail that it actually is. There are two analogous areas of philosophical discourse that expose the inadequacy of Nagel's "solution." First, with respect to the question "Why should I be moral?", there is a distinction of interpreting the question as a first-order one from within the moral point of view (in which case the question is pointless and may be answered only by the vacuous response "Because it is morally right to act and think morally rightly.") vs. a second-order one from outside the moral point of view ("How could there be such a thing as the moral point of view? Why is it rational to accept the moral point of view?"). Admittedly, when one asks the second-order moral question, one is no longer operating from within morality but when one asks the second-order rational question, one is still within rationality. Still, the question "How could there be such a thing as a rational point of view?" is an intelligible question, and as Plantinga has shown and as Nagel acknowledges, naturalistic evolutionary answers to the

second-order question actually provide defeaters for rationality for which theism provides a defeater-defeater. Second, advocates of the design argument sometimes cite as evidence for a Designer the occurrence of various factors necessary for the existence of life (e.g. various cosmic constants, the properties of water, etc.). Critics from Hume to the present have responded in this way: We should not be surprised by these data. If the world had been one in which intelligent life could not have arisen, then we should not be here to discuss the matter. The factors are necessary for people to be around to puzzle over them and, thus, we should not be surprised at their occurrence. This response is analogous to Nagel's defense of reason. To see what is wrong with this objection, let us suppose that an advocate of the design argument cites a number of factors, a–g, that are part of the world and are necessary preconditions for the emergence of life. Hume and his followers interpret the design argument as follows: Theists are supposedly saying, "Isn't it amazing that the factors necessary for life preceded us instead of some other factors that make life impossible preceding us!" In other words, theists are comparing these two different world courses: World Course #1: a through g obtain and human beings appear; World Course #2: alternate factors (say h through n) obtain and human beings appear. Note that worlds one and two differ only in the factors that obtain in them, but the presence of human beings is held constant. Now this is indeed a bad argument, because it is hard to see how humans could emerge in any world other than one in which the factors necessary for their emergence are actualized! But this is not the correct interpretation of the design argument. Advocates of the design argument are offering the following comparison: World Course #1: a through g obtain and human beings appear; World Course #2: alternate factors (say h through n) obtain and no human life appears. Advocates of the design argument are claiming that the emergence of any life, including human life, was incredibly unlikely and required the actualization of a delicately balanced set of preconditions, and the realization of these preconditions require explanation provided by the existence of a Designer. Even the atheist J. L. Mackie saw the flaw in Hume's criticism: "There is only one actual universe, with a unique set of basic materials and physical constants, and it is therefore surprising that the elements of this unique set-up are just right for life when they might easily have been wrong. This is not made less surprising by the fact that if it had not been so, no one would have been here to be surprised. We can properly envisage and consider alternative possibilities which do not include our being there to experience them." See J. L. Mackie, *The Miracle of Theism* (Oxford: Clarendon Press, 1982), 141. Nagel confuses parallel cases of these two interpretations of the design argument by dismissing questions about rationality as though they were like the first interpretation. But questions about rationality are like the second interpretation and Nagel's "solution" not only fails to address this question, it actually provides grounds that strengthen the force of it. For more on this, see J. P. Moreland, "The Twilight of Scientific Atheism: Responding to Nagel's Last Stand," in *The Future of Atheism*, ed. by Robert Stewart (Philadelphia: Fortress Press, 2008).

8 See Richard Connell, *Substance and Modern Science* (Notre Dame: University of Notre Dame Press, 1988) 89–100; Geoffrey Madell, *The Identity of the Self* (Edinburgh: Edinburgh University Press, 1981), 49–77. Unfortunately, Madell claims that the I should be taken as the property of being a self and not as a substance. Consequently, the I is something that, like redness, can be exemplified. See Madell, 134–38. Cf. J. P. Moreland, "How To Be A Nominalist in Realist Clothing," *Grazer Philosophische Studien* 39 (1991) 75–101.

9 Stewart Goetz, "Modal Dualism," delivered at the Midwestern Meeting of the Society of Christian Philosophers, March 9, 1996. Madell, *The Identity of the Self*; cf., Madell, *Mind and Materialism* (Edinburgh: Edinburgh University Press,

1988) 103–25. Cf. J. P. Moreland, "Madell's Rejection of a Substantial, Immaterial Self," *Philosophia Christi* 2:1 (1999): 111–14.

10 Richard Swinburne, *The Evolution of the Soul* (Oxford: Clarendon, 1986) 145–73.

11 I omit temporal indexicals like "now" and "then" because on my view, they are two primitive indexicals that cannot be reduced to or eliminated in favor of the other: "I" and "now". "Now" expresses an irreducible fact about temporal reality—presentness—and it implies an A-series view of time. The fact that "I" and "now" are both primitive may have something to do with the fact that finite, conscious beings are intrinsically temporal entities.

12 See Madell, *Mind and Materialism* 103–25.

13 See Madell, *The Identity of the Self*; Hywel David Lewis, *The Elusive Self* (Philadelphia: Westminster Press, 1982).

14 See John Foster, *The Immaterial Self* (London: Routledge, 1991) 266–80; Grant Gillett, "Actions, Causes, and Mental Ascriptions," in *Objections to Physicalism*, ed. by Howard Robinson (Oxford: Clarendon, 1993) 81–100; J. P. Moreland, "Naturalism and Libertarian Agency," *Philosophy and Theology* 10 (1997) 351–81. But cf. Timothy O'Connor, "Agent Causation," in *Agents, Causes, & Events* (N. Y.: Oxford, 1995) 178–80.

15 Foster, *The Immaterial Self*, 266–80.

16 Paul Tidman, "Conceivability as a Test for Possibility," *American Philosophical Quarterly* 31 (October 1994) 297–309.

17 See James van Cleve, "Conceivability and the Cartesian Argument for Dualism," *Pacific Philosophical Quarterly* 64 (1983) 35–45; Charles Taliaferro, *Consciousness and the Mind of God* (Cambridge: Cambridge University Press, 1994) 134–39,

18 A. D. Smith points out that if we sever our beliefs in possibility entirely from conceivability, we shall land in extreme Megareanism where the possible and the necessary collapse into the actual. Se A. D. Smith, "Non-Reductive Physicalism," in *Objections to Physicalism*, ed. by Howard Robinson (Oxford: Clarendon Press, 1993) 243.

19 Cf. Keith Yandell, "A Defense of Dualism," *Faith and Philosophy* 12 (1995) 548–66; Charles Taliaferro, "Animals, Brains, and Spirits," *Faith and Philosophy* 12 (1995) 567–81.

20 Paul Churchland, *Matter and Consciousness* (Cambridge, Mass.: MIT Press, rev. ed., 1988)

21 Paul Churchland, *Matter and Consciousness* (1988), 10.

22 See J. P. Moreland and Stanley Wallace, "Aquinas vs. Descartes and Locke on the Human Person and End-of-Life Ethics," *International Philosophical Quarterly* 35 (September 1995): 319–30. In the article we address and offer a Thomistic solution to causal pairing. Kim may be forgiven for missing a specific journal article since we all do that regularly. But our solution is not unusual among Thomistic dualists, and it is difficult to see how Kim could fail to interact with this view if he knew of it.

23 Anthony O'Hear, *Beyond Evolution: Human Nature and the limits of Evolutionary Explanation* (Oxford: Clarendon, 1997).

24 Searle, *Rediscovery of the Mind*, 9,

25 Ibid., 9.

26 Ibid., 4.

27 Ibid., 4–5.

28 Ibid., 5.

29 Ibid., xii.

30 Ibid, 27.

31 Richard Swinburne clearly distinguishes substance dualism and immortality. He claims to provide a compelling case for the former independent of Christian revelation, but not for the latter. See Swinburne, *The Evolution of the Soul*,

introduction and chapter fifteen. Searle's comments occur six years after Swinburne's, and it is either dishonest or ignorant for Searle to use his rhetoric in light of a clear, powerful counterexample in the literature, a counterexample that is typical of substance dualists and not idiosyncratic to Swinburne.

32 Searle, *Rediscovery of the Mind*, 90–91.
33 Quentin Smith, "The Metaphilosophy of Naturalism," *Philo* (2001).
34 Ibid.
35 Ibid.
36 Richard Gale, *On the Nature and Existence of God* (Cambridge: Cambridge University Press, 1991), 387.
37 Quentin Smith, "The Metaphilosophy of Naturalism."
38 John Searle, "An Interview with John Searle," *Free Inquiry* 18:4 (Fall 1998): 39. See the equally puzzling summary of Peter Watson's hernia-enducing eight-hundred page tome *Ideas: A History of Thought and Invention, from Fire to Freud* (N. Y.: HarperCollins, 2005), 746.

39 J. P. Moreland and Kai Nielsen, *Does God Exist? The Debate between Theists & Atheists* (Buffalo, N. Y.: Prometheus, 1993).
40 Ibid, 79–86.
41 See P. C. Vitz, *Faith of the Fatherless: The Psychology of Atheism* (Dallas, Texas: Spence Publishing, 1999). Cf. Benjamin Beit-Hallahmi, "Atheists: A Psychological Profile," in *The Cambridge Companion to Atheism* ed. by Michael Martin (Cambridge: Cambridge University Press, 2007), 300–317.
42 Jaegwon Kim, "Lonely Souls: Causality and Substance Dualism," in *Soul, Body and Survival*, ed. Kevin Corcoran (Ithaca, N. Y.: Cornell University Press, 2001), 30.
43 Frank Jackson, *From Metaphysics to Ethics* (Oxford: Clarendon Press, 1998), 45.
44 Joshua Hoffman and Gary S. Rosenkrantz, *Substance: Its Nature and Existence* (London: Routledge, 1997), 7. Cf. 77–79. Unfortunately, Hoffman and Rosenkrantz fail to follow their own advice, or so it seems to me. For they claim that, while souls are intelligible and, thus, *possibly* exist, there is no sufficient reason to postulate their existence, given the natural scientific view of living organisms and their place in the natural world. Cf. 6–7. But this judgment reverses the epistemic order between science and "folk" ontology and removes the burden of proof about the soul that science has not, and perhaps cannot meet, given the nature of the issue.
45 Ned Block "Consciousness" in *A Companion to the Philosophy of Mind*, ed. Samuel Guttenplan (Malden, MA: Blackwell, 1994), 211.
46 John Searle, "The Mystery of Consciousness: Part II," *New York Review of Books* (16 November 1995), 61.
47 Colin McGinn, *The Mysterious Flame: Consciousness Minds in a Material World* (New York: Basic Books, 1999). 14.
48 Colin McGinn, *The Problem of Consciousness* (Oxford: Basil Blackwell, 1991), 10–11.
49 David Chalmers, *The Conscious Mind* (New York: Oxford University Press, 1997), 93.
50 David Papineau, *Philosophical Naturalism* (Oxford: Blackwell, 1993), 119.
51 Ibid., 106, 114–18, 120, 121, 126.
52 Leibniz, *Monadology* 17, in *Leibniz Selections*, ed. Philip Weiner (N. Y.: Charles Scribner's Sons, 1951), 536.
53 Jackson, *From Metaphysics to Ethics*, 6 n. 5.
54 Jeffrey Schwartz and Sharon Begley, *The Mind and the Brain* (N.Y., N.Y.: HarperCollins, 2002), 37; Cf. 28, 30–31, 43, 44, 46 48–49, 142, 143, 148.
55 Jaegwon Kim, "Mind, Problems of the Philosophy of," s.v. *The Oxford Companion to Philosophy*, ed. Ted Honderich (New York: Oxford University Press, 1995), 578.

56 Jaegwon Kim, *Mind in a Physical World*, 96.

57 Ibid., chapter 4, especially pages 118–20. Curiously, Kim has become an emergent epiphenomenal dualist regarding phenomenal conscious. See his *Physicalism or Something Near Enough* (Princeton, N. J.: Princeton University Press, 2005). This is curious because Kim has always been sensitive to emergentist questions (Why does pain instead of itchiness emerge on certain brain states? Why does consciousness emerge at all?) and, as far as I can tell, he does not believe there is a clear naturalistic answer to these questions. In this case, it is likely that his ontology has lots and lots of brute facts, a curious admission for a philosopher who accepts ontological simplicity as a guide for doing ontology. Cf. J. P. Moreland, "If You Can't Reduce, You Must Eliminate: Why Kim's Version of Physicalism Isn't Close Enough," *Philosophia Christi* 7 (Spring  2005): 463–73; "The Argument from Consciousness," in *Rationality of Theism*, ed. by Paul Copan and Paul Moser (London: Routledge, 2003), 204–20.

Bibliography

Adams, Robert. "Flavors, Colors, and God," reprinted in *Contemporary Perspectives on Religious Epistemology*, edited by R. Douglas Geivett and Brendan Sweetman. N.Y.: Oxford University Press, 1992.

Alexander, Samuel. *Space, Time and Deity: The Gifford Lectures at Glasgow, 1916–1918, vol.* 2. New York: Dover Publications, 1920, 1966.

Aquinas, Thomas. *Summa Contra Gentiles*. Translated by Anton C. Pegis. Notre Dame; London: University of Notre Dame Press, 1975.

—— *Summa Theologica*. Translated by Fathers of the English Dominican Province. Allen Texas: Christian Classics, 1981.

Armstrong, D.M. *A Materialist Theory of Mind*. London: Routledge & Kegan Paul, 1968.

—— "Naturalism, Materialism, and First Philosophy," *Philosophia* 8 (1978): 261–76.

—— *Nominalism & Realism: Universals & Scientific Realism. Volume I*. Cambridge: Cambridge University Press, 1978, 1988, 1990.

—— *A Theory of Universals: Universals & Scientific Real*ism, *Volume II*. Cambridge: Cambridge University Press, 1978, 1980, 1990.

—— "Can A Naturalist Believe in Universals?" in *Science in Reflection*, edited by Edna Ullmann-Margalit. Boston: Kluwer Academic Publishers, 1988.

—— *A World of States of Affairs*. Cambridge: Cambridge University Press, 1997.

—— *The Mind-Body Problem: An Opinionated Introduction*. Boulder, Colorado: Westview Press, 1999.

Aune, Bruce. *Metaphysics: The Elements*. Minneapolis: University of Minnesota Press, 1985.

Bealer, George. "On the Possibility of Philosophical Knowledge," in *Philosophical Perspectives 10: Metaphysics*, edited by James E. Tomberlin. Cambridge, MA: Blackwell, 1996.

Bedau, Mark. "Cartesian Interactionism," in *Midwest Studies in Philosophy X: Studies in the Philosophy of Mind*, edited by Peter A. French, Theodore E. Uehling, Jr., and Howard K. Wettstein. Minnesota: University of Minnesota Press, 1986.

Behe, Michael J. *Darwin's Black Box: the biochemical challenge to evolution*. N. Y.: The Free Press, 1996.

Beilby, James K., editor. *Naturalism Defeated? essays on Plantinga's evolutionary argument against naturalism*. Ithaca, N. Y.: Cornell University Press, 2002.

Beit-Hallahmi, Benjamin. "Atheists: A Psychological Profile," in *The Cambridge Companion to Atheism*. edited by Michael Martin. Cambridge: Cambridge University Press, 2007.

Bennett, M.R. and Hacker, P. M. S. *Philosophical Foundations to Neuroscience*. Malden, MA: Blackwell Publishing, 2003.

Bhaskar, Roy. *The Possibility of Naturalism*. New Jersey: Humanities Press, 1979.

Bishop, John. *Natural Agency*. Cambridge: Cambridge University Press, 1989.

Block, Ned. "Consciousness" in *A Companion to the Philosophy of Mind*, edited by Samuel D. Guttenplan. Malden, MA: Blackwell, 1994.

Bringsjord, Selmer. "Swinburne's Argument from Consciousness," *International Journal for Philosophy of Religion* 19:3 (October 1986): 127–43.

Brown, Patterson. "Infinite Causal Regression," in *Aquinas: A Collection of Critical Essays*. edited by Anthony John Patrick Kenny. Notre Dame, IN: University of Notre Dame Press, 1969, 1976.

Burge, Tyler. "Philosophy of Language and Mind; 1950–90," *The Philosophical Review* 101:1 (January 1992): 3–51.

Campbell, Keith. "Abstract Particulars and the Philosophy of Mind," *Australasian Journal of Philosophy* 61:2 (1983): 129–41.

—— *Abstract Particulars*. Oxford: Blackwell, 1990.

Cantori, Enrico. *Atomic Order: an introduction to the philosophy of microphysics*. Cambridge, Mass.: MIT Press, 1969.

Casdorph, H. Richard. *Real Miracles: indisputable evidence that God heals*. Gainesville, Florida: Bridge-Logos, 2003.

Chalmers, David John. *The Conscious Mind: in search of a fundamental theory*. New York: Oxford University Press, 1997.

Chene, Dennis Des. *Life's Form: Late Aristotelian Conceptions of the Soul*. Ithaca, N.Y.: Cornell University Press, 2000.

Chesterton, G.K. *Orthodoxy*. John Lane Company, 1908; repr., San Francisco: Ignatius Press, 1950.

Chisholm, Roderick M., *Theory of Knowledge*. Englewood Cliff, N. J.: Prentice-Hall, 2nd. ed., 1977.

—— *The First Person*. Minneapolis: University of Minnesota Press, 1981.

—— *Brentano and Intrinsic Value*. Cambridge: Cambridge University Press, 1986.

—— *On Metaphysics*. Minneapolis: University of Minnesota Press, 1989.

—— *Theory of Knowledge*. Englewood Cliff, N. J.: Prentice-Hall, 3rd. ed., 1989.

—— "Mind," in *Handbook of Metaphysics and Ontology*, edited by Hans Burkhardt and Barry Smith, vol. 2. Munich: Philosophia Verlag, 1991.

—— *A Realist Theory of Categories: an essay on ontology*. Cambridge: Cambridge University Press, 1996.

Churchland, Patricia Smith. *Neurophilosophy: Toward a Unified Science of the Mind-Brain*. Cambridge, Massachusetts: MIT Press, 1986.

Churchland, Paul. *Matter and Consciousness*. Cambridge, MA.: MIT Press, 1984.

—— *Matter and Consciousness*. Cambridge, MA: MIT Press, rev. ed., 1988.

Clark, Stephen R.L. *From Athens to Jerusalem: the love of wisdom and the love of God*. Oxford: Clarendon, 1984.

Clayton, Philip. *Mind & Emergence*. Oxford: Oxford University Press, 2004, 2006.

Clifton, Robert and Hans Halverson. "No place for particles in relativistic quantum theories?" *Philosophy of Science* 69 2002: 1–28.

Connell, Richard J. *Substance and Modern Science*. Houston, Texas: Center for Thomistic Studies, 1988.

Copan, Paul and Paul K. Moser, editors. *Rationality of Theism*. London: Routledge, 2003.

Cover, J.A. and John O'Leary-Hawthorne. "Free Agency and Materialism," in *Faith, Freedom, and Rationality: philosophy of religion today*, edited by Jeff Jordon and Daniel Howard-Snyder. Lanham, Md.: Rowman & Littlefield, 1996.

Craig, William Lane. *Reasonable Faith*. Wheaton, Illinois: Crossway Books, 1994.

—— editor. *Philosophy of Religion: A Contemporary Reader*. Edinburgh: Edinburgh University Press; N. Y.: Rutgers University Press, 2002.

—— and Quentin Smith. *Theism, Atheism, and Big Bang Cosmology*. Oxford: Clarendon Press, 1993, 1995.

Crick, Francis and Christof Koch. "Consciousness and Neuroscience," *Cerebral Cortex* 8 (1998): 97–107.

Cross, Richard. *Duns Scotus on God*. Hants, England: Ashgate Publishing Limited, 2005.

Cudworth, Ralph and Johann Lorenz Mosheim. *The True Intellectual System of the Universe: wherein all the reason and philosophy of atheism is confuted, and its impossibility demonstrated*, Vol. 1. Translated by John Harrison. London: Thomas Tegg, 1845.

Dembski, William. *Intelligent Design: the bridge between science and theology*. Downers Grove, Illinois: InterVarsity Press, 1999.

Dennett, Daniel C. *Consciousness Explained*. Boston: Little, Brown and Co., 1991.

—— *Elbow Room: the varieties of free will worth wanting*. Cambridge, Mass.: MIT Press, 1984.

Dickason, C. Fred. *Demon Possession & the Christian: A New Perspective*. Wheaton, Illinois: Crossway, 1987, 1993.

Fales, Evan, "Naturalism and Physicalism," in *The Cambridge Companion to Atheism*, edited by Michael Martin. Cambridge: Cambridge University Press, 2007.

Foster, John, "A Defense of Dualism," in *The Case For Dualism*, edited by John R. Smythies and John Beloff. Charlottesville: University of Virginia Press, 1989.

—— *The Immaterial Self: a defence of the Cartesian dualist conception of the mind*. London: Routledge, 1991, 1996.

Gale, Richard M. *On the Nature and Existence of God*. Cambridge: Cambridge University Press, 1991.

Gillett, Grant, "Actions, Causes, and Mental Ascriptions," in *Objections to Physicalism*, edited by Howard Robinson. Oxford: Clarendon, 1993.

Goetz, Stewart, "Modal Dualism," delivered at the Midwestern Meeting of the Society of Christian Philosophers, March 9, 1996.

—— "Modal Dualism: A Critique," in *Soul, Body & Survival: Essays on the Metaphysics of Human Persons*, edited by Kevin Corcoran. Ithaca, N. Y.: Cornell University Press, 2001.

—— "Naturalism and Libertarian Agency," in *Naturalism: A Critical Analysis*, edited by William Lane Craig and J.P. Moreland. Routledge, 2000.

Goodman, Felicitas D. *How About Demons? Possession and exorcism in the modern world*. Bloomington, Indiana: Indiana University Press, 1988.

Habermas, Gary R. and J.P. Moreland. *Beyond Death: exploring the evidence for immortality*. Wheaton, Illinois: Crossway, 1998.

Haldane, John. "The Mystery of Emergence," *Proceedings of the Aristotelian Society* 96 (1996): 261–67.

Hasker, William. *The Emergent Self*. Ithaca, N. Y.: Cornell University Press, 1999, 2001.

Herbert, Nick. *Quantum Reality*. Garden City, N. Y.: Anchor Press/Doubleday, 1985, 1987.

Hoffman, Joshua and Gary S. Rosenkrantz. *Substance: Its Nature and Existence* London and New York: Routledge, 1997.

Horgan, John. "Can Science Explain Consciousness?" *Scientific American* 271:1 (July 1994): 88–94.

Horgan, Terence. "Nonreductive Materialism and the Explanatory Autonomy of Psychology," in *Naturalism*, edited by Steven J. Wagner and Richard Warner. Notre Dame: University of Notre Dame Press, 1993.

Hudson, Hud. *A Materialist Metaphysics of the Human Person*. Ithaca, New York: Cornell University Press, 2001.

Hurtado, Larry W. *Lord Jesus Christ: devotion to Jesus in earliest Christianity.* Grand Rapids, Michigan: Eerdmans, 2003, 2005.

Jackson, Frank. *From Metaphysics to Ethics: A Defence of Conceptual Analysis.* Oxford: Clarendon Press, 1998.

Kane, Robert. *The Significance of Free Will*. N. Y.: Oxford University Press, 1996, 1998.

Kim, Jaegwon. "Mental Causation and Two Conceptions of Mental Properties," unpublished paper delivered at the American Philosophical Association Eastern Division Meeting, Atlanta, Georgia, December 27–30, 1993.

—— "Mind, Problems of the Philosophy of," in *The Oxford Companion to Philosophy*, edited Ted Honderich. New York: Oxford University Press, 1995.

—— *Philosophy of Mind*. Boulder, Colorado: Westview Press, 1996.

—— *Mind in a Physical World: an essay on the mind-body problem and mental causation*. Cambridge, Mass.: MIT Press, 1998, 2000.

—— "Lonely Souls: Causality and Substance Dualism," in *Soul, Body and Survival: Essays on the Metaphysics of Human Persons*, edited by Kevin Corcoran. Ithaca, N. Y.: Cornell University Press, 2001.

—— *Physicalism, or Something Near Enough*. Princeton, N. J.: Princeton University Press, 2005.

—— *Philosophy of Mind*. Boulder, Colorado: Westview Press, 2nd. ed., 2006.

Kraft, Charles. *Defeating Dark Angels*. Ann Arbor, Michigan: Servant, 1992.

Leibniz, Gottfried. "Monadology" 17, in *Leibniz Selections*, edited by Philip P. Weiner. N. Y.: Charles Scribner's Sons, 1951, 1979.

Lewis, Hywel David. *The Elusive Self*. Philadelphia: Westminster Press, 1982.

Locke, John. *An Essay Concerning Human Understanding*. New York: Dover Publications, Inc., 1959.

—— *An Essay Concerning Human Understanding*, edited by Peter H. Nidditch. London: Oxford, 1975.

Lowe, E.J. *An Introduction to the Philosophy of Mind*. Cambridge: Cambridge University Press, 2000.

Ludlow, Peter, Yujin Nagasawa, and Daniel Stoljar, editors. *There's Something About Mary*. Cambridge, Massachusetts: MIT Press, 2004.

Lyons, William. "Introduction," in *Modern Philosophy of Mind*, edited by William Lyons. London: Everyman, 1995.

—— *Matters of the Mind*. N. Y.: Routledge, 2001.

Mackie, J.L. *The Miracle of Theism*. Oxford: Clarendon Press, 1982, 1992.

Madell, Geoffrey. *The Identity of the Self*. Edinburgh: Edinburgh University Press, 1981, 1984.

—— *Mind and Materialism* Edinburgh, The University Press, 1988.

Martin, Michael. *Atheism: A Philosophical Justification*. Philadelphia: Temple University Press, 1990.

McGinn, Colin. *Mental Content*. Oxford: Basil Blackwell, 1989, 1991.
—— *The Problem of Consciousness: essays toward a resolution*. Oxford: Basil Blackwell, 1991, 1993.
—— *The Mysterious Flame: Conscious Minds in a Material World*. New York: Basic Books, 1999.
—— *Consciousness and its objects*. Oxford: Clarendon; New York: Oxford University Press, 2004, 2006.
McNutt, Francis. *Deliverance from Evil Spirits: a practical manual*. Grand Rapids, Michigan: Baker, 1995.
Menuge, Angus J.L. *Agents Under Fire: materialism and the rationality of science*. Lanham, Maryland: Rowman & Littlefield, 2004.
Merricks, Trenton. *Objects and Persons*. N. Y.: Oxford: Clarendon, 2001, 2003.
Moreland, J.P. *Scaling the Secular City*. Grand Rapids, Michigan: Baker, 1986.
—— "Keith Campbell and the Trope View of Predication," *Australasian Journal of Philosophy* 67 (December 1989): 379–93.
—— "Nominalism And Abstract Reference," *American Philosophical Quarterly* 27 (October 1990): 325–34.
—— "How to Be a Nominalist in Realist Clothing," *Grazer Philosophische Studien* 39 (Summer 1991): 75–101.
—— "Humanness, Personhood, and the Right to Die," *Faith and Philosophy* 12 (January 1995): 95–112.
—— "A Critique of Campbell's Refurbished Nominalism," *The Southern Journal of Philosophy* 35 (Summer 1997): 225–46.
—— "Agent Causation and the Craig/Grünbaum Debate about Theistic Explanation of the Initial Singularity," *American Catholic Philosophical Quarterly* 71 (Autumn 1997): 539–54.
—— "Naturalism and Libertarian Agency," *Philosophy and Theology* 10 (1997): 351–81.
—— "Searle's Biological Naturalism and the Argument from Consciousness," *Faith and Philosophy* 15 (January 1998): 68–91.
—— "Should a Naturalist Be a Supervenient Physicalist?" *Metaphilosophy* 29 (January/April 1998): 35–57.
—— "Locke's Parity Thesis about Thinking Matter: A Response to Williams," *Religious Studies* 34 (September 1998): 253–59.
—— "Theories of Individuation: A Reconsideration of Bare Particulars," *Pacific Philosophical Quarterly* 79 (1998): 251–63.
—— "Madell's Rejection of a Substantial, Immaterial Self," *Philosophia Christi* 2:1 (1999): 111–14.
—— "Christian Materialism and the Parity Thesis Revisited," *International Philosophical Quarterly* 40 (December 2000): 423–40.
—— "Issues and Options in Individuation," *Grazer Philosophische Studien* 60 (Winter 2000): 31–54.
—— "Topic Neutrality and the Parity Thesis: A Surrejoinder to Williams," *Religious Studies* 37 (March 2001): 93–101.
—— "Reply to Fales," *Philosophia Christi* 3:1 (Summer 2001): 48–49.
—— *Universals*. Bucks, Great Britain: Acumen Press; Canada: McGill-Queen's University Press, 2001.
—— "Naturalism, Nominalism, and Husserlian Moments," *The Modern Schoolman* 79 (January/March 2002): 199–216.

—— "The Absurdities of Mormon Materialism: A Reply to the Neglected Orson Pratt," in *The New Mormon Challenge*, edited by Francis J. Beckwith, Carl Mosser and Paul Owen. Grand Rapids: Zondervan, 2002.

—— "Timothy O'Connor and the Harmony Thesis: A Critique," *Metaphysica* 3:2 (2002): 5–40.

—— "The Argument from Consciousness," in *Rationality of Theism*, edited by Paul Copan and Paul Moser. London: Routledge, 2003: 204–20.

—— "A Christian Perspective on the Impact of Modern Science on Philosophy of Mind," *Perspectives on Science and Christian Faith* 55 (March 2003): 2–12.

—— "Hud Hudson's 4DPartism and Human Persons," *Philosophia Christi* 5 (2003): 545–54.

—— "Resemblance Extreme Nominalism and Infinite Regress Arguments," *The Modern Schoolman* 80 (January 2003): 85–98.

—— "The Knowledge Argument Revisited," *International Philosophical Quarterly* 43 (2003): 219–28.

—— "A Response to a Platonistic and Set-theoretic Objection to the Kalam Cosmological Argument," *Religious Studies* 39 (2004): 373–90.

—— "If You Can't Reduce, You Must Eliminate: Why Kim's Version of Physicalism Isn't Close Enough," *Philosophia Christi* 7 (Spring 2005): 463–73.

—— "The Twilight of Scientific Atheism: Responding to Nagel's Last Stand," in *The Future of Atheism*, edited by Robert Stewart. Philadelphia: Fortress Press, 2008.

—— and William Lane Craig, editors. *Naturalism: A Critical Analysis* London: Routledge, 2000.

—— and Kai Nielsen. *Does God Exist? The Debate between Theists & Atheists*. Buffalo, N. Y.: Prometheus, 1993.

—— and Scott Rae. *Body & Soul: Human Nature and the Crisis in Ethics*. Downers Grove, Illinois: InterVarsity Press, 2000.

—— and Stan Wallace. "Aquinas vs. Descartes and Locke on the Human Person and End-of-Life Ethics," *International Philosophical Quarterly* 35 (September 1995): 319–30.

—— and Michael Wilkins, editors. *Jesus Under Fire: Modern Scholarship Reinvents the Historical Jesus*. Grand Rapids: Zondervan, 1995.

Morse, Melvin and Paul Perry. *Closer to the Light: Learning from the Near-Death Experiences of Children*. N.Y.: Random House [Villard Books], 1990.

Murphy, Nancey. "Human Nature: Historical, Scientific, and Religious Issues," in *Whatever Happened to the Soul?* edited by Warren S. Brown, Nancey Murphy and H. Newton Malony. Minneapolis: Fortress Press, 1998.

—— "Nonreductive Physicalism: Philosophical Issues," in *Whatever Happened to the Soul?* edited by Warren S. Brown, Nancey Murphy and H. Newton Malony. Minneapolis: Fortress Press, 1998.

Nagel, Thomas. *Mortal Questions*. New York: Cambridge University Press, 1979, 1991.

—— *The View From Nowhere*. N. Y.: Oxford, 1986, 1989.

—— *The Last Word*. N. Y.: Oxford University Press, 1997.

O'Connor, Timothy. "Emergent Properties," *American Philosophical Quarterly* 31 (April 1994): 91–104.

—— "Agent Causation," in *Agents, Causes, & Events: essays on indeterminism and free will*, edited by Timothy O'Connor. N. Y.: Oxford, 1995.

—— *Persons & Causes: The Metaphysics of Free Will*. N. Y.: Oxford University Press, 2000.

—— "Causality, Mind, and Free Will," in *Soul, Body, and Survival: Essays on the Metaphysics of Human Persons*. Ithaca, N. Y.: Cornell University Press, 2001: 44–58.

—— and Jonathan D. Jacobs. "Emergent Individuals," *The Philosophical Quarterly* 53 (October 2003): 540–55.

—— and Hong Yu Wong. "The Metaphysics of Emergence," *Nous* 39:4 (2005): 658–78.

O'Hear, Anthony. *Beyond Evolution: Human Nature and the limits of Evolutionary Explanation*. Oxford: Clarendon, 1997.

Otis, George, Jr. *The Twilight Labyrinth: why does spiritual darkness linger where it does?* Grand Rapids, Michigan: Chosen Books, 1997.

Papineau, David. *Philosophical Naturalism*. Oxford: Blackwell, 1993.

Peacocke, Arthur and Grant Gillett, editors. *Persons and Personality: A Contemporary Inquiry* Oxford: Basil Blackwell, 1987.

Peck, Scott M. *People of the Lie: the hope for healing human evil*. New York, New York: Touchtone, 2nd. ed., 1998.

Perry, John. *Knowledge, Possibility, and Consciousness*. Cambridge, Massachusetts: MIT Press, 2001, 2003.

Pivec, Holly. "Exorcizing Our Demons," *Biola Connections* (Winter 2006): 10–17.

Plantinga, Alvin. *Warrant and Proper Function*. N.Y.: Oxford University Press, 1993.

—— "Methodological Naturalism," in *Facets of Faith and Science, Vol. 1: Historiography and Modes of Interaction*, edited by Jitse M. vander Meer. Lanham, Maryland: University Press of America, 1996.

Poland, Jeffrey. *Physicalism*. Oxford: Clarendon, 1994.

Rea, Michael. *World Without Design: the ontological consequences of naturalism*. Oxford: Clarendon Press, 2002, 2004.

Rescher, Nicholas. *The Limits of Science*. Berkeley: University of California Press, 1984.

Robinson, Howard. *Matter and Sense: A Critique of Contemporary Materialism*. Cambridge: Cambridge University Press, 1982.

Rosenberg, Alex. "A Field Guide to Recent Species of Naturalism," *British Journal for the Philosophy of Science* 47 (1996): 1–29.

Ross, Hugh. *Beyond the Cosmos: the extra-dimensionality of God*. Colorado Springs, CO: NavPress, 1996.

Rumph, Jane. *Signs and Wonders in America Today*. Ann Arbor, Michigan: Vine Books, 2003.

Schwartz, Jeffrey and Sharon Begley. *The Mind and The Brain: Neuroplasticity and the Power of Mental Force*. N.Y.: Regan Books, 2002.

Searle, John. *The Rediscovery of the Mind*. Cambridge, Mass.: MIT Press, 1992, 1994.

—— "The Mystery of Consciousness: Part I," *The New York Review of Books*, (November 1995): 60–66.

—— "The Mystery of Consciousness: Part II," *New York Review of Books* 16 (November 1995): 61.

—— *The Mystery of Consciousness*. N.Y.: *The New York Review of Books*, 1997.

—— "An Interview with John Searle" *Free Inquiry* 18:4 (Fall 1998): 39–41.

—— "Why I am not a Property Dualist," *Journal of Consciousness Studies* 9:12 (2002): 57–64.

—— *Mind: a brief introduction*. Oxford; New York: Oxford University Press, 2004.

Sellars, Wilfrid, *Science, Perception, and Reality*. London: Routledge & Kegan Paul, 1963.

—— *Naturalism and Ontology*. Atascadero, CA: Ridgeview Pub. Co., 1979.

—— "Towards a Theory of Predication," in *How Things Are*, edited by James Bogen and James E. McGuire. Dordrecht: D. Reidel, 1985.

Shafer-Landau, Russ. *Moral Realism: A Defense*. New York: Oxford University Press, 2005.

Shockey, Peter. *Reflections of Heaven: a millennial odyssey of miracles, angels, and afterlife*. N. Y.: Doubleday, 1999.

Sider, Theodore. "What's So Bad About Overdetermination?" *Philosophy and Phenomenological Research* 67 (November 2003): 719–26.

Skinner, B.F. "Can Psychology Be A Science of Mind?" *American Psychologist* 45 (November 1990): 1206–10.

Skrbina, David. *Panpsychism in the West*. Cambridge, Mass.: MIT Press, 2005.

Smith, A.D. "Non-Reductive Physicalism," in *Objections to Physicalism*, edited by Howard Robinson. Oxford: Clarendon Press, 1993.

Smith, Barry, editor. *Parts and Moments: Studies in Logic and Formal Ontology*. Munchen: Philosophia Verlag, 1982.

Smith, Quentin. "The Metaphilosophy of Naturalism," *Philo* 4:2 (2001). www.philoonline.org/library/smith_4_2.htm. Accessed 6/19/07.

Sperry, Roger. "In Defense of Mentalism and Emergent Interaction," *Journal of Mind and Behaviour* 12:1 (Spring 1991): 221–45.

Strawson, Galen. *Freedom and Belief*. Oxford: Clarendon Press, 1986.

Stroud, Barry. "The Charm of Naturalism," reprinted in M. DeCaro and M. Macarthur editors, *Naturalism in Question*. Cambridge University Press, 2004.

Swinburne, Richard. *The Existence of God*. Oxford: Clarendon, 1979.

—— *The Evolution of the Soul*. Oxford: Clarendon Press, 1986.

—— "The Origin of Consciousness," in *Cosmic Beginnings and Human Ends*, edited by Clifford N. Matthews and Roy Abraham. Varghese Chicago and La Salle, Illinois: Open Court, 1995: 355–78.

—— *Is there a God?* Oxford: Oxford University Press, 1996.

Taliaferro, Charles. "Animals, Brains, and Spirits," *Faith and Philosophy* 12 (1995): 567–81.

—— *Consciousness and the Mind of God*. Cambridge: Cambridge University Press, 1994, 2005.

Tennant, F.R. *Philosophical Theology I: The Soul and Its Faculties*. Cambridge: Cambridge University Press, 1956.

Tidman, Paul. "Conceivability as a Test for Possibility," *American Philosophical Quarterly* 31 (October 1994): 297–309.

Tyndall, John. "Scientific Materialism," in his *Fragments of Science Vol. II*. New York: P. F. Collier & Son, 1900.

van Cleve, James. "Conceivability and the Cartesian Argument for Dualism," *Pacific Philosophical Quarterly* 64 (1983): 35–45.

van Fraasen, Bas C. *The Scientific Image*. Oxford: Oxford University Press, 1980.

—— "To Save the Phenomena," in *Scientific Realism*, edited by Jarrett Leplin. Berkeley: University of California Press, 1984: 250–59.

van Inwagen, Peter. *Material Beings*. Ithaca, N. Y.: Cornell University Press, 1990, 1995.

—— *Metaphysics*. Boulder, Colorado: Westview Press, 2nd. ed., 2002.

van Till, Howard J. "Special Creationism in Designer Clothing: A Response to The Creation Hypothesis," *Perspectives on Science and Christian Faith* 47:2 (June 1995): 123–46.

—— "Basil, Augustine, and the Doctrine of Creation's Functional Integrity," *Science and Christian Belief*, 8:1 (April 1996).

—— "Basil and Augustine Revisited: The Survival of Functional Integrity," *Origins & Design* 19:1 (Summer 1998): 1–12.

Vitz, Paul C. *Faith of the Fatherless: The Psychology of Atheism*. Dallas, Texas: Spence Publishing, 1999.

Wagner, Steven and Richard Warner, editors. *Naturalism: A Critical Appraisal*. Notre Dame, Indiana: University of Notre Dame Press, 1993.

Watson, Peter. *Ideas: A History of Thought and Invention, from Fire to Freud*. N. Y.: HarperCollins, 2005.

Williams, Clifford. "Christian Materialism and the Parity Thesis," *International Journal for Philosophy of Religion* 39 (February 1996): 1–14.

—— "Topic Neutrality and the Mind-Body Problem," *Religious Studies* 36 (2000): 203–7.

Williams, Peter S. *The Case for Angels*. Carlisle, U. K.: Paternoster Press, 2002.

Wilson, Colin. *The Occult: the ultimate book for those who would walk with the Gods*, new edition. London: Watkins Publishing, 2003.

Wright, Crispin. "The Conceivability of Naturalism," in *Conceivability and Possibility*, edited by Tamar Szabo Gendler and John Hawthorne. Oxford: Clarendon, 2002.

Wright, N.T. *The Resurrection of the Son of God*. Minneapolis: Fortress Press, 2003.

Yandell, Keith. "A Defense of Dualism," *Faith and Philosophy* 12 (1995): 548–66.

Yolton, John W. *Thinking Matter: Materialism in Eighteenth-Century Britain*. Minneapolis: University of Minnesota Press, 1983.

Author index

Adams, Robert 69, 186, 199n6, 221
Alexander, Samuel 200n33, 221
Aquinas, Thomas 55, 100, 101, 202n15, 207n54, 210n6, 211n21, 218n22, 221–22, 226
Armstrong, D.M. 8, 22–3, 59, 61, 69, 100, 108, 196n21, 198n45–9, 199n14, 202n27,n29 210n5, 221
Aune, Bruce 8, 196n20, 221

Bealer, George 160, 186, 214n8, 221
Bedau, Mark 186, 211n21, 221
Begley, Sharon 215n30, 219n54, 227
Behe, Michael J. 211n25, 221
Beilby, James K. 200n20, 221
Beit-Hallahmi, Benjamin 219n41, 221
Bennett, M.R. 159, 214n9, 222
Bhaskar, Roy 4, 195n10, 222
Bishop, John 46–7, 70, 91, 200n19, n30,n31, 203n1, 204n2,n12,n19, 209n85, 222
Block, Ned 192, 219n45, 222
Bringsjord, Selmer 200n19, 222
Brown, Patterson 210n6, 222
Burge, Tyler 201n5, 216n5, 222

Campbell, Keith 5, 8, 108, 196n15, n23, 206n52, 222, 225
Cantori, Enrico 213n73, 222
Casdorph, H. Richard 211n13, 222
Chalmers, David John 192, 210n1, 219n49, 222
Chene, Dennis Des 213n57, 222
Chesterton, G.K. 155, 222
Chisholm, Roderick M. 24, 26, 39–40, 50, 100, 121, 165, 186, 196n30, 198n50,n54, 200n22–4, 201n43, 210n4, 215n21, 222
Churchland, Patricia Smith 161–2, 214n11–13, 215n14–15, 223
Churchland, Paul 5, 61–2, 162–3, 185, 196n14, 199n15, 202n30, 204n19, 214n7, 215n16, 218n20–1, 222
Clark, Stephen R.L. 201n36, 222
Clayton, Philip ix–x, 135–55, 212n1–46, 213n47–9,n51–2, n54–56, n58,n64–6,n69–72, 214n74–83,n85, 222
Clifton, Robert 196n19, 222
Connell, Richard J. 213–14n73, 217n8, 222
Copan, Paul x, 195n6, 211n13, 220n57, 222, 226
Cover, J.A. 209n84, 223
Craig, William Lane 195n6, 196n25, 204n3, 209–10n3, 210n10, 211n13, n30, 223, 225, 226
Crick, Francis 170–1, 173, 215n34, 216n39–40, 223
Cross, Richard 210n7, 223
Cudworth, Ralph 67, 177, 216n3, 223

Dembski, William 211n25, 223
Dennett, Daniel C. 8, 156, 196n22, 214n1, 223
Dickason, C. Fred 213n62, 223

Fales, Evan 30, 199n3, 216n41, 223, 225
Foster, John 183, 186, 200n28, 209n84, 211n21, 218n14–15, 223

Gale, Richard M. 189, 219n36, 223
Gillett, Grant 202n30, 218n14, 223, 227
Goetz, Stewart x, 92, 182, 186, 204n3, 205n23, 209n91, 215n22, 217n9, 223
Goodman, Felicitas 213n62, 223

Habermas, Gary R. 213n61, 223
Hacker, P. M. S. 159, 214n9, 222
Haldane, John 197n36, 223
Halverson, Hans 196n19, 222
Hasker, William x, 144, 172, 186, 206n50, 207n53, 213n59, 216n37, 223
Hoffman, Joshua 192, 219n44, 224
Horgan, John 215n35, 224
Horgan, Terence 59, 209n16, 202n26, 224
Hudson, Hud 211n14, 224
Hurtado, Larry W. 211n13, 224

Jackson, Frank viii, 9–10, 13, 23–5, 83, 89, 91, 142, 191, 193, 196 n26–9, 197n34, 198n 53, 207n56, 208n61, 209n81,87, 213n53, 219n43,n53, 223

Kane, Robert 70, 204n3, 209n84, 224
Kim, Jaegwon viii, 8–9, 13–14, 16–18, 24–5, 31, 48, 56, 68, 91, 149, 163–5, 185, 194, 196n24, 197n35, n37, 198n41,n51,n52, 199n4, 200n34, 202n17–18, 203n41, 204n19, 208n69, 209n86, 211n22, 213n67, 214n2, 215n17,n20, 218n22, 219n42,n55, 220n56–57, 224
Koch, Christof 171, 173, 215n34, 216n39–40, 223
Kraft, Charles 213n62, 224

Leibniz, Gottfried 1, 193, 195n1, 219n52, 224
Lewis, Hywel David 183, 218n13, 224
Locke, John 65–6, 78, 176–7, 202n15, 203n37,n38, 207n54, 211n21, 216n2, 218n22, 224
Lowe, E.J. 202n32, 224
Ludlow, Peter 200n26, 224
Lyons, William 2, 177, 195n5, 215n18, 216n4, 224

Mackie, J.L. 46–47, 65–6, 68, 202n35, 203n36,n43,n44 217n7, 224
Madell, Geoffrey 1, 48, 125, 182–3, 186, 195n2, 201n37, 211n23, 217n8,n9, 218n12,n13, 224
Martin, Michael 199n3, 201n42, 219n41, 221, 223, 224
McGinn, Colin ix–x, 1, 6, 51, 62, 81, 95–113, 140, 180, 192, 195n3, 196n17, 207n56, 209n1, 210n9, 219n47,48, 225
McNutt, Francis 213n62, 225
Menuge, Angus J.L. 199n5, 225
Merricks, Trenton 11, 196n31, 197n38, 225
Moreland, J.P. 182, 195n6, 196n25, n30,n32, 198n42,n44, 200n25, n32, 201n1,n5, 202n15,n35, 203n43–4, 204n3–4, 206n49,n52, 207n52,n54, 209n3, 210n10,n14, n5, 211n13–14,n21–2,n30, 213n57, n61,n68, 214n84,n2, 215n19,n22, n28, 216n41, 217n7–8, 218n9,n14, n22, 219n39–40, 220n57, 223, 225–26
Morse, Melvin 147, 213n60, 226
Moser, Paul K. x, 211n13, 220n57, 222, 226
Mosheim, Johann Lorenz 216n3, 223
Murphy, Nancey 157, 166–9, 214n5–6, 215n25–6,n29, 226

Nagel, Thomas 48–9, 58, 60–2, 64, 68–9, 178, 200n35, 201n38–9, 210n1, 216n7, 217n7, 226
Nielsen, Kai 191, 203n43–4, 211n13, 219n39–40, 226

O'Connor, Timothy ix–x, 27, 33, 51, 70–94, 152, 198n55–6, 199n11, 204n4–11,n13–18,n20–2, 205n22–38, 206n39–47,n51–2, 207n52,n54–5, 208n56–60,n62–8, n70–1,n73–5, 209n77,n79–80,n82–4, n88–90,n92–3, 226–7
O'Hear, Anthony 186, 213n50
O'Leary-Hawthorne, John 209n84, 223
Otis, George, Jr. 213n62, 227

Papineau, David xiii, 3–5, 8, 35, 56, 66, 161–2, 166, 193, 195n7, 196n13,n16, 199n13, 200n29, 202n19, 203n39, 204n19, 214n10, 215n24, 219n50–51, 227
Peacocke, Arthur 200n28, 202n30, 227
Peck, Scott. M. 213n62, 227
Perry, John 96, 209n2, 227
Perry, Paul 213n60, 226
Pivec, Holly 213n63, 227
Plantinga, Alvin 169–70, 186, 200n20, 215n31–2, 216n7, 227
Poland, Jeffrey 8, 210n9, 227

Rea, Michael 195n6, 216n1, 227
Rescher, Nicholas 106, 210n8, 227
Robinson, Howard 186, 200n28, 218n14,n18, 223, 227, 228
Rosenberg, Alex 195n6, 227
Rosenkrantz, Gary S. 192, 219n44, 224
Ross, Hugh 210n15, 227
Rumph, Jane 213n62, 227

Schwartz, Jeffrey x, 169, 186, 193, 215n30, 219n54, 227
Searle, John ix, x, 4, 7–8, 50–1, 53–69, 88, 157, 171, 177, 186–90, 192, 195n11, 196n18, 200n27, 201n1–10, 202n11–14,n20–1,n28,n31,n33–4, 203n42, 209n78, 214n3–4, 215n23, n36, 216n5–6, 218n24–30, 219n31–2,n38,n46, 227–8
Sellars, Wilfrid 4, 8, 108, 195n8, 210n11–12, 228
Shafer-Landau, Russ 214n88, 228
Shockey, Peter 213n61, 228
Sider, Theodore 197n38, 228
Skinner, B.F. 69, 203n45, 228
Skrbina, David ix–x, 51, 115–19, 122–3, 125–6, 128–9, 133, 210n2–4,n6–10, 211n12,n15–16, n18–20,n26,n28, 212n31, 228
Smith, A.D. 218n18, 228
Smith, Barry 196n30, 215n21, 222, 228
Smith, Quentin 33, 188–9, 199n10, 209n3, 219n33–5,n37, 223, 228
Sperry, Roger 17, 170, 198n39–40, 228
Strawson, Galen 77, 206n48, 228
Stroud, Barry 175, 216n1, 228
Swinburne, Richard x, 32, 60, 69, 182, 186, 199n7–8, 199n17–18, 200n21, 201n40, 202n16, 218n10,n31, 219n31, 228

Taliaferro, Charles 184, 186, 218n17, n19, 228
Tennant, F.R. 168, 215n27, 228
Tidman, Paul 218n16, 228
Tyndall, John 172, 216n38, 228

van Cleve, James 218n17, 238
van Fraasen, Bas C. 169–70, 215n33, 228
van Inwagen, Peter x, 11, 196n31, 202n22–5, 229
van Till, Howard J. 154, 214n86, 229
Vitz, Paul C. 219n41, 229

Wagner, Steven 4, 195n6,n9, 199n16, 202n26, 224, 229
Warner, Richard 4, 195n6,n9, 199n16, 202n26, 224, 229
Watson, Peter 229
Williams, Clifford 202–3n35, 206n49, 225, 229
Williams, Peter S. 213n62, 229
Wilson, Colin 213n62, 229
Wright, Crispen 1, 195n4, 229
Wright, N.T. 211n13, 229

Yandell, Keith 184, 211n21, 218n19, 229
Yolton, John W. 67, 203n40, 206n49, 210n11, 216n3, 229

Subject index

abstract object 5, 8, 99, 108, 122; *see also* ontology
academe 33, 52, 157, 188, 193
action: basic and non-basic 49–50, 75, 107, 201n40–41; causal theory of 46–47, 203n1; desiderata for an adequate theory 205n23; *see also* agency; libertarian
agency; common sense concept of 46; libertarian 46, 47, 49, 183, 185, 203n1; agent-causal 75, 82, 102, 134; agent causation account of 7, 21, 70–71, 74, 75, 94, 102, 124, 153, 167, 173, 185, 200n19, 209n88, non-agent-causation 204n3; notion of freedom vs. free agents 205n22 *see also* action; causation; dualism; libertarian; naturalism
anomalous monism 45, 133
Argument from Consciousness (AC) 45, 49, 50–51, 55, 58, 59, 60, 66, 80, 81, 102, 106, 109, 118, 133, 154, 155, 176, 186, 190, 191, 192; agent causation 47, 200n19; explained ix–x, 32–51; inference to the best explanation 32; C-inductive vs. P-inductive arguments 32–33 175; deductive argument 37–51; supervenience of moral properties 203n44; theism/dualism x, 3, 30, 31, 34, 51–52, 59, 62, 64–65, 78, 96, 97, 99–107, 110, 113, 115, 119, 135, 142, 145, 154, 156; *see also* consciousness; dualism; fear of God; God; naturalism; panpsychism
Aristotelian 8, 29, 149–50, 154, 158, 169, 197n33, 206–7n52
Armstrong, D.M. existence 8, paradigm-case naturalist 22–23; falsification of naturalism 59 emergence of consciousness 61, 69, vicious infinite regress 100, general ontology 108; *see also* naturalism
Atheism 35, 45, 104, 178–79, 188, 191, 217n7; *see also* dualism; naturalism; God; secularization
atomic theory of matter 3, 6–7, 14, 26, 54, 188; *see also* evolution; naturalism; science
Authority Thesis *see* philosophy
Autonomy Thesis *see* philosophy

Big Bang cosmology 1, 6, 14, 35, 98, 110, 132, 138, 155; *see also* science
Biola University x, 148
biological naturalism 54–58, 60, 62, 65–66, 114; *see also* naturalism; physicalism; Searle, John; science
brain: body and 144, 157; evolution and 97, 98, 137, 140; faculties of the soul attributed to 167; internal relations and 23; introspective acquaintance with 89; Knowledge Argument and 42; mental/consciousness (correlations, emergent on, process, properties, states) 18, 45, 54–55, 57, 58, 60, 62, 86, 96, 98, 102, 103, 105, 107, 143, 146, 168, 171, 172, 182, 197n38, 220n57; mind/brain supervenience 18, 64; near death experiences 147; neurobiological features of 57; quale and 173; split brain phenomena 167; *see also* mental entities/properties/states; mind/body problem; introspection; Knowledge Argument; consciousness; supervenience

burden of proof ix, 3, 5, 21, 25, 28, 46, 55, 69, 71–73, 81, 87, 90, 104, 120, 128, 136, 156, 166, 192, 209n88, 219n44
brute facts 12, 14, 21, 34, 47, 59, 110, 140, 154, 220n57; *see also* ontologically basic

Campbell, Keith: abstract objects 5; emergent entities 8 general ontology 108; *see also* emergent; naturalism; ontology
Cartesianism 8, 16, 38, 40, 54–55, 59, 63, 83, 86, 91, 108, 117, 124–25, 130, 144, 157, 161–62, 178, 185, 187, 191; *see also* dualism; mind/body problem; naturalism
causal closure 13–17, 21, 76, 88, 97, 135, 140, 143; *see also* naturalism; physicalism
Causal Unity of Nature Thesis 72–74, 76; *see also* naturalism; O'Connor, Timothy; physicalism
causal correlation 47, 59, 107; *see also*, causation; supervenience
causal necessitation 25–27, 58, 60–61, 87, 105; *see also* determinism
causation: agent 7, 21, 70–71, 74, 94, 102, 124, 153, 167, 173, 185, 200n19, 209n88; bottom/up or top/down or outside/in 2, 7, 12, 13, 14, 15, 16–17, 18, 19, 21, 78, 79, 80, 81, 96, 135, 136, 143, 149, 150; causal pairing problem 207 n54; event 75, 93; impotent 19; realist view of 25–27; *see also* determinism; necessity/necessitation
Chinese Room thought experiment 42–44, 85; *see also* conceivability; Searle, John; thought experiments
Chisholm, Roderick M.: a leading dualist 186; epistemological particularist 24, 121; epistemic appraisal 26–27, 50; self-presenting properties 39–40; vicious infinite regress 100, first-person introspective knowledge 165; *see also* dualism; ontology; self-presenting properties; third-person perspective
Churchland, Paul: advocates strong physicalism viii; replaces the first-person ontology 5; reasons for strong physicalism 61–62; semantic and epistemic issues 162–63; substance dualism 185; *see also* first-person perspective; naturalism; physicalism; substance dualism
Clayton, Philip: AC and theism 154–55; dualism misrepresented 143–45; emergence, employment of 145–49; methodology 139–43; individual, category of 149–54; minimalist vs. strong naturalism 139; ontology 143; pluralistic emergentist monism: features 135–39; *see also* Argument from Consciousness; dualism; emergence; ontology; theistic dualism
compatibilism 92, 204n12; *see also* agency; libertarian
conceivability 36, 60, 68, 97, 110, 127, 183, 205n4, 218n16–18; conceivable not identical to imageable (pictureable) 57, 62, 68, 183; strong vs. weak 26, 85, 110, 180, 182, 184; *see also* thought experiments
conceptual supervenience 18; *see also* supervenience
consciousness: brain and 60, 64, 98, 103, 107; consciousness as emergent 80, 87–90, 131; divine 99; epiphenomenal 96–97; problems for naturalism, evidence for theism viii–ix, 1, 2, 29, 34, 35, 45, 47, 51, 109, 119, 120; emergence of 1, 34, 35, 36, 57, 61–62, 65–68, 73, 87–90, 95, 98, 145, 155, 192, 220n57; explanatory gap 9, 11, 19; finite viii, 29, 32, 34, 96, 99, 110, 121, 131–32; hard problem of 11, 141, 145; imageability of 57, 61–62; mystery of 97, 99; naturalistic approaches to 30, 34, 35, 53–69, 70–94, 95–113; nature of 157, 159, 171, 176; neurotic to deny 54, 62, 65, 177–78; origin of ix, 1, 30, 34, 35, 36, 37, 57, 66, 79, 95, 101, 103, 105, 107, 127, 128, 131, 139, 142, 176; phenomenal viii, 15, 43, 128, 133, 200n27; problem of 6, 11, 109, 110, 141; secondary qualities in 67–68; self-159, 163; space and 98; unity of 129, 167; *see also* Argument from Consciousness; brain; conceivability; dualism; emergentism; naturalism; physicalism

Consciousness and the Existence of God: overview of viii–x, 11, 51–52, 114, 156, 157 175–76, 192–94; *see also* Argument from Consciousness; consciousness; dualism; God; naturalism; physicalism
constituent/whole relation 20, 110, 181; *see also* ontology
Constitution Thesis 72–74, 76, 90–92; *see also* naturalism; O'Connor, Timothy; physicalism
contingent correlations 51, 53, 140, 143, 156; *see also* Searle, John
cosmic authority problem: *see also* fear of God; Nagel, Thomas
counterfactuals 26, 53, 197n38; *see also*, ontology

determinism: dependence and 16, 18–19, 86; diachronic or synchronic 7–9, 16; Grand Story and 14; novel emergent property and 15; vertical 16; *see also* necessity/necessitation
dualism: argumentation and theism 179–86; emergent property viii, ix, 133
disembodiment 167; dismissive rhetorical moves by naturalists 186–89; proponents, list of 186; weak 45; *see also* agency; Argument from Consciousness, consciousness; emergent property dualism; property dualism; substance dualism

ego 80, 159, 167, *see also* self
eleatic principle of existence 8 *see also* ontology
eliminativism 11–12, 13, 20, 30, 151, 151; *see also* physicalism
emergence: emergence$_{0-1}$ 21; emergence$_{2a}$ 21, 28, 56; emergence$_{2b}$ 22; emergence$_{2c}$ 21, 22, 77, 81; emergence$_{3}$ 21, 28, 81; strong vs. weak 136; *see also* consciousness; Clayton, Philip; emergentism; O'Connor, Timothy; Searle, John
emergentism 33, 82, 136, 137, 138, 140, 145, 148, 149, 150, 155, 165, 193; *see also* consciousness
emergent necessitation 83–87, 156; *see also* O'Connor, Timothy
emergent property ix; 3, 6, 11, 15, 17, 19, 25, 27, 34, 47, 57, 62, 67, 68, 71, 72, 73, 74, 75, 76, 78, 80, 83, 84, 85, 86, 87, 88, 89, 91, 92, 130, 131, 136, 137, 139, 140, 141, 142, 143, 145, 146, 148, 150, 152, 153, 154, 155, 205n23; epistemically characterized 33; naturalistically inexplicable or dismissive of 6, 7, 14; ontological status of 74; *see also* Clayton, Philip, consciousness; O'Connor, Timothy; *sui generis*
emergent supervenience 15, 86, 105, 108, 137, 150; *see also* supervenience
empirical 24, 34, 173 causal questions 173; emergence and 148, 159–60; empirically established 73–74; 87, 91, 92, 161; equivalent philosophical models 20, 87–88, 165–66, 168, 170; evidence 92, 148, 164, 185, 208n76; knowledge 79; naturalism and 133; point of view 34; philosophical arguments and 73; philosophy of mind 2; research 89, 106; theories 4; *see also* Causal Unity of Nature Thesis; Constitution Thesis; naturalism; philosophy of mind; quantum; scientism
epiphenomenal(ism) 15, 18, 19, 21, 96, 97, 104, 105, 136, 149, 165, 193, 200n57; *see also* consciousness, naturalism; physicalism
epiphenomenal property dualism 56; *see also* dualism; Kim
epistemic appraisal 26–27, 50–51; *see also* Chisholm, Roderick; naturalness and theory
epistemic values 30–31; *see also* naturalness and theory; theory acceptance/adjudication
epistemic virtues 106, 165; *see also* naturalness and theory; theory/ acceptance/adjudication
epistemological particularism 24, 121; *see also* epistemological methodism; epistemology; Chisholm, Roderick; first-person perspective
epistemological methodism 5–6, 23; *see also* epistemological particularism; epistemology; Chisholm, Roderick; third-person perspective
epistemology: Descartes 40; externalist 22–23; foundationalism 102; naturalist/naturalized 3, 5–6, 8, 10, 12, 13, 21, 22, 24, 25, 59, 64, 95,

109, 161, 162, 164, 166, 176, 199n3; *see also* Cartesianism; externalist epistemology; foundationalism; naturalism
event-causation 75, 93; *see* causation
evolution: a "seamless garment" 2, 177; Clayton's emergentism 137, 140, 154; consciousness or mental states and 1, 38, 135, 137, 141, 154, 177; cultural 143; epistemic limitations from 95; neo-Darwinism 7, 30; *see also* causal closure; consciousness; God; emergentism; naturalism
explanation: causal 7, 22, 25, 26, 46 53, 54, 62; combinatorial modes of 6, 7, 10, 14, 25, 35, 96; covering law form of 26, 49, 59; natural scientific 22, 37, 47, 48, 60, 62; personal 37, 38, 46, 47, 48, 49, 50, 105, 197; realist 195n12; worldview superior ix, 3, 5, 7, 9, 10, 14, 21, 24, 26, 31, 51, 53, 65, 83, 90, 110, 118, 119, 128, 132, 133, 139, 140, 141, 145, 154, 156, 160, 167, 176, 199n3; *see also* necessity
externalist epistemology 22, 49; *see also* epistemology; foundationalism; internalist epistemology; naturalism; scientific

Faith and Philosophy x, 201, 202, 211, 218, 225, 228, 229; *see also* philosophy; philosophy of religion
fallacies: *ad hoc* 29–30, 32, 34, 59, 61, 65–66; 109, 113, 133, 141, 148, 176, 198n1, 199n3; genetic; question-begging 29–30, 31, 34, 37, 46, 58, 59, 65, 66, 106, 109, 126, 130, 142, 144, 169, 176, 198n1; *post hoc ergo propter hoc* 148–55; *see also* philosophy
fear of God ("cosmic authority problem") ix, 176–79, 188, 190–92; *see also* Argument from Consciousness; God; Nagel, Thomas
first-person perspective 4–5, 9, 31, 38, 40, 42, 44–45, 79, 81–82, 89, 92–95, 121–22, 124, 135, 149, 156, 158–59, 163–68, 171–72, 174, 182–83, 202n20, 203n37, 215n18,n28; *see also* third-person perspective
first-philosophy 3, 5, 159, 160–62, 165; *see also* philosophy; foundationalism
folk philosophy/psychology 91, 162–63, 191; *see also* dualism
functionalism 21, 44, 45, 86, 133, 124, 172; *see also* naturalism; physicalism
foundationalism 40, 160–62; *see also* epistemological particularism; first-person perspective; first-philosophy; internalist epistemology
fulfillment structure 44; *see also* Chisholm, Roderick; first-person perspective; self-presenting properties

generalization problem 17, 18; *see also* naturalism; physicalism
God: as spirit 59, 86, 116; created by 102–3, 104, 105, 109, 119; consciousness in 29, 96, 99; evil 104; existence of viii, ix, 32, 35, 52, 54, 85, 104, 119, 152, 156, 175, 176, 177, 188, 189, 190; finite 116; human persons analogous to 152–53, 186, 213n50; hypothesis 96, 105; intentions (wantings) or model of 46, 50, 101–4, 105; libertarian power 85–86; metaphysically impossible 86–87; necessary being 101–2, 103, 132, 138; not "dead" 33, 188; omnipotence of 66; omnipresence 122–23; persons and 33; purely spiritual substance 78; Spirit of 58; "superadd" thinking 65–66, 203n37; transcendent 119, 138; unembodied mind in 32, 116; *see also* Argument from Consciousness; consciousness; dualism; fear of God; naturalism; theism

haecceities 12–13; *see also* metaphysics, ontology
higher order 18–19, 181; *see also* mereological hierarchy; supervenience

indexical 9, 22, 149, 160, 167, 182–83; 218n11; *see also* first-person perspective; self; self-presenting properties
inseparable/separable parts 11–12, 22, 144, 151, 181; (monadic) property-instance 5, 11, 19–20, 64, 80, 129; *see also* ontology

intentional actions: three kinds 201n41; *see also* agency, intentionality
intentionality ix, 38, 40, 44, 54, 64, 124, 164; *see also* first-person perspective; self-presenting properties
intra-level higher order functional properties vs. inter-level micro-based properties 19; *see also* mereological hierarchy; supervenience
internalist epistemology 40, 42, 190; *see also* epistemology; externalist epistemology; foundationalism
introspection 5, 62–64, 81, 82, 88–89, 94, 95, 157, 158, 161, 163, 164, 165, 166, 168, 171–72, 174, 180, 215n28; *see also* first-person perspective; self-presenting properties; self
intuitions 10, 60, 77, 119; dualist/pre-philosophical 37, 73–74, 82, 87, 90–94, 172, 187, 205n22, 209n88; modal 37; panpsychism 117, 125; *see also* dualism; first-person perspective; self-presenting properties
irreducibility viii–ix, 1, 7, 16, 18, 22, 31–32, 35–36, 41, 45–46, 50, 57–58, 74, 75, 90, 114, 124, 126, 133, 134, 136, 138, 149–50, 163, 168, 178, 182–83, 192, 204n3, 205n23, 207n56, 211n25, 218n11; *see also* consciousness

Jackson, Frank: advocates strong physicalism viii, 10, 193, 198n53; eliminative or reductive approach 142; "location problem" 9–11; constraints for naturalist ontology 10–11; folk conception of personal identity 91, 191; haecceities 13; Kim and 24–25; necessitation by subvenient base 89; serious metaphysics vs. shopping-list approach 23–24, 83, 207n56; O'Connor and 83; *see also* metaphysics; naturalism; physicalism; reductionism

Kalam cosmological argument for the existence of God 99, 111; *see also* God; philosophy of religion
Kim, Jaegwon: causal closure 13–14, 17, 56; causal powers 8; emergent approach 48; emergent epiphenomenal dualist 220n57; emergent mental properties 149; epistemological/ontological simplicity 24–25, 31, 165; "dualism of personhood" 91; Grand Story 14; mental vs. agent causation 185; mereological hierarchy 149; Nagel-type reductions 68; naturalist, a strong physicalist 56, 194; supervenient, a label 9; generalization problem 17–18; substance dualism 185, 218n22; supervenience argument ("exclusion argument") 16–19; top/down mental causation 16–17; 149; type identity physicalism 163–66; *see also*, dualism; emergentism; naturalism; physicalism; reductionism; supervenience
Knowledge Argument ix, 39, 40, 41, 42, 43, 44, 85, 87, 95, 166, 173, 215n22; *see also* consciousness; dualism; first-person perspective
know-how 42; *see also* epistemology; knowledge by acquaintance; propositional knowledge
knowledge by acquaintance 5, 40–44, 88; *see also* epistemology; first-person perspective; propositional knowledge; know-how
knowledge of other minds 163; *see also* dualism; Knowledge Argument
Kuhnian paradigm crisis 2, 192; *see also* philosophy of mind

law 6, 13; law-like ix, 48, 51, 58, 102, 124, 126, 134, 140; natural 10, 111; psycho-physical 45, 129, 132, 200n28; strong physicalism ix, 8, 13; *see also* physicalism; physical
libertarian: acts 132, 173; agents 76, 132, 205n22; freedom 38, 49, 70, 94, 183 204n3, 205n23; free acts 39; indeterminism 204n3; intuitions 91; personal explanation 46, 47; power 85; *see also* action; agency; dualism; naturalism
location problem 9–10, 83; *see also* physicalism; naturalism; Jackson, Frank
Locke, John: thinking matter 65–66, 78, 203n37; pneumatophobia 176–77; *see also* fear of God

lower order 18–19; *see also* higher order

Madell, Geoffrey 1, 48, 125, 182–83, 186, 195n2, 201n37, 211n23, 217n8,n9, 218n12,n13, 224; *see also* consciousness; dualism
matter: consciousness arise from or linked to 37, 57, 61, 69, 95, 97–98 105, 109, 110, 123, 131; creatures of 62; Leibniz and 1, reality and 7, mental potentialities in 36, 98, 123; ontology and 108; naturalistically described 120; panpsychism 82, 133; thinking 65–67, 68, 78, 203n37, 206n49; universe and 2, 34, 36, 98, 110, 112, 114, 155, 177; *see also* atomic theory of matter; evolution; naturalism; physical
Matter and Consciousness 163; *see also* Churchland, Paul
materialism 1, 2, 4, 12, 20, 54, 59, 67, 115, 117, 127, 133, 136, 157 172, 177, 178, 195n5; mechanistic 1, 4, 13, 133; *see also* naturalism
McGinn, Colin AC/theistic dualism and 99–107; cognitive closure 97; critique of 98–108; dismissal of theism 180; hyperdualism 107–8; mysterianism, description and problems of 1, 6, 51, 95, 109–13, 140–41, 192, 195n3, 209n1; naturalism/anti-naturalism 96–97; panpsychism 81, 207n56; property/event dualism 95; Searle and causal necessitation 62–65; *see also* Argument from Consciousness; dualism; God; theism; naturalism; panpsychism; physicalism; Searle, John
mental entities/properties/states: causation 16–18, 185; holism of 44, 200n28; proto-48; *sui generis* viii, 2, 3, 11, 12, 13, 14, 15, 19, 23, 33, 59, 64, 82, 83, 89, 102, 110, 130, 131, 135, 139, 140, 141, 142, 175; *see also* brain; evolution
mereological hierarchy 10–24; Clayton and 136, 143, 145, 149–51; 154; Kim and O'Connor and 76, 79, 83; *see also* naturalism; Clayton, Philip; Kim, Jaegwon; O'Connor, Timothy
metaphysics: anthropocentric subject-matters 2; central dilemma in 2; descriptive vs. explanatory 207–8n56; essentialism 103; indexcal "I" 167; possibility/modality 105, 108; principle of simplicity 23, 24–25, 79, 165, 166; science and 169–71; serious; 23–25, 35, 83–84, 114; *see also* Chisholm, Roderick; Jackson, Frank; ontology
micro-macro: constitution 14; relation 18–19; *see also* mereological hierarchy; supervenience
micro-physical 11–14, 18–21, 23, 25, 27, 73, 82, 90, 208n60; *see also* physical
mind/body problem ix, 54–55, 62, 97, 149, 178; *see also* dualism; physicalism
mind/brain supervenience 18; *see also* supervenience
minimal physical duplicate 9–10, 83, 208n76; *see also* Jackson, Frank; psychological duplicate
modal 19–20, 37, 73, 87; argument for substance dualism 85, 91, 132, 184; epistemic vs. metaphysical 45; intuitions 37; skepticism 37; necessity 123; status of Harmony Thesis 205n22, *see also* metaphysics; ontology, substance dualism
moral: point of view 216n7; properties 9, 68–69, 203n43,44; *see also* mental entities/properties/states; Nagel, Thomas
Murphy, Nancey: physicalism, a hard-core research program 157; 169; science makes dualism implausible 166–68; *see also* dualism; naturalism; physicalism; science

Nagel, Thomas: emergence of the mental 69; "fear of God" (cosmic authority problem) ix, 178–79; Nagel-type reductions 68; panpsychism 48; Searle and 58, 60–62, 64; "solution" 216n7; universal, normative objective reason 216–17n7
naturalism: attempts to deflate, deny, eliminate or reduce ontological matters 5, 15, 28, 31, 35–37, 45, 65, 109, 187, 192, 193, 194, 203n43; central features 3–10; defense of dualism and theism 179–86; dualist

literature dismissed 186–90; epistemic attitude 4–6; epistemology 3, 5–6, 8, 10, 12, 13, 21, 22, 24, 25, 59, 64, 95, 109, 161, 162, 164, 166, 176, 199n3; etiological account ix, 3, 64; global vs. local 8; Grand Story 6–8, 9, 12–14, 16, 18, 19, 21–23, 24–25, 29, 30, 33, 34, 35, 59, 96, 128, 139, 141, 142, 142, 151, 154, 199n3, 209n76; hegemony of x, 2, 10, 133; inner logic of ix, 23, 156; ontology ix, 3, 6, 7, 8–10, 11, 13, 14, 19–22, 25–27, 30, 34, 50, 51, 59, 60, 69, 70, 71, 86, 108, 109, 110, 138, 143, 199n3; philosophical monism 7, 192; positive ix, 31, 49, 79, 133, 154, 176; strong ix, 8–9, 10, 22, 115, 117, 118, 120–21, 128, 131, 133, 138–39, 155, 157, 178, 179, 192; weak ix; *see also* Causal Unity of Nature Thesis; Constitution Thesis; dualism; epistemology; evolution; mental entities/properties/states; physicalism; O'Connor, Timothy; reductionism

naturalized epistemology *see* epistemology; naturalism; physicalism

naturalness and theory 29–30, 59, 64, 204n12; *see also* epistemic appraisal, epistemic values

necessity/necessitation 11; causal 58–65; *see also* causation; determinism

network theory of meaning 162–63; *see also* Churchland, Paul

neuroscience 157, 159, 167, 170, 171, 172, 173, 193; *see also* science

nominalism 108, 206n52 *see also* naturalism; physicalism

O'Connor, Timothy: ix–x, agent causation (AGC) and 71, 72–73, 74–75, 77–81, 84, 90, 91, 92, 93, 94, 204n22, 209n88; approaches to properties 152, 206–7n52; Christian theist 71; causal pairing problem 207; consciousness as emergent 34, 87–90; contingent correlations 51; emerging naturalist picture of the world (N) 71, 72–73, 74, 76–77, 82, 83–84, 86, 88, 89, 90, 91, 92, 205n22, 207n56, 208n68; emergent necessitation/contingency 27, 83–87; Harmony Thesis, logical and epistemic status explained 71–74, 83, 84, 85, 86, 89, 90, 91, 92, 94, 204n22, 208n68; panpsychism 81–83; pre-philosophical intuitions, role and nature 90–94, 209n88; *see also* agent-causation; dualism; emergent necessitation; naturalism; physicalism

ontologically basic 28–29, 76, 88; *see also* ontology

ontological simplicity 24, 25, 31, 140, 220n57; *see also* epistemic values

ontology: categories 12, 59–60; causal criterion of existence 15; constituent 12, 19, 122, 207n52; essence 12–13, 31, 63, 73, 74, 78, 80, 98, 151–52, 158, 160, 182, 203n37; existence 4, 5, 7, 8, 11, 15, 22, 23, 32, 36, 37, 38, 60, 61, 101, 139, 184, analysis vs. nature of 8; individual 11, 13, 14, 20, 60, 76, 78, 80, 84, 130, 143, 149, 151, 152, 154, 195n5; individuation 13; particulars ix, 8, 10, 21, 22, 25, 26, 35, 45, 70, 76, 83, 85, 87, 108, 119, 125, 127, 131, 142, 150, 208n76; serious 23–24, 35, 83, 84; shopping-list 12, 13, 24, 137, 139, 140, 151; subject 21, 22, 40, 41, 42, 63–64, 77, 182; *see also* Chisholm, Roderick; metaphysics; Jackson, Frank

ontological pluralism 12, 143; *see also* naturalism; physicalism; evolution

Overdetermination 16–19, 197n38; *see also* determinism; necessity/necessitation

Panpsychism: as a version of naturalism 133–34; strong vs. weak 115; theological influence 115, 116, 123, 126; *see also* McGinn, Colin; naturalism; O'Connor, Timothy; Skrbina, David

Panpsychism in the West 115, 116; *see also* panpsychism; Skrbina, David

Papineau, David: advocates strong physicalism xiii, 35–36, 56, 193; Autonomy Thesis 166; conduct philosophy within empirical theories 3–4, 5; epistemic methodism 5–6; matter/physical 66; rejects first philosophy 5, 161–62; weak vs. strong naturalism 8, 35, 56, 66, 161–62, 166, 193, 195n7, 196n13,

n16, 199n13, 200n29, 202n19, 203n39, 204n19, 214n10, 215n24, 219n50–51, 227; *see also* empirical; epistemology, philosophy, physicalism
persons 40–41, 42, 43, 50, 70, 74, 78, 80, 152–53, 158, 168, 169, 183, 184, 191, 206n50; *see also* dualism; self; soul
Persons & Causes 71, 78, 89; *see also* O'Connor, Timothy
phenomenological 41, 42, 92, 136, 146, 215n28
pluralistic emergentist monism ix, 49, 51, 135–37, 154, 156, 199n9; *see also* Clayton, Philip
Philosophia Christi x, 211, 216, 218, 220, 225, 235, 226, 226; *see also* philosophy; philosophy of religion
Philosophical Foundations of Neuroscience 159; *see also* philosophy; neuroscience; science
philosophical naturalism *see* naturalism
philosophy: analytic viii; Anglo-American philosophy 33, 188; Authority Thesis 159–60; Autonomy Thesis 159–60, 162–66; first vs. second order issues 158–59; science and 166–74; *see also* philosophy of mind; philosophy of religion
philosophy of mind viii, 31, 35, 53–54, 62, 85, 115, 145, 157–63, 166, 169–70, 172–73, 176–79, 185–86, 192, 196n19, 208n72; central issues/ questions 2, 158–59; *see also* Argument from Consciousness; Churchlands Paul and Patricia; consciousness; Kim, Jaegwon; naturalism, Papineau, David; physicalism
Philosophy of Mind (Kim); *see also* philosophy of mind
philosophy of religion viii, 99, 162, 180, 189; *see also* philosophy; philosophy of mind
physical entities: 14, 32, 34, 35, 38, 45, 59, 64, 76, 83, 85, 108, 132, 200n28; events 14, 16, 17–18, 37, 38, 45, 47, 123, 158, 197n38, 200n19; properties 13, 35, 48, 55, 84, 86, 88, 89, 90, 94, 107, 141, 144, 158, 197n38, 208n60; states ix–x, 7, 30, 38–39, 45, 47, 51, 53, 58, 66, 68, 69, 172; *see also* micro-physical; science
physicalism: emergent 45, 123; minimal 86; non-reductive 45, 168, 169; scientific research program 169–74; strong or strict form viii, ix, 7, 31, 35, 45, 51, 54, 62, 65, 69, 90, 95, 114, 115, 124, 135, 146, 156–74, 175, 176, 177, 178, 179, 192, 193; token 45; type 149, 163; weak form 35; *see also* Kim, Jaegwon; naturalism
Plantinga, Alvin 169–70, 186, 216n7; *see also* philosophy of religion
pluralistic emergentist monism ix, 49, 51, 135–45ff, 156, 199n9; *see also* Clayton, Philip
primary or secondary qualities 3, 9, 23, 43, 67–68, 130, 142, 164
principle of sufficient reason 132; *see also* epistemology; ontology
principle of naturalist exemplification 19–20; *see also* naturalism
principle of simplicity *see* ontology
problem of epiphenomenalism 15; *see also* consciousness; physicalism; Searle, John
properly functioning faculties 190–91; *see also* epistemology
property entailment and inclusion 39–40; *see also* Chisholm, Roderick
property dualism ix, 38, 44, 55, 71, 103, 133, 141, 156, 172, 185, 192; *see also* dualism; substance dualism
property identity 164, 215n19
property-instances 5, 11, 19–20, 80; *see also* ontology
propositional knowledge 40, 42, 43; *see also* knowledge by acquaintance
psychological duplicate 10, 83; *see also* minimal physical duplicate

qualia 67, 85, 87–88, 105, 132, 146, 171, 203n43, 208n72; *see also* mental entites/properties/states
quantum 20, 126, 129–30; *see also* science

Rediscovery of the Mind 189, 201n5, 202n20; *see also* Searle, John
reductionism: linguistic 6; Nagel-type 67, 49; naturalistic 2, 23, 24, 31, 35, 90, 179, 200n28; psychological 48; *see also* naturalism; physicalism

religion viii, 99, 162, 178, 180, 185, 189–9; neurotic physicalism and 177–78; *see also* Searle, John; theism

Searle, John: AC 55, 58, 59 60, 62, 64, 65, 66, belief in the supernatural 190; biological naturalism 55, 56–58; Cartesian dualism 59; causal explanations 7; contingent correlations 51, 53, 59; emergent (different senses) 88; empirically equivalent views 164–65; epiphenomenal property dualism 56; dismissive rhetorical devices 186–90; future correlation/ideal physics 61, 69; imageability of consciousness 61, 62, 78; intellectuals secularized 190; introspection 63–64; Mackie and 65–66, 68–69; McGinn and 62–65; Nagel and 58–62; philosophy of mind 53–54, 157, 177–78; property dualism 55; self 64; Quentin Smith on 189; unity of science is the unity of all knowledge 4–5; weak naturalist 8, 54 *see also* Argument from Consciousness; consciousness; contingent correlation; dualism; emergence; philosophy of mind; science; supernatural

secularization 179, 189–90; *see also* Atheism; religion; theism

self 8, 48, 64, 77–78, 81, 91, 92–93, 94, 128, 129, 149, 152, 153, 157, 163, 165, 167, 168, 171, 172, 180, 181, 182, 203n37, 217n8, *see also* first-person perspective; soul

self-presenting properties 39–41, 43, 63–64, 102, 163; *see also* Chisholm, Roderick; first-person perspective; intentionality

science: causal explanations as a kind of causal necessity 25–26; "completeability of physics" 13–14; evidence of x, 139, 146, 148–49, 166, 169; hard 5; natural 4–5, 25, 153; philosophy and 5, 166–74; physical 2, 169; soft; unity of 4, 135; *see also* physical

scientific: explanation 37, 47–48, 58, 64, 138, 143; knowledge 4–5, 87, 161, 167; materialism 2, 172, 177, 195n5; *see also* explanation

scientism 3–5, 23, 127, 179; *see also* naturalism; physicalism

Skrbina, David: AC/theism and panpsychism 51, 115–21, 125–26; arguments for panpsychism 116–17; arguments not supportive of panpsychism 121–25; defeaters for defeaters of arguments against panpsychism 126–33; Pierce, C. S. 123; Seager, William 129; Strong, Charles 128; *see also* Argument from Consciousness; panpsychism

spatio-temporal 3, 8, 22, 38, 48, 59, 108, 111; *see also* physical

soul 54, 96, 102, 116, 119, 123, 129, 133–34, 137, 143, 147, 156, 157–58, 167, 176, 178, 182, 195n5, 203n37, 219n44; faculty of 167–68; *see also* person, self

strong physicalism: *see* physicalism

substance dualism 33, 55, 70, 74, 84, 85, 86, 87, 88, 91, 92, 93–94, 122, 135, 141, 144, 149, 166–68, 170, 172, 175, 179, 180–86, 188, 190, 193, 203n37, 204n3, 204n22, 205n22, 208n68, 209n88, 218n31; thomistic 144, 149, 154, 185, 207n54, 218n22; *see also* Argument from Consciousness; dualism

supernatural 2, 120–21, 148, 189–90; *see also* religion; theism

supervenience: causal 64 conceptual 18; dependency 45, 123, 137; explanation or solution of vs. label for a problem 9, 59, 150, 193; global 83; levels 13; moral properties 68, 203n44; properties 135; relation 18, 38, 59, 60, 84, 182; strong 84; structural 14, 15, 17, 18, 83; *see also* emergent supervenience; Kim, Jaegwon

Swinburne, Richard x, 32, 60, 69, 182, 186, 199n7–8, 199n17–18, 200n21, 201n40, 202n16, 218n10,n31, 219n31, 228; *see also* Argument from Consciousness; philosophy of religion; theism

theism 28, 29, 33, 51, 59, 66, 84, 110, 153, 179; arguments/evidence/justification for viii–x, 1, 2, 33, 38, 59, 64–65, 68–69, 104, 112, 113, 118–21, 125–26, 131, 138, 143, 188, 191, 203n44; Christian 33, 177, 186, 211n13, 213n50; atheism and 191; critique/dismissal of 179–80,

189; dualism and argumentation 179–86; emergent 123, 134, 137–38; explanatory power/presence/ resources of 2, 28, 29, 30, 31, 32, 34, 68, 79, 85, 109, 128, 131–33, 135, 156, 192, 199n3; finite 134; ordinary response of the persons to creation 191; panpsychism and 48, 49, 115, 118–21, 124, 125–26; 128, 131–32; persons and 33; *see also* Atheism, God; religion
theistic dualism ix–x; 96, 98–99, 102–5, 107, 110, 124, 138–39, 141–42, 145, 152, 154; *see also* Argument from Consciousness; dualism
The Mysterious Flame 179; *see also* McGinn, Colin; panpsychism
theory acceptance/adjudication basicality 28–29; epistemic values 30–31; naturalness 29–30; *see also* epistemic appraisal
third-person perspective 4–5, 10, 25, 31, 34–35, 49, 89, 94, 122, 134, 140, 158, 162–65, 182, 202n20, 215n18; *see also* first-person perspective; naturalness and theory
thought experiments 85–87, 91, 146–47, 159, 163, 166, 173, 183, 208n72; *see also* conceivability

unified subject ("I") 21, 38–39, 127, 128, 129, 171, 180–83, 191; *see also* property dualism; substance dualism
universals 8, 75, 78–80, 84, 108, 116, 122, 147, 160, 191, 206–7n52, 216n7; *see also* mental entities/ properties/states; nominalism; qualia

world: actual 10, 26, 35, 84, 87, 105, 132, 148, 173, 205n22, 208n76; possible 26, 46, 73, 84, 87, 105, 110, 132, 146, 160, 180–81, 197n38, 205n22; *see also* conceivability,
worldview viii–ix, 2–3, 14, 21, 26–28, 34–35, 51, 54, 60, 90, 110, 115, 118–19, 133, 138, 140, 154, 156, 176, 186, 188, 190, 193, 199n3, 213n50; *see also* atheism; naturalism; theism

0 – Upanishads Vedanta

1) Descartes – Doubt – the dreams [illegible]

2) Kant – [illegible]

(Hegel, Schelling)

3) James – [illegible]

Phenomenology – SEP

4) Husserl, Ricoeur, Derrida, Merleau-Ponty

Locke
Berkeley
Hume

Transcend [illegible]

Faith – Brahman

HP – [illegible]

[illegible] – [illegible]

Logos – [illegible]

St. John
Those who love [illegible]
Paul – [illegible]
[illegible] love

My Heart [illegible]

Eros

Eckhart

Other
Religions
Islam – Sufi
[illegible] – Buddhism
Sufi
Tao – Zen

Comparative Religions

#0154 - 280417 - C0 - 234/156/14 - PB - 9780415989534